NATURE AND POLITICS

NATURE AND POLITICS

Liberalism in the Philosophies of Hobbes, Locke, and Rousseau

Andrzej Rapaczynski

CORNELL UNIVERSITY PRESS

ITHACA AND LONDON

First published 1987 by Cornell University Press.
Second printing, 1989.
First published, Cornell Paperbacks, 1989.

International Standard Book Number 0-8014-1992-1 (cloth)
International Standard Book Number 0-8014-9606-3 (paper)
Library of Congress Catalog Card Number 87-5451
Printed in the United States of America
Librarians: Library of Congress cataloging information
appears on the last page of the book.

The paper in this book is acid-free and meets the guidelines for
permanence and durability of the Committee on Production Guidelines
for Book Longevity of the Council on Library Resources.

For Nicola Chiaromonte

In memoriam

Contents

Contents

Preface

The meaning of the philosophical foundations of liberalism must be understood against the background of the world views it superseded. In the classical, Aristotelian view the production of material goods was a degrading necessity and a source of human enslavement. The medieval outlook deemed the satisfaction of bodily needs at best a distraction from the pursuit of salvation. In contrast to these traditions, early liberal theory insisted that human productive capacity is the main focus of self-realization: through it human beings transform alien nature into a world of their own, assure themselves of both dignity and comfort, and achieve the highest form of freedom.

This book investigates the philosophical presuppositions of the liberal world view and seeks to bring to the surface the connections between liberal political theory and the rise of modern natural science. The crucial link between these two bodies of thought is constituted, the argument goes, by Hobbes's and Locke's theory of man as an acquisitive creature of desire rather than as a seeker of truth or immortality.

The analysis of Hobbes with which the book opens differs from most prevailing modern readings of his thought in that it takes seriously his attempt to give a purely descriptive and mechanistic account of human nature (Chapter I) and to base on it a theory of the nature of moral obligations and political institutions (Chapter II). It further claims that the social contract in Hobbes's thought should be understood not as an artificial (and most likely hypothetical) agreement from which the legitimacy of the state is to be derived, but rather as an actual (and thoroughly unintended) coincidence of many persons' beliefs which, through a form of self-fulfilling prophecy, gives rise to the power of the state to coerce obedience. It is because human beings have a unique propensity toward error and absurdity (rather than because of their rationality) and because they can make some of their mistaken beliefs come true that they first face each other as mortal enemies and then join together in a political community.

Whereas Hobbes was the first to use modern science as a foundation for political theory, Locke was the first to attempt to reconcile it with an expansive conception of human freedom. The section devoted to Locke shows how several seemingly disconnected strands of his philosophy—his theory of action, his mixed-modes theory of morality, and his theory of appropriation—come together in a complex and powerful conception of autonomy (Chapter III). In light of this conception, Locke's famous theory of property may be understood in a new way (Chapter IV). Locke was indeed, as some have claimed, an early ideologue of capitalist accumulation, but he viewed accumulation as a moral calling, an activity that liberates man from the forces of nature and results in human autonomy.

No one interested in a deeper understanding of the philosophy of liberalism can ignore a series of criticisms provided by Rousseau. For Rousseau did not simply reject liberalism in favor of an alternative political world view; rather, he provided an immanent critique of it, a formidable challenge that began from liberal assumptions in order to refute their consequences. Claiming that natural science leaves no room for freedom, Rousseau argued for a theory of man which breaks with Hobbes's and Locke's view of the human condition and foreshadows most later critiques of liberalism (Chapter V). His theory of the relation between the individual and the community (Chapter VI) and his historicist attack on the naturalistic presuppositions of early liberal theory (Chapter VII) are the enduring antiliberal paradigms with which later liberals had to come to terms if the tradition begun by Hobbes and Locke was to retain its long-term intellectual vitality.

In quoting works originally written in English, I have retained the original spelling and punctuation. In quoting translations, however (even if, as in the case of some works of Hobbes, I have used the author's own translation), I have not followed this rule, but have employed modern conventions. Wherever possible, I have referred to chapters, paragraph numbers, and so forth rather than to the pages of a single edition.

For Hobbes's *Leviathan*, I have used the reprint of the original edition edited by C. B. Macpherson (Penguin Books, 1968), but I refer to the original pagination (indicated in Macpherson's edition). For Locke, I have used the long overdue critical edition of the *Essay Concerning Human Understanding* by Peter H. Nidditch (Oxford, 1975) and Peter

Laslett's edition of the *Two Treatises of Government* (published originally by Cambridge University Press and reprinted in paperback by the New American Library). Neither of these works is referred to by page numbers; the *Essay* is cited by book, chapter, and paragraph numbers, while references to the *Second Treatise* are to paragraph numbers and are inserted in the main text. For Rousseau, I have used the four-volume Pléiade edition, citing titles of particular works and indicating in the initial citation for each the appropriate volume of the *Oeuvres complètes*. In quoting from *The Social Contract*, I have helped myself to Maurice Cranston's translation (Penguin Books, 1968); for *Emile* I have used the translation of Barbara Foxley (London, 1911); and for the *Second Discourse*, I have used that of Lester G. Crocker (New York, 1967). In many places, however, especially in *Emile*, I have departed from the English translations if it seemed to me that the text could be rendered more adequately.

My friend and colleague Bruce A. Ackerman has given me constant advice and encouragement. Patrick Riley read an early draft of this book, and his criticisms led me to a thorough revision. Piotr Hoffman read the entire manuscript and gave me valuable comments. Kay Scheuer's careful editing made the language much smoother than it would have otherwise been and saved me from a number of embarrassments. Wanda Rapaczynski and Rebecca Berlow were very generous with their patience and advice. To all of these persons I owe a great debt of gratitude.

I also thank Bernard H. Kayden Research Fund for its generous support during the summer of 1983.

ANDRZEJ RAPACZYNSKI

New York, New York

NATURE AND POLITICS

Introduction

Since the publication, in 1971, of John Rawls's *Theory of Justice*, political philosophy seems to have reclaimed much of the terrain it had lost to political science in the preceding three or four decades. Whereas in the optimistic climate of the 1950s the future of the study of politics had been supposed to lie largely in empirical research and the application of the methods of the "hard" sciences, the decade of the seventies witnessed a striking renewal of interest in the most basic normative, foundationalist questions of traditional political philosophy. What is justice? Do men have rights? What should be the role of the state in structuring relationships among individuals? Such are the pressing questions to which the most influential political writers of recent years have addressed their work.

Moreover, the recent renewal of interest in political philosophy has, by and large, coincided with a renewal of interest in liberalism. Indeed, liberalism has become quite fashionable: many of the most eminent political philosophers today, such as von Hayek, Rawls, Nozick, and Ackerman, despite all the differences among them, identify themselves with the liberal tradition.[1] Others, such as Roberto Mangabeira Unger and Michael Sandel, have thought it worthwhile and timely to try to show that liberal political thought is fundamentally incoherent.[2]

Given the renewed interest in liberal political philosophy and the debate about liberalism's overall viability, one might have expected

[1] F. von Hayek, *Law Legislation and Liberty*, 3 vols. (Chicago, 1976); J. Rawls, *A Theory of Justice* (Cambridge, Mass., 1971); R. Nozick, *Anarchy, State, and Utopia* (New York, 1974); B. A. Ackerman, *Social Justice in the Liberal State* (New Haven, 1980).

[2] R. M. Unger, *Knowledge and Politics* (New York, 1975); M. Sandel, *Liberalism and the Limits of Justice* (New York, 1982).

that the work of historically oriented scholars would have been similarly animated by the search for the foundations of liberalism and that this interest would inform the historians' own inquiry into the origins of the liberal tradition. Nothing of the kind has happened, however. Indeed, political philosophy and the history of ideas have obviously traveled in different directions. When political philosophy seemed to be declining in favor of political science, historical studies of political thought, such as the works of Leo Strauss and C. B. Macpherson, were looking to past thinkers in order to inform contemporary concerns.[3] Just as philosophy turned to a new examination of the values and principles underlying the liberal tradition, however, historians embarked on a "revisionist" course, refusing to allow us to kidnap classical figures for present-day purposes and attempting, in painstaking detail, to demonstrate the enormous differences between our concerns and theirs.[4]

This book proceeds on two basic assumptions: first, that a historical dimension, largely missing from recent work in political philosophy, is indispensable to political theory and, second, that "pure" history of political thought, which ignores all but its most immediate intellectual context, is an essentially misguided enterprise. Thus, by engaging in what is (let us hope, temporarily) a disparaged form of inquiry into the origins of liberalism, I want to bridge the widening gap between the history of ideas and political philosophy. In fact, the very idea that there is a strong distinction between these two disciplines is what I want to dispute.

At first sight, the historical and the systematic approaches to political theory seem to be quite distinct and unproblematic modes of inquiry. On the one hand, the historian of political thought may focus attention on a past thinker and attempt to reconstruct his views as faithfully as insight into the mind of a dead person will allow. An enterprise of this kind is supposed to be basically descriptive, and its truth is to be tested by the usual devices available for an empirical inquiry into the past: textual adequacy, investigation of the factual context in which the work came into being, the psychological plausibility of the proffered interpretations, and so on. On the other hand, one may be interested in the truth or falsity of an *idea* and ignore its historical origins. For example, a

---

[3]L. Strauss, *Natural Right and History* (Chicago, 1953), and *The Political Philosophy of Hobbes* (Oxford, 1936); C. B. Macpherson, *The Political Theory of Possessive Individualism* (Oxford, 1962).

[4]Among the revisionist historians writing on the origins of liberalism are J. Dunn (*The Political Thought of John Locke* [Cambridge, 1969]), J. Tully (*A Discourse on Property: John Locke and His Adversaries* [Cambridge, 1980]), J. G. A. Pocock (*The Machiavellian Moment* [Princeton, 1975]).

writer may formulate a point of view called "liberalism" and engage in an investigation of all kinds of arguments that make it plausible or implausible. An inquiry of this kind may be focused on the articulation that a particular historical figure, say, Locke, gave to "liberalism," but its accuracy with respect to what Locke *actually* said is of no special interest.[5]

There are many reasons to believe, however, that the distinction between the historical and the systematic approaches, if pushed beyond a certain point, is basically unsound. Underlying it is a simple-minded cleavage between questions concerning truth and those concerning the genesis of political positions and an equally questionable separation of matters of fact from problems of normative validity.[6]

It is by now a truism that all observation is "theory-laden," that is, conditioned by the frame of reference within which facts are apprehended. It is, of course, possible for a historian to abstract from one or another aspect of his own world view as he examines the thought of the past, but the very necessity of making the past intelligible requires that it be put within a conceptual framework that relates the subject of the inquiry to some meaningful concerns of the inquirer and his public. To be sure, one may investigate the seemingly political views of, say, Hobbes for the purpose of, say, constructing a psychological picture of their author, and thereby push their narrower political significance into the background. But the very necessity of recognizing some of Hobbes's views *as* political requires that the researcher have a more or less elaborate (though usually implicit) theory of what counts as political, together with various criteria of relevance—a theory as to what kinds of problems are addressed within the political sphere and what in that context constitutes a valid or invalid argument. Even to say that Hobbes "really meant" this or that implies that we know what it is "to mean" something, and this, in the context of a historical inquiry, raises the highly problematic question of *who* is the proper interpreter of meaning. Thus, though a history of political thought may be "neutral" enough to be neither Republican nor Democratic, it can hardly rest on "hard facts" alone.

Similarly problematic is the idea that one can meaningfully conduct a

---

[5]In the context of Locke scholarship, for example, Dunn's *Political Thought of John Locke* is a work of the first kind, oriented toward a historical reconstruction. The parts devoted (in a Pickwickian sense) to Locke in Nozick's *Anarchy, State, and Utopia* rather strikingly exemplify the systematic approach.

[6]The problem of the is-ought distinction is, as we shall see presently, quite germane to the thought of Hobbes, Locke, and Rousseau. It was, in fact, the original understanding of modern science that brought the issue into sharp relief. But the distinction has been repeatedly criticized and largely undermined in modern philosophical discussions.

purely systematic, doctrinal inquiry into the validity or invalidity of political theories and proposals. The best way to see the difficulty is to ask what success in such an enterprise would look like. Suppose, for example, that someone were to "prove" that democracy (defined as a way of solving certain types of problems by a certain class of procedures involving voting, representation, and so forth) is *the* legitimate ("right") political system. Such a "proof" might be very interesting, of course, insofar as it would clarify the logical consistency or inconsistency of certain commonly used arguments and devise new argumentative strategies in political theory. But by definition nothing more than the logical relationships among various propositions could be tested in this way. In order to make the more general claim that the conclusions derived from this exercise indeed apply to the existing circumstances of political life, one would have to show further that the accepted diagnosis of the very *problems* to be solved by politics is itself correct.[7] In certain narrow circumstances, of course, a sufficient consensus on this matter might exist to make the conclusions of practical significance. But I would find it a very dubious proposition if someone were to claim that the nature of the problems politics is supposed to solve—and thus the very meaning of politics itself—is a matter that can be determined without historical inquiry. Problems faced by mankind do not seem to be eternal and imposed by purely objective circumstances of the human condition. Instead, these problems arise only in the context of what historical agents perceive as worth pursuing and are relevant only with respect to a socially and historically determined assortment of concerns. Even the seeming immutability of such problems as that of scarcity has been questioned in the history of political philosophy,[8] and the articulation of the tasks this problem poses seems to differ quite radically from one society to another. To believe, then, that an ahistorical, systematic inquiry into the nature of politics may yield a criterion of legitimacy that can be applied regardless of historical circumstances is to impose a straitjacket on political thought and to deny the most fundamental feature of human action: its creativity. It is not surprising, therefore, that those who view political theory in ahistorical terms tend to pronounce all known forms of political organization, except the one they advocate, illegitimate or at least to explain that the legitimacy of the "undemocratic" system of, say, Elizabethan England hinges on the

[7] I abstract here from still another empirical question, namely, the need to show that the methods of solving political problems proposed by the hypothetical proof can be actually implemented with the help of the available "technology of justice," i.e., that the solutions are themselves practicable. For the concept of the "technology of justice," see Ackerman, *Social Justice in the Liberal State*, 21–24.

[8] See below, Chap. IV, section 3.2.

imperfect "technology of justice" available to Shakespeare's contemporaries.

For these and other reasons, in my study of the origins of the thought-formation known as "liberalism," I have tried to avoid locating myself unequivocally at either the "historical" or the "systematic" extreme of the continuum between them. Historical accuracy is important to my study, and I cannot dismiss as irrelevant an objection that, say, Locke could not have meant what I say he did mean. But I have not felt bound by the strictures that would constrain a more narrowly historical work, for what Locke "meant" is not determined for me exclusively by what the man called Locke actually thought he was doing or even by what he or his contemporaries could fully articulate. Tests of this kind are not, to be sure, without importance, for it is after all *Locke's* text that I am reading and interpreting. But it is also important that it is Locke's *text* that I am reading, and in this respect Locke's own reading is not the only relevant *con*text that determines the meaning of what Locke said. The reason I am writing about Locke is that he largely defined the problematic of liberalism (or so, at least, I claim) not only for his contemporaries but also for many generations to come. The continuing interest of these later generations is what has assured the lasting vitality of Locke's writings, and it provides an indispensable part of the context in which he must be read. My concern with Locke's continuing vitality does not, however, shift my inquiry into the purely abstract domain of the question "Was Locke right?" I do not know what it would mean to say that Locke was "right" in the abstract, and I therefore propose a somewhat more manageable inquiry than might be pursued by someone who believes that such questions are meaningful.[9] Rather than consider Locke's arguments *in abstracto* or in the context of narrowly defined contemporary standards, I try to locate them in the context of the political tradition to which Locke's readers have belonged: the intellectual tradition of liberalism.

Many historians may object to this relatively vague formulation, and to some extent I share their reservations. "Liberalism" means many different things to different people. In our more sober times, the grand Hegelian generalizations of the historians and philosophers of the nineteenth century appear (often justifiably) indefensible. To be sure,

[9]Neither do I ask whether Locke's political proposals would be viable if they were written today and judged according to purely contemporary standards. Unlike some representatives of the revisionist school, I clearly believe that Locke's ideas are not "dead" and that Locke has something to "say" to us, despite all the differences between his modes of expression and ours. But his relevance for us has more to do with helping to explain how we got to where we are in our intellectual predicament than with providing us with definitive answers to the problems we face.

Introduction

liberalism is not a simple idea and its definition cannot be given in a few words at the beginning of this book. Furthermore, one of the most characteristic, and in fact "liberal," features of liberalism is that while it has many founders and progenitors, no single person can pass as *the* founder of its doctrine. Without any one of such diverse thinkers as Hobbes, Locke, Montesquieu, Smith, Hume, Burke, and Mill, the intellectual character of present-day liberalism would be significantly different. Nevertheless, I think there exists both need and room for an inquiry that neither treats the term "liberalism" as referring to a confused motley of ideas nor reduces its meaning to one or another of its particular versions. In particular, I maintain that it makes sense to speak of liberalism as a genuine *tradition* of political thinking and that by clarifying its origins, which I believe are to be found primarily in the work of Hobbes and Locke, we may gain an insight into a general style of thinking which continues to shape our own intellectual formation.

While the contours of the liberal tradition, as I understand it, will emerge from my specific discussions of Hobbes, Locke, and Rousseau, it might be useful at this point to explain why I chose to deal primarily with these three thinkers and why I believe them to be of particularly seminal importance in the development of political theory.

In a complex and sometimes implicit three-way dispute, Hobbes, Locke, and Rousseau thrashed out the most important issues concerning the reconstruction of the philosophical foundations of politics, shattered by the birth of modern science and the destruction of the basic intellectual framework of the premodern era. The belief which Hobbes, Locke, and Rousseau all shared, and which unifies their thought, was that the Aristotelian or medieval world view could no longer provide an adequate framework within which to situate the political life of their time; the realities of modern politics stood in need of a new conceptualization.

Once liberalism became firmly established, the difficult circumstances of its birth were largely forgotten. As in the case of modern science, the very success of liberal politics allowed one to forget the philosophical presuppositions without which the liberal doctrine could not have arisen. During the nineteenth century, the fusion of political individualism with the economic doctrine of *laissez-faire* (the doctrine initially advocated by the Physiocrats, in the same breath with a defense of royal absolutism) yielded a social system that seemed as impregnable as the laws of Newtonian physics. Even such thinkers as John Stuart Mill, who were quite unhappy about the consequences of classical liberalism, looked upon its tenets as so firmly rooted in the "laws of nature" that they despaired about the possibility of change. With the notable exception of the Marxists and the less notable one of the utopian socialists, critics of liberalism could not help viewing themselves as reactionaries, born at a wrong time. It is not surprising, therefore, that most defenders of liberalism who lived during the time of its triumph did not feel the need to go into far-reaching philosophical speculations to justify their stand. Their philosophy was somewhat uncritically utilitarian and positivistic—on both counts unwilling to engage in a dispute concerning the ultimate meaning of individual life and its relation to political institutions.

Seventeenth-century England and eighteenth-century France, however, had been deeply troubled lands, and the future shape of their political institutions was by no means settled. Despite the vital importance of religious controversies in the politics of Stuart England, the most important political thinkers of the time saw that, whatever the nature of the political structure that would finally crystallize, its legitimacy could not rest on predominantly theological foundations. Neither could they assume that future economic developments would settle the questions of political organization; on the contrary, they believed that the material prosperity of the nation depended on the finding of the right political solutions. The problem they faced was not merely to find such solutions, but also to *justify* them, that is, to situate them within the context of a broader system of beliefs to which their contemporaries (or at least the more educated and open-minded among them) could subscribe. Not surprisingly, they turned to what seemed to them the most distinctive and most promising feature of seventeenth-century culture: the mechanistic science of nature and its philosophical foundations.

The new way of looking at nature suggested to them a new way of looking at society. The stress on efficient, as opposed to final, causation made them cautious about assuming that social and political institutions had a fixed purpose, independent of prior arrangements among the individuals who made them up. The scientific procedure of substituting an ideal model of nature for the apparent world of perception made them look for a similar distinction in human affairs and oppose the natural state of man to the contingent products of historical circumstances. The empiricism of modern science made them sensitive to the distinction between the way things actually are and the way they ought to be. The concept of rationality entailed by modern science made them rethink the meaning of the concept of humanity and reappraise the expectations that individuals have with respect to political institutions. The hope that science would one day allow human beings to control the natural world made them much more attentive to the relation between man and his environment, and they came to view knowledge not as a form of disinterested contemplation, but as a tool in the human productive effort, directed at the comfort and convenience of life. Consequently, they could no longer subscribe to the Aristotelian distinction between inferior *techne* and superior *episteme*, together with the underlying separation of free action (*praxis*) from the subservient domain of production (*poesis*). Finally, the nominalistic presuppositions of the new scientific method, consisting of the resolution of all composites to their simple elements, confirmed the proponents of the new social science in their attempt to explain the meaning and function of social institutions with reference to the individuals that constituted their elements. This nominalism, which by itself did not necessarily lead to a liberal political outlook, was of great importance for early liberalism, since it no longer allowed for the Aristotelian insistence on the natural priority of society over its individual members. From this time on, the legitimization of even the most authoritarian forms of government had to appeal to individual interests, and it became exceedingly difficult to claim that society *as such* constitutes the main benefit of individuals' participation in it. In order to explain the relation between the individual and society, one had to *begin* with the concept of human individuality. Consequently, one had to be able to specify the latter's constitutive elements without reference to the social interaction that was going to be derived from them. Man's humanity, far from being derivative with respect to social and political relationships, became their foundation.

It is against this background that the theory of presocial man originates. Whether the postulation of the original state of nature is a historical hypothesis or a philosopher's fiction, its meaning derives from the crucial postulate of the natural priority of human individuality to social interaction. The task of the new political theory was to describe, with the help of the conception of the natural state of man, what this individuality consists in, and to translate the outcome of such analyses into a theory of the *rights* and *obligations* of a citizen. Explaining the possibility of such a translation is the essence of the whole contractual approach to social and political phenomena.

The three contractarians discussed in this book set out to explore the possibilities of such a general approach. All three assumed that a system of political legitimization could not appeal to any natural phenomena, unless by "nature" was meant the mechanical system indicated by modern science. A theory of natural law and natural right, for example, had had a very long standing in political philosophy. But what distinguished the appeal to natural law in Hobbes, Locke, and Rousseau from the older political theories was their view that nature does not operate with the help of moral or quasi-moral norms: it does not prescribe, allow, or condemn, but forces, inclines, or incapacitates. The question that they, therefore, thought had to be answered before any natural law was used to legitimize a political system was whether the operation of the mechanical laws of nature provided a sufficient ground for inferring a system of normative principles. It is this question that defines the crucial issue of early liberal theory.

There is also an important element of substantive, and not only formal, agreement in Hobbes's, Locke's, and Rousseau's perception of the task of political philosophy. All three believed that the first, spontaneous form of social interaction, at least insofar as it transcends the confines of the family, is not cooperation but *competition*. This primacy of difference over identity in the relations between the members of the human species, together with the insistence on the activity of production visible in Locke, prepared the ground for the later marriage of liberal politics with classical economics. Initially, however, competition was seen not as a socially beneficial form of interaction but as the main centrifugal force that a contractually established social order was supposed to counteract. The immediately presocial condition of man is that of a struggle for survival that makes *security* the paramount concern of each individual. Human rationality, according to the three contractarians, is characterized by the human capacity for responding to possible deprivations as if they were actual. Consequently, human needs and desires do not have any inherent or natural limitations, and this leads to a situation of conflict among men. Each of the three thinkers responds to the resulting *bellum omnis contra omnem* in a different way: Hobbes believes that only the establishment of an overawing power above men can provide a solution; Locke believes that the essential insecurity of human beings is overcome by appropriation, so that a free union among them is enough to counteract the aggressiveness of the irrational few; Rousseau maintains that a thoroughgoing remaking of man is needed to eliminate the misery and unhappiness engendered by human selfishness. But the most important difference between them is one that ranges Hobbes together with Locke against Rousseau. For according to the former two, the fact that human needs and desires are unlimited is necessary and natural, while Rousseau views it as an unnatural aberration, though nonetheless possessed of inner dynamics. Thus, whereas Hobbes and Locke (despite the former's political authoritarianism) opt for a defense of the expansive conception of human individuality which will provide the most basic feature of liberal theory, Rousseau sets out to explore the possibility of reimposing some limitations on human acquisitiveness and proposes a revolutionary alternative to the system established on liberal, individualistic assumptions. The arguments in their dispute, especialy if they are not confined to a narrow historical context but extrapolated so as to make them relevant to later discussions between critics and defenders of the liberal system, concern what seem to me the most basic *philosophical* issues of liberalism—issues that are often lost in analyses that reduce the differences between the liberals and their opponents to purely pragmatic or economic considerations.

Before concluding these introductory remarks, I would like to add a few words concerning the interpretations I offer of each of the authors discussed in this book.

Generally speaking, I have tried to present the writings of each of my authors as consistently as I could, and I am aware that sometimes the text, while providing numerous confirmations of my own readings, may admit of several others. In my polemical zeal, I sometimes dismiss these perhaps more brusquely than the "liberal" side of me would like. This same polemical zeal sometimes makes me look for readings that go against the grain of established scholarship: I chose the least obvious reading of Locke, where I find most previous interpretations rather unimaginative, and the most obvious one of Hobbes, where previous scholars have reached a highly sophisticated consensus that the text cannot be taken to mean what it seems to mean. But my aims were not merely polemical; the choices I made were motivated by my desire to make the authors fit with my own insights into the alternative viewpoints defining the problems of early liberalism, and I hope that the reader will find in them a least modicum of enlightenment, in addition to an *esprit de contradiction*. I have also deemed it worthwhile sometimes to pursue certain idiosyncrasies of my authors, even if it detracts somewhat from the overall flow of my argument. Political theory is not a science like physics, where the discoveries of different scientists can be reformulated without loss of content to fit an impersonal textbook presentation of the subject matter. In political theory, as in art (though to a lesser extent), the personality of the author is inseparable from his work; not only does it influence his style or exposition of the problem, but also, by giving different weight to different issues, provides a peculiar flavor to the whole enterprise. Political theories arrange themselves into certain series and form certain "traditions" of thinking, not unlike the "styles" of writing or painting. But they are always produced by individuals and not by traditions. In the cases of outstanding specimens of such theories it is often worthwhile to follow their inner dynamics, reflecting an author's individuality, as well as to look at them as filling a "slot" in a given series.

Finally, contrary to the prevailing fashion, I analyze the political doctrines of my authors in terms of their wider philosophical commitments, such as their views on some general issues in ontology or epistemology, their theories of subjectivity, and their understanding of the nature of science. My purpose is not to reduce political philosophy to other branches of philosophical investigation or to argue that one's political orientation actually originates in some ontological or epistemological commitments. Nonetheless, as a general matter, these broader commitments greatly enlighten the narrowly political dimension of philosophy, and they are particularly important in the thought of the early liberals who, as I have already indicated, faced the problem of providing new philosophical foundations for the very enterprise of political theory. To take one obvious example, all three of my authors talk about something they call "the state of nature." The meaning of this concept has been widely discussed in the scholarly literature and many different questions have been raised. Does the hypothesis of the natural state of man imply a historical claim? Is it a legal fiction? Is it a hypothetical device for testing the legitimacy of political arrangements? Is it a result of the quest for some universal human characteristics? What is the status of moral obligation in the state of nature? And so on. But at least one crucial question, the answer to which may provide a key to answering most of the others, is often overlooked: What do these authors mean by "nature"? Not "the state of nature," not "the nature of man," but "nature" *tout court*. This question is bound, of course, to lead us beyond the confines of ordinary political problems. To answer it we must inquire into our authors' views on science, their evaluation of teleological and mechanistic accounts, their view of the relation between description and prescription, and the like. Once we have made these inquiries, however, our discussion of the idea of the state of nature is likely to be much better informed.

The method advocated here presupposes, of course, that the authors one examines had wide philosophical commitments. In the case of Hobbes and Locke (as well as Plato, Aristotle, Hegel, and Marx) this requirement causes no problem. But in the case of Rousseau (as well as Machiavelli, Burke, and Tocqueville) one must reconstruct epistemological or ontological positions from relatively few fragments or from the work of other thinkers who took up the theory where our author had left it. The legitimacy of such a procedure is certainly open to doubt: one may be as unpersuaded about the importance of Rousseau's more or less casual philosophical remarks in the context of his political theory as about the adequacy of Kant's or Hegel's philosophy for an *ex post facto* analysis of his thinking. These introductory remarks are certainly not the place to decide this issue. Suffice it to say that I believe that the task is worth attempting.

In my discussion of Hobbes I aim at revealing certain important presuppositions of early liberalism. I do not attempt, however, to make Hobbes into a liberal and in fact find such attempts misguided. What interests me in Hobbes's philosophy is primarily the shift of perspective in the inquiry into the nature of human action and the working out of some of the most important argumentative strategies of liberal individualism. I am not very sympathetic to the efforts of many commentators who deny the radical originality of Hobbes's political and moral outlook and present his thought as an outgrowth of the well-established Christian doctrine of political rights. Further, of the two more plausible interpretations of his theory—the prudentialist and the positivist one—I have chosen to deal primarily with the positivist reading. In doing this, I am returning to the largely abandoned effort to present Hobbes's political theory and his general mechanistic philosophy as a unified body of ideas. This choice was motivated by my belief that the prudentialist reading, which attempts to interpret Hobbes's "laws of nature" as the norms of prudence, is ultimately untenable because it not only forces one to abandon the doctrinal unity of his system, but is also incapable of accounting for some of the most basic features of his properly political philosophy. Most notably, recent game-theoretical studies concerning the so-called free rider phenomena have convinced me that the whole contractarian aspect of Hobbes's political theory, as well as his defense of absolutism, must appear based on a fundamental misunderstanding of the nature of prudence, especially if one wants to read his philosophy as an attempted solution to the so-called prisoner's dilemma.[10]

But my choice of the positivist reading of Hobbes is influenced by other considerations as well. Regardless of the tenability or untenability of the prudentialist interpretation, and of the narrow historical accuracy of one or the other reading, the positivist interpretation is worth pursuing for its own sake, since it provides an important illustration of one of the fundamental philosophical defenses of modern political institutions. As I have already indicated, I do not believe that Hobbes can be made into a full-fledged liberal without seriously distorting the nature of his political theory. In particular, I believe that Hobbes's absolutism is by no means an accidental feature of his political proposals. Nevertheless, Hobbes's very positivism introduces a distinctly modern perspective on human action, against the background of which the liberal theory develops its individualistic philosophy. Hobbes's is the first attempt to examine the political consequences of the thoroughgoing mechanistic world view of modern science and to reject *in toto* the political theory based on Aristotelian or Christian teleology, with its insistence on the primacy of the political (communal) over the individual. Read from this point of view, Hobbes's argument prefigures the one to be adopted by the later "liberal-conservative" school of

[10]See Introduction to Part One, note 15.

political thought, represented by, for example, Hume and Burke. The liberal side of this argument, indeed a crucial tenet of liberalism in general, consists in showing that political legitimization, if it is to be at all meaningful, must, even in advocating a form of absolutist government, appeal to individual interests, irreducible to some purely social, communal values. Accordingly, the government should not take upon itself tasks larger than the already tremendous job of maintaining order which, far from being incompatible with freedom, is in fact the necessary condition of the very security of the citizens' persons and the framework guaranteeing a free pursuit of their happiness. The conservative part of this argument consists in showing that the necessary stability of a social order does not—and cannot—rest on a legitimization that all rational men must accept, but rather must be based on a system of essentially unjustifiable beliefs, the questioning of which, if too radically pursued, may lead to the collapse of the civilized forms of existence.

Hobbes's derivation of political philosophy from modern natural science is in yet another sense of crucial importance for the political philosophy of liberalism: it is a form of political theory that the *critics* of liberalism took for the paradigmatic liberal approach. As I try to make clear in my treatment of Rousseau, the most important critics of liberalism argue that modern natural science cannot provide a foundation for a truly normative theory of right and that, consequently, liberalism, being the outgrowth of positivism, lacks the essential philosophical foundation for its moral outlook. The charges of relativism, nihilism, narrow materialism, and other alleged sins of liberalism, leveled by critics from Rousseau through Marx to Strauss and contemporary Marxists, are rooted precisely in the conviction that the purely descriptive and analytic character of modern science is inherently incapable of doing justice to social and political phenomena, intertwined as they are with the question of norms and values. In this respect, Hobbes, positivistically interpreted, provides an ideal focus for an antiliberal critique: on this interpretation, Hobbes indeed refuses to infuse his political system with any element of teleology and transforms the traditionally normative account of political life into a purely descriptive political science. Thus, even though there may be some legitimate disagreement as to the extent of Hobbes's positivism, I have decided to sharpen the contours of his thought and engage in the thought experiment of reading his work as a consistent attempt to reduce all de jure considerations to de facto analyses. Beyond what I believe to be the historical value of the positivist reading of Hobbes, my choice of interpretation serves, therefore, three additional functions: it focuses the dispute concerning the philosophical foundations of liberalism; it shows that the turn from de jure to de facto questions opens up an entirely new and independently interesting dimension of political theory; and it prepares the way for the claim, pursued in the second part of this book, that not every form of liberalism, even if closely connected to the world view of modern natural science, is positivistic in its spirit. As much as positivism is itself a questionable reading of modern science, it is equally questionable that the rigid distinction between facts and values, description and prescription, is a tenable proposition. But if this distinction is abandoned or modified, the allegedly insurmountable difficulty of bridging the gap between the world view of modern science and the normative social and political theory of liberalism turns out to be spurious. With it also disappears the allegedly unavoidable relativism or nihilism of the liberal outlook. The move from positivistic reductionism toward establishing the moral foundations of liberalism is to be found, in my opinion, in the philosophy of Locke.

My discussion of Locke is the centerpiece of this book, in more than just the literal sense. Locke is the only unqualified liberal among the three contractarians. Despite his tremendous influence on people who actually made politics, however, he has received rather curious treatment from those who write about him. There are, of course, some very good books on Locke's political philosophy, but it seems that Locke's critics have given him credit for somewhat more daring ideas than his defenders. I myself, having been trained originally in the systems of his opponents, began my thinking on Locke by pondering the contrast between the amazing workability of his political proposals and what seemed to me the inadequacy of their philosophical foundations. After savoring for some time this insight into the vicissitudes of history (an insight not unlike Hobbes's or Hume's observation that the best political systems arise out of purely contingent and meagerly justified beliefs), I came to study Locke's philosophy more carefully. To my amazement, I suddenly discovered that Locke's investigations, and especially his account of appropriation, contained some of the most important insights of the practical philosophies of Kant, Hegel, and Marx, without entailing the most serious disadvantages of their theories. In particular, I realized that Locke's theory of property could be read as the most important forerunner of later theories of autonomy, especially those of Hegel and Marx, which link moral self-sufficiency to the process of production by which men transform their natural environment. At the same time, Locke's theory seemed to me to have two essential advantages over its later competitors: it did not involve the intricate, but extremely troublesome element of Hegelian speculation, incompatible with the main insights of empirical science; and it did not entail the collectivist implications of the later theories, so closely linked to totalitarian temptations. As I moved to another study of Locke's *Essay*, I saw that the chapter "Of Power" and the so-called mixed-modes of theory of morality provided the broader philosophical foundations of his conception of autonomy, needed to ground the theory of politics advanced in the *Second Treatise*. Consequently, in spite of the widespread skepticism among Locke scholars about the depth of unity and insight of his work, I try to show that Locke's thought presents a coherent and sophisticated body of ideas behind a seemingly inconsistent and patchworklike facade.

I am quite prepared for the objection that my reading of Locke is highly interpretative and anachronistic. I do bring together several apparently unconnected and seemingly inconsistent features of his moral and political theory in a way that Locke may not have clearly intended. It is in fact quite probable that he was still groping in the dark in developing his theory of autonomy and was not exactly clear as to the relation between the various components of his system. It is also true that I have, to some extent, taken Locke out of the immediate historical context of his time. I did this because his contemporaries could not even *formulate* some of the objections that became dominant in later critiques of his theory and my interpretation, unlike a narrowly contextualist reading, allows Locke's theory to stand up to its later competitors. Moreover, this kind of treatment does not seem to me to violate the spirit of the Lockean enterprise. Locke clearly intended to put forth his moral and political philosophy as more than an occasional political tract in favor of the Glorious Revolution: his ambition was to write a modern equivalent of Aristotle's *Politics*.[11] And the fact that later history of liberalism was to vindicate his ambition seems to me a sufficient warrant for bringing into focus some of the ideas he himself had only somewhat indistinctly envisaged.

Finally, a few words about Rousseau. I do not consider Rousseau a liberal in *any* sense; the reason for including him in my discussions is that the most important *critiques* of liberalism are clearly foreshadowed in his writings. Later important work (above all that of Kant) did, of course, give Rousseau's critique a more solid philosophical foundation, and his political proposals were made somewhat more realistic by Hegel's and Marx's correction of his quite Aristotelian neglect of the concept of production. The main argumentative strategies of antiliberalism, however, are clearly worked out in the writings of Rousseau. Among the most important of these are: his theory of autonomy, constructed in opposition to the alleged liberal reduction of human con-

---

[11]Locke himself, in a letter to Rev. Richard King of 25 August 1703, compares his *Two Treatises* to Aristotle's *Politics*.

cerns to security and material well-being; his antinaturalism and historicism; and his theories of alienation and the general will, with the help of which he attacks the basis of liberal individualism. Admirers of Rousseau have most commonly been unaware of the strengths of the liberal position and quite cavalier about the totalitarian implications of his doctrine. His opponents, on the other hand, have often been too quick in dismissing his objections to liberalism and in viewing him as little more than a frustrated dreamer. Unless his objections are taken seriously, we shall never understand the proper historical meaning of liberal doctrine or the source of the dissatisfaction that liberal political practice is apt to produce. My discussion of Rousseau thus provides the proper perspective for a reading of the work of the early political individualists. It is the challenge of Rousseau that they must meet if their theories are to be of more than antiquarian interest.

Because I have brought in Rousseau not so much for his own sake as for that of formulating the outlines of the main challenges to the natural-right tradition, I have taken two liberties with his work. First, I am much less thorough in my analyses of some of his theories than would be expected of a study in which he was a primary figure. I have especially simplified his account of the moral and historical development of man and limited myself to a discussion of only the major stages of nature, civil society, and the state. Second, I have purposely sharpened certain points of Rousseau's doctrine (especially his theories of autonomy and alienation) by reading them through the eyes of his followers (especially Kant and Marx).

PART ONE: HOBBES

Introduction

For over two and a half centuries after the publication of *Leviathan* (1651), Hobbes's work was taken at face value by most of his readers and interpreters. He was understood to have attacked the Aristotelian, tele-ological conception of the state, undercut the moral and religious basis of political obligation, rejected the validity of religion itself (except as a tool in the hands of authority), and reduced the concept of right to that of might.[1] These interpretations were undoubtedly often crude in their reading of Hobbes, not least because opposition to him, like that to Machiavelli, was influenced by a set of moral presuppositions that Hobbes was seen to have questioned. Hobbes's amorality was com-monly taken for immorality pure and simple. His scientific bent, which could be taken to suggest that he was more interested in describing the nature of political power than in passing value judgments upon it, was not always seen as a sufficient counterweight to his cynical approach to moral and particularly to religious questions.[2] The old-school inter-preters were clearly mistaken in seeing Hobbes's adherence to the doctrine that "might makes right" as merely a cynical rejection of

[1]For a general overview of the literature on Hobbes, see W. H. Greenleaf, "Hobbes: The Problem of Interpretation," in R. Kosseleck and R. Schnur, eds., *Hobbes-Forschungen* (Berlin, 1969), reprinted in M. Cranston and R. S. Peters, eds., *Hobbes and Rousseau* (Garden City, N.Y., 1972).

[2]For a review of contemporary reactions to Hobbes, see J. Bowle, *Hobbes and His Critics* (London, 1951) and S. I. Mintz, *The Hunting of Leviathan* (Cambridge, 1962). For an essential corrective of Bowle's and Mintz's perspective, see Q. Skinner, "The Ideological Context of Hobbes's Political Thought," *Historical Journal*, 9 (1966), and the revised version of the same article in Cranston and Peters, eds., *Hobbes and Rousseau*.

morality. In many matters Hobbes undoubtedly was a cynic, but that might makes right (and vice versa) he claimed impassionately and in earnest. In this respect he may indeed be unique in the history of moral and political philosophy. The Sophists and Machiavelli before him, and some proponents of so-called *Realpolitik* after him, may have come close to maintaining a similar claim. But while the Sophists' theory was a simple consequence of their radical relativism, while Machiavelli was really a moralist for whom there was certainly much more to right than merely might, and while the proponents of *Realpolitik* were most commonly mere cynics, Hobbes presented an elaborate theory designed to show that might and right are two mutually reinforcing and indispensable factors in establishing the legitimacy of any political regime and that they can be understood only when analyzed with respect to their common denominator.

In roughly the 1930s a reaction to the traditional reading set in. The pattern for the new approach to Hobbes's political writings was established by A. E. Taylor[3] and Leo Strauss[4] who, despite many differences in their readings of Hobbes, marked a decisive break with one of the most fundamental claims of the traditional interpretation: the unity of Hobbes's ethical and political theory with his mechanistic theory of nature. Taylor made the less radical claim that these two parts of Hobbes's thought are incompatible with each other and should be read independently; Strauss attempted to show that Hobbes had worked out his basic ethical and political views before he ever became acquainted with the Galilean model of natural science and superimposed his mechanistic philosophy as window dressing on the previously completed political theory.

Another decisive break with the traditional interpretation consisted in an attempt to read a clear moral theory into Hobbes's political thought. Whereas the traditional interpreters had confused Hobbes's amorality with an immoral attack on the prevailing system of values, the new interpreters claimed to have discovered in Hobbes a clearly delineated ethical system. Howard Warrender attempted to show that Hobbes's political theory rested on medieval theological foundations and could not be understood properly if its traditional moral content and presuppositions were neglected.[5] According to Strauss, on the other hand, Hobbes was a radical innovator in the area of moral theory,

---

[3]A. E. Taylor, "The Ethical Doctrine of Hobbes," *Philosophy*, 13 (1938), reprinted in K. C. Brown, ed., *Hobbes Studies* (Oxford, 1965).

[4]L. Strauss, *The Political Philosophy of Hobbes* (Oxford, 1936), and *Natural Right and History* (Chicago, 1953).

[5]H. Warrender, *The Political Philosophy of Hobbes: His Theory of Obligation* (Oxford, 1957). See also F. C. Hood, *The Divine Politics of Thomas Hobbes* (Oxford, 1964).

since he attempted to replace the Aristotelian and Christian model of ethics with a new theory of right rooted in the basic human passions. One way or the other, however, these interpreters came to see Hobbes's political theory as a system of normative claims of a moral nature, and scores of later writers who followed these lines of interpretation have attempted to show that the moral premises of Hobbes's theory not only are incompatible with a view of Hobbes as a detached scientist bent on describing rather than prescribing, but also rule out as inadequate every reading of his work that views it as an examination of social and political organization in the light of a system of prudential calculations.

As with many puzzling texts in the history of ideas (and of political ideas in particular), interpretations of Hobbes's work have tended to become increasingly speculative and progressively further removed from the *prima facie* meaning of the text. Undoubtedly many of these interpretations have enriched our understanding of hitherto neglected aspects of Hobbes's writings and have contributed to a renewal of scholarly interest in his work. But what leaves one dissatisfied with most of them is the fact that their authors seem unable or unwilling to entertain seriously some of the blacker or more skeptical thoughts of the author of *Leviathan*. Indeed, one may be led to suspect that in trying to bring a clear moral content into Hobbes's writings, the majority of his recent interpreters have set out to refute his pessimism with respect to human nature by pointing up the example of their own inability to take (what they saw as) an uncharitable view of his philosophy.

Although the case for Hobbes's being a moralist finds little confirmation in his political writings, the argument that he was a prudentialist seems to abound in textual confirmations. First of all, there seems to be no single place in all of Hobbes's writings where he clearly envisages a possible conflict between morality and prudence and says that a man ought to follow a moral principle over self-interest. The closest he ever comes to a moralist standpoint is in his theory of natural law, and especially in his claim that even in the state of nature men may be under an obligation to adhere to their contractual agreements.[6] But even in this context, Hobbes's defense of the natural law involved can at most be understood as an argument that keeping one's contractual obligations can never be, at least in the long run, against one's own interest. Second, Hobbes clearly appears to have wanted to advise his contemporaries as to the best political arrangements they could arrive at,[7] and since he had made self-preservation the ultimate motive of human behavior, it seems natural that he would appeal to prudence in proposing his

[6]*Lev.*, 68, 69.
[7]See Hobbes's "Preface to the Reader" in *De cive*; and *Lev.*, 193.

solution to the problems of the age. Indeed, it is hard to avoid the conclusion that in both *De cive* and *Leviathan* Hobbes assumes that at least some men are prudentially rational agents and that it is to them that his political philosophy is addressed. The laws of nature that he speaks of, and that he himself identifies with the laws of reason,[8] seem to specify a system of prudential rationality.

It should be noted at the outset that a prudentialist interpretation of Hobbes is no more compatible with a view of him as a protopositivist than is a moralist reading. This sometimes escapes those who assume that prudence, unlike morality, is easily reconcilable with an ordinary causal account of human motivation. Even as careful a writer as Kant made a similar assumption when he claimed that an action in accordance with a hypothetical imperative (above all, a maxim of prudence) involved no difficulty for a mechanistic explanation of human behavior. Because an action of this kind ultimately serves the purpose of satisfying an "inclination" (a desire brought about as a result of processes natural to a human organism, and not a purpose specified by the imperative itself), Kant believed that no appeal to freedom had to be made to explain the possibility of such an action. Nevertheless, precisely the fact that, as Kant says, it is *analytically* true that whoever wants the end wants the means, should make prudential action problematic for him.[9] If, according to the ordinary scientific account of it, human motivation must be viewed as a causal system—and such is the opinion of both Hobbes and Kant—then wanting the end must *causally* imply wanting the means; and the statement "Whoever wants the end wants the means" must by *synthetic*, that is, it must rest on the possibility of pointing to a causal connection between the two desires, since their objects are clearly not the same. By saying that the connection is analytic, Kant could claim only that it would be irrational or illogical to want the end and not the means; but this, even if true, would fall short of showing that a man, regardless of whether or not he is free, could actually follow what his reason suggests to him as the best way of achieving his aims.

Thus, there is some persistent misunderstanding in many people's view of the nature of prudential action both in general and with respect to Hobbes, since the conflict between prudence and morality renders them oblivious to the distinction between prudence and inclination. If the norms of prudence are really *norms* (and not descriptive statements), then one's ability to follow them implies one's ability to do something because it *ought* to be done and not because one is causally

[8]*De cive*, ii, 1; *Lev.*, 64.

[9]Kant, *Foundations of the Metaphysics of Morals* (Prussian Academy edition), 417.

determined to do it. Indeed, for prudential action to be possible, a whole set of conditions, not unlike those concerning the possibility of moral action, must be satisfied. Consequently, although it is for some reason believed easier to be prudent than to be moral, a theory of prudential action should not be reduced to psychology, as has sometimes been done by even the most sophisticated of Hobbes's interpreters. Thus, for example, David Gauthier, in his otherwise excellent .book on *Leviathan*, has claimed that while Hobbes's formal definition of obligation allows for moral duties (that contracts once entered into should be kept regardless of prudential considerations), his naturalistic psychology, by making self-interest into the only viable motive of human action, is destructive of his ethics.[10] It is very important to realize, therefore, that the distinction between prudence and morality entails a choice between two different conceptions of rationality and not between two different psychological theories, and that the possibility of *either* prudence *or* morality is incompatible with the strictly naturalistic psychology with which Hobbes opens his *Leviathan*. The defenders of prudence and the defenders of morality, as two rival systems of norms, do not dispute between themselves whether rationality is best used in the service of one or another set of ends or dispositions (such as self-interest or benevolence) that we happen to have. Neither is the dispute, as Kant had supposed, whether one should follow one's inclinations (with the help of hypothetical imperatives) or the dictates of reason (categorical imperative). Rather, the dispute centers on the question whether it is rational to follow one's self-interest (prudence) or whether rationality implies another set of norms such as morality.[11] Whichever conception of rationality is chosen, one acquires a concept of *obligation* in that both prudence and morality specify what one ought to do and not what one is causally determined to do. The fact that if one opts for prudence the concept of obligation is reduced to a prudential maxim does not change anything here, and a prudentialist interpretation of Hobbes is no more based on Hobbes's naturalistic psychology than is the moralist one.

Theoretically, it is possible to deny the is-ought distinction altogether, insofar as prudential action is concerned:[12] one may say,

[10]D. Gauthier, *The Logic of Leviathan* (Oxford, 1969), 76–98.

[11]D. Parfit, in his excellent book *Reasons and Persons* (Oxford, 1984), has analyzed in great detail the theory of rationality implied in the prudentialist view. Parfit believes, however, that *morality* is not a theory of rationality, but rather a theory of what is "right" and that "we now doubt that acting morally is 'required by Reason'" (ibid., 129).

[12]This may be possible for moral action as well, though hardly anyone is tempted to do it. Kant's idea that for a perfectly rational agent the norms of morality would have the same force as the laws of nature comes to mind as an approximation. So does Hegel's view, in *The Early Theological Writings* (Philadelphia, 1971), that the "fulfillment" of the law by

namely, that prudential calculation is just "built into" the ordinary mechanical process by which the will is determined. In other words, by naturalizing thought processes in general one may "naturalize" prudence as well. But then all talk about prudential *norms* is only a roundabout way of *describing* what happens when we are motivated by self-interest rather than a way of *prescribing* how one ought to behave. The norms of prudence become in this case nothing more than a description of the human machine's proper ways of functioning. It is doubtful, however, whether such a conception can be read into Hobbes's writings. Hobbes's theory of rationality is certainly naturalistic, and reasoning processes are for him directly reducible to mechanically produced motions within the body. It is also true that *some* products of ratiocination contribute, according to Hobbes, to the course of human—but not only human—action by entering into the process of "deliberation" that constitutes a causal chain of mental states leading up to the "last appetite," that is, the act of volition responsible for human behavior.[13] But this does not mean that adherence to the maxims of prudence is built into this causal chain with anything approaching the degree of perfection required for a "naturalization" of prudence. It would be extremely misleading to impute to Hobbes the view that when an agent is really aware of his true interest he will automatically follow the course of action that it prescribes. Quite the contrary, Hobbes seems to believe that human beings in most circumstances act *against* their best interests and that they do so not because they lack sufficient knowledge but because, in view of their vanity, knowledge of their interest is never a sufficient motive for their actions. Even if Hobbes sometimes says that men are made suitable for life in society, and thus presumably for prudential action, by a process of "education,"[14] he does not mean that men need to be *convinced by arguments* as to how they should behave, but only that they must be *trained* or *conditioned* to behave in a certain way. This in turn means, for him, that there must be some great power that induces obedience in them by means of fear and not by presenting them with irrefutable calculations of their own interest. Thus, although some basic elements of prudence may in fact be built into Hobbes's account of the mechanism of human motivation, these elements are

---

Christ (Matt. 5:17) requires that a good person satisfy the Commandments not out of a sense of obligation, but as a result of love, i.e., a disposition that Kant would have classified as an inclination.

[13]*Lev.*, 28.

[14]*De cive*, note to i, 2.

certainly too minimal to justify the claim that he naturalized prudence as such.[15]

In the following inquiry into the meaning of Hobbes's philosophy, I shall consciously oppose the trends prevailing in most recent interpretations and present a qualified defense of the more traditional point of view. Apart from its moralist condemnation of Hobbes's view of human nature, the traditional view of Hobbes as a positivist is, I believe, much more coherent and interesting than the effort to make him into a moralist. Also, I find the attempt to detach Hobbes's political theory from the naturalist background in which he set it and to impart either a moralist or a prudentialist doctrine to his teaching both unnecessary and misguided. I find it unnecessary because I think that a cogent interpretation of Hobbes is possible without denying the unity of his thought or basing his political theory on a moral system; as a matter of fact, I believe that only such an interpretation is compatible with what he actually wrote. And I find it misguided because, contrary to what has

---

[15]The most important objection to the prudentialist interpretation, however, though one that it would take us too far afield to pursue in detail, is not that it is incompatible with Hobbes's theory of action, but that, if pursued consistently, it does not work on its own terms. The most interesting version of this interpretation would see the Hobbesian state of nature as a multiperson version of the prisoner's dilemma, in which the collective interest of all the participants is defeated by the individual interests owing to the absence of social coordination. It is true, of course, that the institution of state authority would be a solution to this problem, but Hobbes's main question is how such an authority could be instituted, given the natural equality of men. If human beings could find a god (someone so powerful that no one could disobey him), they would certainly make him their ruler. But if such a god is not available, the purpose of the social contract must be to create one: the Leviathan, by drawing on the power of all, is supposed to be an artificial god of this kind. Should such a Leviathan be successfully created, the same forces that prevent its original creation would henceforth contribute to its stability, for only *coordinated* disobedience would have a chance of succeeding, while the cost of coordination would be prohibitively high. Still, the transition from the state of nature to the political state presents insuperable difficulties: each person desires the establishment of the state, but no one has sufficient incentive to bear the costs of seeking the agreement with others or adhering to the agreements already made. From the game-theoretical literature (see, e.g., M. Olson, *The Logic of Collective Action* [Cambridge, Mass., 1965]) we know that situations of this kind can be overcome only if (a) individuals can be selectively rewarded for cooperation or punished for noncooperation, or (b) they can be relied to cooperate on moral grounds. The first possibility does not exist in the Hobbesian state of nature, for the very establishment of the power to reward and punish is at stake here. The second possibility is by definition a departure from the assumption that all men act in a prudentially rational manner. The idea that men in the state of nature will cooperate on purely moral grounds Hobbes discounts outright. The only remaining possibility is that they will cooperate because they do not know what is in their interest or are incapable of acting on it and thus stumble on the right solution "by mistake." This, as we shall see, is exactly what the positivistic interpretation implies: the state arises not *because* it is prudentially legitimate, but because people are *incapable* of prudence. Once people commit the "mistake" of cooperating, however, the benefits of cooperation confer a *post factum* legitimacy on their originally "mistaken" beliefs.

been said on this subject, Hobbes's insights become more—and not less—interesting under the more traditional interpretation. His crucial investigation into the problem of legitimacy of political power is, in my opinion, only obscured by confusing the question of de facto legitimacy with moral or prudential considerations. Above all, however, the very importance of Hobbes's philosophy for the development of liberal political thought is, as I shall argue, connected with the positivist, descriptive character of his theory.

I. Theory of Nature and the Nature of Man

1. The Originality of Hobbes

Looking at the strictly political proposals that Hobbes advocated, one would hardly classify him as a "liberal." It is true, of course, that his defense of absolutism moved away from the theory of divine right, and many a Marxist has claimed that absolutism was the first blow the rising bourgeoisie dealt to the political structure of feudalism. But even if one accepts the Marxist claim that Hobbes is an ideologue of rising capitalist society—and much about it is at least defensible—the fact remains that the political arrangements Hobbes proposed are deeply authoritarian.

It is not only Hobbes's authoritarianism that is illiberal; the very idea of absolute sovereignty, whether located in an individual, an assembly, or the people, is in tension with the individualistic premises of liberal politics. The attack on the divine right of kings and the search for a radically new source of sovereignty may certainly be viewed as ushering into a new era of politics—the era that can be described as "modern." But modernity so understood has at least two faces: it implies that all authority, at least all authority that men may have over other men, derives its legitimacy from man-made arrangements, and it may also imply that the will of the people replaces the will of God in that, in principle at least, it no longer knows any legitimate limits. It is the first implication that liberalism thrives on while the other underlies all those movements which, ever since the French Revolution, have insisted that a reference to *vox populi* trumps all other arguments in the political domain. The two strands of modern politics, the liberal and the demo-cratic, have often lived in a somewhat uneasy conjunction: the liberal doctrine must, after all, make some room for the autonomy of the collective, and most democratic regimes have admitted a sphere of privacy into which politics should not intrude. Nevertheless, the basic idea underlying democratic legitimation is that a political aggregation of individuals brings about an entirely new body—the state—which speaks with its own voice and possesses its own will, independently of the cacophony of individual voices and the confusion of individual wills. Thus, in the absence of a separately justified concern for individual prepolitical freedom, there is nothing in democratic ideology that would a priori force one to recognize any particular mode in which the will of the people is to be expressed. A majority of citizens' votes has been one widely used criterion, but it has by no means remained unchallenged. As early as Rousseau in theory and Robespierre in practice, serious qualifications were imposed on the translation of majorities into binding pronouncements of the people.[1] Only shortly afterward the majority criterion was rejected altogether by the Bonapartist regime, which perhaps came closest of all to a Hobbesian polity. Despite his attempts to ape the dynastic tradition of European monarchies and his cynical uses of religion for the purposes of self-advertisement, Napoleon himself could not have for a moment believed that his papal coronation had anything to do with the real meaning of his imperial power.[2] While the coronation was instrumental in controlling the allegiance of the masses, the real legitimacy, if there was any, of the Empire rested on the fact (if one may call it such) that the somewhat mystical entity known as the French nation had invested Napoleon with the right to speak in its name. The difference between the Bonapartist and the earlier republican idea of legitimation is enormous if it stems from the presence or absence of respect for individual autonomy. But it is quite negligible if it concerns merely the most accurate method of ascertaining the will of the nation, i.e., of the entity that is in advance defined as distinct and independent of individual Frenchmen. What unites the two regimes is their belief that once this link between their institutions and the will of the French nation is established, nothing in heaven or on earth can rob them of their legitimacy. The Republic was in fact much more arrogant than Napoleon in this respect. Not only did it believe that it was bound by no norms of international coexistence; it

[1]For an interesting study of the progressive divorce of the concept of popular sovereignty from an empirical ascertainment of majority's wishes through an electoral process, see J. L. Talmon, *The Origins of Totalitarian Democracy* (New York, 1970).

[2]He is reputed to have said that the essence of religion consists not in the mystery of the divine incarnation but in its being a sanction of unequal distribution of wealth. Quoted after A. Aulard, *Histoire politique de la Révolution française* (5th ed., Paris, 1913), 734 (English translation by B. Miall: *The French Revolution: A Political History* [London, 1910], 4:205).

also felt quite free to disenfranchise whole classes of French society, confiscate the property of the church and the *émigrés*, execute the king, and keep the guillotine busy chopping off the heads of its erstwhile proponents. In this sense, the idea of absolute sovereignty makes the Republic closer to the Bonapartist regime than to a liberal state. Indeed, although liberalism shares the democratic hostility to the social divisions of feudalism, its desire for limits on state sovereignty over individuals may make it less disapproving of the obstacles that custom and religion imposed on the feudal king than of unbridled power possessed by even the most democratically elected majority.

Thus, it is not just Hobbes's authoritarianism, but his very insistence on the absolute sovereignty of the artificial person constituting the state that separates him from liberalism in the usual sense of the word. Why then begin with Hobbes if we are interested in the early development of liberal thought?

The answer is quite complex, but we will move along the way toward it if we understand that liberalism was born not as a new answer to an old question, but as a new problem that demanded a solution. No doubt liberal thought has many antecedents earlier than the seventeenth century, but as a *political* doctrine it was new and its rise was meteoric. The civil war in England began and was fought largely as yet another war of religion. To be sure, freedom of conscience was very much at issue and it is an issue that is quite central to liberalism. But the issue did not arise as a secular principle of politics as much as it originated in the demand of religious dissidents to be free from the requirement of conformity with an established church. The more "secular" aspects of the conflict, such as the struggle over the rights of Parliament and the extent of the royal prerogative, whatever their deeper social meaning, were a natural consequence of the fact that the House of Commons represented the classes attached to the chapel and the presbytery, while the Crown stood for the Church of England and the specter of the pope. It is easy to exaggerate this view, of course, but this much at least seems obvious: if the religious component of the struggle had been removed from the picture, the participants themselves would have been unable to articulate their positions,[3] and, if they had to clothe them in exclusively secular terms, they would have been frightened by their own political demands. If the civil war was still a war of religion, however, the English government's dominant mode of legitimation

---

[3]Imagine, for example, Charles I trying to defend his absolute power without reference to divine right or the Puritans trying to articulate their defense of individual autonomy without recourse to the idea that man's relation to God is not mediated by a terrestrial church.

forty years later is hardly conceivable without a decisive triumph of liberal thinking. In this transition, Hobbes's role is absolutely central, for it was he who reformulated the very task of political philosophy and defined the problem-setting characteristic of early liberal theory.

Although Hobbes clearly believed that religion was an extremely important element in preserving or undermining governmental stability, he did not believe that the legitimacy of a government—and he saw an intimate connection between legitimacy and stability—in any way depended on the *truth* of the religious justification from which the government may derive support. Quite the other way around, in fact: it was the legitimizing function of religion that he appears to have used as a criterion of the worthiness and acceptability, if not the truth, of religious beliefs. There has been, of course, a substantial amount of controversy concerning the extent to which Hobbes's own philosophy still rests on religious foundations. But he seems to have had little doubt that the originality of his approach to politics was to consist in rejecting the theological foundations of political philosophy and replacing them with a rooting in natural science.[4]

In rejecting the rooting of politics in theology Hobbes was not entirely without precedent. At least Machiavelli, among the great modern thinkers, had done this before him. Neither was Hobbes original in attempting to look at politics in the context of a broader philosophical view, including a theory of nature. In fact, most prior political philosophies since Plato and Aristotle were of this kind. Given the fact that both politics and science are fundamental elements of advanced cultures, it would be surprising to discover that a connection between them was missing throughout most of our history. Nevertheless, Hobbes was an absolutely seminal thinker in realizing that political philosophy in the seventeenth century had to be grounded in *modern* natural science, with its mechanistic approach, rather than in outdated Aristotelian teleology. In this way, Hobbes did not merely "update" political philosophy for his time; he confronted it with a body of knowledge which seemed to rule out most of the preexisting argumentative strategies in the field. More than that, in many fundamental ways the new science transformed the very problems faced by political philosophy and, at the

---

[4]This view has, of course, been questioned by H. Warrender, *The Political Philosophy of Hobbes* (Oxford, 1957). More recently, a very interesting and more balanced study of Hobbes on religion was provided by E. J. Eisenach's *Two Worlds of Liberalism* (Chicago, 1981). No one can free himself entirely from such a dominant feature of one's tradition as was religion in Hobbes's time. It is therefore not surprising that some traces of religious thinking may be found in his work; it is in fact surprising how few of them there are. Fastening onto them as a key to an overall interpretation of his thought appears to me even less promising than past attempts to make Descartes into a medieval philosopher.

extreme, seemed to threaten the very possibility of political philosophy as a coherent intellectual enterprise.

2. Hobbes's Conception of Desire. His Critique of Aristotle

The substitution of modern mechanistic natural science for the old philosophical background of political theory enabled Hobbes to give a radically new theory of the nature of *man*. To be sure, Hobbes himself did not draw all the liberal political conclusions from his new scientific approach to the study of man. But his new theory provided some of the fundamental premises of liberalism that future political philosophy could not ignore, even if it wanted to avoid the liberal outcome on the political level. I do not claim, of course, that a theory of man similar to that Hobbes gave could not be maintained without the mechanistic presuppositions of seventeenth-century natural science. Nevertheless, Hobbes clearly believed that his effort to derive one from the other greatly enhanced the plausibility of his theory and we must, it seems to me, take his effort seriously. In a number of places Hobbes's derivation may appear artificial, and in others, especially when he uses terms normally associated with moral discourse, it may seem to break down altogether. But its importance will become clear if we begin our inquiry into Hobbes's theory of man in the place where the interrelationship between the various components of his philosophical system is perhaps the most obvious. His account of the nature of desire is, I believe, just such a place: in it, on the basis of insights derived from Galilean physics, Hobbes gives us the general contours of his revolutionary— and, in its implications, liberal—theory of human nature, which in turn will serve as a foundation of his own political philosophy.

Nowhere is Hobbes's radical break with the traditional theory of man more clearly visible than in the following passage from *Leviathan*:[5]

> The Felicity of this life, consisteth not in the repose of a mind satisfied. For there is no such *Finis ultimus*, (utmost ayme,) nor *Summum Bonum*, (greatest Good,) as is spoken of in the Books of the old Morall Philosophers. Nor can a man any more live, whose Desires are at an end, than he, whose Senses and Imagination are at a stand. Felicity is a continuall progresse of the desire, from one object to another; the attaining of the former, being still but the way to the later.

As the novelty of this statement has dwindled since the publication of *Leviathan*, its implications may be best understood when viewed

[5]*Lev.*, 47.

against the background of the theories that it criticizes. The "old Morall Philosophers" are, of course, the Aristotelians, whose theory of man had been woven into the whole structure of their teleological world view. To ask about the content of human "felicity," about the ideal of happiness for which men strive, was for them to ask about the essence of humanity or a state the realization of which constitutes the fulfillment of human aspirations. This very way of asking the question, and not only the content of the answer, is what Hobbes intends to reject.

Let us look at what is assumed in the Aristotelian way of asking about human happiness, even if this analysis does not promise any strikingly original results. First, the Aristotelian manner of asking questions implies a certain view of *nature*. The most characteristic feature of the Aristotelian conception of nature is the blurring of the is-ought distinction: "nature" is a *normative* concept that does not refer to a continuous process of change in which any particular state is only a fragment, but rather to the *terminus ad quem*, in other words, a state that constitutes the culminating point of a process. For Aristotle and his followers, a process was always a process of *becoming*, in the sense of *becoming something*. Thus, to account for a process was not so much to uncover the "how" of the operating mechanism as to point to the *end* of the process, both in the sense of a point at which the process comes to a stop and in the sense of the purpose of the movement. This end was, for the Aristotelians, identical with the essence of the thing in process and its "good" (what it "ought" to be "according to its nature"). Hence, insofar as this view postulated that every process culminates at the point of its completion, the Aristotelian theory of nature assigned a priority to rest over motion; insofar, however, as the end point was supposed to specify a *norm* for the process of becoming, the Aristotelians viewed moral norms, which specify the good toward which men ought to strive, as only a species of a more general principle of nature, namely, that each thing has its own "good" to which it tends in accordance with its nature.

It is not particularly relevant whether Hobbes had first come to his views concerning human psychology and only then discovered the Galilean theory of nature, which he could use to support them, or whether he actually derived the former from the latter. The important consideration is that the two remain in close relation to each other. The Galilean rejection of the Aristotelian priority of rest over motion undermines the whole structure of Aristotelian physics and, with it, the conception of man built around the concept of man's "essence."[6] With the claim that a body in motion will continue to move with uniform

[6]Without the additional assumption that every process of change is a form of physical motion, the move from Galilean physics to the Hobbesian theory of man would remain only an analogy. But this assumption is, of course, one Hobbes made.

velocity unless an application of some external force results in its acceleration or deceleration, the concept of essence, as the Aristotelians understood it, becomes useless in explaining the nature of the process that a given thing is undergoing, since it is no longer true that a body has its "natural place" at which its motion is going to cease, regardless of other considerations. The only properly physical characterstic of a body—its inertia—is not something that propels the body to move toward a certain point that could be seen as the purpose of its movement, but rather something responsible for a continuation of the present velocity and direction of movement, no matter what this velocity or direction may be. "Self-preservation," whether applied to physical motion or a living body, is ultimately resistance to change and not a force responsible for a change leading to some future state in which the essence of a thing or an organism is fully realized. Thus, being able to specify the characteristics of the present state of a thing (together with the nature of the underlying mechanism) is much more pertinent to the knowledge of its "nature" and of its future states than trying to determine the meaning of the present state on the basis of some "good" or essence peculiar to the thing in question.

Hobbes's theory of desire is hardly understandable except against the background of this modern conception of nature. His rejection of a *finis ultimus* or a *summum bonum* is not predicated on the simple psychological observation, known to the ancients, that a man always wants more than he already has; it is not the possibility of some end's being ultimate or some good's being the *greatest* that bothers him, but the very concept of *finis* and *bonum* as the Aristotelians understood them. What he wants to question is the very conception of desire as being raised by some good, as much as some good's being in itself the most desirable. In a strikingly novel turn, Hobbes insists that what we call "good" must be *defined* in terms of desire and must be understood as a function of the activity of desiring, rather than the other way around. For Aristotle, the statement that a good raises a desire functions as an explanation, a causal account. For Hobbes, it is merely a tautology, and in order to explain how a desire is brought about, we must look for its efficient cause in the mechanism of human action.

As applied to his conception of man, Aristotle's general theory of nature prejudges much of the answer concerning the nature of human happiness and desire. It would be a mistake to say that Aristotle or his followers did not envisage the possibility that a man may desire more than he can ever achieve. On the contrary, Aristotle himself says that "the naughtiness of men is a cup that can never be filled," and he even adds that "it is the nature of desire to be infinite."[7] Moreover, he does

---

[7]*Politics*, 1267b, trans. E. Barker (Oxford, 1946).

not believe that the greatest good is the state of passivity, since he sees happiness to consist in an "activity of the soul."[8] Thus, Hobbes would be trivially wrong if he meant to accuse the Aristotelians of holding a theory of happiness that would make happiness equivalent to a cessation of life functions.[9] But what Hobbes aims at is the *necessity* for desire to transcend any given state of satisfaction and not the mere Aristotelian possibility of a man's wanting more than he already has. What makes, in Aristotle, for a conflict between happiness and desire and precludes their identification along Hobbesian lines is that he views desire as caused by the absence of something indispensable (or perceived as such) for the realization of man's essence, while he defines happiness in terms of self-sufficiency. Self-sufficiency, or the gist of the good life for which an Aristotelian man strives, is a state "which taken by itself makes life something desirable and deficient in nothing."[10] Hence, even though Aristotle may describe happiness as an "activity of the soul," this sense of "activity" must be distinguished from "motion," or "process," or "striving for," since it implies no external purpose; this is what is meant by its being "desirable for its own sake" or "good in itself." Its having an internal purpose, or better still, its being its own purpose, implies that it is an activity that does not involve any change or process of becoming. Consequently, despite its being an activity, it corresponds to the state of rest or completion (perfection). A happy man may perform all kinds of actions, but he cannot be said to desire something that he does not already "have": his happiness rests in the totality of his dispositions (brought about by habits, education, and so on) that make nothing outside his control an object of his volition.

Within this framework, desire plays the same role with respect to living organisms as the inherent propensity of a physical body to occupy its natural place does for that body. In the same way as a body will move if it is "outside" with respect to its natural position, a living organism endowed with a will is motivated to act by a desire raised by an external object the organism perceives as necessary for the realization of its essence. The only relevant difference between the two situations is that a desiring organism perceives its good as such, while a body does not. Thus, insofar as a desire constitutes the initiation of any process of *change*, it is always an effect of some *privation*. In other words, a good *necessarily* raises a desire only when it constitutes some external object perceived as indispensable to happiness as a state of

---

[8]*Nicomachean Ethics*, 1098a, trans. M. Oswald (Indianapolis, Ind., 1962).

[9]Aristotle specifically addresses this issue in connection with his discussion of Solon's dictum that the term "happy" cannot be applied to a man during his lifetime; *Nic. Eth.*, 1101a10–1101a20.

[10]*Nic. Eth.*, 1097b.

"rest" in which all human aspirations are essentially fulfilled. Once this state is reached, we can still speak of a man's having desires, as, for example, when a man "desires" to learn a new truth, to undertake some political activity, or even to go for a walk;[11] but at this point desire no longer limits the extent of human freedom: it flows from the spontaneity of human agency and its object no longer *constrains* the will. This is what is meant by saying that a happy man can no longer desire anything that he does not already "have."

Thus, the Aristotelian conception of desire clearly allows, and in fact calls, for a limit on the extent to which desire can create a state of "restlessness" in a being endowed with a will. Aristotle's statement that "it is the nature of desire to be infinite" does not mean that desiring beings must constantly be pushed from one pursuit to another. To begin with, each *particular* desire has an obvious limit in the good by which it is raised. Hence, "infinity" does not define a particular desire but rather the whole category, the class of desires. To say that desire is by nature infinite means that the (general) *concept* of desire does not contain within itself the determination of its limit; in other words, it does not by itself specify the whole class of objects that could be desired. Limitation is inherent not in the nature (definition) of desire, but in the nature of each particular organism capable of desiring. Thus, for example, it is the nature of man, and not of desire, that prescribes a limit to what a man may properly want. To be sure, the existence of this limitation is still not enough to guarantee that all men will actually desire only that which their true nature prescribes to them, since by an error of judgment (lack of knowledge about the nature of happiness) they may view as necessary to their happiness something that is in fact not such, or by a habit of indulgence they may pervert their natural constitution in such a way as to make it require more than they are ever able to provide. This is why the "cup that can never be filled" is the "naughtiness" (a refraction from the norm and not the norm itself) of men. But even in these cases a limit is always implied, since otherwise no desire could actually arise and move the will. The reason none could arise is embedded in the whole philosophical framework of Aristotle's system. As his physics precludes the possibility of infinite motion, so does his teleological account of human volition preclude limitless desire. Desire is, for Aristotle, always raised by its object, so that the good to which it tends is the proper final cause of the action that desire effects. If this object is desired for its own sake, then its fulfillment puts an end to the chain of actions that desire for it effects. On the other hand, when an object is desired for the sake of something else, the chain

---

[11]As opposed to his "having to go somewhere."

of desires to which it gives rise cannot be infinite, for then, in the absence of the final good to be desired, no intermediate object of desire could be fully determined as such. This is not only a result of Aristotle's rejection of the concept of actual infinity, but also a simple consequence of his view of motion as requiring constant renewal by its *terminus ad quem*.

The central point of Hobbes's critique of the Aristotelian conception of happiness is his claim that desire cannot be understood as an *effect of privation*. Whereas for Aristotle, desire is always to be accounted for with respect to the state of rest and fulfillment to follow, for Hobbes it is essentially an indeterminate state insofar as its ultimate satisfaction is concerned; it is an attitude toward the external world *as such*, so that no particular object (or set of objects) is capable of removing it. The Aristotelian, teleological model of explanation is not merely inadequate, according to Hobbes, to account for the behavior of men and other natural agents; when used for the purpose of constructing a theory of human action, it leads—unless one distorts the real motives that make men act—to a network of absurdities.

To begin with, the concept of the ultimate purpose of human action cannot, according to Hobbes, be given any realistic or even meaningful positive content. If we are to suppose that the actions of men are indeed directed toward an end established for them by some natural order, then the "good" for which men strive must be described as "security." But the goal of absolute security contradicts itself in its very achievement. It is the nature of man to be able to perceive anything independent of his volition as a potential danger to his life. Consequently, absolute security would be made possible only by the acting organisms' achieving a total mastery over the natural world and annihilating the latter as an entity independent of itself. Success in such an enterprise would in fact transform the organism into a fully self-enclosed cosmos. Like the real cosmos, however, the organism could no longer be said to be "alive" in the ordinary sense of this term, since in the absence of any interaction with the environment, all voluntary and cognitive processes would have to come to a halt.

The absurdity does not end here, however. Suppose that by "security" one does not mean absolute security but a relative state of peace, such as that brought about by the institution of a commonwealth. The question that now arises concerns the *means* that nature provided men with to achieve this goal, or the kind of motivational principle that is operating to allow them to realize the good toward which they are said to strive. No careful reader of Hobbes will have any difficulty in determining from his work the only available candidate for this position: it is the *fear of violent death*, which is the driving force of human behavior and an always overriding factor in human motivation. But while security, in its relative form, is a state that in the natural condition of men (and it is only of the natural condition that we may speak so far) may be brought about only by following a course of behavior resulting from a careful calculation of risks involved in any particular situation, fear of violent death is an instinctual reaction of man to any possible danger, no matter how close or remote it might be. Fear, according to Hobbes, is a *passion* or *emotion*,[12] and it does not allow for reasoning; it operates entirely indiscriminately and, by forcing man to react to every danger he perceives, makes it impossible for him to trade the acceptance of some risks for the sake of avoidance of others. The *summum malum* that a man avoids through his fear of violent death is not one evil among many (only the greatest) or an aggregate of these evils, both of which would involve more or less complex calculations incompatible with an instinctual reaction. It is, rather, an indeterminate representation of danger that calls for an immediate response. The general outcome of this mode of functioning is the human organism's insatiable desire for power, a desire that is obviously irrational, in that it most often does not contribute to the organism's goal of security or even to a real increase of its power. But this statement does not have, for Hobbes, the normative significance that it acquires in a moralist or a prudentialist reading. Rather, it is a consequence of the analysis of the way human motivation operates by virtue of man's natural constitution. Hobbes's basic point is not so much that men do not always know what is best for them in the long run or that there is an objective conflict between their individual interests and some kind of interest that may accrue to them from following a policy designed to foster collective security; it is that the actual precedence among the various factors determining a particular act of volition is given to an irrational fear of violent death that makes men inherently incapable of following those principles which prudence may recommend to them as ways to security.

Thus, the generalized effect of the fear of violent death is an *indiscriminate* desire for power, a result very different from security viewed as an optimal outcome of a calculation of gains and losses involved in any type of behavior. Absolute power and absolute security do in fact coincide, but (to say nothing about the hopelessness of all efforts to achieve them) they result in a state that defeats their purpose, since it annihilates the very subject that was supposed to have been preserved and protected. Relative security and man's desire for power, on the other hand, contradict each other outright: in his behavior toward the environment, and especially in the context of competition with his

---

[12]*Lev.*, 70; *De homine*, xii, 3.

fellow men, each man's desire for power creates a vicious circle of *bellum omnis contra omnem*, which is the exact opposite of the security he needs and desires. If we want, then, to give a teleological account of human behavior, the result is quite surprising: the means (or power) that nature has put at man's disposal to achieve the end of security has in fact a quite contrary effect. It is as if nature contradicted itself in its most sublime product and revealed a jarring discord in its choice of ends and means—a curious phenomenon to ponder for those who believe that it acts according to a perfect design and embodies the principles of rationality. An even more curious phenomenon, perhaps, is that the remedy for this situation is to be found in a human artifact: a social contract that yields an artificial person capable, by its overawing power, of rechanneling men's efforts and effecting the harmonization of naturally conflicting ends and means. The final irony of Hobbes's theory of man is that the social contract itself is brought about, as we shall see in the discussion of his political theory, not by virtue of men's finally coming to their senses and acting rationally, but as a result of their propensity to error and absurdity.

3. Self-Preservation: Mechanistic and Functionalist Accounts

In place of Aristotle's teleological world view, Hobbes substitutes a mechanistic theory of nature on which he constructs his own theory of man. He analyzes the nature of human behavior from two essential and mutually complementary points of view. On the one hand, his ontology commits him to a radical mechanistic reductionism. Accordingly, he adopts for his theory of man the rather cumbersome vocabulary of a mechanistic theory and attempts to redescribe the phenomenon of life, including its most developed forms such as sensation, imagination, and reason, as species of physical motion. On the other hand, however, an inquiry into the life of man in general and into his social behavior in particular does not easily lend itself to a completely "value-free" investigation, like that attempted in the natural sciences. Human beings are emotionally and passionately involved in those aspects of inquiry which concern themselves, and the outcome of their actions, determined or not, is rarely indifferent to them. Besides, whether or not they are in fact only very complicated machines, they never *think* of themselves as such, and this fact is not theoretically unimportant: it not only calls for an explanation, but also allows for a phenomenological or functionalist account, in addition to the mechanistic one. Consequently, Hobbes leaves room in his theory of man for an account that admits of language in some respects not unlike that of a normative or teleological theory: it can treat of such subjects as the "self" (and not merely a body), evaluate different types of behavior from the point of view of their "functionality" with respect to the overall "purpose" of an organism, and so on. Nevertheless, it must be kept in mind that Hobbes's "functionalist" account of human action has no ontological status independent of his mechanistic theory, with which it must always be compatible; it derives its validity entirely from the *fact* that men attach emotional significance to certain outcomes of their actions. Hobbes may have been sometimes guilty of a terminological inconsistency, but he was not guilty of the more serious confusion of combining the incompatible claims of mechanistic and teleological accounts. A good case in point is his treatment of the concept of self-preservation, which organizes his whole theory of man and provides a bridge between its mechanistic and functionalist aspects.

The teleological implications of the concept of self-preservation, insofar as this concept is to play an explanatory role in a theory of life, are obvious enough not to require extensive discussion. The very fact that an action may be done "for the sake of" some future state implies a theory of ends and means as a basic element of explanation. The first point at which Hobbes frustrates this mode of explanation is connected with some consequences of his radical nominalism. The traditional understanding of the concept of self-preservation, deriving from Aristotle, required that some ontological status be conferred on the not yet realized state of affairs that exerts causal influence on the present state of the organism. The future states of the organism do not exist in the same way that the present states do, and yet they are supposed to exert some influence on the latter. Aristotle's answer to this problem lay, of course, in his notion of essence, in the *concept* of a thing, which, unlike the thing itself, is eternal and indestructible. The essence of an organism provided the always existing standard of perfection for the organism in its development and constituted the norm that specified the state of affairs toward which the organism was supposed to strive to develop. Thus, within the Aristotelian framework, self-preservation had the meaning of a striving toward the realization of the essence of a given thing. In the case of man, for example, it was the idea of rationality that determined the meaning of human development. According to Hobbes, however, concepts are merely words or names, and as such they cannot by any stretch of the imagination play the role Aristotle assigned to them. Concepts are essentially artificial collections of particulars subsumed under a common name for reasons of convenience, and not objectively existing patterns to which things must conform. They arise as a matter of conventional definition and have no independent ontological status.

This fact has rather fundamental implications for Hobbes's understanding of the concept of self-preservation. To begin with, whatever else it might be (and it is too early for us to inquire into this problem in more detail), the "self" that is the subject of self-preservative behavior is primarily a *particular* and not a member of some indestructible species. Second, self-preservation is not primarily a future-oriented activity, but a *conservative* force, the meaning of which is determined by the status quo and resistance to change. As a consequence, the concept of self-preservation in Hobbes is immediately severed from the notion's traditional setting. In the context of Aristotelian theory, the connection between the concept of man's self-preservation and the essence of man resulted in an account of human action in which self-preservation had the sense of a striving for the self-sufficiency of a species—a state of fulfillment of all human aspirations deriving from the fact that human beings are essentially rational. For Hobbes, on the other hand, self-preservation is a largely blind organismic drive that aims at the mere perpetuation of natural existence.

But Hobbes's reduction of the teleological implications of the concept of self-preservation goes even further. Within a norminalist framework, it is still possible to view human behavior at least as guided by a *representation* of some future state (viewed as desirable by the organism) and in this sense "purposeful." Hobbes will not deny, of course, that a representation of some future state plays a role in the motivational process of voluntary action, but he intends to defeat the teleological implications of this fact by effecting an identification of mental phenomena with species of internal motion and thus to substitute ordinary mechanical causation for a seemingly purposeful behavior. As a result, voluntary and involuntary motions become for Hobbes only two subspecies of the same phenomenon.[13]

There is no need here to go into the details of Hobbes's rather crude mechanistic reduction, especially since what interests us most is not, after all, its success or failure, but its influence on Hobbes's political philosophy. In general, with some refinements the significance of which will be discussed later, Hobbes presents a simple model of man as a machine reacting to certain kinds of external stimulation. Senses are, for him, receptacles of external motion that "by the mediation of Nerves, and other strings, and membranes of the body, continued

---

[13]*Lev.*, 23. For a very interesting discussion of the nature of voluntary motions in Hobbes, see J. W. N. Watkins, *Hobbes' System of Ideas* (London, 1965).

inward to the Brain, and Heart, causeth there a resistance, or counter-pressure, or endeavour of the heart, to deliver it self: which endeavour because *Outward*, seemeth to be some matter without. And this *seeming*, or *fancy*, is that which men call Sense."[14] Imagination, which plays a crucial role in actions directed toward an absent future goal, is in turn "nothing but *decaying sense*,"[15] and understanding is but "Imagination that is raysed in man . . . by words, or other voluntary signes."[16] It is here that the proper mechanistic reduction of voluntary motions takes place. Since "Voluntary motions, depend alwayes upon a precedent thought of *whither*, *which way*, and *what*; it is evident, that the Imagination is the first internall beginning of all Voluntary Motion."[17] But since imagination is but "decaying sense," that is, the decaying movement by which the organism resists external pressures, the origin of voluntary motion may be explained with the help of purely physical phenomena. The psychic or mental quality of the endeavor that leads to a voluntary motion and that, "when it is toward something which causeth it, is called APPETITE, or DESIRE," is only an epiphenomenon of the "small beginnings of Motion, within the body of Man, before they appear in walking, speaking, striking, and other visible actions."[18] Thus, desire is nothing but a mechanical response to certain types of stimuli, even if the action in which it results may be called voluntary and involve deliberation. Deliberation, according to Hobbes, is "the whole summe of Desires, Aversions, Hopes and Fears [all of which are similarly reduced to internal motions], continued till the thing be either done, or thought impossible," and the will is "the last Appetite, or Aversion, immediately adhaering to the action, or to the omission thereof."[19] With this, the mechanistic reduction of voluntary motions is in fact completed.[20]

The effect of Hobbes's mechanistic reduction of mental phenomena on his understanding of the concept of self-preservation is, despite the crudeness of his account and the absence of any evolutionary considerations, not unlike the effect of Darwin's theory of evolution on his concept of the survival of the fittest. In the same way that Darwin's theory explains a given species' ability to survive by pointing to a

[14]*Lev.*, 3.
[15]Ibid., 5.
[16]Ibid., 8.
[17]Ibid., 23.
[18]Ibid.
[19]Ibid., 28.
[20]For a critique of Hobbes's mechanistic reductionism, see R. S. Peters and H. Tajfel, "Hobbes and Hull—Metaphysicians of Behaviour," *British Journal for the Philosophy of Science*, 8 (1957–58), reprinted in M. Cranston and R. S. Peters, eds., *Hobbes and Rousseau* (Garden City, N.Y., 1972).

contingent development of its particular organs, abilities, and so forth, the Hobbesian mechanistic theory explains man's ability to avoid death with reference not to the purpose of his behavior, but to the particular constitution of his organism. The human machine is constructed in such a way that its voluntary responses to environmental stimulation tend (though by no means invariably) to prolong its existence and are *always* perceived as at least not incompatible with survival. But the "purpose" of the machine's continuation in existence is a function of the machine's mode of operation and not vice versa. Self-preservation is an *outcome* or *effect* of the organism's constitution, and it cannot *causally* account for the organism's behavior. That an organism's responses tend to prolong its existence is a matter of fact and not a norm, and statements about self-preservation are as much normative pronouncements as, say, a statement that a certain material tends to break in certain circumstances.

Nevertheless, without a violation of the result of such analyses, it is not impossible—and in many respects it is in fact desirable—to speak of self-preservation within a context of not merely a mechanistic but also a functionalist theory. In general, the phrase "tends to," which we often use in describing man's self-preservative behavior, does not have to refer to any inner striving; in the example of the material that "tends to break in certain circumstances" it expressed nothing more than a significant frequency of a certain outcome. But in some sense men do, of course, strive to preserve themselves, since even if they are fundamentally only very complicated machines and, being as determined to act the way they do as a stone is determined to fall,[21] they can hardly choose to act otherwise, the success or failure of their self-preservative tendency has for them a very strong emotional significance. That they are not indifferent in this respect is, of course, also only a fact (about their psychic makeup), and that it plays a role in their motivational process does not change very much here (since their thoughts, feelings, and so on are but internal motions of their bodies). Nevertheless, if we approach human behavior at the level of a phenomenological analysis, not as it *is*, but as it *appears* to the subject (especially in view of the necessarily limited knowledge the subject has about himself and others like him)[22], we may say that the subject's self-preservation appears to him as a norm, as something that provides a standard of the conformity of his behavior to his innermost desire. Now, so long as one does not

[21]*De cive*, I, 7.

[22]In view of Hobbes's claim that the perceptive "seeming" is in fact *identical* (and "in fact identical" is for him the same as "necessarily identical," i.e., not only coextensive, but also synonymous) with the underlying physical motions, he would have to say that for a perfect knower the level of reality and the level of appearance would be indistinguishable.

infer from this that the mere logical value of such statements about conformity has anything to do with the real causes of men's actions, there is nothing wrong in adopting this way of speaking. The fact that men care about their own preservation and that their behavior does tend in this direction allows us to take self-preservation as the proper *function* of the human organism, as an aspect of human behavior that has special significance for the scientist as well. That men's success in preserving themselves is by no means invariable then allows us to classify some of their actions as functional and others as dysfunctional and to speak, in the case of the latter, of periodic "breakdowns" of the human machine.

It is in this light that many passages in Hobbes that seem to suggest a normative interpretation of his theory should be read, especially those in which he speaks about the laws of nature or of reason and about its being wrong to break them, even in the absence of an enforcing authority. When Hobbes says that a certain course of action is dictated by a law of reason, he has two things in mind: first, that what the law says is conducive to self-preservation, and hence universal conformity with it is functionally rational; second, that in accordance with man's concern for his own security, the "Lawes of Nature . . . bind [him] to a desire that they should take place."[23] Rather than imposing on this "binding" the strong sense of moral or prudential obligation, we should understand it for what it is: a statement of the *fact* that what men, by their reasoning, view as conducive to their security, they necessarily (in accordance with the laws concerning the *causal* determinants of their beliefs) desire, even though this desire may never be strong enough to overcome their instinctual craving for power and influence their actual behavior.[24] It is only in this sense of a factual connection (mechanical association) between security and an inner state of approval and desire that the laws of reason are natural; for what they postulate is brought about by a convention, by an artificial device designed to harmonize the naturally incompatible ends and means of human behavior.

4. Hobbes on Human Nature

It is time for us to consider those aspects of Hobbes's theory of man in which he presents his substantive views of human nature (as distinct

[23]*Lev.*, 79.

[24]In Chapter 26 of *Leviathan* (p. 138) Hobbes expressly states that the laws of nature "are not properly Lawes, but qualities that dispose men to peace, and to obedience." See also *De cive*, III, 31, where Hobbes says that "good and evil are names given things to signify the inclination or aversion of them, by whom they were given" and then proceeds to explain that moral laws are founded in the natural coincidence of individual judgments concerning good and evil.

from the nature of animals and physical bodies) and, by characterizing the presocial condition of man, sets the stage for his properly political theory. Several important characteristics that have traditionally been used to distinguish humans from animals Hobbes specifically discounts as either common to many kinds of organisms (sometimes even to all things in existence) or empty and meaningless. In particular he discounts all those features that were supposed to capture the uniqueness of human nature by ascribing to man, and man alone, the ability to act freely and escape the necessity of mechanical determination. To begin with, Hobbes clearly believes that absolutely everything is subject to mechanical necessity, so that the traditional concept of freedom is meaningless. Freedom, according to Hobbes, is simply "the absence of Opposition," where by "opposition" are meant "externall Impediments of motion."[25] Consequently, he says freedom "may be applyed no less to Irrationall, and Inanimate creatures, than to Rationall." But even voluntary action is not unique to humans. We have already seen that Hobbes defines the will as the last appetite in the chain of deliberation and deliberation as the "summe of Desires, Aversion, Hopes and Fears." Animals, he believes, are perfectly capable of all these, and he specifically ascribes to them not only will and deliberation, but the capacity for understanding as well, even though he views that capacity as inseparable from the use of speech.[26]

4.1. Language

Still, it is with reference to the human use of speech that Hobbes defines the difference between humans and animals. Although the difference in question is a matter of degree rather than a radical discontinuity, it is sufficiently marked to set man apart from the rest of the world. While a dog, says Hobbes, must be said to possess understanding (which he defines as "Imagination that is raysed ... by words, or other voluntary signes"), since it can respond to the call of its master, the "Understanding which is peculiar to man, is the Understanding not onely [of] his will, but [of] his conceptions and thoughts, by the sequell and contexture of names of things into Affirmations, Negations, and other formes of Speech."[27] Althought at first sight Hobbes's view of the role of language in human life does not appear particularly novel or striking, it is indeed so upon closer examination.

The significance of speech in general, according to Hobbes, is "to

---

[25]*Lev.*, 107.
[26]For will and deliberation, see *Lev.*, 28; for understanding, *Lev.*, 8.
[27]Ibid., 8.

transferre our Mentall Discourse, into Verbal; or the Trayne of our Thoughts, into a Trayne of Words."[28] His own explanation of the usefulness of language is that it allows for communication and for a "registring of the Consequences of our Thoughts; which being apt to slip out of our memory, and put us to a new labour, may again be recalled, by such words as they were marked by."[29] The importance of such a mnemonic device is, of course, not negligible; it allows for a process of storing past experiences and using them in the future. As a result, men are capable of a far-reaching generalization of their experience and of organizing a mass of past perceptions into a simplified system of knowledge. The fact that men reproduce past perceptions of connections between, say, two events when only one of them (or rather an event similar to one of them) is actually present is not due to their linguistic ability, and, thus, they possess a certain capacity of generalization before the introduction of speech. But this adaptive mechanism (of which animals are also not ignorant) is most severely limited until a fully developed system of signs transforms it into human wisdom and prudence.

Nevertheless, the real meaning of the "transfer" of mental discourse into a verbal one lies elsewhere, and Hobbes gives an indication of it in those passages in which he speaks of abuses, rather than the proper use, of language. What Hobbes calls "Mentall Discourse" is in fact a mechanical succession of images, which, though sometimes regulated by a desire that a subject may possess, is limited to a reproduction of actually perceived past connections between things or events.[30] Once the "Trayne of Thoughts," however, is replaced by a "Trayne of Words," the number of possible permutations of connections increases beyond all comparison. Associations between words or sentences are, of course, considerably easier to come by than associations between things or events: they can be suggested by hearsay, by education in which other people communicate their knowledge and experience, by accidental conjunctions of words or phrases because of their similarity, or by combinations connected with metaphorical uses of language. The very fact that the same event may be classified in many different ways opens a multitude of possibilities as to how it may be associated with other events and influence men's behavior. Thus, while the increase in the capacity for generalization that language introduces certainly allows for an ordering and, consequently, for a simplifying of a man's picture of the world around him, the loss of concreteness involved in

[28]Ibid., 12.
[29]Ibid., 12–13.
[30]Ibid., 8.

this process also increases the number of expectations that may arise in the mind of the perceiver upon any given occasion. And it is *this* feature of language that, above all, determines for Hobbes the difference between men and other organisms. It is, of course, trivial to say that language facilitates generalization or opens new possibilities for its user, but in view of the strictures imposed by Hobbes on the extent of human spontaneity (strictures that make all association a matter of mechanical necessity), the difference that this triviality makes in his account of human behavior cannot be exaggerated, because it is responsible for the unpredictability of human action and releases man from a fixed pattern of behavior characteristic of lower species. The very possibility of an absurd response to a relatively familiar stimulation and a great increase in the capacity for erring, which is characteristic of man, according to Hobbes, as a result of his abuses of language, will prove crucial in accounting for human behavior. As we shall see presently, this characteristic is responsible for man's insatiable desire for power which is at the root of the universal condition of war in the Hobbesian state of nature. And as the next chapter will in turn make clear, man's capacity for error is also absolutely instrumental in explaining the origin and stability of political power.

4.2. Desire for Power

The net effect of the introduction of language can be characterized as an enormous increase in the variety of responses that a man is capable of when faced with a particular stimulation and, consequently, an enormous increase in man's *powers*.[31] The exact sense in which powers may be predicated of objects (and of men in particular) will receive a more detailed treatment later. But what should be clear even now is that the increase of the extent of human powers brought about by the introduction of language cannot mean that a man now has a greater variety of possible responses to choose from when faced with some external stimulation, at least not if "choice" is taken as implying "freedom of the will." Rather, what is meant is that man will *actually* reveal an incomparably greater variety of responses, as compared with members of lower species. The best way of describing this difference is by pointing to the fact that man, to an infinitely greater extent than animals, reacts to possible dangers as if they were *actual*.[32] Of course, insofar as an animal can respond defensively to a certain stimulus that, like the

---

[31] In *De homine* (x, 3) Hobbes says that "by speech man is not made better, but only given greater possibilities."

[32] Cf. Hobbes's statement, ibid., that "man is famished even by future hunger."

hunter's voice, may not in itself present any danger but has been associated with danger in the past, it can be said to "predict" one event upon an observation of another and, since no prediction is infallible, to react to an only possible danger as if it were actual. But on the whole, an animal has a very limited power of making such "predictions," and the type of danger signals it reacts to is so restricted that in effect a completely unequivocal reaction to any type of stimulation may be considered to be built (as an "instinct") into every member of a given species. Some of these responses may in fact be very complicated (nest building, for example) or flexible to a degree (such as some animals' hunting habits), but the point is that they are all uniform throughout the life of each individual and the same for the whole species. In the case of man, however, no such simple "programming" is either operating or generally possible. This is not to deny, of course, that man is, for Hobbes, nothing but a very complicated machine, but he is a machine that reacts with an entirely different response to even the slightest variation in environmental stimulation, and—what is much more important—constantly adds new patterns to his arsenal of responses, so that continuous "reprogramming" (or learning) may make the same individual react entirely differently to virtually the same kind of stimulation at different times. Finally, the amount of information stored in the "human machine" is so great that the machine is capable of "mistaken" (ultimately harmful) reactions or even periodical breakdowns in the form of completely dysfunctional (absurd) responses.

Man's capacity for responding to possible dangers as if they were actual is by no means an unequivocal blessing. To begin with, the number of expectations that a man may have with respect to the future course of events around him creates in him a general feeling of insecurity and accounts for many forms of his dysfunctional behavior. A further consideration that only heightens this feeling of insecurity concerns the fact that the agent himself is aware that his predictions are fallible and may take this into account in deciding upon the course of action he is going to follow. In this sense, the huge area of the unknown comes to plague man more heavily than any other species, and perhaps not surprisingly, this fact is due to the greater extent of what he does know. An animal may react with fear to the unknown, but most of its habitat is familiar to it. Man, on the other hand, knows that familiarity is deceptive: the abstractness of his reasoning makes him always capable of picturing some possible consequences of any familiar event that will make it look ominous and threatening to the highest degree. And since his self-preservation mechanism, involving an obsessive fear of violent death, always makes him expect the worst and prepare for it, he is incapable of tranquil enjoyment of anything he now has and constantly strives to *anticipate* future deprivations.[33] It is this feature of man's desire that makes it independent of any concrete object that may even momentarily satisfy him and transforms desire from the result of a temporary and particular deprivation (which it was for Aristotle) into a general attitude toward the world *as such*. Desire in general (and not just human desire) is an organism's response to any kind of external interference with its internal state. No matter what stimulation enters the organs of sense (unless it is too weak to be perceived), it produces the "counter-pressure, or endeavour of the heart, to deliver it self."[34] The phrase "to deliver it self" is very significant here, for it shows that even ordinary sense perception (from the account of which this passage is taken) refers to a *practical* organismic function of self-preservation: the perceptive "seeming" or "fancy" is only a by-product of the organism's inertia that opposes any danger the external world may bring. In this sense the "generality" of desire, that is, its being a general function of life, incapable of being extinguished by any particular satisfaction, is characteristic not only of men, but of all organisms endowed with a will. But in the case of man, "to deliver it self" acquires an added, special significance, since it indicates an organismic impulse of self-assertion in which the world *as such* is perceived as a danger. While animals are only unconsciously subject to the never-ending chain of desires, without realizing the underlying unity of their pursuits (the unity due to the self-preservative function of their organisms), men, by virtue of their awareness of future and hypothetical dangers, effect the process of an *explicit* generalization of their desire: they transform it into the *desire for power*, that is, an explicitly indeterminate striving for absolute mastery over the world and not a particular attitude directed toward a specific satisfaction.

With this ideal of "mastery over the world" Hobbes has reached one of the most basic features in the self-understanding of the modern man. It is often said that the effect of early modern science, beginning with the Copernican revolution in astronomy and continued in the Galilean

[33]Cf. the following passage in *Lev.*, 52:

"First, it is peculiar to the nature of man, to be inquisitive into the Causes of the Events they see. . . .

"Secondly, upon the sight of any thing that hath a Beginning, to think also it had a cause, which determined the same to begin, then when it did, rather than sooner or later.

"The two . . . make Anxiety. For being assured that there be causes of all things that have arrived hitherto, or shall arrive hereafter; it is impossible for a man, who continually endeavoureth to secure himselfe against the evill he fears, and procure the good he desireth, not to be in a perpetuall solicitude of the time to come. So that every man, . . . like . . . *Prometheus*, . . . in the care of future time, hath his heart all the day long, gnawed on by feare of death, poverty, or other calamity; and has no repose, nor pause of his anxiety, but in sleep."

[34]Ibid., 3.

mechanistic theory of nature, was to undermine the centrality of man's position in the universe. Man was said to come to be seen as one natural object among many, more complex and more gifted perhaps than other organisms, but not in any way exempt from the same immutable laws that determine the fate of every other natural object. No one, perhaps, drew this conclusion with as much force and consistency as did Hobbes, who firmly located all human action in the domain of inexorable necessity. But from the very beginning of modern times another revolution has been taking place resulting in a much more radical subordination of nature to man than had ever been envisaged in medieval theology. We usually associate with Kant this second, (anti-)Copernican revolution, since it was Kant who first explicitly claimed that nature is, at least in part, a human artifact. It had started earlier, however, and is clearly visible in all those thinkers, including Hobbes and Locke, for whom the "disenchantment" of the natural world—its severance from the idea of a higher spiritual order that nature had been supposed to reflect—made that world an open arena for human manipulation. The premodern era had envisaged man as living in two more or less separate realms. For Aristotle, man's interaction with nature had been only that aspect of life—the pursuit of mere necessities—which man shared with animals; truly human life was supposed to take place in the pursuit of rationality among man's equals— other men. For Christians, the chasm between the spiritual and "natural" life was even deeper, and the concerns of salvation came to be viewed as almost entirely cut off from most worldly concerns. The modern turn, however, initiated and exemplified by Hobbes's mechanistic theory of man, at once located human life in man's interaction with the natural world and endowed that interaction with a deeper meaning, which liberal theory was later to infuse with new moral significance. The very possibility of a separate Aristotelian domain of "action"—the moral pursuit of the good life—was undermined by Hobbes with his thorough deterministic naturalism. But the equivalent of the Aristotelian domain of "production"—the domain of the satisfaction of needs—was correspondingly enlarged by the Hobbesian idea that human desires are in principle insatiable and transform nature as a whole into a sphere of human self-assertion.

Hobbes's consistent refusal to accept any but a trivial meaning for the concept of freedom imposed severe limitations on his ability to perceive the fascinating new potentialities implied by this new concept of "production," and he focused on its more nefarious consequences. The idea of human mastery over the world, however, was to acquire crucial significance in the work of Hobbes's immediate successor, Locke, who viewed it as a way in which man can, in a process of appropriation, "humanize" his environment and transform the external determination of his actions into a new form of independence and autonomy. As we shall see in Part Two of this book, the very foundation of Locke's liberal conception of human personhood is rooted in the move foreshadowed by the Hobbesian idea that the infinity of human desire transforms the concept of human acquisitiveness from a satisfaction-oriented attitude into a posture in which nature as such becomes a medium of human self-assertion. It is very important to keep firmly in mind, therefore, that the Hobbesian "restlesse desire of Power after power,"[35] far from being, as some have claimed,[36] an aberration of human nature, was in fact conceived by Hobbes as constitutive of the very nature of man. Whatever conception of subjectivity can be constructed within the mechanistic framework of Hobbes's ontology must be based on this feature of human behavior.

4.3. The Self

Hobbes never specifically allows for any conception of subjectivity that would ascribe to man a mode of being independent of his bodily existence. His mechanistic reductionism does not envisage any autonomous ontological status for the mental or the spiritual, and his polemic against Descartes's *Meditations* rests on the claim that the *cogito*, if understood as an immediate awareness of one's own present mental acts (and not a remembrance of past cogitations), involves an infinite regress in every act of thinking.[37] The subject of psychic processes, according to Hobbes, cannot be identified with an entirely empty act of self-awareness but must be looked for in man's bodily substance and its interaction with the external world. Nevertheless, Hobbes's theory of man's *practical* attitude toward the external world is not entirely blind to that aspect of human existence which Descartes referred to as the "cogito," Rousseau as "reflection," and others as "self-consciousness" or the "self." The aspect of Hobbes's theory that implicity allows for a not entirely reductionist theory of human subjectivity is precisely his claim that desire, in man, takes the form of desire for power, since it introduces a certain element of self-reference into his description of human nature. The fact that the normally outward-directed activity of desire takes in man the form of desire for power means that human

[35]Ibid., 47.
[36]See for example, L. Strauss, *Political Philosophy of Hobbes* (Oxford, 1936), 8–12.
[37]See Objection II in Hobbes's "Third Set of Objections" to Descartes's *Meditations*, *The Philosphical Works of Descartes*, ed. E. S. Haldane and G. R. T. Ross, (Cambridge, 1955), 61–62.

consciousness is not a mere immersion in the present particulars of the external world and is not accessible to itself only through memory, but that, by taking its *own* power as its object, it opposes itself as a conscious striving for domination to the contingent circumstances of its life, whatever those circumstances may be. The explicit "generality" of desire implies a self-conscious continuity of human action and the unity of all mental acts in the underlying self-referential structure of volition. Thus, although the *real* subject of desire consists in man's bodily substance, in functionalist or phenomenological terms we may speak of it as self-consciousness. Within this functionalist or phenomenological framework, the desire for power amounts to a general self-awareness: the generalization of desire from an attitude toward a particular to an attitude toward power itself is responsible for the fact that man not only acts so as to foster his own preservation, but—as his desire for power implies—is also immediately aware that he acts in this way.

This conception of the self, though only implicit in Hobbes's discussion of the nature of man, is quite original, and several of its features distinguish it from the Cartesian theory of the soul. First, it allows us to speak of the self in purely phenomenological terms but does not involve any ontological commitments comparable to those implied by the Cartesian *res cogitans*. Second, it ties the self to the practical concerns of self-preservation and does not locate it in a purely theoretical act of knowledge. Third, and most important, it makes the term "subject" refer to a dynamic and expansive function of life and not to any static substratum of mental acts that could then be identified with a "soul" and analyzed in terms of its mortality or immortality, essential or accidental characteristics, potential or actual capacities (talents, faculties, and so on). In fact the Hobbesian "self" is not a residuum of any human "nature" or "essence" but an in itself contentless striving for self-assertion; it is an occasional term referring to a purely individual and particular focus of the self-preservative activities of a given organism. Any "content" that this concept may acquire derives entirely from the contingent events of life; it denotes not an essence but only a unified biography.

4.4. Equality

Hobbes's belief that the natural human condition is characterized by a universal state of war is also explicable primarily with reference to man's capacity to respond to possible dangers as if they were actual, with the consequent "defamiliarization" of the environment and indiscriminate desire for power. As a matter of fact, in the context of an interaction among many human beings, the capacity for responding to remote and hypothetical dangers is not only the immediate cause of the conflict among men, but also a relatively rational (from a functionalist point of view) mode of responding to external stimulation. For in view of the insatiable desire for power characteristic of human nature, the danger that a man faces when confronted with another man is no longer remote or merely hypothetical. Whereas the fear that nature instills in man may be "paranoid" to the extent that nature is in fact predictable, the wildest suspicions that a man may harbor with respect to another man are apt, according to Hobbes, to be borne out more often than not.

The resulting state of universal war, which Hobbes postulates as characteristic of the human condition, is more than just an expression of his pessimistic and, some would say, cynical view of human nature. For beyond the more sinister aspects of the Hobbesian view of rivalry among men, his description of the state of nature introduces a relatively new conception of social relations, which will become extremely influential among many later political, social, and economic theorists, regardless of their actual opinion of the merits of Hobbes's political philosophy. The novelty of Hobbes's conception of social relations consists in acknowledging the primacy of *competitive* relations among men over any bonds that unite them into one society. Most previous political thinkers started from the alleged fact of *natural inequality* among men and thought of society as an institution that replaces a system of human relations based on force with a system of moral and legal norms allowing for *political equality*. According to these thinkers, human individuality could acquire its proper significance only within the context of a real community, that is, a system of shared moral, legal, and traditional norms that endowed each individual with dignity, rights, and obligations. As opposed to all such theories, Hobbes postulated a radical priority of individuality over all forms of communal existence. Whereas other theories concentrated on defining the nature of human individuality within the context of a shared language (rationality) and values, for Hobbes, the dividing principle becomes primary and fundamental: it is not a *principium individuationis*, but rather the source of unity among men, that is a problem for him. His nominalism made "humanity" into a mere *name* and not an essence of the species. Consequently, he identified individuals with isolated, atomistic, and self-centered particulars the purely individual "nature" of which is for all practical purposes unknowable. Human interaction, so far as it comes about at all, must therefore be explained as a contingently arising system of relations among individuals who are fully constituted as such prior to any social interaction. And in this connection, human competitiveness is the first and foremost feature of their relationships.

The interesting aspect of Hobbes's analysis of the competitiveness of human relationships is that it yields a highly original conception of equality. Far from being the unifying bond among men, equality is, for Hobbes, the most important dividing principle, responsible for the fact that men are pitted against each other in their struggle for survival. Men are equal, according to Hobbes, because even "the weakest has strength enough to kill the strongest, either by secret machination, or by confederacy with others, that are in the same danger with himselfe."[38] The nearly infinite variety of responses of which a man is capable when faced with any external stimulation makes his behavior for all practical purposes absolutely unpredictable, and it is this feature of his behavior that determines the nature of his relationships with other men. There may be rules and manuals for dealing with one's inferiors; but no set of rules, no matter how complicated, can ever capture the scope of human resourcefulness, and the equality among men is defined by their capacity to surprise one another. Consequently, the deadly contest among men, which is the first form of their interaction, is a contest without any rules, since even the relations of power among the participants are not sufficient (at least initially) to impose any semblance of order. The problem that this state of affairs poses for Hobbes's political theory is paramount. Unlike previous political thinkers, Hobbes, with his nominalistic account of equality, cannot look for the origins of society in any system of shared, universal values entailed by a common human essence. On the other hand, unlike such later social thinkers as Smith and Mandeville, he cannot envisage a natural coincidence of purely individual human pursuits (such as that observable in the behavior of ants or bees), because men's insatiable desire for power precludes any natural foundation for order. Thus, Hobbes cannot think of the concept of social cohesion as either logically prior to the diversity of individual pursuits or as a natural consequence of individual behavior. The only way out of this dilemma open to him is to think of social unity as embodied in another *particular*: the artificial person of the sovereign who, by his possession of an overawing power, is able to enforce peaceful coexistence among his subjects. But the establishment of such an artificial person and the source from which he might derive his power are problems that require a not inconsiderable amount of ingenuity to solve.

[38]*Lev.*, 60.

5. Hobbes on Power

The most fundamental problem of Hobbes's political philosophy is how, given the natural equality of men, there can ever arise a situation in which one man, or a small minority of men, may be strong enough to command the obedience of all. Put in this way, it is clear that the concept of *power* is the focal point of Hobbes's theory. This becomes even more evident when one reads closely Hobbes's definitions of some of the most important terms of his political philosophy—as we shall see later, his concept of right is intimately linked to that of the power a man has at his disposal, and his concept of obligation refers to a peculiar process by which a man can deprive himself of a power to resist another man by virtue of holding certain kinds of beliefs.

I could, perhaps, move directly now to a discussion of Hobbes's political philosophy and hope that my readers' ordinary intuitions concerning the meaning of the term "power" would sustain their understanding of Hobbes's argument. To do this, however, would not do justice to my conviction that Hobbes's attempt to derive his political theory from a general mechanistic account of natural phenomena should be taken seriously. Nor would it do justice to the rather subtle way in which the mechanistic and functionalist approaches are intertwined in his theory of human action.

"Power" is a very broad category for Hobbes, applicable not only to human beings but also to inanimate objects, and it is clear that in at least two contexts the sense in which he ascribes powers to men differs from the sense in which he ascribes them to natural objects. First, in speaking of powers "of a Man," Hobbes defines power as "the eminence of the Faculties of Body, or Mind,"[39] that is, as the "*excess* of the power of one above that of another."[40] This expression is "curiously paradoxical," as one commentator observed,[41] "for if power is the excess of power, what is it an excess of?" Consequently, Hobbes's account of the powers of man can be understood only when placed in the context of another, more general theory of the ascription of powers to objects which it presupposes. Second, when speaking of powers in general Hobbes clearly believes that they are predicated of *bodies*, and his materialism might lead one to believe that the same is true insofar as ascriptions of powers to men are concerned. Nevertheless, as I shall show presently, Hobbes's account of political power requires that powers be predicated of persons and not of their bodies.

[39]Ibid., 41.
[40]*De homine*, viii, 4.
[41]S. I. Benn, "Hobbes on Power," in Cranston and Peters, eds., *Hobbes and Rousseau*, 210.

5.1. Powers of Objects and Powers of Men

"THE POWER *of a Man*," says Hobbes in *Leviathan*,[42] "is his present means, to obtain some future apparent Good." This definition contains an inherent ambiguity: it can be understood as saying that "power" refers to some qualities of the agent that *explain* his ability to achieve something he desires or as tying the concept of power *by definition* to the effect it is going to produce. This ambiguity is, indeed, quite common in ascriptions of powers to objects. On the one hand, when we ascribe to some object O the power to produce some effect E we may be indifferent as to the occurrence of E, but interested in accounting for it, *should* it occur. This would, in general, be the attitude of a (courageous) scientist who spoke about the "dormitive power" of opium: he would be interested not in putting anyone to sleep, but only in *explaining* why administering opium puts one to sleep. In order to be able to do so, he would, of course, have to define the "dormitive power" of opium independently of the effect of putting one to sleep—say, with reference to the chemical composition of opium. Then he could claim that, owing to the interaction of the chemical with the patient's organism, the patient's falling asleep is a predictable consequence of its administration. On the other hand, when we ascribe to O the power to produce E, we may not care about why O produces E, but may be intensely interested in controlling E's occurrence. This might be the attitude of a doctor for whom the "dormitive power" of opium simply *identifies* opium as that which he can use to put his patient to sleep. Whereas for the scientist that "dormitive power" of opium referred to some property that opium could still be said to possess even if it turned out that it does not put anyone to sleep (although the scientist would, of course, not persist in calling it by that name), for the doctor the link between "dormitive power" and "putting one to sleep" is *definitional*: failure to produce sleep would *mean* that opium does not have "dormitive power."

Given Hobbes's general commitment to mechanistic scientific explanations and his concurrent tendency to switch to a functionalist account in the context of discussing human action, one should not be surprised to find that both accounts of power ascriptions coincide, and sometimes fade into each other, in his philosophy. One would also expect, however, that ultimately the functionalist account, which definitionally links power ascriptions with their intended effects, would be entirely dependent on the underlying mechanistic (causal) explanations. But, in fact, the matter is somewhat complicated by Hobbes's rather confused view of ordinary power ascriptions.

In general, Hobbes conceives of "power" as a concept complemen-

[42]*Lev.*, 41.

tary to "liberty"[43] and, unlike our ordinary speech, he ascribes the two concepts both to men and to inanimate objects. While he defines liberty as an absence of external impediments to motion (or action), he says that power consists in the absence of similar impediments "in the constitution of the thing it selfe," Thus, "when a stone lieth still, or a man is fastened to his bed by sicknesse," they may lack not the liberty to move, but only the power to do so.[44]

Hobbes gives his scientific account of power in *De corpore*, where he identifies powers as internal properties of objects, causally responsible for bringing about certain effects upon the occurrence of some external events.[45] All power, according to him, is either active or passive. "Whensoever any agent has all those accidents which are necessarily requisite for the production of some effect in the patient," he says, "then we say that the agent has [active] *power* to produce that effect, if it be applied to a patient." Correspondingly, "whensoever any patient has all those accidents which it is requisite it should have, for the production of some effect in it, we say that it is in the *power* of that patient to produce that effect [that is, it has the corresponding passive power], if it be applied to a fitting agent." If all words used here were to be taken in their ordinary sense, there would be no problem: power ascriptions would refer to properties of objects that could constitute possible partial causes (efficient causes in the case of active powers; material causes in the case of passive powers) of future events. However, for reasons connected with his strict determinism, Hobbes believed that he could not allow for a concept of *possible* cause. Since the course of natural events was, for him, strictly determined, he viewed every actual event as strictly necessary and, thus, every counterfactual hypothetical as assuming an *impossibility*. He therefore thought that he was forced to exclude as false every ascription of power that did not amount to a prediction that an appropriate effect would *actually* be brought about. Thus, for Hobbes, power was not to be viewed as a potential cause, but simply as a *future* cause.[46] To say that a match, for example, has the power to ignite gasoline means that it *will* do so; should the match burn out before it is brought in contact with the gasoline, then we must say, according to Hobbes, that it never had the power in question, since otherwise, he thought, a genuine contingency would have to characterize natural events.

It is easy to see that Hobbes was simply wrong in drawing such

[43]Ibid., 107.
[44]Ibid.
[45]*De corpore*, x, 1.
[46]Ibid., "*Cause* is so called in respect of some effect already produced, and power in respect of some effect to be produced hereafter."

radical conclusions from his determinism.[47] If "powers" refers to certain properties of objects that are capable of producing certain effects, then these objects do not cease to have such properties even if the effects are never produced. Nor is it true that saying that a match had the power to ignite gasoline, even though it had burnt out before it was brought into contact with the flammable liquid, necessarily implies that the match really *could* have come into contact with gasoline, in violation of the strict necessity characteristic of all natural events. Instead, all that could be meant is that the property of the match to which the "power" in question referred was the same property as that also possessed by *another* match which actually did (or will) ignite some gasoline and that this property was (will be) a partial cause of the relevant effect. So long as an assumption is made that different natural events are comparable and that nature is uniform in its activities, there is nothing in what I have just said that could not be made compatible with strict determinism.[48]

Still, even if we make the necessary corrections in Hobbes's scientific account of power, it is clear that in speaking of the powers of *man* he often uses the word in a different sense. A scientist is usually indifferent to the occurrence or nonoccurrence of a given effect that he investigates and merely wants to be able to explain it. But an ordinary agent placed in the Hobbesian struggle for survival is not a detached investigator. For him, power is his "means to obtain some future apparent Good"[49] and his success or failure in this attainment is all that matters. From *his* point of view, power is not an object of inquiry, but an object of a "perpetuall and restlesse desire."[50] Since the focus of this "desire of Power after power"[51] is the *effect* of those things, such as strength, riches, and reputation, which are viewed as powers, their failure to produce the desired effect makes them into no powers at all.

When Hobbes talks about human powers, he shifts back and forth between the scientific account and the one that definitionally links power and its effect. It is in this way that he arrives at the seemingly

[47]For a fuller account of Hobbes's views on this subject and their pertinent critique, see Benn, "Hobbes on Power."

[48]The solution proposed here may, of course, run into some problems with Hobbes's nominalism, and it may be this, rather than his determinism alone, that is responsible for his strictly actualist account of power. For if one accepts the radically nominalist claim that each individual object is unique and that nothing in nature corresponds to our general terms, then all comparisons among different objects are only *de dicto* and not *de re*—so it might be impossible to ascribe any powers to one object by virtue of something that happens to another object. But it would lead us too far astray to try to inquire into Hobbes's position on this issue.

[49]*Lev.*, 41.

[50]Ibid., 47.

[51]Ibid.

paradoxical definition of human power as the "*excess* of the power of one above that of another."[52] That of which human power is an "excess" is power in the scientific sense of *De corpore*: it is the strength of a man, his mental ability, motivational drive, and so on. But unlike inanimate objects, which are indifferent to the powers they possess, man views his natural endowments as tools for survival and in the natural course of events desires those effects of his powers that he thinks contribute to his survival. It is important to stress in this context that the intellectual and motivational factors in man's makeup are themselves powers of a peculiar kind, in that they confer an inner teleological order on all human actions and subordinate all other human powers to the overall goal of survival. Furthermore, unlike inanimate objects, men find themselves in intense competition with one another. From this perspective, not only wasted powers are viewed as no powers at all, but also those powers that are insufficient to overcome the resistance of one's competitors. Strictly speaking, an external frustration of an effect of a certain power is, according to Hobbes, only a limitation of the agent's liberty and not of his power, but from the agent's own perspective it can be said indeed that "equal powers opposed, destroy one another."[53] Thus, while the "Faculties of Body, or Mind" are the primary powers of man in the scientific sense of *De corpore*, it is only the "eminence" of these faculties,[54] that is, "the excess of powers of one above that of another" that makes for the actual effectiveness of human actions from the point of view of the agent.

5.2. Subjects of Power Ascriptions

A shift from the mechanistic, scientific account of power to a functionalist one, geared to take into consideration the subjective perspective of the agent, also has another consequence, one that distinguishes the way in which powers are ascribed to men from that in which they are predicated of everything else. This can be seen from the fact that while Hobbes clearly believes that powers should be predicated of *bodies* (material objects being the only ones capable of exerting any kind of causal influence), certain contexts in which powers are ascribed to men make it imperative that the subject of such predication be understood as not identical with his own body. A series of examples may lead us to the considerations that make this obvious.

Consider first the example of the power to walk in a man who is either

[52]*De homine*, viii, 4.
[53]Ibid.
[54]*Lev.*, 41.

paralyzed or bound. In the case of a man who is paralyzed, we are clearly entitled to say that he does not have the (passive) power to walk (that is, the power to respond by walking to a certain kind of stimulation that produces this effect in healthy people under ordinary circumstances), since he does not possess the working organs necessary to produce such an effect. The case of a man who is bound, however, is more ambiguous. One would want to say that, all his internal organs being intact, he has the power to walk but is not free to do so. Indeed, if, when given the appropriate kind of stimulation, the man will produce some tension on the ropes that restrain him, we may say that he has the power to walk but is simply prevented from walking by some external circumstances (i.e., is not *free* to walk). But if the man in question realizes that all his efforts to walk would be futile and refrains from even trying, then—a proper system of motivation being an integral part of the human constitution necessary for walking—Hobbes will have to say that the belief the man has concerning his inability to walk effectively "cripples" (at least temporarily) his constitution and therefore the man is neither free nor *able* (has no power) to walk.[55] Now, these changes in what must be called the "internal constitution" of a man which are due to changes in his motivation (such as the acquiring of new beliefs or habits) can be of an amazing variety. Consider, for example, the following case, which will become extremely important in Hobbes's account of the nature of obligation and the source of political power. Antony for some reason comes to believe that Caesar is irresistible, that an action which might displease Caesar has a very good chance of being suicidal for whoever is foolish enough to perform it. This belief will certainly influence Antony's behavior and thus be decisive with respect to the question as to which powers we may truthfully ascribe to him. Accordingly, we must say, for example, that Antony has the (passive) power to do what Caesar orders him to do, but that he has no power to do what Caesar forbids him to do. But if Antony has no power to disobey Caesar, *this very fact* makes us ascribe some power to Caesar. Hobbes calls this power "reputation."[56] But what kind of power is it? It is not the power to issue orders, for Caesar could issue those to Cassius as well, even though Cassius (not sharing Antony's belief about Caesar's power) will probably not obey them. Similarly, it is not the power to *enforce* his orders, for it may be that Antony's belief is groundless, in the sense that if Antony changes his mind about Caesar he will be able to disobey him with impunity. Caesar has, of course, the power to "make himself obeyed" (at least in the case of Antony), but this power is entirely a

---

[55]This is significantly different from Benn's view ("Hobbes on Power," 198).
[56]*Lev.*, 41.

function of Antony's belief. The problem with this kind of power becomes even more obvious when we ask whether it is passive or active. It cannot be a passive power; for Caesar, by issuing orders, is supposed to be an agent and not a patient. Yet, it is not clear how it could be an active power, since active power is always a form of motion for Hobbes,[57] and the only change in, and "addition" to, Caesar's power is due to something that happens to *Antony*.

Hobbes undoubtedly allows for the fact that the power of one man can be "added" to or "subtracted" from the power of another. His whole political theory in fact rests on this assumption. But while the "subtraction" of powers does not create serious problems (it simply amounts to the frustration of a portion of one man's power), the case of "addition" makes for difficulties in determining what constitutes the proper subject of power ascriptions in the case of human powers. If Caesar's active power really increases as a result of the fact that he will be obeyed by Antony, then the power that Caesar releases in Antony by his commands must now be predicated of *Caesar*. This, in turn, means that the ascription of such a power to Caesar is no longer an ascription of a power to a *body*, at least not to *his* body in any usual sense of the term. As long as Caesar and Antony are identified with their bodies, the power that Caesar releases in Antony is a motion of Antony's and not of Caesar's. It is only when an intermediary is used as an *instrument* by the initiator, that is, when the initiator acts *purposively*, that the initiator may be said to be the *agent* with respect to the final result. However, while actions of this kind may, within the context of a functionalist account, be ascribed to agents endowed with a will and a *self*, they cannot be ascribed to bodies in general. In fact, it is only in the context of *human* powers that Hobbes speaks of "instrumental powers,"[58] such as reputation, riches, and friendships, and this usage shows, again, a switch from the mechanistic to the functionalist account.

All this tends to show that our reading of a theory of the self into Hobbes's general theory of human nature is by no means an external or unnecessary addition to his explicitly stated views on this subject. The foundation of Hobbes's political theory lies, of course, in his mechanistic account of the way the actions of atomic individuals can coalesce into a more or less harmonious system guaranteeing the survival of a great number of individuals—something that does not obtain in the "state of nature." But the translation of this mechanistic account into the language of a *political* theory requires that the locus of human agency be shifted away from bodily substance and into the "fiction" of

[57]*De corpore*, x, 6.
[58]*Lev.*, 41.

the self. The Leviathan that men create when they form a political society is, according to Hobbes, an *artificial* person precisely because the power of which it is a focus is not the same as the bodily motion of the person who embodies the state. It is only the *will* of the ruler that belongs to the particular person who wields the supreme power. But the power itself at his disposal is, strictly speaking, the power of *all* the members of the state and only in the functionalist sense his own.

II. Political Theory

Despite the fact that I am about to present a positivistic interpretation of Hobbes's political philosophy and defend its intellectual interest and coherence, I am not prepared to claim that such an interpretation, which eliminates the normative content of such crucial terms as "right," "duty," and "obligation," is the only possible one. In fact, I am prepared to admit that Hobbes was occasionally inconsistent and slipped into the more familiar use of these terms. He was a passionately political man and sometimes spoke not as a scientist analyzing, but as an advocate wanting to convince his contemporaries, torn by a civil war, to treat his writings as a practical guide in their actions.[1] Nevertheless, a good argument can be made that the prevailing tenor of Hobbes's philosophy, at least as he presents it in *Leviathan*,[2] is that of radical positivism. The mechanistic account of human nature that precedes the exposition of his political philosophy indicates at minimum that Hobbes *intended* us to understand him as a positivist. His definitions of such terms as "liberty," "right," and "obligation," when taken literally, imply a purely *descriptive approach*. He delights in telling us that in the state of nature concepts such as "Right and Wrong, Justice and Injustice have . . . no place" and that "Force and Fraud, are in warre the two Cardinall vertues."[3] It seems at least fair, therefore, to make a serious attempt to read his philosophy in the spirit in which he intended it to be read.

But it is not primarily the spirit of fairness that motivates me to

---

[1] *Lev.*, 194.
[2] *De cive* is less consistent on this score than *Leviathan*. See below, section 3.
[3] *Lev.*, 63.

attempt to develop a positivistic interpretation of Hobbes's political philosophy. At least two other considerations are equally decisive. The first is connected with the fact that overcoming the positivistic implications of modern science in the domain of political theory is an important problem in the development of liberal thought. The second is that the hypothesis that Hobbes was, indeed, engaging in a purely descriptive and scientific, rather than a normative, inquiry into the origin and maintenance of political authority, far from being unfruitful or inconsistent, yields what I believe to be a highly interesting and sophisticated account of the nature of political power. A few words ought to be said on both these scores before we go any further.

1. Positivism and Liberalism

It was a fundamental premise of early liberal political theory that all political authority derives from the consent of the governed. The fact that if one takes this premise to be decisive then Hobbes must be counted among the liberals should be enough to show that the belief in the origin of authority in consent is not a sufficient condition of liberalism. Although it may be a little more difficult to see, the derivation of authority from consent is not a necessary condition of liberalism either. Clearly, tying liberalism to a contractarian theory of government would saddle it with a commitment that would greatly decrease its viability. Any claim that governments actually originate in a contract or that each person actually consents to becoming a citizen is unlikely to make much sense if the notion of consent is used in any way that would meaningfully legitimize political authority.[4] Moreover, despite some interesting attempts to give new meaning to the contractarian approach by using the concept of hypothetical rather than actual consent, it would be very risky to limit liberal political theory to such a controversial justification.[5]

[4]At least insofar as de jure legitimacy is concerned. Insofar as de facto legitimation (i.e., legitimation on the basis of a mere belief in the government's right to command obedience, regardless of how this belief is induced) is concerned, the claim is somewhat less unacceptable. Indeed, I shall argue that Hobbes gives us a rather strong argument in its favor, perhaps the strongest that ever has been given.

[5]Obviously, this is not the place to take issue with the recent revival of the contractarian idea. It may not be out of place, however, to point to one aspect of hypothetical contractarianism that, far from supporting the idea of the liberal state, is in fact in tension with it. To say that a rational person (under some definition of rationality, be it tied to the concept of prudence, economic calculation, utilitarianism, or a Kantian deontology) would, under certain circumstances (such as the Rawlsian "original position" or the Habermasian community of language speakers), agree to one or another arrangement of power relations, amounts to saying that that system of power relations is simply dictated by the

What the contractarian metaphor implies, however, is the quintessentially liberal belief that individuals possess a sphere of autonomy that no government can violate. At minimum, this means that the life plan of an individual, while it may be restricted in a variety of ways to make it compatible with those of other individuals, cannot itself be made a function of the interest of the community. In mature liberal thought this statement has a normative and moral meaning *par excellence*: it conveys the idea that governments are instituted to prevent conflicts among individuals, but that their function goes no further, since individuals are autonomous agents endowed with the fundamental right to live according to their own lights. What came to be a basic insight in its maturity, however, was not so obvious in liberalism's early history; on the contrary, the idea went against the grain of the most entrenched theory of man as essentially a communal creature incapable of individual self-sufficiency and dependent for his most basic human traits on some supraindividual institutions. In the ancient Aristotelian framework, it was the institution of the *polis*, a community of speakers expressing the specific element of rationality in human nature. In the Middle Ages, it was the institution of the terrestrial church, without the mediation of which an individual was incapable of salvation, and the institutions of secular authority which embodied the divinely ordained hierarchy designed to protect the members ·of the community in their journey through the temporal world.

The first wholesale assault on the indispensability of communal institutions, whether temporal or spiritual, for the very maintenance of man's humanity did not occur in the name of individual self-sufficiency. On the contrary, it arose within the context of radical Protestantism, which held human nature to be of itself so weak that no earthly institutions were capable of lifting it from its fallen condition. The salvation of man—the most basic purpose of life—was seen as a matter wholly beyond what human institutions could affect. This position had two consequences with seminal importance for the future development of liberal thought. First, the most important part of man's life was seen as concerning his relation to God, which now became an essentially private relationship, unaffected by the community and encompassing all that was truly moral and dignified about human nature.

---

accepted concept of rationality and the relevant statement of the problems to be resolved. Beyond the fact that the definitions of both rational behavior and the relevant criteria of decision can be very controversial, the concept of consent is, at bottom, superfluous in all such attempts. To say that all would agree to something means that all would *have* to agree or their vote would not count. Thus, the move from actual to hypothetical consent uses "consent" in a Pickwickian sense and hides an essentially nonliberal belief, namely, that "there is only one truth" in matters political.

Second, the earthly community, and especially political authority, was no longer seen as more than a series of pragmatic arrangements which should concern itself with the external (and thus infinitely less important) conditions of human life.

Although the Puritan outlook was, of course, crucial for creating the atmosphere in which liberal thought could arise, it should not be mistaken for the liberal outlook. Only when its religious perspective became secularized and the value of human individuality became decoupled from its theological foundations could individuals be seen as truly autonomous agents, forging their own destinies according to their own lights. Only then can we speak of that fundamental dignity of human individuality which characterizes liberal thought.

This process of the secularization of Puritan individualism was by no means straightforward. A fundamental feature of secular liberalism is its move away from the otherworldliness characteristic of the fervently religious movements of the seventeenth century. While the pursuit of salvation concentrates on the inner aspects of life and focuses on the role of faith and divine grace, liberalism attempts to infuse with dignity those aspects of life that are concerned with the pursuit of happiness through the productive activity by which man becomes a master of the world around him. It may be true, of course, that some such perversion of Calvinist theology as that described by Weber[6] made anxious Puritans look to worldly success as a sign of election and thus released the productive forces of capitalism. At least on the level of theory, however, there is (quite literally) a world of difference between this attitude and that represented by the liberal outlook.

The inspiration to look at man as at once a worldly creature and an essentially independent agent whose life plan is shaped without an indispensable reference to human community came from quarters very different from, and politically opposed to, Puritanism. It came from Hobbes and his attempt to expound a theory of man rooted in modern science. Hobbes did not intend, of course, to provide the foundation of anything like later liberal political theory, any more than he intended to give a new justification to Puritan demands. But the conclusions he believed to be implicit in the mechanistic account of human nature were in many respects instrumental in the rise of liberalism. The very nominalism he associated with the reductive method of science made him look at the state (and, indeed, society) as a collection of individuals rather than as a natural and organic unity, so that it had to be accounted for in terms of the properties of individuals and not vice versa. But more important, the substantive account of human nature that he thought

[6]M. Weber, *The Protestant Ethic and the Spirit of Capitalism* (New York, 1958).

followed from the application of the principles of natural science yield-ed a view of man for whom the Aristotelian separation of production, i.e., the domain concerned with the reproduction of life, from action, i.e., the domain of activity unrelated to the necessities of survival, no longer made sense. Whatever else the Hobbesian conception of man, for whom "felicity" was no more than the "continuall progresse of the desire, from one object to another," may mean, it and the overarching striving for security define the purpose of life (so far as one is allowed to speak of purposes in Hobbes) as inherently tied to the concerns of production. The fact that life itself ceases when "Desires are at a stand" means that man is an outward-oriented being who finds his satisfaction in the never-ending process of making the world serve his insatiable needs. Even if the destructiveness involved in this attitude is somehow tamed by political institutions, the nature of man is not radically trans-formed by this fact. Political power may alleviate the feeling of danger that the world represents to a man, but does not result in the "repose of a mind satisfied," the leisure that Aristotle believed to be the necessary condition of truly human existence. On the contrary, it merely allows for a more systematic pursuit of happiness and ever more elaborate expressions of human acquisitiveness.[7]

This turn away from viewing the meaning of human life in terms of pure rationality, unencumbered by the concerns of material existence, and toward a definition of man as a creature of *interest* I view as the most basic premise that Hobbes introduced into the development of liberalism. It is true that this feature of liberalism was most often stressed by its opponents, since it tended to present liberals as crude materialists, while supporters of liberalism tended to focus on individ-ual freedom and the dignity it confers on man. As a result, liberals—though most commonly non-Anglo-Saxon liberals, such as Kant—often went so far in defending the idea of individual freedom as to locate it in a purely disembodied self (Kant's transcendental apperception being the most extreme example) and introduced a host of metaphysical com-plications that ultimately weakened the doctrinal coherence of liberal theory. Nevertheless, the idea of man as a creature of interest does not necessarily have the crude materialistic implications so gladly seized on by opponents of liberalism. It merely opposes the traditional dualis-tic account of human nature which degraded those aspects of life that concern most of us throughout our daily pursuits. And it does so not by assuring us that interests, inclinations, desires, and so on "also" have a

---

[7]Hobbes puts this rather succinctly in *De cive*, 1, 2; "We do not . . . by nature seek society for its own sake, but that we may receive some honour or profit from it; these we desire primarily, that secondarily."

place in human life—a rather common ploy of those who add "but . . . " and then proceed to ignore them—but by stating that interests do not have to be conceived as expressions of merely animalistic impulses and that whatever "higher purposes" may be found in life must be integrated into the context of man's productive activity.

Nevertheless, the specter of crude materialism or moral nihilism is one that tends to haunt liberals, both because of liberalism's insistence on the crucial role of interest in human life and because its condemnation of communal impositions on individuals is so easily confused with the belief that all conceptions of the good are of equal value and, perhaps, of no real value at all. Given the grounding of early liberal theory in natural science, this specter arose in very striking form in the positivistic implications of Hobbes's deterministic account of human nature, and had to be faced in the very first period of liberalism's doctrinal development. In this sense, Hobbes's legacy to liberalism was not free of ambiguity. On the one hand, by grounding political philosophy in arguably the greatest intellectual achievement of modernity— mechanistic natural science—he provided a strong foundation and an extremely powerful argumentative strategy for the new theory of man which came to underlie much of liberal thought. On the other hand, precisely because he looked to modern science for support for his theory and drew out its positivistic implications, he also posed the challenge of integrating that theory into a doctrine that would go *beyond* what he himself thought it capable of. In facing this task, Hobbes's successors—Locke, above all—had to show not only that the authoritarian model Hobbes presented was not a necessary implication of his new theory of man, but also that the theory itself, as well as the political theory built upon it, was not limited to a purely descriptive account, precluding any normative or ethical content. To see this enduring challenge, one will find it at least useful to pursue Hobbes's professed commitment to the positivistic version of his new political science.

2. "The Right of the Strongest"—An Outline of Hobbes's Political Argument

I have already said that one reason why the positivistic interpretation of Hobbes is worth attempting is that Hobbes's theory becomes more, not less, interesting when seen from this perspective. But before I make the reader embark on the journey through the dense forest of Hobbes's theory, it might be helpful to provide an outline of the argument that I believe he makes in his political philosophy.

Many readers of Hobbes who object to interpreting his political philosophy as a descriptive and not a normative theory argue that were his theory purely descriptive, his use of concepts such as "right," "duty," "obligation," and "contract" would be meaningless. Thus, no doubt with Hobbes among others in mind, Rousseau, displaying his usual rhetorical skill, attacked the so-called "right of the strongest," which he took to be the essence of the positivistic position:

> I suggest it [the right of the strongest] can only produce a tissue of bewildering nonsense; for once might is made to be right, cause and effect are reversed, and every force which overcomes another force inherits the right which belonged to the vanquished. As soon as a man can disobey with impunity, his disobedience becomes legitimate; and as the strongest is always right, the only problem is how to become the strongest. But what can be the validity of a right which perishes with the force on which it rests? If force compels obedience, there is no need to invoke a duty to obey, and if force ceases to compel obedience, there is no longer any obligation. Thus the word "right" adds nothing to what is said by "force"; it is meaningless.[8]

With those parts of Rousseau's statement in which he restates the doctrine that "might makes right" Hobbes could not disagree. It is well known that Hobbes's insistence on the unity of de facto authority with political legitimacy made his own theory of greater use to a Cromwell than to a Charles II. But in the main, Rousseau's statement shows its author to be singularly insensitive to the realities of political power— something that interests Hobbes above all. "How to become the strongest" is indeed "the only problem" for a political theorist intent on explaining the nature of authority, but it is by no means an easy problem if one begins, as do both Hobbes and Rousseau, by postulating the initial equality of all men. "For as to the strength of the body," says Hobbes, "the weakest has strength enough to kill the strongest, either by secret machination, or by confederacy with others, that are in the same danger with himselfe";[9] and since the sovereign is most often greatly outnumbered by his subjects, the secret of the stability of political power is what Hobbes wants most to discover.

Rousseau was, of course, not unaware of the difficulty that natural equality poses for all those who want to equate legitimacy with the "right of the strongest," and he makes this into one of his main objections against the proponents of legal positivism. "The strongest man is never strong enough to be master all the time," he says, "unless he

[8]J. J. Rousseau, *The Social Contract*, I, 3 (the translation is M. Cranston's).
[9]*Lev.*, 60.

transforms force into right and obedience into duty."[10] But Rousseau's error, which makes his whole argument question-begging at this point, lies in his strict dichotomy between force as a "physical power" and right as a moral concept. "Force," he says, "is a physical power; I do not see how its effects could produce morality. To yield to force is an act of necessity, not of will; it is at best an act of prudence. In what sense can it be a moral duty?"[11] But what Rousseau has also failed to see is that his assertion of a cause-and-effect relationship between right and power ("for once might is made to be right, cause and effect are reversed"), while necessary to make the problem of legitimacy relevant to considerations concerning the stability of political authority, will work as much against his own view as its reversal does against the "right of the strongest." For no causal connection between right and power can be inferred at all as long as "right" is taken in its purely normative or moral sense. From the fact that someone has a right (in this sense) to command, it no more (causally) follows that he will be obeyed than that the effects of physical force "could produce morality."

Clearly, what counts in the context of a political theory is what people *believe* with respect to the sovereign's authority; and only this, rather than the truth or validity of some purely normative proposition, can *causally* produce the effect of obedience. Thus, for example, when a long-standing process of compulsion (in the narrow sense of physical power) creates a habit of obedience or a belief in an obligation to obey, even though the physical power of enforcement may no longer be present, we may talk of might (causally) producing "right" (at least in the sense of de facto legitimacy); or (to consider the case of reverse causation) when a widespread belief in someone's right to command constitutes the main source of the "physical" power that this person can in fact command for his purposes we may talk of right (causally) producing might. It is not meaningless, therefore, to treat right as homogeneous with power, so that each may sometimes be viewed as produced by the other, rather than to think of them as two ontologically heterogeneous types of entities. Moreover, it is only within the framework of a *descriptive* theory that we can capture the causal connection between might and right, and no theory of political legitimacy will be complete without such an account. If we limit the idea of the "right" to govern to the idea of de facto legitimacy, no further account is needed at all; if, on the other hand, we are interested in the idea of de jure legitimacy, a purely descriptive account will constitute only a part of the story, but still an indispensable part. (As a matter of fact, Rousseau's own charac-

---

[10]*Social Contract*, I, 3.
[11]Ibid.

terization of most existing governments of his time as "illegitimate" should have made him realize that his concepts of both power and legitimacy were too narrow. Some of these governments, which according to Rousseau endured by keeping men "in chains," were surely not unstable, and clearly "chains" could not be meant literally as the sole source of their power. And yet, according to Rousseau's own view of their illegitimacy, the governments in question could not rely on their subjects' moral duty to obey them. How, then, were they able to maintain themselves?)

In view of his mechanistic reduction of psychic processes to internal motions, Hobbes would have to agree, of course, with Rousseau's statement that "force is a physical power," and he could not claim that a government's capacity to make itself obeyed is an exception to this rule. But as a political thinker, he understood that the constraints imposed by a government upon its subjects could not be reduced to what is *usually* referred to as "physical force." In fact, the fundamental meaning of his effort was to show that no government could subsist by mere force in the narrow sense of the word, and that the stability of any government implies the consent of the governed. Nevertheless, unlike Rousseau, he was too keen an analyst of the concept of power to conclude that the power accruing to a government from its legitimacy and the power it has by virtue of its control of the means of repression constitute two wholly different kinds of authority. On the contrary, the entire framework of his theoretical commitments inclined Hobbes to search for the common denominator of these two phenomena. That a man comes to *will* to obey a government could not, according to him, be accounted for differently from the fact that the government has the *power* to make itself obeyed.

It does not make much sense, therefore, to try to show that Hobbes had to be a moralist of one kind or another just because throughout his political writings he used terms such as "right," "obligation," and "duty," which are usually infused with moral content. As we have seen, there is clearly room, and indeed need, for an investigation into the relation between, on the one hand, the mere existence of people's beliefs concerning the legitimacy and limits of political authority and, on the other hand, the existence and extent of the power that such authority has at its disposal. Further, it is clearly possible to give a de facto account of the nature of such beliefs without committing oneself to an evaluation of their de jure validity. Finally, it is clearly not absurd, and may be quite interesting, to try to explain how people come to have these beliefs and act on them, without making their validity one of the elements in the (causal) explanation—indeed, rejecting as meaningless some aspects of the very question about validity. A scientist who, like

Hobbes, undertakes an inquiry of this kind neither perverts the ordinary vocabulary of political philosophy nor renders it useless, though one may, of course, disagree with the result.

The basic argument I take Hobbes to be making is that the power of the state results from what is sometimes called "self-fulfilling prophecy," i.e., a situation in which the very fact of believing something causes the belief in question to become true. A person's belief, for example, that he or she is going to fail in some activity may actually cause that person to fail. (The same is sometimes true about success.) More interesting, there are some situations in which any one person is incapable of significantly affecting the actual state of affairs by either action or belief; but the very fact of many people's holding a similar belief, regardless of the validity or invalidity of the justification of that belief, makes the object of their belief come about. Thus, for example, a general belief that the stock market is going to collapse may in fact cause its collapse. This basic observation, known to any economist interested in the relation between expectations and economic performance, was, I believe, first made by Hobbes and used by him to account for the ability of a government to ensure social peace and security.

There are three situations in which the phenomenon of self-fulfilling prophecy plays a decisive role in Hobbes's political philosophy. First, the natural equality of men plus the irrational (i.e., dysfunctional) belief that all men threaten my life at any point and without the slightest provocation make me try to preempt their aggression by striking first. But since all men share the same belief, the belief becomes true: each man is, indeed, a wolf to every other man. Second, if for some reason I come to believe that another person possesses sufficient power to enforce his control over some object in dispute between us (be it his control over some resource, an aspect of his personal security, or some behavior of mine)—that is, if I come to believe that he can overpower and kill me if I attempt to interfere with his wishes in some respect— then, according to Hobbes, my fear of death will make it impossible for me to resist that person in that respect and that person will indeed have the power in question.[12] Again, given Hobbes's account of human action, the very fact of believing something makes the belief come true. Finally, if sufficiently many people (though not necessarily all) were to be persuaded that we were all obliged to obey some particular person because of that person's superior power to enforce his commands, then by this very fact this person would acquire superior power (since he could now dispose of the power of all those who are not prepared to disobey him) and *all* (not just some) people within the reach of the

[12]See above, Chap. I, section 5.2.

sovereign's power would be obliged to obey him, since he could now back up his commands with enforceable threats. This particular version of the phenomenon of self-fulfilling prophecy is what lies at the basis of Hobbes's contractarian argument.

These three situations of self-fulfilling prophecy define three essential stages in Hobbes's account of the origin of political institutions, and an important quasi-moral concept is connected with each of them. The first situation defines the Hobbesian state of nature, with its war of all against all, and connected with it is a very peculiar concept of *right*. The second one defines the way in which a derogation of right is possible in the state of nature and gives rise to an equally peculiar concept of obligation that Hobbes calls "natural" (and I shall sometimes call "pre-political") obligation. The third defines the social contract by which natural obligation is transformed into what I shall call "political obligation."[13]

It is important to note at the outset that in each of these cases a *causal account* is given to explain how what we usually take to be a moral concept influences human behavior. There are according to Hobbes, only two ways in which the concept of praise or blame may be attached to human actions: either because such actions directly relate to the achievement of security or because a superior power is prepared to reward or punish them. In the first case, praise or blame merely reflects the assessment of the functionality, or lack of it, of the way people behave with respect to a goal they themselves desire. Given Hobbes's strict determinism, there is no peculiar moral significance to such an assessment and, given his skepticism about the way ratiocination affects human behavior, no prudential advice is implied by a judgment of praise or blame in this sense. In the second case, when a political authority is prepared to reward or punish some actions, praise or blame may or may not attach to actions that directly contribute to the achievement of security (depending on the reasons a government chooses to reward or punish the actions in question and the wisdom of its choice); but the attachment of praise or blame is directly related to the causal determinants of men's action (since it is the fear of the government's enforcement of its value judgments that motivates a person's behavior in this context). If we choose to, as Hobbes does, we may speak in this context of an "obligation" that an individual may have to obey authority and, while this is not the only meaning in which Hobbes uses this concept (it corresponds to what I called "political obligation"), it is the one that comes as close as anything ever will in his philosophy to the

---

[13]There is still another sense in which Hobbes uses the term "obligation," corresponding to what I shall call "civil obligation," but there is no need to introduce it at this point.

common normative use of that term. Even here, however, no more "moral" sense is intended than that which is acceptable to legal positivists. Hobbes's concept of natural obligation, on the other hand, as well as his concept of right, do not have even this weak normative sense and because of this their use is quite foreign to an ordinary reader. The concept of right is a purely descriptive category referring to the power that a man, acting in self-defense, has at his disposal because of the absence of internal or external impediments to his actions.[14] The concept of natural obligation is equally descriptive, since it merely refers to the lessening of a man's power that may result from the presence of that particular impediment to his actions constituted by the belief that some action is physically impossible or fraught with an imminent danger of death.[15] It is of course, possible to evaluate those actions that a man undertakes "as of right" or "out of a (natural) obligation" from the point of view of their functionality with respect to the achievement of security, and indeed Hobbes sometimes does so. But this evaluation is apt to be confusing (especially when Hobbes's evaluation is mistaken, as it sometimes is on his own grounds), if we do not keep his own definitions firmly in mind. What characterizes Hobbes's use of quasi-moral concepts is not that he attaches to them normative significance, but that he views them as tied to certain types of beliefs that causally affect the outcome of human action in that particular way we call "self-fulfilling prophecy."

The explication of the complex web of relations among the concepts of right, natural obligation, and political obligation will have to await further discussion. But a few words must now be said concerning what Rousseau believed to have been the main problem of Hobbes's political philosophy: how is it that someone may acquire that superior power which allows the sovereign to exercise the much disputed "right of the strongest"? The phenomenon of self-fulfilling prophecy explains how the fact that many people come to believe in the superior power of one person (that they contract a natural obligation to that person, to use the language of Hobbes's philosophy) indeed confers such power on that person (and transforms natural into political obligation). Why, however,

[14]For the sake of simplicity, several distinct meanings of the concept of right have been fused in this definition. They will be discussed further below. Also, note that, given Hobbes's deterministic account of power, his concept of right is even more descriptive than would be the case if he allowed for any implication of *choice* in the way in which a man can make use of his power.

[15]In *De cive*, xv, 7, Hobbes also speaks of another meaning of "natural obligation," namely, "when liberty is taken away by corporal impediments, according to which we say that heaven and earth, and all creatures, do obey the common laws of their creation." It is clear, I suppose, that no normative meaning is intended here, since a mere *physical restraint* on man's actions is meant.

would a sufficiently great number of people ever acquire such a salutary but nonetheless entirely unfounded belief? The difficulty involved in this question is the one that must plague the prudentialist interpreter of Hobbes. Given the prisoner's dilemma-like situation in which an individual finds himself in the Hobbesian state of nature and the endemic problem of free riders who would not be willing to contribute to the costs of establishing and maintaining the authority of the state, an enforceable agreement of the type seemingly contemplated by Hobbes under the rubric of "social contract" appears so unlikely as to be doomed from the start. A rational individual, no matter how much it may be in his interest to live in a political community, after all *knows* that no one has or is likely to have the required superior power. It would therefore be impossible to count on rational individuals ever to leave their wretched existence in the state of nature.[16] The answer I believe Hobbes provides to this problem is that men are *not* rational and that the same irrationality which plunged them into the *bellum omnis contra omnem* also takes them out of it and into the political community. It will be remembered that the capacity for *error* was, according to Hobbes, the distinctive characteristic of the human species, attendant on man's ability to use speech. Hobbes was only partly ironic, however, when, in his final attack on Aristotle, he defined man as an irrational animal. In part, he was preparing the ground for his strikingly novel claim that man's irrationality, far from being a departure from the norm, is the very reason that humanity survives. This move bears the unmistakable sign of modernity, though it is not the confident modernity of a liberal. Hobbes's skepticism about the idea that the world is a well-ordered place makes him, like many modern conservatives, skeptical that political institutions can be founded on the power of reason, much as his skepticism about modern man's ability to preserve the moral content of the basic terms of political philosophy makes him skeptical that political power can be safely founded on man's obedience to the norms of morality. He is therefore aware of the fragility of political institutions and this awareness underlies much of his theory, as it underlies those of many other modern thinkers, such as Hume and Burke; the specter of revolution is indeed never absent from modern political philosophy.[17] Like many later conservatives, Hobbes also feels

[16]See Introduction to Part One, note 15.

[17]One could indeed make the radical claim that revolution, as we know it, is a modern phenomenon. To be sure, premodern times knew struggles for power, and established authorities were overthrown in the past. But a revolution that abolishes an established *regime*, i.e. a whole system of social relations, and tries to build "from scratch" presupposes that society is a human artifact and can be remade to suit men's wishes. Thus, because of this sense of the absence of some deeper foundation for social and political order, modern conservatism is different from its ancestors: it defends customs and the

that no replacement can be found for the web of often ill-justified beliefs and customs that hold the social fabric together. And like another later thinker, he believes that the invisible hand which aggregates individual actions into a social outcome often transforms less than laudable individual features into highly desirable social characteristics. The social contract as a self-fulfilling prophecy is exactly such a marketlike mechanism.

The type of error that Hobbes thought could bring men to a set of beliefs capable of sustaining political power is what we call "religion." While Hobbes believes that the advanced form of religion represented by Christianity also has other advantages, such as the fostering of the scientific search for ultimate causes,[18] the main function of religion lies, for him, in its ability to make man obey authority. In the first truly secular account of the role of religion, Hobbes wove his account of belief into his theory of social contract, which was to explain how the mysteries of religion acquire a qualified validity.

According to Hobbes, as I read him, the social contract conferring legitimacy on political power does not, except for some unusual cases, refer to any unitary historical event, nor does it refer to a hypothetical consent given by the ruled to the actions of the rulers. It refers rather to the continuing process by which the *actual* consent of the governed (in the sense of their belief in the government's right to command obedience) becomes a self-fulfilling prophecy and confers both power and de facto legitimacy on the exercise of political authority. Obviously, this explanation of the source of governmental authority cannot have the significance that is most often expected from a contractarian account: that of explaining the moral rightness—de jure legitimacy—of the use of political power. Whatever approval or disapproval exercise of political power may receive from Hobbes depends on that power's ability *vel non* to contribute to the achievement of social peace and security—in other words, Hobbes's is a consequentialist and not a deontological political philosophy. But the interpretation presented here has the merit of making more enduring sense of Hobbes's contractarianism, since by explaining the source of power in *actual* consent, it avoids the inherent difficulties of both the hypothetical consent theories and the claim that the social contract is a specific historical event. Instead, the contractarian idea becomes a category of historico-political analysis which can be employed in explaining the secret of legitimacy of any stable political arrangement.

---

status quo for their *own* sake, not for the sake of something more profound that they may reflect.

[18]*Lev.*, 52.

3. Right

The term "right" is rarely, if ever, used in a nonnormative sense. In moral contexts, it has two distinct, though perhaps not unrelated, meanings. In the first meaning, "right" is opposed to "wrong" and it carries a clearly prescriptive sense. Used in this way, the word "right" is most commonly an adjective and it expresses approval. Thus, for example, when we say that someone "has done the right thing" we mean that he acted the way he should have and that by acting otherwise he would have done something wrong. Consequently, the prescriptive sense of "right" implies the existence of some law (moral or political) and of an obligation to act in a certain way. In its second meaning, "right" is also thought of as incompatible with "wrong," but not as a positive term of opposition to "wrong," not related to it as "good" is related to "bad," or as "hot" is to "cold." "Right" used in this way, most often as a noun, has a mainly negative sense, and it expresses the absence of disapproval. Thus, for example, when we say that a man "had a right" to do something, we do not necessarily approve of his action, but merely believe that he was under no obligation to act otherwise.

The tradition of political thought against which Hobbes argues at length in *De cive* and *Leviathan* rested on a conception of right which viewed the noun form of the word "right" (as in "he has a right") as inherently tied the adjectival form (as in "it is right to do this"), so that the concept of right was intimately linked to that of obligation. In this view, deriving from Aristotelian philosophy, man was essentially a social being and the conditions of his truly human existence entailed proper respect for the superior claims of the community. It was only in the context of the shared idea of the "right way of life," which was basic to any worthwhile individual life plan and implied a whole system of obligations toward the state, that a man could be said to possess any rights of his own.

The conception of right inspired by classical antiquity, according to which a right always presupposes an obligation, still has many proponents among those critics of liberalism who see the severing of the link between right and obligation as one of the cardinal sins of modern political philosophy.[19] It is important, therefore, to note at the outset that Hobbes explicitly warns his readers against what he viewed as the confusion of the two meanings of "right." "They that speak of this subject," he says, "use to confound *Jus* and *Lex*, *Right* and *Law*; yet they

[19]One of the prime examples of such people is L. Strauss (see his *Natural Right and History* [Chicago, 1953], especially chaps. 4 and 5). C. B. Macpherson (*The Political Theory of Possessive Individualism* [Oxford, 1962]) and many Marxists belong here as well.

ought to be distinguished; because RIGHT, consisteth in liberty to do or to forebeare; Whereas LAW, determineth, and bindeth to one of them: so that Law and Right, . . . in one and the same matter are inconsistent."[20] He who acts in accordance with the commands of a law or fulfills an obligation may earn some "merit" in this respect, but he is not exercising a right.[21]

To be sure, the fact that right and obligation "in one and the same matter are inconsistent" does not preclude the existence of some connection between them. In fact, in addition to his general philosophical discussion of the concept of freedom (with reference to which he defines the concept of right), Hobbes also introduces the concept of the "liberty of subjects," to which he attaches a more specific, political meaning, referring to the extent of freedom that a man enjoys after he has joined political society and renounced his *natural* rights.[22] In this context, Hobbes defines the liberty (and hence also the rights) of subjects as their freedom to do anything that the sovereign does not forbid them to do. Thus, in political society, rights are defined with reference to the absence of the sovereign's disapproval; they may not have to be explicitly granted, but they certainly imply acceptance by the subject of a corresponding system of obligations.[23]

Nevertheless, when speaking of *natural* rights, Hobbes wants to do more than just warn us against an innocuous confusion between right and obligation: he intends to sever the concept of right completely from any idea that it may rest on, or imply, some underlying system of obligations. In contradistinction to the Aristotelian tradition, Hobbes means to elevate the concept of natural right to the position of absolute priority in the hierarchy of his quasi-moral concepts and thus assert the absolute priority of an individual life plan over any claims of the human, and in particular the political, community. What this means, of course, is not that rights cannot be overridden by the demands of the community, but only that any claim that the community or another individual may make on an individual's allegiance must be accounted for as derogation from a preexisting right to refuse that allegiance and not vice versa. Political society, in particular, begins when the natural rights of citizens end; it is in fact their nearly total renunciation that gives rise to the power of the state. Consequently, natural rights have to be defined without any reference to the power of enforcement that constitutes the

---

[20]*Lev.*, 64.

[21]Ibid., 67.

[22]Ibid., Chap. XXI.

[23]Hobbes also acknowledges that a renunciation of right results in an obligation of one party and a new, acquired right of another party, thus acknowledging the reverse order of dependence between right and obligation: ibid., 65.

foundation on which moral judgments (or whatever Hobbes substitutes for them) must rest. It would be superfluous, I suppose, to explain in any detail how revolutionary this claim was and how important for laying the foundations of the liberal outlook.

For reasons intimately linked to his positivism, Hobbes went in fact much further than most later liberals in assigning a priority to right over obligation and in the process rendered his concept of right quite idiosyncratic and rather difficult to understand. In distinguishing between the prescriptive and the negative senses in which the word "right" is ordinarily used, I explained its negative (noun-form) sense as expressing the absence of disapproval. Even this explanation, however, becomes rather vacuous if it does not imply that there are (or could be) some things that one *does* (or *would*) disapprove of, be they only actions that violate other people's rights. Such, however, is not the case for Hobbes, who claims that "Right and Wrong, Justice and Injustice have . . . no place"[24] in the state of nature and that "there is nothing to which every man had not Right by Nature,"[25] so that no objectively valid condemnation of any action is implied by the concept of natural right.[26]

The only point at which the Hobbesian concept of natural right connects with some of our intuitions concerning its normative significance is when one considers it from the *subjective* point of view of the agent endowed with what Hobbes calls "right." In defining the right of nature as "the Liberty each man hath, to use his own power, . . . for the preservation of his own . . . Life,"[27] Hobbes makes an explicit reference to the subjective purpose of all actions that a man may perform as of this kind of right. Since every action that the agent perceives as necessary for his security he also perceives as passionately desirable, the course of action he chooses acquires *for him* the significance of an imperative. Consequently, in the private world he inhabits, the goal of his security constitutes a supreme value and anything within or without that interferes with this goal is viewed with intense disapproval. But even this subjective disapproval in no way carries over to actions that may interfere with rights of *other* people; not only because the agent's normative

[24]Ibid., 63.

[25]Ibid., 65. See also ibid., 64: "in such a condition [state of nature], every man has a Right to everything; even to one anothers body," and *De cive*, I, 10: "Nature hath given to *every one a right to all*; that is, it was lawful for every man . . . to do what he would, and against whom he thought fit, and to posses, use, and enjoy all that he would, or could get." Nevertheless, in a footnote in *De cive*, Hobbes qualifies this statement by saying that a man may offend God or natural laws in the state of nature. As I shall show presently, Hobbes's views evolved significantly between *De cive* and *Leviathan*.

[26]This is not to say that Hobbes is entirely consistent on this score. See *Lev.*, 71–74, and my discussion in the next section for what at least appears to be such an inconsistency.

[27]Ibid., 62.

world is private (it is only *his* security that is a value for him), but also because the security of other people necessarily entails a threat to his own. In fact, it is precisely because he places such a high emotional value on his own rights that a man has no respect for the rights of others. From an objective point of view, however, characteristic of the scientific observer that was Hobbes, the value that an individual attaches to his self-preservation dissolves to a mere observation concerning the natural functioning of the human machine. While the definition of right as that which expresses absence of disapproval entails a commitment to some *normative* laws specifying that which is disapproved of, the Hobbesian use of the world "right" entails only that limitation on the scope of behavior which is provided by the set of *natural* laws making certain actions *physically* impossible. Consequently, the meaning of the word "right" resolves, as we shall see presently, to some such neutral and descriptive expression as "favorable external conditions for man's use of his power."

Still, the fact that what the agent sees as contributing to his self-preservation acquires for him the nature of an imperative is not irrelevant and, indeed, the agent's view of his own rights has a peculiar property of self-validation. The main distinctive feature of quasi-moral concepts in Hobbes is not that they *derive* from some objectively valid system of norms, but that they *causally influence* human behavior in such a way that they *result* in a system of objectively valid rules, controlling interpersonal relations. Quasi-moral concepts differ from other determinants of human action in that they are *self-fulfilling prophecies*: they specify a certain set of norms that acquire validity not *qua* moral norms, but *qua* laws of nature. They are figments of human imagination which human behavior *makes* true. Thus, a man's belief that all other men are his enemies is an outcome of the natural human propensity toward absurdity, the inability to understand the potential as merely possible, and not real. From this belief, the man derives an imperative that subjectively justifies his claim to every possible resource as indispensable to his security. But precisely *because* all men share the same belief, the belief becomes *true*: each man *in fact* threatens the security of other men and each man's subjective justification of his behavior acquires objective validity. Although the Hobbesian scientist's understanding of the meaning of "right" is purely descriptive (or at most functionalist), his analysis of the actual *scope* of actions performed "as of right" is determined by his analysis of the conditions that men create on the basis of their beliefs. Hobbes's theory of the state of nature is precisely such an analysis. In the process of constructing it, however, Hobbes purifies the concept of right of its subjective coloration and lays bare its descriptive residue.

It was only in *Leviathan* that Hobbes realized the full implications of his positivist commitments for his definition of natural right. In *De cive* (written in 1642), which in other respects contains a more or less complete exposition of his later political views, the definition of natural right is still significantly different from the form in which it appears in the later English treatise. In *De cive* Hobbes defined right as "that liberty which every man hath to make use of his natural faculties according to right reason."[28] It is, of course, the expression "according to right reason," which will disappear from the definition of natural right in *Leviathan*, that points to the still persisting lack of clarity on this subject in Hobbes's mind. To begin with, the adjectival use of the word "right" may be taken to imply a confusion of right and law. In fact, immediately after his definition of right Hobbes says that "the first foundation of natural right is this, that *every man as much as in him lies endeavour to protect his life and members*," and this sounds very much like a prescription (law) and not a right. But even if we take this as a merely ambiguous formulation, the expression "according to right reason" still strongly suggests a moral quality implicit in Hobbes's concept of natural right. "Right reason" clearly implies that there may be "wrong reason" on which a man is not permitted to act, at least not "with right."[29] The criterion for distinguishing between right and wrong reasons is, as Hobbes himself tells us a few pages later,[30] the law of nature, "some certain truth collected by right reasoning from true principles." The reappearance of the word "right" in the definition of natural law certainly does not help in determining the meaning of the *definiendum*, and the note that Hobbes adds to his definition can only confuse us further. By "right reason," he says, he does not mean "an infallible faculty, but the act of reasoning, that is, the peculiar and true ratiocination of every man." Unfortunately, his understanding of the word "peculiar" (referring to the fact that in the state of nature every man is a judge of what is right) contradicts his use of the word "true" (for the latter is meant to imply that some men judge falsely). One thing that is clear, however, is that Hobbes is thinking of natural laws here not as merely mechanical products of internal motions that constitute an element of the motivational process of human behavior, but as normative statements discovered by men when they think rationally. Natural rights are then seen as arising within the context of such laws as that which the laws do not forbid. A man may be said to act "with right"

---

[28]*De cive*, i, 7.

[29]It is perhaps possible to avoid this conclusion if one understands the expression "right reason" as synonymous with "sanity," so that the word "right" would be given the same meaning as in "he is not in his right mind." I thank Joel Honig for this suggestion.

[30]*De cive*, ii, 1.

when there actually exist some norms specifying a system of obligations and when an assertion of right on his part implies his acceptance of these obligations (the most important among them being that he be ready to renounce certain of his rights when other men are also prepared to do so). Even if no confusion of *jus* and *lex* is involved here, certainly the primacy of law over right, and a derivation of the former from the latter, are implied.

When Hobbes defines the concept of natural right in *Leviathan*, on the other hand, he clearly goes out of his way to exclude all moral implications. "THE RIGHT OF NATURE," he says, "is the Liberty each man hath, to use his own power, as he will himselfe, for the preservation of his own Nature; that is to say, of his own Life; and consequently, of doing any thing, which in his own judgement, and Reason, hee shall conceive to be the aptest means thereunto."[31] No mention is made here of "right reason." On the contrary, it is stressed that the man's judgment or reason is *his own*; that it may in fact be "wrong" or faulty does not seem to matter, and Hobbes makes no effort to distinguish between "true" and "false" ratiocination. The reference to judgment and reason is clearly not meant as a possible limitation of the extent of natural right in any other sense than as pointing to the fact that only *voluntary* actions could be said to be done "with right." Since the will must be determined, and since the mechanical process by which it is determined, according to Hobbes, involves those internal motions he identifies with deliberation, judgment and reason are obviously involved in all actions falling within the scope of a man's natural rights. But that a voluntary action involves deliberation is a *fact* and not a norm.

Similarly, the reference to self-preservation in Hobbes's definition of natural right is not meant as a qualification of the extent of a man's rights, but should be read as an explanation of the phrase "as he will himselfe." Each man desires his own preservation, according to Hobbes, and although he may act against what is "objectively" the best judgment, he is absolutely incapable of truly willing his own death (at least as long as he is sane at all). Even in *De cive* Hobbes says that "every man ... shuns ... death ... by a certain impulsion of nature, no less than that whereby a stone moves downward,"[32] and he certainly had not changed his mind on *this* point when he wrote *Leviathan*. Consequently, Hobbes cannot consistently claim that a man acts *sine jure* if some of his actions are objectively detrimental to his self-preservation, and he cannot make the right of nature dependent on the law of nature understood as a normative statement obliging a man to try to stay alive.

[31]*Lev.*, 62.
[32]*De cive*, I, 7.

There is in fact no reason to believe that Hobbes had any such claim in mind when he gave his definition of natural right in *Leviathan*. To begin with, had he wanted to make natural rights dependent on a prior system of obligations, it would have been difficult to take seriously his claim that a man has a right to *everything* in the state of nature.[33] Second, in marked contrast to *De cive*, Hobbes follows his definition of natural right in *Leviathan* with the already quoted specific disclaimer concerning the confusion of *jus* and *lex*. Finally, a few lines later, he specifically *derives* the fundamental law of nature from the fact that the natural rights of men are so extensive that they involve them in a universal conflict with one another.

To forestall any normative implications of his concept of natural right, Hobbes, having defined natural right as "the Liberty each man hath, to use his own power," hastens to add a paragraph explaining his general philosophical meaning of liberty: "By LIBERTY," he says, "is understood . . . the absence of externall Impediments: which Impediments, may oft take away part of a mans power to do what hee would; but cannot hinder him from using the power left him, according as his judgement, and reason shall dictate to him."[34]

The replacement of the expression "Liberty each man hath," in the definition of right by its equivalent expression will clearly reveal the neutral meaning of "right." "THE RIGHT OF NATURE," the definition will now run, "is the absence of externall Impediments to [a man's] use [of] his own power, as he will himselfe . . . " etc. When the passage is read in this way, the concept of natural right becomes completely devoid of its objective moral significance and has no consequences involving free choice or moral responsibility. The only type of law the existence of which is relevant to the extent of a man's natural rights is the law determining the way in which the environment of human action is shaped, that is, a rule of nature ascertainable by a physical theory. Within the context of a mechanistic theory of nature, "natural right" sounds like a contradiction in terms, but the Hobbesian interpretation makes it quite consistent. Given Hobbes's view of liberty (in terms of which he defines "right"), ascriptions of right refer at most indirectly to any property or accident of an agent; in their immediate significance they refer to the absence of external opposition and thus to a property (or, to be more precise, a privative characteristic) of the agent's *environment*.

What, then, is ultimately the content of Hobbes's conception of natural right? As we have seen, the concept is primarily *negative*, in that it

[33]*Lev.*, 64, 65.
[34]Ibid., 63.

refers to an absence of external, environmental impediments to a man's action. In this negative sense, "right" is not opposed to "wrong," but to a "counteracting force" or "unfavorable environmental conditions," where by these expressions is meant not only the purely natural conditions in which a man acts, but also any insuperable opposition he may encounter when faced with actions of other men. But is there no *positive* sense of "right" implied in Hobbes's account, that is, a sense in which ascriptions of right may refer to some property of the agent and not of his environment? The prime candidate for this position is, of course, some such characteristic as "the scope of possibilities of action" that a man may have at his disposal, which is to say, his *power*. Nevertheless, given the differences between Hobbes's understanding of the terms "freedom" and "power" and the way in which they are generally used, the identification of the positive sense of "right" with "power" is apt to be misleading. In ordinary parlance, the extensions of the terms "freedom" and "power" are roughly the same. For Hobbes, however, they are very different, at least from a logical point of view. To begin with, his concept of freedom is much broader than that in ordinary use, since his identification of freedom with the absence of external impediments allows one to say that a man may be free to do all kinds of things that he is absolutely unable to do, to fly, for example, or to stop breathing for an hour. Thus, freedom is not a *power* of man, but a negative feature of the world in which he lives. Second, Hobbes's concept of power is much narrower than that in ordinary usage, since the ontological limitations he imposes on the concept of possibility do not allow one to say that a man really *can* do something that he is not actually going to do or that he has any freedom of choice with respect to the way he is going to act. Consequently, from a logical point of view, both the meanings and the extensions of the terms "right" and "power" are significantly different.

Still, it is not incorrect to say that right, insofar as it has any positive sense, is the same as power. While, in purely logical terms, Hobbes's negative concept of freedom leaves room for more than his positive concept of power, his deterministic ontology will make the two concepts, insofar as they concern human action, exactly coextensive. Whatever happens happens necessarily, according to Hobbes. Hence, actions that are never going to take place are not really possible and do not constitute meaningful subjects of predication. Although Hobbes does not forbid us to say that, e.g., Mozart was free to complete his *Requiem* (which he in fact did not complete), our saying this amounts to a statement of the fact that Mozart was not poisoned (as he thought he was) when composing his last piece of music. But such an expression as "Mozart's act of composing the *Benedictus*" (one of the parts of the *Requiem* that Mozart did not compose) is for Hobbes entirely

81

meaningless. Thus, insofar as the term "right" may be used to single out a class of actions that an agent "has a right" to perform, the class in question will contain only those actions that he is actually going to perform, and it will be exactly the same class as the one composed of all the actions that are within the scope of his *power*. The positive and the negative meanings of "right" must still be distinguished—and the importance of this distinction will become clear in our discussion of obligation—since the result of a denial of right is different for each meaning of "right." The opposite of "right" in either sense, so long as the concept of *natural* rights is concerned, is not "wrong"; in the case of "right" in the negative sense (freedom), however, its opposite must be thought of as "presence of external opposition," while in the case of "right" in the positive sense (power), its opposite must be thought of as "incapacitation (by internal obstacles)." But that Hobbes does indeed effect the identification of right with power is obvious from his discussion of the state of nature. Not only is the war of all against all not mitigated by the fact that each man is vested with fundamental natural rights, but the universal state of war is indeed *derived* from this fact. The natural rights of one man imply no obligation not only on his own part, but also on the part of another man, and this leads to a conflict between their respective rights and to a contest between their powers. As long as the state of nature persists, it is absolutely impossible to trample on another man's right. To thwart the power of another man to achieve that good which he desires is to take away his right to it at the same time and to leave him without any legitimate *claim*. A right of one man limits that of another only to the extent that he has the power to impose his will on that of another. Not only does a natural right not add anything to a man's power (though an acquired right will), but it is for all practical purposes coextensive with it. If a man's right is his liberty to do what he wills, and if, further, an act of volition is only the last appetite in the chain of his desires, and if, finally, liberty is the absence of external impediments, then the statement that a man has a right to do what he thinks conducive to his self-preservation means nothing more than that he will actually do whatever he is impelled to do by his mechanism of self-preservation, regardless of whatever rights other people may have. It is difficult to see how Hobbes could be more explicit in making "natural right" a descriptive category or how he could tie it more closely to the concept of power.

4. Obligation

I have already stressed the originality of Hobbes's idea of the primacy of right over obligation and its seminal importance for the development of liberal political theory. The very way Hobbes posed the problem of the legitimacy of the state required that the state's authority be rooted in some set of circumstances that derogates from a preexisting right of each person to live entirely by his own lights and refuse allegiance to any will but his own. Consequently, any theory of obligation, at least insofar as obligation of one man to another or of a man to the state is concerned, had to be derived from the initial situation of equality which, in the strange definition Hobbes gives to it, entailed each person's having rights, but not duties.[35] Contractarianism was such a popular move with early liberals precisely because of this derivative status of obligation: given the primacy of right, the concept of *consent*, by which an individual could renounce a part of his natural liberty, seemed perhaps the only way obligations (and political authority) could be legitimized in the early liberal framework.

As I have also stressed, however, Hobbes's positivism made him go further than most liberals in delimiting the scope of natural rights, to the point at which the concept of right lost its usual moral and normative implications. In this sense, Hobbes posed a further challenge for the early political philosophy based on liberal foundations, since he made the very normative character of political concepts problematic. Not only did the specific concept of political obligation have to be reconciled with the concept of individual rights, but also the very possibility of obligation *as such* came under a cloud of doubt. Although later liberals, beginning with Locke, devoted much of their effort to overcoming the positivistic implications of Hobbes's theory of right, rooted in the mechanistic science of nature and man, Hobbes himself rested satisfied with them and constructed, accordingly, a positivistic theory or obligation.

A word of caution is required before we proceed further. Hobbes defines "obligation" in Chapter xiv of *Leviathan* and immediately moves on to his discussion of the concept of *contract*. He then gives us a general exposition of most of his quasi-moral concepts and, after a short detour, follows it with his theory of the commonwealth. As a result, the treatment of obligation is extremely compressed and, except for a few misleading examples, no attempt is made to analyze the effect of obligation in the state of nature separately from its effect in the context of a political community. Some commentators have concluded from this that Hobbes recognizes only one essential type of obligation and always uses this concept in the same sense.[36] Although, as will be seen from my

[35]This formulation of the problem of obligation, restricted to obligation *toward other men*, applies to Hobbes's account in *De cive*, which may leave some room for independent obligations to God or for some purely moral laws of reason, as well as to his account in *Leviathan*.

[36]See H. Warrender, *The Political Philosophy of Hobbes* (Oxford, 1957), 8–10. Warrender admits that Hobbes distinguishes two concepts of natural obligation, but says that only one of these is really important in his political philosophy.

discussion, the several meanings in which Hobbes uses the word "obligation" are linked to each other, I believe that no proper sense can be made of his theory if one fails to distinguish them. The most important of these distinctions is between political and civil obligations, on the one hand, and prepolitical or natural obligations, on the other hand. Political obligation in Hobbes is a concept relatively familiar to legal positivists—it derives its binding force from the presence of the overwhelming power of a state prepared to enforce its commands by punishments or rewards. While Hobbes has a very original account of this type of obligation, it is a concept relatively easy to grasp intuitively and should pose no special difficulties for the reader. Hobbes is quite aware, however, that the possibility of state power is the main problem that his more general theory of obligation is supposed to solve, so that he would be guilty of rather crude question begging if *all* obligations were to reduce to political obligations. Consequently, Hobbes must give us an account of *prepolitical* obligation that explains the possibility of a derogation from the natural rights of men and makes the creation of state power possible to begin with. This prior concept of prepolitical obligation, however, is, like the concept of right, quite idiosyncratic in Hobbes, and the reader must keep in mind the reason why it needs to be introduced. The outline of Hobbes's argument, given in section 2 of this chapter, should be helpful in this respect: with the concept of natural or prepolitical obligation, Hobbes wants to account for the motivational mechanism that enables him to explain how the natural equality of men is transformed into a system in which one man can command over others.

4.1. Natural Obligation

In *De cive* Hobbes says that

> there are two species of *natural obligation*. One when liberty is taken away by corporal impediments, according to which we say that heaven and earth, and all creatures, do obey the common laws of their creation. The other when it is taken away by hope or fear, according to which the weaker, despairing of his own power to resist, cannot but yield to the stronger.[37]

There are several differences between these two types of natural obligation, the most important being that one is an effect of an external power, while the other is an effect of a voluntary act of the agent. The first, which, following Warrender,[38] I shall call *physical obligation*, does

---

[37]*De cive*, xv, 7.
[38]Warrender, *Political Philosophy of Hobbes*, 9.

not play a very important role in Hobbes's political philosophy, but it is a strange concept, worth noting precisely because of its strangeness. I said in the previous section that while the normal use of the word "right," as that which expresses the absence of disapproval, entails a commitment to some *normative* laws specifying that which is disapproved of, the Hobbesian use of the word "right" entails only that limitation on the scope of behavior which is provided by the set of *natural* laws making certain actions *physically* impossible. Now, that physical impossibility may be of two kinds: one, when the operation of natural laws restricts the scope of the agent's *freedom* (defined by Hobbes as absence of external impediments), the other, where the operation of such natural laws restricts the scope of the agent's *power* (defined by Hobbes as a feature of the agent's inner constitution). As can easily be seen, the concept of physical obligation refers to a subset of these limitations, encompassing those restrictions on the agent's freedom and power which are not due to the agent's voluntary acts. I shall argue in a moment that those limitations of the agent's rights in the state of nature which are due to his voluntary acts are also to be understood as a species of physical impossibility. But since this understanding makes the concept of obligation in Hobbes rather unusual, it is important to note that, in introducing his concept of physical obligation, Hobbes himself clearly uses the term "obligation" in this way: to say that a man is held prisoner by another man or that he is paralyzed is the same, for Hobbes, as to say that he is *obliged* not to walk. And note that this concept of physical obligation is not in any easy way translatable into a prescriptive ("ought") statement.

It is the other kind of natural obligation, the one that results from a voluntary act of the agent, that interests us most here, and from now on I shall use the term "natural obligation" to refer exclusively to this kind of obligation, unless otherwise indicated. Indeed, in *Leviathan*, Hobbes does not speak of physical obligations at all and, instead, gives us (65) a general definition of obligation, the terms of which could apply to both natural and political obligations:

> [W]hen a man hath . . . abandoned, or granted away his Right; then he is said to be OBLIGED, or BOUND, not to hinder those, to whom such Right is granted, or abandoned, from the benefit of it: and that he *Ought*, and it is his DUTY, not to make voyd that voluntary act of his own: and that such hindrance is INJUSTICE, AND INJURY, as being *Sine Jure*; the right being renounced, or transferred.

Precisely because this definition is phrased in general terms, certain parts of it may not apply without qualifications to natural obligations. Thus, for example, Hobbes's statement that to "hinder" those to whom one is obliged is "injustice and injury" is not easily reconciled with his claim that "Justice and Injustice have ... no place" in the state of nature.[39] In fact, Hobbes's wording may leave one with the impression that his definition refers to a rather standard concept of moral obligation arising out of a free commitment to a certain course of action.[40] It is important therefore to analyze the meaning that Hobbes assigns to the particular expressions he uses to introduce his concept of obligation.

The most important feature of Hobbes's definition of obligation is that it arises out of a renunciation or transfer of a *right* by which another person gains a new right that he did not have before—to distinguish this new right from a person's natural right, I shall call it "acquired right."[41] Now, suppose that the right renounced is a natural right. As will be remembered, "natural right" has two meanings in Hobbes. In the negative sense, it is a "liberty to do, or to forebeare" and, given the definition of "liberty" as absence of external impediments, "right" is equivalent here to some such expression as "favorable external environment for man's action." In the positive sense, natural right is the same as the agent's power, i.e., some property of his internal constitution which enables him to pursue a certain course of action. It is clear, then, that a denial of one man's right in either of the two senses increases the scope of another man's right, since in view of the universal conflict among men, it makes the situation more favorable to the other's designs.

The strange notion of physical obligation apart, however, the denial of right that gives rise to an obligation does not arise from the fact that a man may be overpowered by another, but from a *voluntary act* of the agent. Again, two possibilities arise as to the way one should understand how a voluntary act of an agent may result in a derogation of right, depending on which of the two meanings of "right" is meant. Insofar as the negative sense is concerned, the agent would have to do something to change his *objective position*, so as to curtail his freedom of action. How this can be done is not immediately clear. Suppose that I promise not to exercise an option to act in a certain way. So long as my freedom to exercise that option is defined as a feature of the world around me, however, the mere promise, no matter how sincere, will not materially affect the continued existence of my option; I can "undo" my right only

---

[39]*Lev.*, 63.

[40]This is the understanding of D. Gauthier. See Gauthier, *The Logic of Leviathan* (Oxford, 1969), 76–98. See also above, Introduction to Part One.

[41]The person who acquires such a right had a preexisting natural right to everything he could get, so that, in a way, nothing new seems to be added here, especially if the promisee had originally enough power to overcome the one who now promises to refrain from hindering the promisee's exercise of his original right. Cf. *Lev.*, 65. But if the promisee did not have such power in the first place and the promise gives him such power, there is a clear increment in the promisee's arsenal of rights.

if I actually change the environment in such a way as to make the action in question objectively impossible (or at least its successful performance highly improbable). Contracting a political or civil obligation, according to Hobbes, amounts to precisely such a process of effecting a change in the objective conditions of man's action, and I shall discuss this later in more detail. Insofar as the positive meaning of "right" is concerned, on the other hand, it is much easier to understand what Hobbes has in mind when he speaks of obligation as a voluntary renunciation of right. To renounce a right in this sense is to curtail one's own power to pursue a certain course of action, without materially affecting the state of one's environment, and thus to increase the freedom of another man (and also his power in those cases where the promise is not only to refrain from resisting the other man, but also to assist him in obtaining some good[42]). It is this type of the renunciation of right that Hobbes means by his concept of natural obligation.

What is, more precisely, the nature of the voluntary act by which a man may renounce his rights? Hobbes says, immediately following his definition of obligation in *Leviathan*, that "The way by which a man either simply Renounceth, or Transferreth his Right, is a Declaration or Signification, by some voluntary and sufficient signe, or signes, that he doth so Renounce, or Transferre ... And these Signes are either Words onely, or Actions onely; or (as it happeneth most often) both Words and Actions."[43] Then he adds: "And the same are the BONDS, by which men are bound, and obliged."[44] Clearly, insofar as political and civil obligations are concerned—and we should remember that Hobbes's definition in *Leviathan* applies to both natural and political obligations—an overt act of promise making is both a necessary and a sufficient condition of obligation: once the overt act is performed, the state is prepared to enforce the promise. Equally clearly, however, in the case of a natural obligation, a mere act of promise making, unless sincerely meant, does not in any significant way limit the power of the agent. Someone who promises in bad faith may be guilty of lying (Hobbes even likens such false promises to absurdity[45]), but he certainly cannot be said to have truly renounced his right—indeed, Hobbes tells us that "Force and

---

[42]For the sense in which such incremental power, resulting from an obligation of assistance on the part of other men, can be ascribed to an agent, see section 5.2 of the preceding chapter.

[43]*Lev.*, 65.

[44]Ibid.

[45]Ibid. A loose comparison must be meant, since there is no real contradiction between promising and breaking the promise at some future time. Still, the comparison is interesting in the case in which one has a sufficient motivation to make a promise but not to keep it *at the same time*. It may also be interesting to speculate whether Hobbes toyed with an idea similar to Locke's mixed-modes theory of morality, to be discussed in Part II, below.

Fraud, are in warre the two Cardinall vertues."[46] Hobbes is, of course, fully aware that he cannot premise the objective validity of promises on the *overt act* of promise making. A statement of promise is only a mere *utterance* or an *action*, the "nature" of which is no different from other events of this kind, and it cannot, without more, be transformed into a norm. Thus, Hobbes adds immediately following the statement that "Words and Actions. . . . are the BONDS, by which men are bound, and obliged": "Bonds, that have their strength, not from their own Nature, (for nothing is more easily broken than a mans word,) but from Feare of some evill consequence upon the rupture."[47] The overt signs of promise making may thus be a necessary but not a sufficient condition of a natural obligation.

Hobbes's view that obligations are kept out of fear concerns more than just his theory of motivation; it lies at the very core of his theory of natural obligation. An indispensable element of a man's power to perform any voluntary action is the mechanism by which he forms an intention to act. Now, the main moving force of the human motivational system is fear of violent death. But that fear may determine not only an intention to act, but also an intention to refrain from a certain course of action and in this case fear plays a role comparable to a paralysis. An act of will, as we have seen, is an important link in the causal chain leading to an action and, although it involves the activity of ratiocination, it is essentially of the same kind as the involuntary determinants of behavior. Thus, an act of will by which an agent, for whatever reasons, forms an intention not to pursue a certain course of action effectively deprives him of his *power* to act, in the same way as another deficiency in the internal constitution of the agent, such as paralysis, deprives him of his power to walk.[48]

Leaving aside such outlandish behavior as a self-maiming designed to prove one's good faith in promising,[49] we can say that the voluntary act by which a man may renounce his rights is the act of forming an *intention* to adhere to the promised course of action as a result of the agent's fear of the consequences "upon the rupture." What is distinctive about natural obligation (physical obligation aside) is that a certain

---

[46]*Lev.*, 63 (emphasis added).

[47]Ibid., 65.

[48]See above, section 5.2. of the preceding chapter.

[49]Somewhat less outlandish would be the case in which an agent *disarms* himself to prove good faith. Whether this would be a case of an agent's changing the objective conditions of his actions (thus renouncing his right in the negative sense of freedom from external impediments) or a case of the agent's diminishing his power to act (renouncing a right in the positive sense) depends on how one views the relation between a man and his tools. I see no way of deciding what answer Hobbes would give to this question, but the resulting obligation would probably be natural and not political.

belief, namely, that the agent has no power to resist another in the competition for some resource, *causally determines* the action of the agent, so as to make the belief *true*. Thus, in the case when a man simply lacks the power to do something because of some other-than-motivational deficiency, say, a lack of wings that would enable him to fly, Hobbes still insists that the man has a "right" (in the sense of "freedom") to do it, since he can still form an intention to fly and only then experience its impossibility. On the other hand, the same man may have no power to take another man's crop, not because he lacks the strength to pick it or because the owner of the crop actually has the "physical" power to restrain him, but because the first man, believing the other has such power, has formed the intention not to try to take the other's property. Of this man Hobbes will now say that he is under a natural obligation not to take the other's crop because of the effect of the voluntary act that can be classified as "consent."

Hobbes's concept of natural obligation has several rather peculiar features. First of all, his deterministic account of human motivation disassociates the concepts of obligation and consent from any meaningful *choice* that an agent may exercise in deciding upon a certain course of action, and thus the voluntariness of the act by which a man contracts an obligation serves as an element in a *causal* explanation of human behavior, rather than as a source of norms. Second, Hobbes's theory of natural obligation implies that obligations preserve their validity only so long as the agent adheres to his original intention; the agent's very *ability* to break his promise means that he is no longer obliged. Nevertheless, as was true with Hobbes's concept of right, some of the counterintuitiveness of his theory diminishes, though it may never entirely disappear, if one looks at it, once again, from the perspective of the agent. In the "mere state of nature," no one ever recognizes the superior power of another man if that power is "naked" since men are naturally equal and capable of seeing that no one is strong enough to enforce his wishes over time. Most acts of promise in such a situation amount to a form of trickery and the life of a man who trusts them is even shorter than the usual. Situations can exist, however, in which obligations are more or less viable, even in the absence of a political authority willing to enforce them. These obligations derive their strength from the fact that people's belief in the power of those to whom they make promises is often embedded in a web of other beliefs which, regardless of their objective justification or lack of it, tend to support the fear that underlies the decision to make a sincere promise in the first place. The most important of these "supportive" beliefs are connected with religion. I shall discuss the subject of religion in Hobbes's philosophy a little more closely in the next section, and I shall explain there how it comes about that a man, ridden by the anxiety that his struggle for survival engenders, comes to postulate the existence of a supernatural power from which emanates a code of moral behavior.[50] Regardless, however, of the justification that a man may have for reaching a system of religious beliefs, Hobbes claims that he naturally comes to have it. Thus, after giving his definition of natural obligation, in *De cive*, as the state in which "when [liberty] is taken away by hope or fear, . . . the weaker, despairing of his own power to resist, cannot but yield to the stronger," Hobbes goes on: "From this last kind of obligation, that is to say, from fear or conscience of our own weakness in respect of the divine power, it comes to pass that we are obliged to obey God in his natural kingdom; reason dictating to all, acknowledging the divine power and providence, *that there is no kicking against the pricks.*"[51]

The fear of "evill consequence upon the rupture," which makes men adhere to their promises, is therefore not limited to the fear of retaliation by the promisee, but also includes the fear of punishment that God or gods are prepared to mete out to those who do not keep their obligations.[52] Thus, although Hobbes never truly commited himself as a scientist to conferring any truth value on most religious beliefs, and in fact his account of the origin of religious beliefs indicates that he did not believe they had any in a scientific sense,[53] he never doubted the *causal* efficacy of the belief in the fiction of divine power. From an agent's

[50]In anticipation of further discussion, it might be helpful to note here that Hobbes believes that "the Gods were at first created by humane Feare" (*Lev.*, 52). Men, living "in a perpetuall solicitude of the time to come," search for something "to accuse, either of their good, or evill fortune" and cannot find anything, "but some *Power*, or *Agent Invisible*" (ibid.). This personification of the power of nature makes men believe that they are faced not only with their potential human enemies (to whom they may rightly consider themselves equal), but also with a much more powerful being, who cannot be offended with impunity.

[51]*De cive*, xv, 7.

[52]Cf. *Lev.*, 70: The force of Words being . . . too weak to hold men to the performance of their Covenants; there are in mans nature, but two imaginable helps to strengthen it. . . . The passion to be reckoned upon, is Fear; whereof there be two very generall Objects: one, The Power of Spirits Invisible; the other, The Power of those men they shall therein offend. . . . The feare of the former is in every man, his own Religion: which hath place in the nature of every man before Civill Society. The latter hath not so; at least not place enough, to keep men to their promises; because in the condition of meer Nature, the inequality of Power is not discerned, but by the event of Battell. So that before the time of Civill Society . . . there is nothing to strengthen a Covenant of Peace agreed on, . . . but the feare of that Invisible Power, which they every one Worship as God; and Feare as a Revenger of their perfidy."

[53]Cf. ibid., 74: "because there is no naturall knowledge of mans estate after death; much less of the reward that is then to be given to breach of Faith; but onely a beliefe grounded upon other mens saying, that they know it supernaturally, or that they know those, that knew them, that knew others, that knew it supernaturally; Breach of Faith cannot be called a Precept of Reason, or Nature."

subjective perspective acknowledgment "of the divine power and providence" makes it perfectly reasonable to believe that, indeed, mere words have some power, and that, as Hobbes says in his definition of obligation in *Leviathan*,[54] when a man has renounced his right, "he *Ought*, and it is his DUTY, not to make voyd that voluntary act of his own: and [such violation of duty] is INJUSTICE, and INJURY, as being *Sine Jure*." This is what Hobbes means when he says that "The Lawes of Nature," which for him are "not properly Lawes, but qualities that dispose men to peace, and to obedience,"[55] "oblige *in foro interno*; that is to say, they bind to a desire that they should take place."[56] Only in society, however, the same laws acquire *objective* validity and bind *in foro externo*, for only then the desire for peace and its consequences is transformed into a system of *civil laws*.[57]

If the agent believes in God, then, his mental processes accompanying behavior in situations when the agent is under an obligation look, from the agent's own perspective, much the same as they look from the perspective of a moralist, and Hobbes is perfectly justified in speaking about "obligations" when explaining how one man may come to confer acquired rights on another man. As a *scientist*, however, searching for a causal explanation of human behavior, Hobbes is not obliged to, and indeed does not, subscribe to the view of the common man. Instead, like a physicist of his (and our own) time, he substitutes for the world of appearances the mechanistic construct of scientific theory: the world of motion and causation. From *this* perspective, natural obligation amounts to a process by which intention formation causally determines human behavior, making the agent's underlying belief in the

[54]Ibid., 65.

[55]Ibid., 138.

[56]Ibid., 79.

[57]The system of natural laws that bind *in foro interno* is also the system that, if adhered to by everyone, produces peace and security. Even in the absence of state power to enforce them *in foro externo*, therefore, "the laws of nature" are viewed by a scientist such as Hobbes as *functional* with respect to the goal that all men desire, so that their unjustified breach is viewed as counterproductive. Although Hobbes is sometimes not sufficiently clear in distinguishing this scientific evaluation of human behavior from a moralist's evaluation that would view the laws of nature as genuine obligations, he is not guilty of this confusion when he comes to treat explicitly of "Morall Philosophy." "Good, and Evill," he says there (ibid., 80), "are names that signifie our Appetites, and Aversions; which in different tempers, customes, and doctrines of men, are different." But, he says (ibid., 81), "all men agree on this, that Peace is Good, and therefore also the way, or means of Peace, which . . . are . . . the Laws of Nature." Consequently, "the true Doctrine of the Lawes of Nature, is the true Morall Philosophie. But the Writers of Morall Philosophie, though they acknowledge the same Vertues and Vices" do not see "wherein consisted their Goodnesse." This is so because "These dictates of Reason, men use to call by the name of Lawes; but improperly: for they are but *Conclusions, or Theorems concerning what conduceth to the conservation and defence of themselves*; whereas Law, properly is the word of him, that by right hath command over others" (ibid.; emphasis added).

power of another man into a self-fulfilling prophecy. In the same process, certain religious beliefs of the agent, insofar as their truth value is measured by the difference they make in the world of human action and not by their metaphysical content, also acquire some validity. But more about that later.

4.2. The Fool and the Robber

Everything I have said so far, even if it somewhat sharpens the contours of Hobbes's theory, seems to me not only compatible with Hobbes's overall project, but also the best way to make sense of it. It is, however, impossible to ignore certain passages in *Leviathan* in which Hobbes seems rather clearly to contradict the interpretation I have so far given of his concept of natural obligation. I shall discuss, therefore, two of the most important of these passages: the story of the fool and the story of the robber.

To begin with the fool. Hobbes gives us quite a few examples of "covenants entered into . . . in the condition of meer Nature"[58] and of obligations that arise from them, such as those toward one's parents or masters.[59] But all these obligations do not contradict the fact that there is no room for an objective concept of injustice in the state of nature. In fact, even political obligations lose their validity, according to Hobbes, when the state no longer has the power to enforce them.[60] A careful reader, then, has every right to be surprised when he or she finds Hobbes adopting a modified version of the biblical story of the fool who said in his heart that there is no God.[61] The same fool, Hobbes says, "hath sayd in his heart, there is no such thing as Justice."[62] Then, in a straightforward contradiction of his statement that there is no justice in the state of nature, Hobbes proceeds to argue that covenants under which one party has already performed are sources of valid obligations for those who were trusted to perform in the future. In the context of

[58]Ibid., 69.

[59]For filial obligations, see ibid., 102–3; for servant's obligation, see ibid., 103–4. Cf. also *De cive*, note to I, 10, where Hobbes states that a son, by virtue of his filial obligation, is no longer in the state of nature. Obviously, however, the "state of nature" is no longer understood here as merely that which precedes *political* association, and as such it is not relevant in the present context. Nevertheless, the statement is very interesting. First, it may be an indication of a distinction between political and civil society in Hobbes: any human relationships which arise out of contractual agreements are man-made and thus no longer strictly "natural." Second, the remark may be very important in view of Hobbes's argument, to be presented in the next section, that political society originates in paternal dominion.

[60]*Lev.*, 174.

[61]*Psalms* 14:1 and 53:1.

[62]*Lev.*, 72–73.

political society, there is clearly nothing wrong with this view (although it does not deserve to be singled out from among other valid contractual situations). But insofar as the validity of the obligation in question in the state of nature is concerned, Hobbes seems to be confused on several scores. First, if covenants of mutual trust are invalid in the state of nature (as Hobbes says they are[63]), then so are covenants of one-sided trust, since the covenant itself must *always* precede performance by *either* party. Otherwise there would be no reciprocity of obligation and thus no real covenant: if I do something for you, I can justify demanding that you do something for me in exchange only if we have previously agreed to exchange our services. But if the original covenant is invalid before either one of us has performed, it cannot acquire validity from the performance of one party, since in view of the covenant's prior invalidity, the performance of the first party amounts to an unintended (and imprudent) *favor*.[64] If I enter into an agreement that I know to be invalid, I cannot suddenly become bound by it on the grounds that the other party was irrational and allowed itself to be tricked. Trust, within the context of prepolitical obligations, can at best amount to *foresight*, but disappointing someone's prediction cannot be deemed an injustice or an offense.[65] Second, the outcome of Hobbes's argument against the fool is at most that it is *irrational* not to reciprocate in the performance of a covenant of one-sided trust (since Hobbes argues that such nonperformance cannot be ultimately beneficial to the violator), and this, perhaps, is the reason why the fool is a fool. If, as Hobbes argues (though his argument is fallacious[66]), violation of covenants of one-sided trust is

[63]Ibid., 71, 73.

[64]Lawyers do allow for recovery on the basis of justified reliance, but no reliance can be justified in the state of nature, in view of the obvious initial invalidity of mutually executory promises.

[65]Hobbes's argument for the validity of covenants of one-sided trust is often explained with reference to his alleged belief that covenants of mutual trust are invalid in the state of nature only because each contracting party always has good reasons to believe that the other party does not intend to adhere to its promise (cf., for example, Brian Barry, "Warrender and His Critics," *Philosophy*, 42 [1968], 164, reprinted in M. Cranston and R. S. Peters, eds., *Hobbes and Rousseau* [Garden City, N.Y., 1972], 37–65; see especially pp. 50ff.). This argument, which derives some support from *Lev.*, 68, where Hobbes says that "the cause of feare, which maketh . . . a Covenant invalid, must be alwayes something arising after the Covenant made," is hardly convincing, for the reasons given for the invalidity of covenants of mutual trust could be extended to cover, *mutatis mutandis*, the case of covenants of one-sided trust. Granted, of course, that when one party has already performed, the other could not reasonably suspect nonperformance in *this* particular instance. But still, in the state of nature, one always has every reason to suspect the other party of all kinds of nefarious designs, and hence also of having performed on this particular occasion in order to set an elaborate trap for the one who has not yet performed. If this is the case, however, there can be no obligation arising out of *any* covenants in the state of nature.

[66]Hobbes's argument assumes that a man who breaks covenants of one-sided trust will earn a bad reputation that will make others refuse to admit him to a future community

imprudent, all that he can say is that, from an objective point of view, the fool's behavior is *dysfunctional* (not at all a rare or surprising occurrence among human beings) and that, from a subjective point of view, any man who perceives the imprudence of the fool's behavior, must desire, according to the laws of nature, to adhere to covenants of one-sided trust (i.e., they have some validity *in foro interno*). But even that does not assure that a non-fool will keep them, since the desire in question may be easily overridden by some fear of a greater danger. What Hobbes *cannot* consistently say is, first, that any other sense of blame may attach to the fool's behavior so long as no state exists to punish him, and, second, that the fool had any choice to act differently from the way he actually did.

I have already indicated that Hobbes's treatment of obligation in *Leviathan* is extremely compressed and that he pays insufficient attention to his distinction between political and natural obligations. In fact, a confusion between a natural obligation and a civil one (an obligation contracted by private parties living in a political society) seems to lie at the root of all the others concerning the argument about the fool. Hobbes's main reason for the binding character of obligations arising from covenants of one-sided trust is that the would-be violator may have a justified fear that he will earn a reputation for wanton hostility and may not be admitted to society at some future time. But then the fool's allegedly natural obligation is already being considered in the context of a political compact that will yield the appropriate power of enforcement, and not really in the context of the state of nature. The only difference between natural and civil obligation becomes a matter of the degree of the *remoteness* of enforcement, and the "punishment" the fool will incur in the natural sequence of events is the very same punishment that allows us to assign blame to asocial conduct in a political society. If, however, the norms of political society spill in this way into the state of nature, then the whole distinction between the two states loses much of its value. Hobbes does not, of course, have to be committed to the claim that the state of nature ever existed in its pristine form. But the whole value of this concept rests in allowing us to isolate the *nature of man* from the requirements of political life, so that the latter can be explained out of the former. It is *this* aspect of the theory that loses its persuasiveness if the requirements of social life loom large over the state of nature from its very inception.

If a confusion between a natural and a civil obligation was at the root

---

that would be his best chance of achieving security. But an *intelligent* promise breaker will make sure that others do not learn about his treachery or that they find it justifiable on grounds similar to those discussed in the immediately preceding note.

of Hobbes's story about the fool, a similar confusion between a natural and a properly political obligation is at the root of his story about the robber. In this story Hobbes wants to argue that "in the condition of meer Nature, . . . if I Covenant to pay a ransome, or service for my life, to an enemy; I am bound by it."[67] Despite certain similarities to the more general argument about the fool (since the obligation of a victim to a robber seems to be based on the validity of covenants under which one party has already performed), Hobbes could not possibly argue for the validity of this obligation in the same way. In every society the validity of obligations is regulated by law, and no civilized law will be prepared to enforce covenants among the subjects that are clearly extracted by the use of force. No one, then, but the robber himself may consider a person untrustworthy on the ground of his breaking his word in *this* instance and thus think him disqualified for admission into some future society. No one, that is, unless one is prepared to think of the *ruler* of the future society as akin to the robber who will not trust a person to be a loyal subject if he does not adhere to covenants entered into because of a threat of force. Was Hobbes prepared to think this?

The actual context in which Hobbes introduces the example of the robber deals with the problem of whether covenants entered into because of fear are invalid. Hobbes is intent on showing that this cannot be the case, and he has good reasons for his claim. Fear, in his theory of man, is the most important motivating force of human action, and it is with the help of a man's fear of violent death that Hobbes explains most or even all of his behavior. Thus, to say that covenants entered into by reason of fear are invalid would leave no room for obligation at all: we incur a debt because we are afraid of starvation, and we pay it back because we are afraid of imprisonment;[68] we promise to help another person because we are afraid that otherwise he will not help us when we need it; we promise, in international relations, not to develop certain kinds of weapons because we are afraid that we shall be destroyed in case of war. Most important, we enter into a social pact because we are afraid of the one whom we promise to obey (the case of sovereignty by acquisition) or because we are afraid of each other (the case of sovereignty by institution). But Hobbes is carried away by his rhetorical zeal: to say that all covenants are entered into by reason of fear (that this fact cannot by itself invalidate a covenant) does not mean that all promises given out of fear are in fact valid covenants. Even in society, only those promises are valid which the law is prepared to enforce. Similarly, in the state of nature, there are all kinds of promises that

[67]*Lev.*, 69.
[68]Ibid., 108.

Hobbes himself admits do not bind anyone. Why then does he insist on the validity of the promise extracted by the robber?

One possible reading of the robber case will not create any problems, namely a reading under which the obligation of the victim is an ordinary instance of a prepolitical obligation. The victim may be afraid that the robber will get him in his hands once again and not trust him the second time. The victim may therefore form the appropriate intention to pay and in fact do so. If this was indeed what Hobbes had in mind—though it is doubtful that this is the case—his claim is much less provocative than it seems. But if Hobbes claims that the victim has an obligation to the robber even if he does not have the appropriate motivation to keep his promise, then he must claim that the validity of this obligation is independent of the fear that motivated the man to contract it. He can claim this only if he indeed confuses the robber-victim relation with the relation between the sovereign and the subject, just as we have suspected.

The confusion of natural and political obligations of which Hobbes is undoubtedly guilty here is especially interesting because the ruler-robber analogy has long been the favorite example of those who claim that political legitimacy cannot rest on the threat of force. Rousseau was to use exactly this analogy in order to show that right and might are two different things and that legitimacy must derive from a *moral* right to command.[69] Like Rousseau, Hobbes has shown himself, in choosing this misleading example, uncharacteristically oblivious to the difference between social and individual phenomena. But unlike Rousseau, who took the robber's case to be paradigmatic and argued from it that a government cannot legitimize itself by a threat of force, Hobbes, politically minded and English as he was, took the case of the legitimacy of sovereignty by conquest as paradigmatic and then mistakenly applied the result to the domain of individual relationships. At first sight, the two cases of extorted consent are indeed quite similar. A conquering despot is very much like a robber on a big scale; he keeps a gun to his victim's head and demands a promise of future obedience. But the differences are crucial as well. The conqueror never really lets his victim go free but watches over him constantly even after the promise has been extracted, and is always ready to strike again. We must assume, of course, as Hobbes clearly does, that no government could survive in the long run without the consent of the governed; as in a master-servant relationship,[70] the cooperation of the subjected party is always re-

---

[69]Rousseau, *The Social Contract*, I, 3. See also above, section 2.
[70]*Lev.*, 103–4.

quired. But this is so only in the *long* run, and the process of legitimization that then takes place consists in the fact that most people cease to question the conqueror's right to rule, independently of the force with which he threatens them. It is this *consent of a great number of people* that transforms the conqueror into a sovereign, that is, a *political* person. His dominion is a state not because he was able to overpower his subjects, but because he was able to translate his military advantage into their allegiance. It is only against this background of the government's legitimacy that we can introduce the concept of political obligation in which an overt act of promise, even if extracted under duress, may imply a real obligation, the validity of which *derives* from the ruler's continuous ability to enforce his commands. In the robber's case, on the other hand, nothing other than the victim's own intention could validate the obligation he may have, and there is no plausible reason why the victim should ever form such an intention.

4.3. Political and Civil Obligations

Only against the background of Hobbes's peculiar concept of natural obligation may his concepts of political and civil obligation be properly understood. The concept of natural obligation explains how a voluntary act of an agent may derogate from the agent's natural right and confer new power on another agent, giving him a new, "acquired" right. The concept of political obligation, in turn, explains how natural obligations can be compounded to allow for the creation of state power with binding authority over all subjects, including those who may not otherwise have a sufficient motivation to obey. Finally, civil obligation explains how a private party may be bound in favor of another private party in a political society.

I have already said that political obligation is equivalent to a renunciation of right in the negative sense of "freedom from external impediments," a renunciation that results from a voluntary act through which the agent changes the objective environment of his action, so as to make a certain course of action objectively impossible. Natural obligation is a very unstable phenomenon precisely because it arises out of some changes in the purely internal constitution of the agent—his motivational system. As a result, the beneficiary of this obligation can never be sure that he is not being tricked and may be quite justified in not suspending his hostile attitude toward the promisor. It is this instability that the political obligation eliminates. When the agent's success in the course of action he promises not to pursue is impossible, or at least extremely unlikely, as a result of perfectly ascertainable objective conditions in which the agent will have to act, the reasons for the universal mistrust responsible for the *bellum omnis contra omnem* simply disappear and war is replaced by peace.

In most situations, it is clearly impossible for an individual agent to provide sufficient objectively ascertainable proofs of his good faith, short of some act of self-maiming or some uniquely effective continuous disarmament. Therefore only a *social compact* in which *many* people participate can provide an effective transformation of natural into political obligation. It would be a mistake, however, to believe that Hobbesian agents can resolve the problems plaguing them in the state of nature by simply agreeing to institute an external power of enforcement and bootstrap themselves out of the situation resulting from the necessary natural forces that control their behavior. The Hobbesian social contract, which I shall discuss in more detail in the next section, is not a free act that simply ushers man into a new *modus operandi*. Rather, it is a natural outgrowth of the same forces that operate in the state of nature.

We have already seen how "self-fulfilling prophecy" transforms natural into political obligations when many people come, for one reason or another, to share the belief that some particular person has a right to command others. By the very fact that Antony believes Caesar has an irresistible right to command all Romans, Antony actually deprives himself of the power to resist Caesar. But Antony's belief may still be quite erroneous, insofar as he believes that Caesar has a right to command Cassius and Brutus. If most Romans came to share Antony's belief, however, Caesar could, by being able to rely on the joint forces of all those who dare not resist him, concentrate in himself their combined power and become indeed irresistible. At this point Caesar's right to command *everyone* would become a fact, no matter how absurd Antony's initial belief. By giving up their own freedom, the Romans would give up the freedom of all, including Cassius and Brutus. With respect to Antony and most other Romans, Caesar would have an *acquired* right to command, i.e., a right based on their obligation; whereas with respect to Cassius and Brutus, Caesar's right would still be *natural*. Brutus and Cassius would now face a choice: either to join Antony and others in making themselves coauthors of Caesar's authority or to face the consequences of Caesar's anger. Despite some hesitation that my choice of names may induce, Hobbes's theory of man leaves no doubt what the normal Brutuses would do. It is at this point that *political* obligation enters into play: whether Brutus and Cassius pledge their allegiance sincerely or not no longer matters, as it does not matter whether Antony changes his mind at some time in the future. The validity of their obligation now rests on the fact that Caesar is able and willing to enforce his commands and punish anyone who acts in violation of his merely *overt* act of promise. At this point Caesar ceases to be just one individual among others and becomes the ruler. One of the uses, that, as such, he will make of his power will certainly be to strengthen in any way possible—by civic education and the imposition of state religion, for example—his subjects' belief in his right to command and thus further strengthen both his legitimacy and the power that flows from it.

The ruler, once established in his position, will also be naturally interested in enforcing not only the subjects' obligations toward him, and especially the obligation of obedience, but also the obligations that the subjects contract among themselves. The extent of his power is, of course, predicated on the unity of his subjects and will be adversely affected by conflicts among them. Consequently, the establishment of political authority will also modify the character of obligations among the subjects themselves: they will now become *civil* obligations, since the overt act of promise will be validated no longer by the formation of an appropriate intention on the part of the promising party, but by the fact that the state is now prepared to enforce any promises implied in those overt acts that the state by law declares to have such implications.

What this transition from natural to political obligation represents is Hobbes's quite refined and sophisticated theory of the interdependence of force and legitimacy, power and consent. He does not claim in any *simple* sense the "might makes right." Neither is his account of political power, despite his nominalistic requirement that the nature of the state be explained in terms of its individual components (the subjects and their interests) and not vice versa, insensitive to the differences between individual and social phenomena. The viability of political power does not rest exclusively on mere application or even a constant threat of force. On the contrary, it rests on the *consent* of a great number of people: a consent that comprises both the overt act of the signification of promise and the formation of an appropriate voluntary intention to obey on the part of a great majority of the citizenry. To be sure, their consent has its ground in fear, but most often their fear of "naked" force is mediated by a belief in the ruler's *right* to command. On the other hand, however, once a political compact exists, a new set of rules, specifically characteristic of group phenomena, becomes applicable, and the formation of the appropriate intention on the part of any particular individual becomes irrelevant with respect to the validity of the promise he overtly signifies. It is only as *such* that his obligation becomes *political*. Naturally, the subjective motive of actual obedience is still fear and the formation of the appropriate intention to obey that follows as a consequence of this fear is still the immediate cause of obedience. But the formation of such an intention is no longer the *source* of the obligation's validity, but rather its *effect*. It is in *this* sense that justice, which comes onto the scene only with the state, is a result of power. But even here the relation between might and right is not that of one-sided dependence. For a scientific observer like Hobbes, the idea of justice objectively resolves to the sovereign's readiness to enforce his commands. But while, in the case of a natural obligation, breach was just a matter of *fact* and ended the obligation in question, there is an objectively meaningful sense in which a breach of a political obligation violates an established legal *norm* and constitutes an *injustice*. The law in question is still, of course, positive law, but it, and the threat of punishment, allow for a meaningful use of the concepts of blame, praise, merit, and so forth. The subjective effect of this moral vocabulary, the effect certainly intended by the ruler, is to strengthen, in turn, the subject's belief in the sovereign's right and thus to increase his power.

5. Contract

One of the most important differences between natural and political obligations is that a man may at any time in the state of nature enter into the former but not the latter. Only a large group of people may enter into a political compact. Thus, although a man may at any time possess all the rights that he renounces upon entering a political society, some very special conditions must be met in order for him to renounce them in the sense implied by the concept of political obligation. What these conditions are we must now investigate in some detail.

It is a common error in interpreting Hobbes's political doctrine to view the social contract in the light of our ordinary ideas about the nature of contractual obligations. From a superficial reading of *Leviathan* one may assume that when Hobbes speaks of the original social pact he alludes to a more or less historical phenomenon. One imagines a large assembly of all the people inhabiting a certain territory who decide in common upon the future organization of their state. Arguments are heard on all sides before the best option is chosen and accepted. Even if an actual meeting of this kind was not what Hobbes had in mind, he might, it seems, have argued that questions of political legitimacy could be settled on the basis of a quasi-historical supposition—that *should* all the people meet together and discuss the form of their association, each rational human being would *have* to agree to a certain form of government. Whether a meeting actually took place or is only a hypothetical device for adjudicating the questions of justice is not terribly important; questions of legitimacy are questions of right and not of fact, and their resolution does not depend on actual historical events.

An approach of this kind may be very useful for a philosophical analysis of the problems of legitimacy in general, and there have been some recent attempts to return to this method.[71] Nevertheless, its applicability to Hobbes's political theory is very questionable. If there is any merit in my discussions thus far, it consists in showing that Hobbes effects a far-reaching transformation of the problem of legitimacy and that his view of the origin of the state cannot be made into a problem of rational decision making. His main problem is not to explain what kind of government *ought* to be obeyed, but what kinds of governments *are* obeyed and *why*. The whole framework within which Hobbes poses the question of legitimacy makes it impossible for him to speak of a deliberate choice concerning the most rational form of association, that is, a choice that would entail several viable alternatives as to the future course of action. Indeed, Hobbes's choice of the very form of government he presents as the most suitable to man's nature is determined by the fact that he believes men incapable of sustained rational conduct and of forming a viable association on the basis of rational choice.

Thus, the first thing to be understood about Hobbes's contractarianism is that the social pact is not a reference to either an actual or a hypothetical event connected with a problem of rational decision making. The social-contract metaphor is, rather, a category in terms of which a social or a political philosopher analyzes a certain set of continually operating factors in social life, and not at all a term referring to any unitary event. Like a psychoanalyst's category of "the murder of the primeval father" or Hegel's "master-slave dialectic," Hobbes's category of social contract is a synchronic representation designed to bring together a multitude of features responsible for what is in reality a very complex phenomenon. A psychoanalyst does not have to claim (as Freud unfortunately came to do) that Jews actually killed Moses in order to use the category of the murder of the primeval father in explaining the complex set of factors determining the meaning of Jewish culture. Hegel does not have to claim that his category of the struggle for life and death refers to an actual historical event (though the wars in which slaves were taken provide a certain historical background to his views) in order to be able to use it in explaining the dilemmas of Greek political thought. Similarly, Hobbes does not have to refer to any real or hypothetical assembly of all people to be able to use the social-contract metaphor to explain the nature and the

[71]See J. Rawls, *A Theory of Justice* (Cambridge, Mass., 1971).

origin of a government's legitimacy. It is true, of course, that in some particular circumstances, such as the reestablishment of authority after a political revolution—a concern that was clearly prominent in Hobbes's mind—the actual course of events bears some resemblance to a situation described in the social-contract metaphor. Nevertheless, the considerations with which Hobbes intends to deal in representing the contractual origins of political society are of a much more general nature than those that concern the problems involved in eliminating the chaos introduced by a revolution; and Hobbes's own analysis of the way a society is founded in a contract is very different from the perception that most, if not all, revolutionaries have of their own actions. Hobbes does not think of the social contract as a means of legitimizing only a certain kind of society, so that the consent implied in the contractarian origin of a given state could provide a means for distinguishing it from other stable political associations and for calling the former "just" or "legitimate" and the latter "unjust" or "illegitimate." On the contrary, all stable societies, according to him, derive their stability from some form of social contract, and unless they differ in the extent of their stability, all are equally legitimate, regardless of whether they originate in conquest, grow out of a tribal or paternalistic system of authority, or are founded by an originally popular assembly.[72] Democracies, monarchies, oligarchies, and all other stable political systems must be accounted for in terms of the social-contract metaphor. In our ordinary understanding, a legitimizing consent must be *free*. For Hobbes, however, this kind of freedom is meaningless. All our voluntary actions are strictly determined, and all are determined in the same way, as mechanical effects of mechanically arising fear; so there is no reason to distinguish in principle among various kinds of motives that can give rise to legitimizing decisions. So long as the direct cause of an action lies in the corresponding act of volition (as opposed to having one's body moved by an external force or an involuntary muscle contraction), all actions are on a par. Consequently, the legitimacy to which consent gives rise is a matter of *fact*, namely the fact that accounts for a government's *stability*.

I have already analyzed the most general features of the process of the foundation of political authority that Hobbes intends to capture with the help of his category of social contract. At that point, I explained that the social contract consists in a coincidence of the formation of prepolitical obligations of the same kind on the part of a great number of individuals. As a result of such a coincidence, the belief vesting a particular person or group of persons with powers incompatible with

[72]*Lev.*, 102.

the natural equality among men acquires, provided it is shared by a sufficient number of people, the character of a self-fulfilling prophecy. No matter how absurd the initial reasons for holding such a belief, once it is held by a sufficient number of people, the belief becomes in fact *true*. I have also indicated that the reason, according to Hobbes, that people ever come to form beliefs of this kind in the first place is that they are prone to religious superstition. We now have to look more closely at the role of religion in the formation and maintenance of political authority.

5.1. Religion

We have seen that the power of man is incomparably greater than that of animals because men are capable of using speech in such a way as to increase beyond all proportion their capacity to respond to possible dangers as if they were actual. When speaking of man's ability to use language, Hobbes points to its being an ambiguous blessing: the privilege of reason allows man to organize his experience, but "this privilege is allayed by another, and that is, by the privilege of Absurdity; to which no living creature is subject, but man onely."[73] We have already seen what might pass as one meaning of this "absurdity": the increase of man's power leads to his desire for power as such and, by means of the universal conflict among men that it introduces, further leads to an undue diminution of the effectiveness with which he can use this power for the sake of his self-preservation, that is, to his having much less power than his individual constitution would lead us to expect. But the primary meaning of "absurdity" that the use of speech brings about is something else; the absurdity Hobbes has in mind in the context of his discussion of language is essentially a *philosophical* type of confusion. When people begin to think abstractly, Hobbes believes, they are apt to lose their footing in reality altogether. They may take grammatical forms to reflect a system of real relationships and thus confuse bodies with accidents, or they may take metaphors literally and ascribe entirely inappropriate characteristics to some objects.[74] What is perhaps especially interesting in the context of our discussion is that Hobbes classifies among absurdities the "canting of Schoolmen," who talk about supernatural beings and their properties.[75]

When we come to consider Hobbes's account of the origin of societies, we find him adding yet another level of exquisite irony to his

---

[73]*Lev.*, 20.
[74]Ibid.
[75]Ibid., 21.

description of the ambiguous blessings of speech. For it is only by virtue of being able to hold entirely unjustified, and probably also unjustifiable, beliefs about the powers of objects around them (and especially about the power of other men), that men can ever come to grant away their natural rights and to modify the natural relation of equality, so as to create a situation favorable to the rise of a state. Thus, whereas the relatively "rational" use of their power leads men to a state of universal conflict among themselves and accounts for the "absurd" discrepancy between the actual outcome of their actions and the overall goal of security for which they strive, the apparently absurd system of mythical and theological beliefs is ultimately responsible for a harmonization of the ends and means of human life and for the achievement of the greatest degree of security of which human beings are capable.

Hobbes devoted more than half of *Leviathan* to a discussion of religion, but not all the details of this aspect of his theory are pertinent here. The very fact, however, that he felt it necessary to devote such an extensive part of his political work to the subject of religion is significant. His reasons for doing so are not very difficult to discover. To begin with, religion, according to him, is a foundation of an existing government's legitimacy. Without some system of theological beliefs according to which a government has a right to rule, that is, without harnessing men's fear of punishment in the future world to the purpose of extracting their obedience in this one, a government has a virtually impossible task in convincing the citizenry as a whole—and not just any particular individual—that it disposes of a sufficient power to keep them in awe. For this reason, a government must ensure its subjects' religiousness and *orthodoxy*: a belief in a personal God whose commands are interpreted by the temporal, political authority of the state and whose worship is regulated by a uniform, habit-forming liturgy administered by the official clergy. As a scientist, Hobbes is not interested in the truth value of religion. What interests him above all are the political consequences of religious beliefs and their ability to contribute to the stableness of political arrangements. It is true that the power of religion may be as much an obstacle as a help to a government's authority, depending on whether the latter controls it or not. Thus, especially in view of the religious background of the civil war in England, Hobbes feels obliged to explain what features of Christian doctrine are constructive or destructive of political power. He investigates the "Kingdom of Darknesse" contained in Christian doctrine, which allowed the papacy and its proponents to rob the royal power of a part of its prerogatives. He also criticizes the Puritans for their opposition to a state-controlled form of worship and their claims of private responsibility in matters of morality and religion. Finally, and most important

in our context, Hobbes believes that religion or mythology is of fundamental importance for the formation of political associations in the first
place. It is above all with reference to the "absurdities" of primitive
man's system of beliefs that Hobbes must explain the possibility of
overcoming the natural equality among men and the origin of the first
states.

Hobbes envisages the source of religion in the "*Feare* of power invisible, feigned by the mind, or imagined from tales publiquely allowed."[76]
He makes a special allowance for Christianity in that he views the
motives that lead men to a monotheistic system of beliefs as also
connected with human curiosity and interest in science. In a well-
established Christian commonwealth, where the power of the state is
sufficient to protect the citizenry from the dangers they fear most,

> the acknowledging of one God Eternal, Infinite, and Omnipotent, may
> more easily be derived, from the desire men have to know the causes of
> natural bodies, and their several vertues, and operations; than from the
> fear of what was to befall them in time to come. For he that from any effect
> hee seeth come to passe, should reason to the next and immediate cause
> thereof, and from thence to the cause of that cause, . . . shall at last come to
> this, that there must be . . . one First Mover . . . which is that which men
> mean by the name of God: And this without thought of their fortune; the
> solicitude whereof, both inclines to fear, and hinders them from the search
> of the causes of other things; and thereby gives occasion to feigning of as
> many Gods, as there be men that feigne them.[77]

Still, granted the difference between the Christian belief in a personal
God and the "absurd opinion" of the ancients, the original impulse
toward religion proceeds from fear. "It is impposssible," says Hobbes,[78]
"for a man, who continually endeavoureth to secure himself against the
evill he feares . . . not to be in a perpetual solicitude of the time to come."
Consequently, a "man, which looks too far before him, in the care of
future time, hath his heart all the day long, gnawed on by feare of death,
poverty, or other calamity; and no repose, no pause of his anxiety, but in
sleep." The anxiety of man is, as we have seen, by nature indeterminate.
But the state it creates for the agent is in fact intolerable, and he must
find some *object* for his fear. "And therefore when there is nothing to be
seen, there is nothing to accuse, either of their good, or evill fortune, but
some *Power*, or Agent *Invisible*: . . . [so] that the Gods were at first created
by humane Feare."[79]

[76]Ibid., 26.
[77]Ibid., 53.
[78]Ibid., 52.
[79]Ibid.

5.2. Paternal Dominion and the Origin of the First States

To see the exact relation between the formation of mythical or religious beliefs and the operation of those forces that Hobbes intends to capture with the help of his concept of the social contract, we must attempt to reconstruct what must have been for him the most likely scenario concerning the origin of the first states. Hobbes makes a general distinction between two types of commonwealths: those established by "institution" (into which men organize out of the fear of one another) and those established by "acquisition" (in which the direct cause of men's subjection is the fear of the person who is to become their ruler).[80]

Although Hobbes begins his discussion of these types by analyzing "sovereignty by institution," for reasons that will be explained later, his order of exposition may be misleading, and I shall reverse it. Hobbes himself says that the "Rights, and Consequences of Sovereignty, are the same" in both kinds of commonwealths,[81] and the acquisition type, or rather one of its varieties, is clearly the one that corresponds to the origin of the first states.

Within the type of commonwealth established by acquisition, Hobbes distinguishes two varieties: commonwealths in which sovereignty is acquired by conquest ("despotical dominion") and those in which it arises out of "paternal dominion."[82] It is the latter variety that interests us most here, for a patriarch of a large tribe bound by family ties is the most likely candidate for the first ruler. This is so because the parent-child relationship, at least as long as the child is not yet an adult, is the only natural relation of *systematic inequality*. Parental dominion, according to Hobbes, originates not in the act of generation,[83] but in a radical exception to the principle of natural equality: a parent "may either nourish, or expose" the child[84] and hence possesses the power of life and death over his or her progeny. Hobbes is by no means sentimental about filial obligations; it is not the child's gratitude or other lofty feelings that are primarily responsible for the parent's dominion. Like all sovereignty by acquisition, paternal power is "acquired by Force"[85] and filial obligation derives from an act of submission due to fear. Nevertheless, Hobbes explicitly states that the direct source or the immediate cause of a child's obligation to his or her parent is not the parent's superior force, but the child's *consent*, "either expresse, or by

[80]Ibid., 88, 102.
[81]Ibid., 102.
[82]Ibid.
[83]Ibid.
[84]Ibid., 103.
[85]Ibid., 101.

other sufficient arguments declared."[86] Moreover, he clearly believes that this obligation extends, in most cases, over the child's whole life and even over all future generations.[87] Thus, the covenant by which a child promises obedience to a parent reaches further than the latter's "natural" power and extends even beyond the period of natural inequality between generations. The question is *how* this power is capable of such an extension: what constitutes the *strength* of the filial obligation?

Hobbes's treatment of parental dominion condenses the political and prepolitical filial obligations in a rather short discussion, except for a slightly more detailed inquiry into the relative powers of the father and the mother "in the state of meer Nature."[88] In most political communities with which Hobbes was familiar, parental dominion was legally entrusted to the father. Nevertheless, in the absence of other considerations, Hobbes asserts the priority of the mother's claim which, he says, rests on the facts that fatherhood may be doubtful and that the mother is the primary provider of care. The case of maternal power, however, is always only theoretical: "other" considerations, such as the fact that the father's physical strength makes him the primary defender and provider of the family, puts the mother, and consequently the child, under the father's dominion. Now, so long as human beings live in the state of nature (whatever historical or prehistorical reality this expression is supposed to refer to), filial obligation, insofar as it extends the father's power beyond his natural superiority, must be *natural* or *prepolitical*. This, according to my interpretation, means that the strength of this obligation rests exclusively on the formation, on the child's part, of the appropriate *intention* to act in obedience to the father's wishes. Why does he adhere to this intention beyond the time of physical dependence and thereby deprive himself of the possibility of emancipation upon reaching maturity?

Given what I have already said, this question is not difficult to answer. To make Hobbes's account of the origin of the state more persuasive, one must modernize the context of his discussion of paternal dominion somewhat and introduce some anthropological evidence into the limited perspective of his account of religion. But we do not have to reconstruct the exact details of the theory with which Hobbes could account for the extension of paternal power. It should suffice to see that nothing other than the human "privilege of absurdity" is capable of accounting for this phenomenon. A primitive man, driven by fear of

[86]Ibid., 102.
[87]Ibid., 103.
[88]Ibid.

nature and his enemies, creates a fiction of the afterlife and populates the world with a multitude of ghosts and spirits. His unconscious drive to emulate the ideal of perfection that his father represented for him during childhood makes him conceive a mythical fear of and admiration for living and dead ancestors. In his search for security he turns to the roots of his family life and to the bonds of a clan. A mixture of realistic and mythical considerations leads him to form a system of allegiances to those who afforded him protection in the past, when his life was entirely in their hands. The figure of the father grows to the dimensions of omnipotence, and the religious sanction of paternal power makes it seem greater than anything by which a man could ever be threatened. It is not gratitude or a cool calculation that forms the basis of filial obligation; it is rather the grip of fear that convulses the primitive man when he confronts his future or the possibility of paternal anger, supported by the forces of the dead. A skillful parent may then manipulate these feelings and, with the help of ritual reinforcement, create a very solid power base for himself. Further, if family bonds extend beyond the nuclear family and come to involve uncles, aunts, cousins, and so on, the hierarchical structure of a single family may be gradually extended to include a large number of people of common descent (a tribe). Finally, when the family so extended becomes a politically viable unit, when its power "by its own number, or by other opportunities" is so great that it cannot "be subdued without the hazard of war," it becomes a *state*.[89]

5.3. Sovereignty by Institution

If the foregoing reconstruction of the process of the formation of political authority is correct, the meaning of Hobbes's contractarianism can finally be understood. What is sometimes expressed in the catchphrase "might makes right," Hobbes tries to analyze in the complex fiction of the social contract. The primary function of this fiction is to reveal the intricate network of relationships between power and legitimacy. In his analysis of sovereignty by acquisition, Hobbes makes it clear that political authority rests as much on legitimacy as on force. In discussing sovereignty gained by conquest he makes it clear that even a conqueror's right of dominion derives directly from a covenant and not from the fact of victory,[90] and in the case of paternal dominion, he explains that it derives not from generation but from the child's consent. Nevertheless, force and fear are always in the background of a

[89]Ibid., 105.
[90]Ibid., 104.

covenant: the subject's political consent is an internalization of external relationships of power that in turn derive from a mixture of force and prepolitical consent. The meaning of the social contract is above all that of an interplay and mutual reinforcement of right and power, and it rests in large part on an analysis of the relation between truth and belief in matters of legitimacy. Far from trying to isolate the concept of rational, de jure justification of political authority from actually obtaining relations of power and the de facto modes of their justification, Hobbes is, rather, interested in arriving at a common denominator of power and legitimacy, or of the facts of social life and the norms of political behavior. Not only is he not proposing a political system that a rational agent would have to accept on moral or prudential grounds, but he indeed claims that the element of irrationality present in human motivation is uniquely responsible for the benefits of social cooperation. Acting on those beliefs that they actually have about themselves, men, being the authors of their own actions, *create* the truth of their own beliefs. Political science differs from natural sciences not because an impartial, certain knowledge of our own actions is directly accessible to us as their authors,[91] but because we have the power of conferring truth on some of the most irrational beliefs we hold about ourselves. Political science is, more than any other, concerned with postulates and definitions, because what men postulate with respect to the relations of power among themselves, they very often *ipso facto* bring about.

In his discussion of sovereignty by institution, Hobbes is primarily interested in analyzing these postulates and definitions from the point of view of their internal consistency and persuasiveness rather than from the point of view of their causal efficacy. Even though this perspective is much less important for Hobbesian political science (for men are seldom, if ever, moved to act by persuasion alone), and despite the fact that the establishment of sovereignty by institution is much rarer than by acquisition (it is limited to cases of radical changes in governmental structure brought about by revolutions), Hobbes presents sovereignty by institution as if it were a paradigmatic case of a contractually established social order. One of his reasons for doing so is certainly that the circumstances of his life made revolutions of primary interest. But, more important, in cases of sovereignty by institution, the actual events more closely resemble the theoretical, contractarian model than in the case of the legitimization of a conquest or the rise of paternalistic

---

[91]Strauss (*Natural Right and History*, 172–75) has insisted on the fact that Hobbes considered political philosophy a form of "maker's knowledge." In some sense, this is true of course (see *De homine*, x, 5), but not in the sense that moral or political obligations derive their validity from the very fact of postulation.

political authority. The anarchy created by a revolution approximates in certain respects the Hobbesian state of nature, and the active participation of a large number of people in the process of establishing future authority approximates the "assembly" model of the social contract.

This does not mean that in revolutionary contexts actual events conform perfectly to the theoretical model. In reality, revolutionary changes are far from being as radical as they seem to the agents involved in them, since the revolutionaries are heavily conditioned by having already lived in society and take for granted the benefits of social cooperation. They already *have* the most fundamental beliefs necessary for establishing a stable social order, although they disagree with the particular order that they have abolished. Thus, they are far from having really returned to the "original" state of nature. They seek to found a political order on "rational" principles, but without the experience they have behind them, *no* concept of social order would appear to them defensible on purely rational grounds; for given the truth about human nature, the elimination of the de facto forms of social cooperation leaves no room for any system of obligations that could actually obliterate the ominous features of natural equality and secure men's allegiance to the new order.[92]

Still, in their own understanding, the revolutionaries are creating a genuinely new social order. They see their task as framing new norms of social coexistence. Thus, even though the result may be incomplete and misleading, the analysis of their postulates may, from a purely analytic point of view, yield an outline of the rights and duties of citizens and rulers that the actions of men are going to put into practice. Consequently, Hobbes is not reluctant to step temporarily out of the complex background of his political theory and to adopt the standpoint of the agents involved in the process of "instituting" an entirely new commonwealth, since in this way he can attempt to isolate those substantive views of rights and obligations which have a chance to result in a viable state. This, for example, is the right perspective, according to him, from which to examine the relative merits of different constitutional orders, independently from the problem of the source from which norms of social coexistence derive their motivational strength, and indeed, in Chapter xix of *Leviathan*, he goes on to give us precisely such an analysis. Addressing, as he is, the public of revolutionary England, he is also content at this point (and this is true to a certain extent of his earlier general treatment of obligation as well) to speak about the social con-

---

[92]In this respect Hobbes anticipates the political theories of Hume and some later conservatives. See above, section 2.

tract as if it involved a system of "moral" postulates most conducive to peaceful coexistence. Consequently, he argues for what he views as the "just" terms of the social contract, such as that the contracting parties have no right to change their minds subsequently to the establishment of political authority and that the sovereign's power is not limited by the social contract, as if he was trying to persuade his contemporaries to adopt them.

But what is missing from these discussions is an analysis of the relation between such "moral" postulates and the actual workings of social interaction. It is only later, in the discussion of sovereignty by acquisition, that it becomes clear that the real problem of political science is not to provide an abstract "justification" of such postulates and defend them as the most rational choice in the political decision-making process, but to explain how one, and not another, system of beliefs comes about, how it influences human actions, how it provides for a viable system of political authority, which in turn influences the system of actually held beliefs, and sanctions them as an actually binding system of social norms. Only when this complete circle of influences is fully understood, is the meaning and consistency of Hobbes's philosophical system really laid out before our eyes.

PART TWO: LOCKE

Introduction

The relationship between Locke's and Hobbes's political philosophies has been a subject of much scholarship and controversy. Some of
the earlier interpreters of Locke's *Second Treatise of Government*
viewed that work as mainly a polemic against Hobbes's absolutism.[1] Leo
Strauss, on the other hand, with his usual penchant for the paradoxical,
has argued that Locke was a crypto-Hobbesian who chose to hide some
of his true beliefs.[2] Finally, Peter Laslett, in the introduction to his
excellent edition of the *Two Treatises*, argued that Locke's political
writings were directed against Robert Filmer, and that Hobbes provided
only a general background to Locke's thinking.[3]

It may seem merely an ironic gloss on the scholarly propensity to
argue *any* point of view so long as it is novel and contradicts previous
interpretations, that each of the three conceivable views of Locke's
relationship to Hobbes—that he continued, opposed, or was independent of Hobbes's work—has found its scholarly defenders. In fact,
however, Locke's relationship to Hobbes is very complex and problem-

---

[1]See F. Pollock, "Locke's Theory of the State," *Proceedings of the British Academy*, 1
(1903–4), 237–49; C. Bastide, *John Locke, ses theories politiques et leur influence en
Angleterre* (Paris, 1907), generally; see, e.g., 231. C. E. Vaughan, *Studies in the History of
Political Philosophy before and after Rousseau* (Manchester, 1925), 1:130–203; J. W. Gough,
John Locke's Political Philosophy, Eight Studies (Oxford, 1950).

[2]L. Strauss, *Natural Right and History* (Chicago, 1953), 202–51. For a Straussian interpretation of Locke, see also R. Cox, *Locke on War and Peace* (Oxford, 1960).

[3]John Locke, *Two Treatises of Government*. A Critical Edition with an Introduction and
Apparatus Criticus by P. Laslett (Cambridge, 1963), reprinted by the New American Library
(New York, 1965), 81–92. (The NAL edition is cited here and below.)

atic. Laslett is probably right in claiming that Filmer, with his defense of the divine right of kings, was the immediate target of Locke's attack, and he tells us quite clearly that Locke's notes, diaries, letters, book lists, and so on show no specific preoccupation with Hobbes's work.[4] But there seems to be no doubt that Locke knew Hobbes's writings and that they exercised some degree of influence, positive and negative, on his own thinking. Still more important, the relationship between Hobbes and Locke is of more profound historical and systematic significance than can be surmised from a study of Locke's personal interests and preoccupations. In a somewhat narrower historical sense, a thinker's conscious self-perception should not, of course, be ignored, and a correction imposed on this perspective by an interpreter writing three hundred years later is a risky proposition. Nevertheless, the relation between two thinkers of Hobbes's and Locke's historical importance is not a matter over which they themselves exercise paramount or even primary control, no more, at any rate, than the historical significance of a statesman's actions is purely a matter of the statesman's personal intentions and designs. This is not to imply, of course, that individual thoughts and actions pale before an impersonal *Weltgeist* and the ruse of its reason, but rather to say that the conception of individuality, and of a historical individuality in particular, underlying a scrupulous historical empiricist's approach is partially inadequate to account for the role of an individual in history. Individuals, like events or objects, exist in a public space and under the eyes of the relevant community, be it one of contemporaries or historians, compatriots, kin, or interlocutors. It is a highly debatable proposition that the perspective of an agent or thinker on his own actions or thoughts has any obviously privileged status with respect to truth over the perspectives of other individuals occupying the same relevant intersubjective, public space. That "no man is an *Iland* intire of its selfe," but "a peece of the *Continent*"[5] may be not only a moral but also an epistemological feature of the human condition, so that a reader's encounter with a John Locke is more of a dialogue, in which the very meaning of Locke's individuality is shaped, than a monologue by the thinker which the reader is to accept as given and try to decipher.

From this perspective—which is laden, no doubt with my own philosophical assumptions—it is not necessarily wrong to overlook for the most part Locke's preoccupation with Filmer and to examine

[4]Laslett, "Introduction" to *Two Treatises*, 84–85. But see Cox, *Locke on War and Peace*, esp. 1–44.

[5]J. Donne, *Devotions upon Emergent Occasions* (1624), Meditation xvii.

his thought in the context of his relationship to Hobbes, especially if, as I shall argue, the intellectual origins of liberal social and political thought, to which Locke greatly contributed but which transcend his immediate concerns and his own self-understanding, are thereby placed in stark relief. The rejection of Filmer's argument may have been both politically and intellectually necessary for the triumph of liberalism, but it certainly was not a sufficient condition of liberalism's *intellectual* ascendancy. For unlike Filmer, Hobbes had taken as his point of departure the very asset that was to constitute the foundation of the liberal intellectual edifice—modern science and its conclusions with respect to a new view of man and society—and turned it into a pillar of his own absolutist politics. It is true that in a narrowly political context Hobbes, even though his work was widely read at the time,[6] had made too few friends and too many enemies for his theory to be a serious political contender, compared with either Filmer's or Locke's. But precisely because of the common source of inspiration shared by Hobbes and the liberals, the positivistic and absolutist conclusions of Hobbes's philosophy posed the most serious challenge to the broader enterprise of establishing the intellectual foundations of liberalism, the enterprise that loomed in the background of Locke's more immediate political objectives.[7]

Hobbes is, then, both an important—perhaps the most important—precursor of liberalism and its challenger *avant la lettre*. Although I hope to elucidate both these aspects of his influence in my discussions of Locke's theory, it may be useful to precede the detailed exposition with a more general presentation and to sketch the argument I believe Locke makes in order to avoid some of the Hobbesian conclusions.

Hobbes's anticipation of the liberal approach to political philosophy and of some substantive liberal claims has been stressed throughout my previous discussions. Let us focus now on one aspect of this anticipation and draw from it some conclusions with respect to the tasks of later liberal theory. We have seen that the Hobbesian attempt to root his theory of man and the state in the mechanistic science of his time led him to reject the Aristotelian model of man as a bifurcated creature of

---

[6]Samuel Pepys notes in his *Diary* for 3 September 1668, that *Leviathan* "is now mightily called for" and that in view of the bishops' opposition to a new printing the price of the book went from 8s. to 30s.

[7]In claiming that Locke implicitly responds to the positivistic challenge of Hobbes, my interpretation contradicts that of J. Dunn, *The Political Thought of John Locke* (Cambridge, 1969), 79: "Hobbes's problem is the construction of political society from an ethical vacuum. Locke never faced this problem in *Two Treatises* because his central premise is precisely the absence of any such vacuum." I shall also argue that Locke's response to Hobbes in the *Essay* is by no means "inconsequential and broken-backed," as Dunn believes (p. 80).

essentially animalistic need and rational self-sufficiency. Aristotle's concentration on the specifically human characteristic of rationality, defined as a capacity for what he called "action" (*praxis*), i.e., the capacity to orient one's life toward entirely autonomous and noninstrumental goals, had made him view all activity directed toward the continuation of one's "mere life"—the activity he called "production" (*poesis*)—as a simple function of necessity, falling outside both the moral and the political dimensions of human existence. The Hobbesian response to this division was, as we have seen, to attempt to show that outside the sphere of Aristotelian "production" there is no room for any meaningful talk of human activity. Hobbes's new scientific theory of man, rooted as it was in mechanistic natural science, revealed man as a creature of interest, thoroughly preoccupied with the task of staying alive. Even political institutions, viewed by Aristotle as the forum of purely rational action and deliberation, turned out to be designed to ensure some stability in the competitive pursuit of limited resources.

Quite apart, however, from its scientific origins, Hobbes's conception of man as a "producer" (still in the sense derived from Aristotle) strikes a responsive cord in the modern intellectual framework. Hobbes's and Locke's rather sober contemporaries (and even more so their children and grandchildren) were not likely to find self-realization in constructing Greek temples or delivering flowery orations. They were more likely to be fascinated by the conquest of new virgin lands, transforming the world around them by the development of manufactures, increasing their wealth by trade, and the like. And increasingly, they were likely to confer a moral status on these activities, viewing them as making nature serve the needs and enhance the dignity of man, and to see the state as essentially designed to facilitate this process. The attractions of the leisurely and aristocratic polis were henceforth to be felt only by the nostalgic dreamers from both the reactionary and the revolutionary ends of the political spectrum. In the mainstream, "production" came to be seen no longer as the mere reproduction of life, but as a truly creative activity, shaping both man and his world, until, in the modern use of the term, it came to stand for the greatest part of human activities, including those which endow human beings with their moral worth (and which Aristotle had thought to belong in the totally separate category of "action").

It would be inaccurate, of course, to claim that anything like this developed modern concept of production can be found in Hobbes. On the contrary, despite the quite far-reaching extension of the domain of production by the Hobbesian conception of desire as an essentially infinite quest for power, Hobbes's positivism—his refusal to accord any status to an authentic discourse of moral theory—must have made his

attack on the Aristotelian concept of action look very much
amputation of a crucial dimension of human existence. Inde
the later developments of the "ethos of production," by Locke
others, have seemed to many critics to be basically refinements of an at
bottom nihilistic perspective. That this last objection is unfounded will
become obvious, I hope, as we proceed with the discussion of Locke's
theory, but that it is at least plausible to read Hobbes as a radical moral
reductionist seems hard to controvert.

The reading of Locke I propose here centers around what I take to be
his attempt to demonstrate that a theory of man based on the conceptual framework of modern science involves an indissoluble unity of
moral action and man's productive capacity, but does not result in a
reduction of morality and politics to a simple struggle for self-preservation in a world of limited resources. The Locke that will emerge from
these pages is a strikingly modern philosopher of action: an individualist who sees man through the prism of a secular, scientific outlook,
stressing the precariousness of the human condition amid the vast
expanses of a nature essentially indifferent, and at times apparently
hostile, to the goal of human survival. He is also quite an unabashed
philosopher of capitalism: an apologist for mastery over the natural
world, to be transformed in the process of production into a reservoir of
wealth at the service of human needs. But, finally, he is also a genuine
moralist: a proponent of an "ethics of production" which views human
needs not as a mere necessity of life imposed by immutable and alien
natural laws, but as something autonomously shaped by man in the
process of his encounter with nature. The modernity of Locke's philosophy thus lies not in the elimination of the Aristotelian domain of action
and its replacement with a purely positivist or utilitarian theory of
human interests, but rather in an attempt to fuse the discourse of
interests with the discourse of moral action and to synthesize *praxis*
and *poesis* in a unified theory of human activity.

The distinctive feature of the Lockean synthesis of action and production is its deemphasis of the political dimension of human life. Such
deemphasis, while characteristic of the liberal tradition, goes against
the grain of the previously dominant and still often attractive conception of the political realm as associated with the expression of a community's shared norms and as being a field for the realization of the
community's moral aspirations. Indeed, later theoretical attempts at
such a synthesis have for the most part assumed that liberalism, with its
insistence on the privatization of life in modern societies, was only one
of the extremes (the Aristotelian insistence on politicization being the
other) awaiting a synthetic approach. Thus, both Hegel and Marx, who
consciously undertook the task of bringing together the two points of

117

view, believed that a reconstruction of the ancient *agora* in the context of the modern market was the only way of reinfusing the liberal-dominated society with an undistorted normative content. It would transcend the task of the present work to try to provide a conclusive argument as to whether the moral content of human life essentially requires reference to a political community, as the critics of liberalism have maintained, or whether such content may be found in man's relation to nature and other men in an essentially prepolitical context, as I understand Locke to have claimed. Indeed, I am rather skeptical about the availability of such an ultimate argument, and I limit myself to presenting what seems to me the earliest and most influential articulations of liberalism and its critique: those provided by Locke and Rousseau. But what I think *can* be decided is that we are dealing here with genuine *alternatives* and that most critics of liberalism have missed, or have not taken seriously, Locke's ambition to root his political philosophy in a fully developed moral theory.

Locke's deemphasis of politics and its role in the moral life of man finds its expression in his view that the state is an essentially pragmatic arrangement designed to protect individuals in their private pursuits and prevent conflicts among them from erupting into violence. In a sense, then, Locke's purely *political* theory, his theory of the state, does not go in the direction of extending the Hobbesian view to take into account the more properly moral role of the state, beyond mere self-preservation; it goes, rather, in the direction of retrenching that view by showing that the task of the state is even more limited and correspondingly easier to accomplish than Hobbes envisaged. Like Hobbes, Locke does not believe that men come together under a government to infuse their lives with a new purpose or confer a new dignity on their persons. Political participation, Locke agrees with Hobbes, is not an activity in which men realize their very humanity (as Aristotle believed), nor is the state for Locke (as it was for the medievals) a divinely ordained paternalistic order. Instead, as I have said, it is a pragmatic arrangement designed to assure that men can freely and without interference from each other pursue those goals they already have *before* they enter the state for the first time. Where Locke follows Hobbes, and where the latter had anticipated the quintessentially liberal outlook, is in this insistence that the criteria for the evaluation of a political system are not generated within that system, but rather derive from a preexisting system of individual expectations and depend on a preexisting system of individual values. Where Locke parts ways with Hobbes, however, and attempts to avoid the latter's absolutist and authoritarian conclusions, is in his attempt to show that the state's mediating function is far easier to accomplish than Hobbes had supposed because even prior to their political association men are imbued with a sense of moral order and in a position to pursue their individual aims without the constant threat of violence. A "contract" by which men usher in the domain of politics, according the Locke, is not a Hobbesian metaphor for a combination of force and self-fulfilling deception which permits the overcoming of the nefarious consequences of natural equality and the establishment of the citizen's unconditional subordination to the sovereign. It is rather something much more closely approximating our ordinary understanding of the term, and the very idea of *this* kind of contractual origin or legitimation of a political order presupposes that the men who enter such a contract are more or less fully autonomous moral agents, capable of undertaking all kinds of obligations, before they form a political compact. They do not expect the state to take away their moral agency from them, and since the locus of their moral life remains in their private spheres they expect the state not to interfere too much there, but to limit itself to introducing a minimum amount of regulation into their relations to one another, so that the norms of coexistence, to which all men should independently subscribe, are enforced by an impartial judge. The state, then, has for Locke a limited function and a correspondingly limited power. Its "chief end," says he, is the preservation of "property," which men have in their own persons and their possessions.[8]

It is this conception of property that bears the heaviest burden in Locke's theory and it is here that Locke presents his most powerful arguments against Hobbes. In the first place, the fundamental problem of the insecurity that plagues natural man, according to Hobbes (and Locke agrees with much that Hobbes has to say on this subject), receives its solution, in the Lockean framework, not in the formation of a political compact, but in the process by which man "tames" nature by appropriation and makes it serve human needs. Property thus takes on in Locke the role played by the state in Hobbes, and it is in this way that Locke avoids the authoritarian conclusions of Hobbes's political philosophy. Second, Locke argues against Hobbes that through appropriation man transforms his dependence on nature into a form of self-sufficiency and thus converts his subordination to a preestablished system of natural needs into a condition of *autonomy*, which confers upon his actions a preeminently moral status. The theory of property thus serves to overcome the positivistic implications of Hobbes's theory of man.

These two parallel functions that the conception of property plays in Locke's system—remedying the human condition's inherent pre-

---

[8]*Second Treatise of Government*, §124. The *Second Treatise* is referred to henceforth by paragraph number, in the text in parentheses.

cariousness and infusing moral agency into human life—make it the intellectual cornerstone of his philosophical position. Once this conception is correctly understood, I believe that Locke's properly political views appear rather straightforward and largely self-explanatory. This is not to say that they are not worth some further inquiry, especially insofar as the status of his contractarian hypothesis is concerned. As I indicated earlier,[9] however, I do not take contractarianism to be the essence of the liberal position; I believe the essence of that position to lie rather in its conception of individuals and the limitation on the state's function and power (which may or may not derive from a contract). As a result, Locke's properly political views are not directly discussed in what follows; not because I believe them to be any less important than is usually supposed—on the contrary, I find Locke's defense of the liberal point of view to be one of the most sophisticated theories in the history of political thought—but because the greatest obstacle to their proper understanding seems to me to lie in the philosophical foundations upon which they rest.

Very little of these foundations has found its way into Locke's *Two Treatises of Government*, written with more immediate political objectives in mind, and readers are practically bound to misunderstand them if they do not dig deeper by going to the *Essay Concerning Human Understanding* and to some other writings in which Locke examines the presuppositions of his individualistic philosophy.[10] It is true that the *Second Treatise* contains the crucial chapter "Of Property" (Chapter v), but its significance cannot be properly appreciated without a thorough study of Locke's theory of action and his ethical views, which are to be found in the *Essay*.

The most controversial point of Locke's theory of man is that in which he tries to show that neither man's rationality nor his moral agency implies a constitutive reference to the human community. The relation of man to his *natural* environment, be it in the context of his acquisition of knowledge or of his transformation of the environment through the process of production (appropriation), replaces to a large extent the relation of man to man. It is precisely at this point that the foundations of Locke's political individualism are established because the absence

[9]Chap. ii, section 1.
[10]In viewing Locke's ideas in the *Two Treatises* as flowing from the *Essay*, I go against the opinion of Laslett who, in the "Introduction" to his edition of the *Two Treatises*, 92–105, sees the two as inconsistent. The connection between these two works is observed (though with varying degrees of emphasis) by Dunn, *Political Thought of John Locke*, 92–93; J. Tully, *A Discourse on Property: John Locke and His Adversaries* (Cambridge, 1980), 7–8; R. Polin, "John Locke's Conception of Freedom," in J. W. Yolton, ed., *John Locke: Problems and Perspectives* (Cambridge, 1969), 1; and W. M. Simon, "John Locke: Philosophy and Political Theory," *American Political Science Review*, 45 (June 1951).

of a truly constitutive function of intersubjective rel
that whatever dignity a man has or acquires is largel
his interaction with others, and the community lose
source of its claims on his allegiance: unlike the Aristot
Lockean man always has exit from society as an at lea
available alternative, and it cannot be argued that such a
suicide or puts him outside the class of beings to who
moral obligations.

Two aspects of man's relation to nature are analyzed in the *Essay*: in his theory of knowledge Locke examines how the natural environment shapes the contents of the human mind, and in his theory of action he examines how man influences the natural environment. The first process has a certain priority, for Locke is an antinativist and his theory of *tabula rasa* means that a man is born with very few endowments (any imprints that the Creator has left on his constitution are at most *latent*). Moreover, in his process of acquiring knowledge, man is predominantly a passive receiver of data from the outside world, which shapes the contours of his mental life.[11] In giving this account, Locke follows Hobbes's methodology of basing a theory of the mind on the model of mechanistic science, although he significantly departs from his predecessor's substantive account. Locke agrees with Hobbes that the way in which nature imprints itself on the human mind must be accountable for in terms of a physical theory, and he goes so far as to admit that the original impact by which bodies produce ideas in our minds must be an impulse of the same kind as that of one billiard ball striking another.[12] Nevertheless, Locke does not think that a scientific account of the human mind must proceed by way of a reduction of ideas to physical (or physiological) processes, as Hobbes had supposed. It is still possible, Locke believes, to think of mental phenomena not as bodily motions, but as pictures or other representations which, while also natural phenomena, do not have to be analyzed in terms of bodies hitting one another.

The caveat that ideas are still natural phenomena is important, for Locke does not intent to jump from his distinction between bodies and ideas to the conclusion that the mind operates according to completely

---

[11]Locke's theory of knowledge suffers from his inability to distinguish clearly between innate ideas and innate dispositions. As a result, his attack on the former sometimes seems to include the latter as well, and mental operations often appear mere encounters among the ideas themselves rather than mental activities. While such a view squares rather well with a radically empiricist position, it is probably indefensible in the end.

[12]*The Essay Concerning Human Understanding*, Bk. II, Chap. 8, paragraph 11. The *Essay* is henceforth referred to simply by book, chapter, and (where applicable) paragraph numbers.

...ferent rules from those specified by natural science. In other words, he attempts no move to exempt the mind from the operation of natural laws and to bring back the bifurcation of human nature corresponding to the old body-and-soul distinction. What he intends, rather, is a broadening of a theory of natural causation, so that a parallel "mechanics of the mental" can be constructed as a counterpart of the physical theory. What still remains true is that a scientific account of the human mind specifies a set of natural laws that explain in a more or less continuous form the process by which a physical event (stimulus) produces a series of consequences resulting in a complex mental event, such as knowledge, desire, or volition.

So far no real departure from the positivistic and, indeed, deterministic account of human nature has been made. But then comes the other side of Locke's analysis of the relation of man to nature, namely the way in which man acts on his environment. In analyzing this side of Locke's theory—the task that will occupy us in these chapters—one must bring together three parts of Locke's philosophy: his general theory of action, explained, above all, in the crucial chapter of the *Essay* entitled "Of Power";[13] his rather puzzling "mixed-modes" theory of morality, to be found in several places in the *Essay*;[14] and his theory of appropriation, set forth in the *Second Treatise*. Each of these is often considered separately, and their interrelation is a rather complicated matter. Unless this interrelation is clearly perceived, however, the Lockean foundation of the liberal outlook will remain misunderstood.

The first dent in the positivistic conclusions Hobbes drew from the application of modern science to the theory of man comes in Locke's general theory of human action. Locke agrees with Hobbes that a scientific account of mental events leaves no room for any "freedom of the will"—on the contrary, it must show that an act of volition, being a mental event, must be strictly determined by antecedent mental events and ultimately by external stimulation. Nevertheless, Locke believes that a mental event, being not a body but a "picture"-like entity, cannot constitute a sufficient natural cause of a bodily motion; it is like a shadow that may be produced by a body but cannot in turn produce a movement of that body. If this is so, however, then the translation of a mental event, such as an act of volition, into a physical motion by which we act on the world around us must involve some additional power. This additional power Locke calls "freedom," but we have to be on our guard not to infuse this term with its usual connotations, in particular those of the "free-will" question and its moral significance. What Locke

[13]II, 21.
[14]II, 22; III, 11, 15–17; IV, 3, 18–20.

means by "freedom" in this sense is merely a power that supplen.
the natural chain of causation with an ability to produce motion that
could not arise from the operation of natural laws *alone*. It is not a
power to decide what one wants to do, but merely the power to do what
one wants—the will is still determined, but its manifestation in the
physical world is *contingent* and not necessary.

The next part of the argument is probably the most difficult, and
Locke himself—not a very careful writer, one must admit—is at times
confused about it. It is well known that he made significant changes in
the chapter "Of Power" after the publication of the first edition of the
Essay, and we have some evidence that he felt dissatisfied with some
implications of his earlier theory of action, especially with the fact that
his conception of "freedom" was still insufficient to allow for a meaningful concept of moral responsibility.[15] In his subsequent revision of
this chapter, Locke introduced the concept of "uneasiness" as the
determining factor in the operations of the will and the concept of the
"suspension" of the will's decisions as the key to his new account of
moral action. It has been widely felt, however, that the result was a
patchwork of incompatible claims, which may have placated Locke's
critics but also rendered his theory inconsistent.[16]

One cannot deny that some of the things Locke says about the role of
"freedom" in the "suspension" of the will's decision—namely, that we
can use our freedom to intervene in the process by which the will is
determined and thus release ourselves from the inexorable operation of
the natural laws of the mind—bring him close to reintroducing the
concept of free will that he had tried to eliminate in the first place. But
this lapse is unnecessary, for Locke also has another theory that allows
him to reconstruct the concept of moral responsibility without giving
up his commitment to a scientific account of mental operations. In
order to understand this properly, one must distinguish two ways in
which Locke uses the words "freedom" and "liberty": one designed to
explain the *contingent* character of the effects of human action in
general, and the other designed to provide a *normative* account of
moral conduct. The resulting two theories of freedom, however, com-
plement, rather than contradict, each other.

The basic idea which allows Locke to reconstruct the concept of
moral agency is that the introduction of an element of contingency into
the world of nature, effected by human action on the natural environment (notably, by the operation of freedom in the sense described

[15]II, 21, 35 and II, 21, 72. See also letter to Molyneux of 15 July 1693.
[16]See R. I. Aaron, *John Locke* (Oxford, 1955), 264. See also A. C. Fraser's edition of the
Essay (New York, 1959), 1:380.

above), opens the possibility that nature, which normally obeys its own independent laws, may be reshaped by man to serve human needs. The process in which this ultimately takes place is that of "appropriation," the one by which, through the application of his labor, man infuses the natural world with his own "personality" and makes it "his own." As a result, the ordinary process in which man is determined by, and dependent on, the vagaries of the natural world (the process described in my account of Locke's epistemology) is reversed: the alien source of the determination of man's will—nature—becomes itself an extension of the human person and in this way heteronomous human action is transformed into *self-determination* or *autonomy*.

In the end, then, my account of Locke's theory of human individuality attempts to show that Locke in important ways anticipated the concept of freedom as autonomy (i.e., as a self-referential determination of the will, rather than the traditional freedom of the will from any determination) to be developed later by Rousseau, Kant, Hegel, and Marx. Moreover, I claim for Locke a particularly happy version of this concept, even if he did not fully and consciously capture it: by tying autonomy to the process of appropriation and production, Locke, like Hegel and Marx and unlike Rousseau and Kant, made autonomy into a dynamic and nonformalistic concept related to the daily pursuits of modern human beings; by tying it to a modern empiricist and individualistic framework, he avoided the potentially totalitarian implications that this concept has in the work of Rousseau and his followers (including Marx and Hegel).

But the move from the concept of freedom as a power of contingency to that concept as autonomy, which provides the foundation of Locke's liberalism, is quite complex and requires a large amount of footwork that will occupy us in much of what follows. First, Locke's theory of how the will operates will have to be explained in some detail and the many factors responsible for its determination, such as pleasure and pain, desire, uneasiness, and understanding, will have to be analyzed. Then the role played by the ideal of happiness, which organizes human action, will have to be examined, and I shall attempt to show that Locke is neither a hedonist nor a utilitarian. Rather, I claim, he believes that we have a large amount of control over what we think will make us happy and that the well-organized life plan of a rational individual involves a striving for self-sufficiency that frees him from the tyranny of daily needs and makes him take a general attitude toward the world of nature that results in appropriation. Finally, the nature of the process of appropriation will be examined in detail. I argue that the view prevailing among Locke's interpreters that appropriation is primarily a way of assuring human survival is largely incorrect and that appropriation had for Locke an essentially moral significance, as an activity in which man transforms his environment and realizes the conditions of his auton-omy. I further argue that Locke was an ideologue of the capitalist form of ownership and that with his theory of appropriation he not only pro-vided the philosophical basis of mercantilist economics but also laid foundations for a modern theory of production capable of withstanding some of the later Hegelian and Marxist attacks.

III. Locke on Freedom and Autonomy

1. The Problem

Locke's theory of action, presented in the chapter "Of Power" in the *Essay*, is primarily designed to deal with the dilemma posed by the apparent irreconcilability of freedom and determinism. The problem is very old, of course, and it arose out of the question of how a person can be assigned responsibility for his or her actions. Responsibility had been traditionally defined as involving the possibility of "having done otherwise." But if this definition is accepted, how can it be reconciled with a view that human action follows some laws that would allow us to account for it? The dilemma is, of course, most obvious if man's actions are seen as Hobbes saw them—as subject to ordinary natural laws operating through mechanical necessity. But even when actions are viewed as motivated, i.e., not mechanically caused but induced by *reasons*, the problem does not disappear. For clearly, if a person had a reason for doing one thing rather than another, then how could he have done something that ran counter to his motivation? Can a person act only on those motives or reasons he actually has, or is his will undetermined (or incompletely determined) by any specific set of motives, so that he could still decide upon a different course of action?

The problem of "undetermined choice" is a real can of worms. If the agent's choice of reasons is ultimately determined, then he cannot be responsible for his actions. If, on the other hand, his choice is not determined, then it is also unmotivated and arbitrary. If this is the case, however, responsibility will not make much sense either, for the agent is not "rational." Should he have "done otherwise," either he would have been determined to do what he did or the justification of *either* of his actions would ultimately have been the same, namely none. As a result, much of the Christian tradition has viewed freedom as a very ambiguous blessing at best, since it was at once the basis of all moral action (only free beings are subject to moral evaluation) and the foundation of sin (the only use a man can actually make of his freedom, unless he is assisted by God's Grace, is to *deviate* from divine commandments).[1] It is to this aporetic situation that Locke addresses himself in his chapter "Of Power."

2. The Solution

The basic idea of Locke's theory of action and the gist of his response to the old dilemma of free will and undetermined choice lies in his separation of will and freedom as two different "powers," or faculties, of the mind. The best way of introducing this view is to examine the meaning of the word "choice," which seems to underlie much of the confusion surrounding the free-will problem.

There is clearly some connection between choice and freedom, since beings that are not free with respect to certain actions are said to "have no choice" about them. But choice has two aspects, and only one of them is reflected in this way of speaking. For although I cannot *have* a choice where there is no alternative, neither can I actually *make* a choice where there can be no reason to choose one way or another, or so at least moral philosophers (including Locke) used to believe.[2] For a person to make a choice ("in order for the will to be moved," moral philosophers used to say), it is not enough that two (or more) courses of action be possible; they must also differ with respect to a *criterion* or a *standard* according to which the choice is to be made. Otherwise there would be no difference between choice and chance (the latter understood as something for which no reason or explanation could be given), and either choice would have to be deemed impossible in general (if one denied chance any role in the order of the universe) or nonintelligent beings could theoretically be said to make a choice and be possessed of a will (or not to possess one only contingently). In other words, if choice and chance are different, then it is misleading to say that choice (or volition) does not *have* to be arbitrary; it *cannot* be such.

Locke clearly believed that the two aspects of choice make the word

[1]For a discussion of traces of this view in Locke, see R. Polin, "John Locke's Conception of Freedom," in J. W. Yolton, ed., *John Locke: Problems and Perspectives* (Cambridge, 1969), 3–4.

[2]This does not apply to some nominalists, Descartes among them. For Locke, cf. ii, 21, 34.

unfortunate (and for this reason he often used the word "preference" instead[3]) unless one clearly separates them, and this is what the "separation of mental powers" is supposed to effect. Volition, as an act of willing, is an act of choosing in the sense of "preferment," that is, *making* a choice or picking one course of action. Freedom, on the other hand, is a power of choosing in the sense of "having a choice," that is, a *possibility* of doing one thing or another. We have a choice between two actions, not between two *acts of choice*; although two different courses of action may be in our power (when we are free), two different choices are not. We are *determined* to make the choice we actually make, although we may not be determined to do what we actually do. That the two aspects are, indeed, logically and factually distinct is best confirmed by the fact that I do not really have to *have* a choice in order to *make* a choice; it is enough that I *believe* an action to be in my power to exercise my power of volition with respect to it, even though it may turn out later that my decision was irrelevant with respect to what was to follow.

Locke's own exposition proceeds along similar lines. He does, indeed, talk about the will as the "power of Chusing,"[4] but from his definition of the will it is immediately apparent that he means the power of "*making* a choice":

> This *Power*, which the mind has . . . to order the consideration of any *Idea*, or the forbearing to consider it; or to prefer the motion of any part of the body to its rest, and *vice versa* in any particular instance, is that which we call the *Will*. The actual exercise of that power, by directing any particular action, or its forbearance is that which we call *Volition* or *Willing*. The forbearance or performance of that action, consequent to such order or command of the mind, is called *Voluntary*. And whatsoever action is performed without such a thought of the mind, is called *Involuntary*.[5]

Freedom, on the other hand, is defined in the following manner:

> . . . the *Idea* of *Liberty* is the *Idea* of a Power in any Agent to do or forebear any particular Action, according to the determination or thought of the mind, whereby either of them is preferr'd to the other; where either of them is not in the Power of the Agent to be produced by him according to his *Volition*, there he is not at *Liberty*, that Agent is under *Necessity*.[6]

Thus, while the will is defined as a power of deciding upon a certain course of action (volition being a mental directive that an agent gives to

[3]Cf. II, 21, 15.
[4]II, 21, 18.
[5]II, 21, 5.
[6]II, 21, 8.

himself in this connection), "freedom" refers to the fact that an agent "has a choice" with respect to his actions, in the sense of being able to bring about the state of affairs commanded in the act of willing, whether that state amounts to an action or forbearance (in other words, it is *possible* for the agent either to act or not to act, so that whichever way the will decides, he will be able to carry it out).

Locke believes that his separation of will and freedom as two separate powers does away with the very problem of free will as a matter of logic rather than as a matter of a substantive determination: "free will," according to him, is not just a false, but a nonsensical, idea. To begin with, the very talk about free will rests on a hypostasis of the concept of power, since powers are always attributes, according to Locke, and not substances.[7] It is therefore a mistake to say that a power acts or does something, for example, that the will wills, understanding understands, and the like.[8] It is always the *agent* that uses his power in order to act.[9] Hence powers cannot be predicated of powers and

> ... to ask whether the *Will has Freedom*, is to ask, whether one Power has another Power, one Ability another Ability; a Question, at first sight, too grossly absurd to make a Dispute, or need an Answer. . . . So that this way of putting the Question, *viz.* whether the *Will be free*, is in effect to ask, whether the *Will* be a Substance, an Agent, or at least to suppose it, since Freedom can properly be attributed to nothing else.[10]

But, of course, the problem of "free will" can be reformulated. One may agree that the expression "free will" is unfortunate, but still ask whether an agent is free to will, either in the sense of freedom to will or not to will or in the sense of freedom to will something rather than something else. In order to show that this reformulation does nothing to lessen the absurdity of the question, Locke hastens to add that an examination of the very definitions of will and freedom is enough to make us reject the free-will idea. If freedom is the ability to do or not to do what we please (that is, what we will) then the question "is an agent

[7]ɪɪ, 21, 16. Locke warns us that names of powers are often subject to abuse, since being well entrenched in ordinary language, they are often used without an examination of the ideas for which they stand. He does not propose to eliminate the old *manner* of speaking altogether, but he insists that we must be careful to give our terms only such meanings as may be found in direct experience.

[8]ɪɪ, 21, 17. Locke himself, in view of his already mentioned reluctance to "lay by" completely the ordinary manner of speaking, is not very scrupulous in observing his own injunction against speaking about powers as if they were subjects (see, for example, ɪɪ, 21, 30). I shall sometimes follow him in this "carelessness," but it should always be understood as a *façon de parler* alone.

[9]ɪɪ, 21, 16.

[10]ɪɪ, 21, 16.

free to will?" amounts to asking whether "a Man can *will*, what he *wills*, or be pleased with what he is pleased with."[11] Thus, either the whole question is completely trivial, or it involves a postulation of an infinite regress of wills within a single subject and hence precludes any act of volition whatsoever.[12]

In other words, the impossibility of "free will" is not a matter of the contingent constitution of the human mind, but rather a matter of logical necessity. The nonattributability of freedom to the will does not entail the "unfreedom" of the will, but rather signals that such an attribution rests on a confusion of the logical categories: "Liberty [is] as little applicable to the *Will*," says Locke "as Swiftness of Motion is to Sleep, or squareness to Vertue."[13] This, in turn, not only implies that the will is never "unfree," but also that the will's being "determined" does not make human action either less free or less voluntary. What the "determination of the will" amounts to is the elimination of *arbitrariness* from human action which, being free, may be *contingent*, and yet motivated.

3. Freedom as a Power of Contingency

Locke's separation of will and freedom as two distinct faculties or powers of the mind may do away with the most baffling aspects of the free-will problem, but it is not immediately clear that it substitutes for them a cogent view of human action that would allow for a more successful account of moral responsibility. Indeed, Locke's own view appears increasingly idiosyncratic and paradoxical when one asks oneself what his concept of freedom can possibly contribute to the solution of the problem of moral responsibility. As presented so far, Locke's theory of the will states that acts of volition are mental directives or "commands" that an agent gives to himself on the basis of mental processes that he is not free either to change or not to subject himself to. But if this is so and if freedom is the ability of an agent to follow the commands of his will, then what does freedom add to the mental apparatus required for human actions? Granted that free and voluntary actions are not the same,[14] what sense can we make of saying that a man still "has a choice" to act or not to act when he has already determined (by an act of volition) that he will (or will not) act? Can a man really "do

[11] II, 21, 25.
[12] Ibid. Cf. also another argument in II, 21, 23.
[13] II, 21, 23.
[14] II, 21, 11.

otherwise" if his will is already determined, and even if he can, would this be anything more than arbitrary behavior that has nothing to do with moral responsibility?

One possible way of approaching the problem of moral responsibility may be the following: Usually we feel that although a man may have no control over whether or not he desires something, he can refrain from following his desires for reasons of morality, prudence, rational planning, and so on, and this fact may provide a foundation for moral judgment and responsibility. While Locke himself seems to endorse this view later in the chapter "Of Power,"[15] it can hardly explain the role of *freedom* in his theory of action, since the introduction of moral or prudential considerations of this kind clearly takes place prior to the decision of the will; that is, it concerns the relation between the will and desire, rather than the relation between the will and its execution. Freedom, on the other hand, has just been defined as the ability to act or to forbear from acting "according to the determination . . . of the mind" (i.e., of the will). In which sense, then, to repeat the main question, is an agent still "free" if he has already *made up* his mind to do one thing rather than another?

Another possible answer is that an agent is free because, should his will command otherwise, he would be just as able to follow its commands. Locke, again, seems to confirm this interpretation in several places.[16] But it can no more provide a foundation for moral responsibility than can the assumption that a man is not free at all but, like a billiard ball, subject to absolute necessity. For once we accept that a man is not *free to will*, then the fact that he would be able to act otherwise if his will commanded him to would make him no more "free" than a billiard ball that would also move in a different direction if it were struck from a different angle.

Is an agent free, then, because he obeys his *own* will, that is, does what *he* wants, and thus can be held responsible for his actions? We shall see later that Locke does indeed base his moral theory on a concept of autonomy that includes this kind of assignment or responsibility among its vital components. Without more, however, this answer is doubly unsatisfactory. First, some sense would have to be given to the concept of the human subject that would allow for some form of individual control over one's actions of volition, before the mere identification of an agent could give rise to the concept of moral responsibility. For if the human will is determined in the same way as a stone is

---

[15]Locke seems to indicate this solution in II, 21, 47 and in other passages dealing with the problem of "suspension." I shall discuss this below.

[16]See, for example, II, 21, 21; II, 21, 48; or II, 21, 11.

determined to fall, it would be no less sophistic to blame a man for murder than to blame a stone for falling on a victim's head. Second, it is not clear why freedom in the sense that Locke introduces in the chapter "Of Power" should be necessary for this kind of moral responsibility. This is so because the freedom we have been talking about consists in the possibility of forbearance[17] and goes beyond the idea of a merely internal source of motion.[18]

Finally, another possibility has to be considered, namely, that Locke, with his separation of will and freedom, simply intends to deny the reality of moral responsibility altogether. Given our explanation of the concept of freedom as a mere *possibility* of acting or not acting, all that Locke may mean by "freedom" is the Hobbesian absence of external hindrances or impediments to an action, complemented perhaps by a similar absence of internal incapacitation. Locke, in fact, seems to imply this answer by his repeated examples of unfreedom as the presence of a hindrance, as when he talks, for instance, about a prisoner who cannot walk a straight distance longer than his cell.[19] Clearly, Locke is not willing to follow Hobbes in saying that freedom can be predicated of all objects, including inanimate ones, such as billiard balls, and not only of humans. But this may be a purely semantic difference, since Locke's *definition* of freedom includes an explicit reference to the will,[20] so that only beings endowed with a will, such as men, may be said to be free, while billiard balls may not. But this answer, which seems to be the one chosen by those who believe that there is no room at all for a genuine concept of freedom (and not just none for moral responsibility) in the first edition of Locke's *Essay*,[21] is in conflict with Locke's own analysis of the concept of freedom. First of all, at least if only the absence of external hindrances (as opposed to internal incapacitation) is considered, this view seems to negate Locke's repeated insistence that freedom is a power or a faculty *of the agent*, unless one is prepared to say that a mere absence of external impediments can constitute such a power. But even if the absence of internal incapacitation is seen as a requisite component of freedom—thus allowing one to speak of it as an agent's power— clearly Locke intends something more here than the *Hobbesian* con-

[17]II, 21, 8.

[18]Given Locke's view of the will as a "passive power," it is indeed hard to see at first how he can view a person as a genuine originator of his acts of volition. I shall discuss this problem below.

[19]II, 21, 27.

[20]"Where [an action or forbearance] is not in the Power of the Agent to be produced by him according to his *Volition*, there he is not at *Liberty*, that Agent is under *Necessity*," II, 21, 8.

[21]See, e.g., R. I. Aaron, *John Locke* (Oxford, 1955), 268.

cept of power. To see this one needs briefly to compare the Hobbesian and the Lockean views on the nature of power in general.

Like Hobbes, Locke makes a distinction between active and passive powers: "Power . . . " he says[22] "is twofold, *viz.* as able to make, or able to receive any change: the one may be called *Active*, the other *Passive Power*." For Hobbes, however, the distinction between active and passive powers basically tracked the old distinction between efficient and material causes, with no implication that the efficient cause of a given event (say, the match flame that causes a gallon of gasoline to explode) must be the ultimate or the first cause. On the contrary, except perhaps in the case of God's actions, all (natural) causes are secondary or derivative, so that the active-passive distinction is only relative: the match flame that ignites the gasoline is in turn the effect of another cause (say, the human motion of striking the match) and the previous agent (the match) must now be viewed as a patient possessed of an appropriate passive power (the chemical composition of the stuff out of which matches are made) to receive the change (the igniting of the match). For Locke, on the other hand, the idea of active power clearly refers to something that escapes ordinary mechanical explanation, since the idea of active power is the "*Idea* of the beginning of motion."[23] The statement that "whatever Change is observed, the Mind must collect a Power somewhere, able to make that Change"[24] expresses Locke's somewhat Aristotelian belief that behind all mechanical phenomena there lurks an ultimately nonmechanical origin of motion. This becomes quite obvious when we read in the *Essay* that "we have from the observation of the Bodies of our Senses, but a very imperfect obscure *Idea* of *active Power*, since they afford us not any *Idea* in themselves of the *Power* to begin an Action."[25] In other words, observation of bodies leads inferentially to the origin of motion, but does not *provide its idea*. This "we have only from reflection on what passes in our selves, where we find by Experience, that barely by willing it, barely by a thought of the Mind, we can move the parts of our Bodies, which were before at rest."[26]

It is clear that the idea of the active power we have from reflection is no other than the idea of freedom and that this sets freedom apart not only from all the powers of bodies, which are always mechanical and passive, but also from all other mental powers, such as the will and the understanding. Although Locke believes that his business in the *Essay* is "not to search into the original of Power, but how we come by the *Idea*

[22]II, 21, 2.
[23]II, 21, 4.
[24]II, 21, 4.
[25]II, 21, 4.
[26]II, 21, 4.

of it,"[27] he suggests that, according to him, matter is probably "wholly destitute of *active Power*, . . . its Author GOD is truly above all *passive Power*; and . . . the intermediate state of created Spirits [is] that alone, which is capable of both *active* and *passive Power*."[28] Now, the active part of a "created Spirit" is its freedom, since to be free is to have "the power to stop or continue, begin or forbear any . . . Motions of the Body without, or Thoughts within"[29] and hence, conversely, to be under necessity is to be unable to initiate any action, and to be passive. Therefore, the active-passive distinction is coextensive with the free-necessary dichotomy, so that to call, say, the will "active" is the same as to call it "free"—a step Locke clearly forbids. An "order" of the will, being itself determined, does not initiate any action and hence is not active; an action can be perfectly voluntary and yet really be a "passion," or unfree (as when a man in *Chorea Sancti Viti* happens to want to "dance," even though he neither initiates his movements himself nor can stop them[30]), while in the case of an action that is both free and voluntary, it is clearly freedom and not the will that is active. Similarly, to say of any other mental power that it is active is to make one and the same mental act refer back to two different powers.[31]

Thus, while we may still not understand what the Lockean concept of freedom contributes to the solution of the problem of moral responsibility, it should be obvious that this concept is quite different from the Hobbesian idea of freedom as the absence of external impediments to motion.

The best way to understand the Lockean concept of freedom, as it is introduced in the early parts of the chapter "Of Power," is to think of it *not* as directly related to moral action, but rather as a part of a much more general account of *any* human action, from the most trivial, such as a raising of one's hand, to the most complex, such as a cooperative human effort to transform the world around us. Even though the freedom now discussed consists in the agent's ability to act or to forbear from acting, the meaning of this choice is *not* that of the ability "to do otherwise" that would directly support a notion of moral responsibility, but rather that of exempting all action undertaken on the commands of volition, be it a command to raise one's hand or to commit a murder, from the reach of a purely mechanistic account *à la* Hobbes. Hobbes's strict *determinism* is qualified by Locke's concept of freedom, but as we

[27]II, 21, 2.
[28]II, 21, 2.
[29]II, 21, 2.
[30]II, 21, 11.
[31]The problem of whether or not the mind operates as an active power in combining several ideas into a "mixed mode" (as Locke suggests in II, 22, 2) will be discussed below.

have seen from the dilemma posed by the equation of arbitrariness with moral freedom that destroys the consistency of the concept of free will, the rejection of determinism is by no means enough to salvage the concept of moral responsibility. In fact, it is one of the marks of Locke's greatness that he realized this and, without abandoning the concept of moral responsibility, proceeded to reconstruct it along entirely new lines.

But why did Locke believe that a man needs and has the "active power" of initiating motion? The only way of answering this question, without making Locke's theory inconsistent, is to see that the commands of the human will are necessarily always just that: commands that are incapable of self-execution and do not by themselves mechanically force any compliance. The will, according to Locke, only expresses an "ought" and, for this reason, compliance is always *contingent*. Locke himself leaves no doubt about this understanding of freedom when he deals with the so-called indifferency problem:

> I know that Liberty by some is placed in an *indifferency* of the Man, antecedent to the determination of *his Will*. . . . I am not nice about Phrases, and therefore consent to say with those that love to speak so, that Liberty is plac'd in *indifferency*; but 'tis an *indifferency* that remains after the Judgment of the Understanding; yea, even after the determination of the *Will*: And that is an *indifferency* not of the Man, (for after he has once judg'd which is best, judg'd *viz.* to do, or forbear, he is no longer indifferent,) but an indifferency of the operative Powers of the Man, which remaining equally able to operate, or forbear operating after, as before the decree of the *Will*, are in a state, which if one pleases, may be called indifferency; and as far as this indifferency reaches, a Man is free, and no farther: *v.g.* I have the Ability to move my Hand, or to let it rest, that operative Power is indifferent to move, or not to move my Hand: I am then in that respect perfectly free. My *Will* determines that operative Power to rest, I am yet free, because the indifferency of my operative Power to act, or not to act, still remains; the Power of moving my Hand, is not at all impar'd by the determination of my *Will*, which at present orders rest; the *indifferency* of that Power to act, or not act, is just as it was before. . . .[32]

This strange conception of freedom becomes somewhat clearer when one realizes how broad was Locke's conception of "mechanism" and how wide was the scope of things this conception entailed. For both desire and volition, even if physiologically determined, remain *mental states*, not modifications of the body, and Locke's account of the mental, while not dualistic, was also moderately nonreductionist. Em-

[32]II, 21, 71.

piricist that he was, Locke, unlike Descartes or Kant, did not grant the mental a totally special status, apart from the material and the mechanical; he viewed ideas as pictures of the material and not as constituting a world per se. At the same time, however, unlike Hobbes and other materialists, Locke did not feel that this rejection of dualism obliged him to reduce mental operations to their material substratum. Indeed, his conception of *natural law*, and hence of the "mechanical," was broad enough to encompass both the relations between moving bodies *and* between ideas forming a stream of consciousness.[33] A "mechanism" was for him merely a system in which certain events regularly follow upon one another as a result of some causal influence; their "impact" does not have to involve a physical contact between two bodies. Consequently, Locke viewed the laws of association as the "mechanics of the mental," and except for the idea of freedom, reflection, according to him, provided us with essentially the same kind of knowledge as physics, only the entities observed being different. Moreover, this broad conception of mechanism allowed the external world to exert an obvious mechanical influence upon the mental, so that movement in the material world could be transmitted into the mental.[34] Perception, according to Locke, was a paradigmatic case of such transmission from the material into the mental. A physical movement of certain bodies produces in the mind an idea which "resembles," or (in the case of secondary qualities) purports to resemble, the objects in some respects. But emotions, feelings, and desires are also entities of the same kind. The difference between perception on the one hand and emotions, feelings, or desires on the other is that the latter contain some elements that do not even purport to represent the material world or to refer to any object whatever. Desire, for example—whatever its exact nature turns out to be under closer scrutiny—will always remain an idea which, in addition to representing some object, also contains a subjective coloring of its perceptual content. This subjective coloring,

[33]In IV, 3, 6 Locke did come quite close to questioning the immateriality of the soul, and in any case he saw no objection to the idea that matter could think (although he felt that one should not collapse ideas with physical events). Certain formulations in this paragraph gave rise to the attack of Edward Stillingfleet, the Bishop of Worcester (*A Discourse in Vindication of the Doctrine of the Trinity* [London, 1697]). Also, Leibniz, in his first letter to Clarke, says he believes that Locke doubted the immateriality of the soul. See also *Nouveaux essais sur l'entendement humain* in Leibniz, *Philosophische Schriften* (Berlin, 1962), 6:62. That Locke was not a *narrow* physicalist, however, may also be seen from the fact that he was not troubled by the Newtonian concept of action at a distance.

[34]That Locke actually held this view may be seen from II, 8, 11: "*Bodies* produce *Ideas* in us . . . manifestly by *Impulse*, the only Way which we can conceive Bodies operate in." As is usual with Locke, he seems to contradict this in IV, 3, 6 which could, perhaps, be used against my whole interpretation. For reasons that may not be worth going into, however, I do not believe that such an argument would be successful.

even if it turns out to be necessarily connected to some bodily state of the subject, cannot be resolved into a mere perception or representation of that state. This does not change the fact, however, that one way or another, all ideas (including nonrepresentative ones) are included in the chain of natural causality, even if the laws determining the character of this chain are not "mechanical" in the narrow, physicalistic sense of the word and even if some ideas are not *direct* effects of physical events. External stimulation must, in view of the mind's being originally a *tabula rasa*, constitute the origin of each complete chain of ideas. In this sense, Locke agrees with Hobbes that both desire and the act of willing identified with it, as well as all the other ideal elements entering into the motivational circuit of human action (pain, pleasure, uneasiness, desire for happiness), are located in the same causal chain beginning with external stimulation of some kind. Thus, they can all be analyzed in terms of the broad "mechanics" encompassing both the physical and the mental.

But not unlike Newtonian mechanics, which required a periodical intervention of God to "wind" the clockwork of the created universe, the mechanics postulated by Locke's theory of action also involves a "loss of energy" in the process of the transmission from material to mental. It too requires a nonmechanical factor in order to make the reverse process possible. The world of ideas, for Locke, is not a world set totally apart from the material, as the Cartesian *res cogitans* was set apart from the *res extensa*. Nevertheless, ideas do lack an important dimension of physical existence: being essentially "pictures"[35] or "impressions" of reality, they can be mechanically produced by their originals, while their "two-dimensionality" prevents them from exerting a reverse influence in turn. And for this reason, an act of the will is followed by a total break in the usual mechanical process of human action, thus requiring an intervention of human freedom, that is, of "the Power . . . to produce or forbear producing Motion in parts of his Body,"[36] possessed by an agent who can do what his will commands.

The relation between volition and freedom is, thus, the relation between command and execution, so that the nonmechanical, contingent character of the execution confers a semi-teleological status on the course of human action: the act of volition, though *mechanically* produced, cannot be mechanically retransmitted into the realm of the physical. What freedom *adds* do the will is the "is" absent from the "ought" of volition.

It is important to grasp the proper significance of this contingency of

[35]Cf. the "dark room" analogy in II, 11, 17.
[36]II, 21, 16.

human (free) action and not to confuse it with moral freedom. The difference is best explained by reference to the difference between the mechanical and some species of logical or psychological necessity. If one asks the question: may an agent not perform (or attempt to perform) an action that is commanded by his will? the answer will depend on the sense of the word "may." If by "may" we mean "is it physically possible," then the answer is yes; there is no mechanical cause-and-effect relation between volition and action. But if by "may" we mean "does it make any sense" to act that way, the answer is no, for that would mean entirely arbitrary and irrational behavior. It is in this vein that Locke discounts as nonsensical the use of freedom against the commands of one's volition:

> Is it worth the Name of Freedom to be at liberty to play the Fool, and draw Shame and Misery upon a Man's self? If to break loose from the Conduct of Reason ... which keeps us from ... doing the worse, be *Liberty*, true Liberty, mad Men and Fools are the only Freemen: But yet, I think, no Body would chuse to be mad for the sake of such *Liberty*, but he that is mad already.[37]

Although Locke clearly warns us not to confuse the sense of "freedom" just introduced with the moral sense of this word, since that would imply taking it as a license for arbitrary behavior, he does not view madness as something simply "mechanically" impossible. Rather a madman is viewed here as a person who acts without rhyme or reason, that is, uses his freedom not in the service of his will, but in a way that is undirected and arbitrary. It is in a man's *power* to do so, for his power of execution is itself "indifferent" to the demands of his will. But the *man* himself is not indifferent, says Locke,[38] and to use one's power in such a way as to contradict one's own directions with respect to it, means to lose the *unity* of one's mind. Still, the fact remains that the reference to the will in the very definition of freedom ("*Liberty* is ... a Power in any Agent to do or forebear any particular Action ... according to his Volition"[39]) does not imply a mechanical subordination of freedom with respect to the will, but only a *normative* relationship establishing the bounds of sanity. Hence, even in a normal subject, despite the unfailing "obedience" of "operative powers" with respect to the will's commands, the act of the will still remains no more than an "occasion" with respect to action;[40] only, unlike in Malebranche's view,

[37]II, 21, 50.
[38]II, 21, 71.
[39]II, 21, 8.
[40]II, 21, 19.

what makes for the *ad hoc* intervention required in each case of volition is not God, but human freedom. The necessity of this *ad hoc* intervention is due to the fact that in a being possessed of reason (and the will), but deprived of freedom, the commands of the will would always remain entirely ineffectual.[41]

4. The Will

Although Locke broke with Hobbesian strict determinism in introducing his concept of freedom, we have seen that he did not think the

[41]I should point out a problem that may be a limitation of the interpretation of freedom presented here, but may also reflect a confusion in Locke himself. According to Locke, there are "two sorts of Action, whereof we have any *Idea, viz.* Thinking and Motion" (II, 21, 4). The preceding interpretation of freedom explained the need for freedom as an active power initiating physical movement, which cannot result mechanically from an act of volition. However, Locke clearly believes in the reality of freedom with respect to the other "sort" of action as well: "to be able to bring into view *Ideas* out of sight, at one's own choice, and to compare which of them one thinks fit, . . . is an *Active Power*" (II, 21, 72; see also II, 21, 12). This active power is not that of the understanding, for Locke's own definition of the understanding does not make it capable of "bringing into view *Ideas* out of sight." (See the definition of the understanding in II, 21, 5.) Nor is the will such a power, for if the will is "active" then the "free-will" problem will reappear.

At the first sight there seems to be no particular difficulty with the analogy between the initiation by freedom of thought on the one hand and motion on the other: an agent may for some reason wish to consider a certain idea and then freely bring this idea "into view." Things become much more complicated, however, when one inquires more closely into what it is precisely that would *require* the use of freedom for bringing ideas into view and comparing them with one another, especially if one remembers that freedom proceeds not arbitrarily, but rather in compliance with the dictates of the will. Clearly, freedom is not always involved when the will is involved. Indeed, if the object of volition is an idea, the need for any further intervention by freedom seems strange, for to *want* to think something may be equivalent to thinking it *already*, unless we assume that the mind refers to its own thoughts without thinking them at the same time. (This assumption would make some sense if one also assumed that thinking is always done in language. But in view of what Locke says about language in Book III of the *Essay*, it is doubtful that the latter assumption made sense for *him*.) But even if we assume that the mind *can* refer to its own thoughts without thinking them, there seems no need to bring in freedom to explain the bringing of ideas "into view," since it is quite plausible that an act of volition (which is a thought) brings about is desideratum (which in this case is simply another thought) in accordance with the ordinary laws of association (the "mechanics of the mental"). Exactly the same will be true in the case of a comparison or even combination of ideas (which Locke mentions, and calls an "active power," in II, 22, 2). Moreover, to think that something *more* than the "mechanics of the mental" is required for, say, the combination of ideas threatens to introduce an element of arbitrariness into these vital mental operations. For if combination is not a product of association, then in view of Locke's identification of association with reasoning, combination would become haphazard. This may, of course, occur sometimes, but hardly as a rule. Locke himself warns us (II, 21, 72) that active and passive powers are easy to confuse. It is hence likely that he simply lapsed into a mistake against which he warns his readers: since thinking had traditionally been viewed as that about which we are free, he took the words, or the manner of speaking, for reality itself.

rejection of determinism was sufficient to make possible the reconstruction of the concept of moral responsibility. In particular, the reality
of freedom as a power of contingency still left intact the problem posed
by the fact that the voluntariness of an action is a crucial aspect of any
moral evaluation but that the will must be thought of as *determined* in
some way for human action to be possible. Indeed, given Locke's
methodological agreement with Hobbes that a theory of human nature
must proceed on the model of modern natural science, with its insistence on efficient, rather than final, causes as *the* basic element of
explanation, the reconciliation of the fact that the human will is determined with the possibility of moral action becomes particularly difficult. For once this model of explanation is accepted, one can no longer
think, along Aristotelian lines, that the very natural laws which determine the will's operation are normative in character; on the contrary,
such laws are basically descriptive of what is going on and explain an
act of volition in terms of antecedent events which, given that the mind
is originally a *tabula rasa*, are in the end external to, and outside the
control of, the human subject.

Before Locke's ultimate answer to the problem of the possibility of
moral action can be explicated, we have to learn something more about
his theory of the will and the way it is determined. At first sight, this
theory seems to follow that of Hobbes rather faithfully, but there are
some important differences that ultimately allow Locke to part ways
with his illustrious predecessor in a quite radical fashion.

I have already explained that Locke's account of human nature differs
from Hobbes's in that Locke did not think that all mental phenomena
had to be reduced to their material substratum. But except for the
introduction of freedom as a power of contingency which this non-
reductionism necessitates, the difference that this makes with respect
to Locke's account of the *will* is not very pronounced: even if the
mechanism that determines the will is not based on bodily impact, the
will is still determined in accordance with the quasi-mechanical laws of
the mental.

Of more significance is Locke's shift of emphasis from the concept of
desire, which had played the central role in Hobbes, to the concept of
the *will* as a power distinct from desire. Whereas Hobbes viewed the will
as merely "the last Appetite or Aversion [where "appetite" and "desire"
are the same thing[42]], immediately adhearing to the action, or to the
omission thereof,"[43] Locke insists that a clear distinction must be made
between the two:

[42]*Lev.*, 23.
[43]Ibid., 28.

[The] Caution of being careful not to be misled by Expressions, that do not enough keep the difference between the *Will*, and several Acts of the mind, that are quite distinct from it, I think the more necessary: Because I find the Will often confused with several of the Affections, especially *Desire*;... This, I imagine, has been no small occasion of obscurity and mistake in this matter; and therefore is, as much as may be, to be avoided.[44]

Locke is, of course, aware that the will can be effectively distinguished from desire only if the act of the former can go against the urging of the latter:

... the *Will* is perfectly distinguished from *Desire*, which in the very same Action may have a quite contrary tendency from that which our *Will* sets us upon. A Man, whom I cannot deny, may oblige me to use persuasions to another, which at the same time I am speaking, I may wish may not prevail on him. In this case, 'tis plain the *Will* and *Desire* run counter.[45]

But how is the confusion between the will and desire to be avoided if, in Locke's own words, "that which ... determines the Will, and sets us upon those Actions we perform" is the "*Uneasiness* we may call, as it is, *Desire*"?[46] Are we not faced with an obvious contradiction?

We have to consider two factors in trying to solve the riddle of the relation between the will and desire. The first is that desire, especially a very strong desire connected with an acute awareness of deprivation, may determine the will not necessarily in the sense of specifying the particular course of action to be followed, but rather in the sense of forcing a decision as to whether or not to follow it; that is, it may determine the *act* of willing, though not necessarily its *content*. This is doubtless part of what Locke had in mind, but the question remains as to what determines the content of the will's decisions. The second factor to be considered is much more important, therefore, and concerns the reason why the will, as a separate link in the chain of decision making, is needed, that is, why and how the will can refuse to follow the urging of desire. The answer to this question lies in the fact that an agent may have many competing desires at about the same time—a state of affairs that in turn leaves room for a decision as to which course of action to follow. At the very least, such a decision involves a calculation of gains and losses associated with a given course of action, but potentially also much more than that: an evaluation of the place of a given desire in an overall life plan of the agent that would provide an indepen-

[44]II, 21, 30.
[45]II, 21, 30.
[46]II, 21, 31.

dent criterion for the evaluation of each course of action. The calculation of the compatibility of different desires and of the net effect of
actions with respect to a more general set of desiderata Locke calls
"judgment"[47] and it is a function of the understanding as the faculty of,
among other things, "Perception of the Connexion or Repugnancy,
Agreement or Disagreement, that there is between any of our *Ideas*."[48]
Hence, in his conception of the will, Locke attempts both to preserve the
link between the will and desire as the ultimate spring of action, and at
the same time to connect the act of volition with the experience and
knowledge stored in the mind, thus freeing it from automatic subjection to the most pressing desire of the moment. And Locke wants to
have all this without conceding any freedom (at least in the sense
discussed so far) to the will.

The claim that the understanding plays some role in the causal chain
leading up to an action was not, of course, unacceptable to Hobbes. In
fact, it was the understanding, according to him, that in conjunction
with the conversion of the "Trayne of Thoughts" into a "Trayne of
Words,"[49] transformed human desire into the insatiable "desire of
Power after power."[50] Nevertheless the role Locke ascribed to the understanding in the process of human motivation is much more significant. To stay, for the moment, with only the calculations of gains and
losses associated with a given course of action (and we shall see that
this function is in fact much less important than the role of the understanding in the formation of an agent's overall life plan), Locke allows for
a much more developed notion of *prudence* than Hobbes, for whom the
overpowering fear of violent death cast a permanent shadow over man's
ability to consider most positive consequences of his actions. Hobbes
did not insist on a distinction between the will and desire because he
viewed human action as essentially an organismic and largely immediate reaction to external stimulation, and it is this view that Locke, whose
theory of action is much more elaborate and sophisticated, rejected in
stressing that the will must be analyzed as a separate faculty.

In order to grasp better the role played by the understanding in the
chain of human action, one must examine several other components of
that chain. A good point to begin with is the concept of pain and
pleasure.

Pain and pleasure are, according to Locke, simple ideas,[51] so that
their definitions are not really possible. This is not a great problem,

[47]See, for example, II, 21, 48.
[48]II, 21, 5.
[49]*Lev.*, 12.
[50]Ibid., 47. See the discussion above in Chap. I, sections 4.1 and 4.2.
[51]II, 20, 1.

however, since each of us, Locke believes, knows them very well from reflection. In his theory of motivation, Locke again follows Hobbes up to a point, in that he assigns a certain priority to pain over pleasure: it is the avoidance of pain alone that constitutes a *direct* cause of the will's determination[52] and anything an agent does is always in response to an awareness of pain—what Locke calls "uneasiness."[53] Anything other than pain, such as pleasure, prudence, or morality, if it ever determines the will, does so only *indirectly*, as when an absence of pleasure constitutes a pain, when fear of mistakes causes a painful apprehension, or when disapproval of others, fear of God's punishments, or a mental aversion invokes a feeling of uneasiness. Nevertheless, and this difference will ultimately turn out to be crucial, Locke does not intend to draw from the priority of pain over pleasure the Hobbesian conclusion that essentially only negative factors can influence human action. Locke was a modern man and he accepted Hobbes's critique of the somewhat quietist Aristotelian ideal of the *summum bonum*—the state of ultimate rest and satisfaction accompanying the good life. But he did not agree that only a *summum malum*, the fear of death, can infuse some dynamism into human life. Accordingly, he left room for more than the pursuit of "mere life," or rather gave us a more complex idea of what it means to be alive. Consequently, he did not think that pleasure was merely an absence of pain, but rather thought of it as a positive feeling, so that a mere thought of its absence is often enough to give us pain and spur us to action.[54]

It must also be understood and kept in mind that both pain and pleasure are, according to Locke, *ideas* and not bodily states, and that they do not even necessarily involve any bodily states (either as their causes or otherwise): "By Pleasure and Pain," he says, "I must be understood to mean of Body or Mind, as they are commonly distinguished; though in truth they be only different Constitutions of the Mind, sometimes occasioned by disorder in the Body, sometimes by Thoughts in the Mind."[55] This, in turn, does away with the view that all desires (which are connected to pain and pleasure) are physiologically determined, although it remains true that all states of consciousness are ultimately (even if indirectly) related to external stimulation of some

---

[52]II, 21, 31.

[53]II, 21, 31; II, 21, 33; II, 21, 71. The point that only pain is a direct cause of the will's determination is overemphasized by L. Strauss (*Natural Right and History* [Chicago, 1953], 249–51), who sees in Locke's ethics a continuation of Hobbes's idea of life as a purposeless striving for ever new satisfactions. "Life," says Strauss about Locke's view, "is the joyless quest for joy" (251).

[54]II, 21, 31.

[55]II, 20, 2; see also II, 21, 41.

kind. A certain sight may be painful to me not because any "disorderly" state of my body accompanies it, but because I find it offensive to my beliefs, fraught with danger for the future, or the like. But of course my reaction to this sight is an effect of previous experience. I shall come back to discuss this problem later.

The next concept that must be introduced is that of a "good." A good, i.e., something that may be an object of a man's action, Locke defines as that which leads to the absence of pain or to the presence of pleasure. Thus, he again seems to track Hobbes rather closely:

> Things . . . are Good or Evil only in reference to Pleasure or Pain. That we call Good, which is *apt to cause or increase Pleasure, or diminish Pain in us; or else to procure, or preserve us the possession of any other Good, or absence of any Evil.* And on the contrary we name that Evil, which *is apt to produce or increase any Pain, or diminish any Pleasure in us; or else to procure us any Evil, or deprive us of any Good.*[56]

It is important to remember in this context that good is an *object* or an *action*, and not a pleasure or an absence of pain, although a good is a good only "in reference to Pleasure or Pain." Now, how close Locke's position is in reality to Hobbes's is a rather complicated question. The fact that a good is inherently related to pleasure is by itself not determinative of any specific position on the ends of human action. All that it implies is that pain and pleasure are the *motivating* forces of human behavior. But whether the relation between the good and pleasure implies a hedonistic reduction of all *ends* of human action depends on whether one conceives pain and pleasure as merely fixed data of human experience, so that, while people's "tastes" may differ and even undergo changes during the life of one and the same subject, what pleases or pains us is merely "given" at any time,[57] or whether a subject can exercise a certain amount of control over what is pleasant or painful to him.[58] If the first view is chosen, we arrive either at the Hobbesian position that the seemingly moral term "good" merely refers to an unreflective preference of the agent or, at most, at the utilitarian or prudentialist position that recognizes the maximization of pleasure and the minimization of pain as the only valid norms specifying not just

---

[56]II, 20, 2.

[57]On this view, our feelings of pain or pleasure would, except for their nonrepresentative character, be similar to the so-called "secondary qualities" of objects, in that some real properties of objects or thoughts would have a power to produce through our senses, without any intervention of the understanding, an idea of pain or pleasure, the subject remaining purely passive throughout the whole process.

[58]In which case the understanding could have some role in determining what is painful or pleasurable.

a principle of human motivation, but also the ends of human action. Should it turn out that such is also Locke's position, as some commentators have maintained,[59] then the "input" of the understanding into the motivational chain of human action would be restricted to a "cost-benefit analysis" or a prudential calculation. If the second view, that which allows for a certain amount of control by the agent over what gives him pleasure or pain, is chosen, as I shall later argue it must be, then no such restriction is necessary. For it is then still open to us to say that while nothing can be felt by an agent as a good unless it gives him pleasure, it may still be a function of the agent's understanding to determine what assignment of pain or pleasure to particular experiences will maximize his overall life plan (which may be based on nonutilitarian, moral considerations). According to this second view, then, to say that a good must give us pleasure says something related only to a theory of motivation, while according to the first view, it specifies a complete theory of action.[60]

There is, finally, a third concept that plays a very important role in Locke's account of human action, namely, the "desire for happiness." The desire for happiness is not a "desire" in the same sense as other desires. An expression like "will to happiness" would perhaps be more appropriate, but of course Locke does not use it. In any case, the desire for happiness provides a crucial factor in Locke's theory of action, which is entirely missing from Hobbes's account, namely, the link between pain or uneasiness (and the good associated with them) and the generation of ordinary desires. At times Locke seems to use the terms "uneasiness" and "desire" interchangeably[61] and the relation between the two is very close: desire is "always join'd" to uneasiness, is "equal" to it, and "scarce distinguishable from it."[62] But the two are not really the same, for uneasiness is (an awareness of) a pain or discomfort, while desire is a wish for the means to get rid of it. The two are "equal" only in the sense of being equally *intense*; the strength of the uneasiness is in fact responsible for the strength of the desire. The reason desire is "always join'd" to uneasiness, however, is that "we constantly desire happiness; and whatever we feel of *uneasiness*, so much, 'tis certain, we want of happiness; even in our own Opinion, let our state and condition otherwise be what it will."[63] Happiness being "the utmost Pleasure we

---

[59]See, for example, R. P. Brogan, "John Locke and Utilitarianism," *Ethics*, 68 (1959).

[60]The difference between these two points of view will be analyzed later in some detail. See below, section 5.

[61]II, 21, 31: "This *Uneasiness* we may call, as it is, *Desire*"; "Desire [is] nothing but an *uneasiness* in the want of an absent good." II, 21, 32: "*Desire* is a state of *uneasiness*." II, 21, 39: "wherever there is *uneasiness* there is *desire*."

[62]II, 21, 31.

[63]II, 21, 39.

are capable of,"[64] every pain is something which prevents it, and it is "happiness, and that alone" which "moves desire."[65] Hence, desire for happiness is not just one desire among others, only stronger and persisting all the time. Happiness being the chief object of every desire, the desire for happiness is that which makes the removing of pain (uneasiness) or the increasing of pleasure *desirable* in the first place, or that which makes desire into what it is. If a man did not want to be happy, pain and pleasure would hardly have a different status from such mental states as wonder, amazement, or surprise. We desire the good capable of removing pain only because pain makes us unhappy. But even more important, the desire for happiness transcends all particular desires, since it is also a *standard* that determines a *hierarchy of desires*, a hierarchy involving more general considerations than the immediately present uneasiness and its intensity. In view of the "utmost Pleasure we are capable of," a particular desire, even though the most pressing at the moment, may be overridden in the name of other considerations, based on a calculation of present and future satisfactions or on some idea of what a life worth living may be.

It is not very difficult to see why an idea like desire for happiness was absent from Hobbes's account of human action and why its introduction by Locke constitutes a significant departure from the thought of his predecessor. Locke's introduction of the desire for happiness is a fairly direct consequence of his disagreement with Hobbes over whether pleasure is something positive or merely an absence of pain. Given Hobbes's insistence on the latter point of view, happiness itself became for him a merely negative concept, centered around the avoidance of death—the *summum malum* of human existence. Once, however, a more complex view of human motivation is accepted and the Hobbesian unidimensionality of values is eliminated, there arises a real need for the agent's having some criteria of what constitutes the best overall mix of satisfactions that he ought to pursue. It is no longer enough to say that each person wants to stay alive; something like the question of *good* life must also be faced.

The question of what constitutes happiness for Locke will be discussed in some detail below. But what should be noted now is that his reintroduction of the concept of happiness or good life is *not* a wholesale rehabilitation of the Aristotelian concept of *eudaimonia* and certainly not of the concept of *summum bonum* as the state of *ultimate* satisfaction. Locke does not go so far as to reject Hobbes's distinctively modern view that human action must revolve around the concept of

[64]II, 21, 42.
[65]II, 21, 41.

interest, understood as an individual's general attitude toward his environment. Neither does Locke reject the essence of Hobbes's anti-Aristotelian view that what counts as a good is a function of the agent's desire (although it is the desire for happiness that counts in Locke) rather than the other way around. On the contrary, it is this insight of Hobbes's that Locke develops into his distinctly modern theory of autonomy. Consequently, the idea of good life being a product of the agent himself, there is no fixed model of life, defined in terms of a set of necessary external conditions, that must be satisfied for an agent to be happy; nor is it the case that once a certain set of goods is achieved there is no longer anything that an agent may "lack." The ideal of happiness is a dynamic concept that still envisages the "infinity of desire" Hobbes spoke about; but now it is a complex ideal, containing both positive and negative features and not resolving to either a *summum malum* or a *summum bonum*.

I have said that as a consequence of the agent's desire for happiness, a particular desire, even though the most pressing at the moment, may be overridden in the name of other considerations, such as a calculation of present and future satisfactions or an idea of what a life worth living may be. What must be explained, now that the most important concepts have been introduced, is the precise mechanism that allows for this overriding and necessitates the distinction between the will and desire. In order to simplify matters somewhat, I shall consider in this section only the process in which the urgings of a desire are overridden for *prudential* reasons; the more complex question of *moral* reasons, tied to the agent's choice of a rational ideal of happiness (life plan), will be postponed until the next section. What we can assume for present purposes, therefore, is that the *ends* ("goods") of human action are "given" for each subject at a given time; all that is left for his rational powers to do is to observe what these "goods" really are and, with the help of a "calculus of pleasures," to maximize their enjoyment.[66]

Desire, as we have analyzed it, has three essential components: the uneasiness, which gives it its intensity; the representation of the good, that is, of the object to which desire is directed; and the impact of the drive for happiness, which makes the good into a good and thus something desirable. The most pressing (the most intense) desire of the moment is, by assumption, forced upon the will as something that

[66]In other words, we are assuming that the agent does not question the assignment of pain or pleasure to particular experiences, but only wants to engage in a process of utilitarian maximization. It should be noted also that in speaking about the "ends" of human action, we are merely concerned with the perspective of the *agent* (i.e., with what appears to *him* as desirable); no genuine intrusion of teleology into the modern scientific perspective is implied.

demands satisfaction. The decision facing the will is not, properly speaking, a choice between one desire and another (or many others), but between acting and forbearing from acting as urged by the most intense desire, where forbearance is also considered an "action" by Locke.[67] Still, the binary choice characteristic of the will's operation is, of course, only preliminary to other choices in which the will may consider other, competing desires. Now, in the making of this choice, the will is distinguished from desire since the agent's primary concern with his own happiness implies that the understanding's calculation of the overall consequences of a given course of action has a determining influence on the agent's will. In other words, it is the fact that an agent can have many competing desires, together with the fact that the agent must order them according to the criteria provided by his overall strategy of pursuing his most general goal of happiness, that accounts for the necessity of distinguishing the will from desire and for the special use of the understanding in determining the act of volition.

But the role played by the understanding, as an "adviser" interposed between the will and desire, is not supposed, according to Locke, to provide an altogether alternative source of the will's being determined, totally alien to the impulse of desire. It is rather a link *always* present in the motivational chain of human action. The distinction between the good and uneasiness, as different elements of desire, is crucial here. Suppose that a subject feels an uneasiness. This alone does not determine the will in any direction and is not even sufficient to call for an act of volition in general, since no course of action at all is indicated by the uneasiness itself. Before a decision of the will is called for, a desire must arise, and the missing component of it (given the presence of the desire for happiness) is, of course, the representation of the good which determines its direction. This, however, can be provided only by the understanding, with its store of knowledge acquired from experience and capable of providing the required information as to how and where to look for the means of removing the uneasiness. In other words, the understanding, upon the perception of uneasiness and in accordance with the laws of association engendered by experience, specifies the "good" that is to be desired in connection with any given deprivation. Only then can an alternative of acting or not acting be presented to the will.

The understanding is thus clearly involved in the very process of desire formation, and no action could take place without it. What happens when a course of action demanded by desire is rejected by the will is not that the understanding is suddenly introduced into the

[67]II, 21, 28.

motivational mechanism and determines the will independently of the "usual channels," but rather that the role of the understanding, already involved by uneasiness in the process of desire formation, is extended beyond a mere specification of the *particular* good in question. It must be remembered that the specification of any good depends on the desire for happiness as that which moves the understanding to look for some means of removing the uneasiness incompatible with the agent's happiness. It is in this context that the understanding designates, by association, a particular object or action as the good to be pursued. But while every uneasiness strong enough to be considered by the mind evokes the process of association that fixes a corresponding good and gives rise to a desire, the associative process may continue beyond this function.[68] The good specified at first is only prima facie the greatest good, i.e., the one to be pursued immediately. The representation of this good may in turn be associated with another idea, perhaps of some great suffering to be brought upon the agent if the initial good is in fact pursued. This second idea, however, may be sufficient to produce a new uneasiness that is even stronger than the old one and thus generates an even stronger desire, ready to determine the will in the opposite direction. As long as one remembers that pain (uneasiness) is an *idea* and that it may have its source in the mind as well as in the body, there should be no difficulty in comprehending the mechanism described here. This mechanism is, in fact, not very different from the one in which the understanding's idea of an absence of a pleasing object leads to an uneasiness that in turn determines the will to pursue the good in question.[69]

It is quite important to realize that throughout this whole account of the will's operation Locke's departure from Hobbes, despite significant differences between them, is not yet so very radical. What still unites the two thinkers is their commitment to the idea of a mechanistic or quasi-mechanistic account of human motivation. Neither Locke's account of the will nor his account of the understanding requires us to think of either of these faculties as an "active power" that would detract from the deterministic theory of the mental processes involved. The understanding operates according to the usual laws of association which constitute for Locke the "mechanics of the mental." The will still operates as a "power of Chusing" in the sense of "making a choice" based on a standard that *determines* the outcome. Indeed, as may be seen from my analyses, the intervention of the understanding does not even really

---

[68]Locke calls this continuation of the associative process "consideration" or "examination." ii, 21, 46; ii, 21, 50; ii, 21, 51.
[69]ii, 21, 46.

that the strongest desire determines the will, since the
question only substitutes an even stronger desire in the
and in *this* way influences the will's decision.[70] What
between the will and desire indicates is more a shift in
radical departure from Hobbes's methodological com-
entific account of human nature. But as such, the shift
it, for it opens the way for an introduction of a whole
new dimension in the theory of human motivation.

5. The Moral Aspects of Human Motivation

My discussion of Locke's theory of the will has shown that though
Locke did not reject the Hobbesian view that the will is not "free" in the
traditional sense, but instead strictly determined by antecedent mental
events, he has given us a relatively complex account of *how* the will is
determined and left ample room for an intervention of the understanding in providing a direction for the will's decisions. The question which
now arises is whether and how something resembling *moral* considerations can enter into the process of motivation governing human actions.

5.1. Two Readings of Locke's Ethics

There are two directions in which Locke's theory of moral action is
usually interpreted. I shall call them briefly "rationalistic" and "hedonistic."[71] The rationalistic interpretation is based on Locke's theory of
mixed modes and his theory of natural law. The hedonistic interpretation derives from a reading of the chapter "Of Power" in the *Essay*,
according to which a man necessarily desires happiness and happiness
is defined as "the utmost Pleasure we are capable of."[72]

The mixed-modes theory of morality, which constitutes the core of

[70]Although my analysis of the will is designed to show that no interposition of any
"active power" disrupts the quasi-mechanical way in which the will is determined in the
Lockean theory of motivation, Locke quite squarely seems to contradict this when he
speaks of the celebrated power of "suspension" as "Liberty in respect of *willing*" (ii, 21, 56).
While I shall later argue that the word "liberty" is used here and in similar contexts in a
sense quite different from the so-far-discussed "power of contingency" and does not
involve any going back on Locke's critique of the concept of free will, it seems that Locke,
in his eagerness to respond to some critics who had accused him making all moral action
an impossibility, became somewhat confused about what the "suspension" entails. For a
further discussion of the problem of suspension, see below, sections 5.1. and 5.2.
[71]I am following S. P. Lamprecht in this classification. See his *Moral and Political
Philosophy of John Locke* (New York, 1918), chaps. 3 and 4.
[72]ii, 21, 42.

the rationalistic interpretation, says that moral categories are complex ideas to which nothing in the objective world corresponds so that their real and nominal essences coincide, just as do those of mathematical constructs.[73] But if moral categories are products of the mind, then the relations between them can also be known with mathematical precision,[74] and the same should hold for the nature of moral obligations. This, says Locke,

> might place *Morality amongst the Sciences capable of Demonstration*: wherein I doubt not, but from self-evident Propositions, by necessary Consequences, as incontestable as those in Mathematicks, the measures of right and wrong might be made out, to any one that would apply himself with the same Indifferency and Attention to the one, as he does to the other of these Sciences.[75]

Hence, Locke seems to be saying that reason alone can tell us what is morally good and, presumably, move the will in that direction. Immediately, however, the theory runs into problems both because of the way it defines the good (as a construct of the mind) and because of its view of human motivation. First, its definition of the good seems to contradict those passages in which Locke himself defines the good with respect to pain and pleasure, which are not theoretical constructs but simple ideas incapable of definition and knowable only from experience.[76] Second, the theory of mixed modes makes morality into an axiomatic game of definitions and consequences, the relation of which to the reality of human action is left entirely unclear, and thus does not explain why we should treat its conclusions as true obligations or how we may be able to act upon them. Locke himself was perfectly aware of this, for in his "Miscellaneous Papers," he criticizes the Aristotelians for what he saw as precisely the same kind of futile game his mixed theory appears to represent:

> The ethics of the schools, built upon the authority of Aristotle, but perplexed a great deal more with hard words and useless distinctions, telling us what he or they are pleased to call virtues and vices, teach us nothing of morality, but only to understand their names, or call actions as they or Aristotle does; which is, in effect, but to speak their language properly.[77]

---

[73]III, 11, 15.
[74]III, 11, 16.
[75]IV, 3, 18.
[76]II, 20, 1.
[77]The fragment entitled "Thus I think" printed in Lord King, *The Life of John Locke* (London, 1830), 2:120–33. The passage quoted here appears on 126–27.

In other words, as one of Locke's critics put it, "however important he propositions might be which are derived from a system of abstract ideas arranged as Locke would arrange them, these propositions would be assertions of logical implication, but logical implication and moral obligation are not equivalent."[78] In this situation the proponents of the rationalistic interpretation of Locke's ethics must look for some other support, and they usually turn to the *Two Treatises of Government* where Locke talks about natural laws of a moral character (such as injunctions against taking someone else's property).[79] But in view of the widespread opinion that Locke's theory of natural laws is incompatible with his critique of nativism,[80] the "rationalists" have difficulty reconciling it with the rest of his teaching, especially in the *Essay*.[81]

The hedonistic interpretation of Locke's ethics is essentially based on a reading of his general theory of action in the chapter "Of Power." In responding to the critics of the first edition of the *Essay* who claimed that his theory had left no room for morality, Locke introduced in the second edition the new concept of the power to "suspend" a decision concerning the course of action the agent is to follow, in order to allow for the introduction into the chain of human motivation of considerations usually associated with moral concerns. This power of suspension he then identified with the "source of all liberty"[82] that a man has "with respect of *willing*."[83]

Much has been made in the Locke literature about this "power to suspend the act of choice,"[84] but little has been achieved in the way of reconciling it with Locke's view of freedom as a power of contingency and his critique of the concept of free will in the same chapter. In fact, it is not even quite clear what it is precisely that is "suspended" in the cases Locke speaks about, for while in one place he talks about suspending "the act of . . . choice," or the act of volition proper,[85] in other places he speaks about suspending "the execution and satisfaction of

[78]Lamprecht, *Moral and Political Philosophy*, 78. See also Aaron, *John Locke*, 264.

[79]See, for example, *The First Treatise*, § 59.

[80]See P. Laslett's "Introduction" to his edition of *Two Treatises of Government* (New York, 1965), 94–96.

[81]R. Polin, *La politique morale de John Locke* (Paris, 1960), chap. 3), and H. Aarsleff, "The State of Nature and the Nature of Man," in Yolton, ed., *John Locke: Problems and Perspectives*, nevertheless attempt such a reconciliation.

[82]II, 21, 47.

[83]II, 21, 56. Cf. also II, 21, 71.

[84]See, for example, Polin, "John Locke's Conception of Freedom," in Yolton, ed., *John Locke*, 4 . Also, by the same author, *La politique morale de John Locke*, 169. Further, W. Euchner, *Naturrecht und Politik bei John Locke* (Frankfurt/M., 1969), 111–18, and Aarsleff, "The State of Nature and the Nature of Man," 111–26.

[85]II, 21, 56. In the passage in question Locke speaks about the "chusing of a remote Good," and thus, perhaps, about not a situation in which an immediate choice is required.

any of [the mind's] desires,"[86] or even about the "power to suspend any particular desire,"[87] Despite some rather unfortunate formulations, however, there seems to be no need to suppose that Locke meant to go back on his rejection of the concept of free will when he talked about the "suspension"; on the contrary, he seems merely to restate his main point about the reasons necessitating the distinction between the will and desire—namely, the role played by the understanding in introducing an element of "consideration" or "examination" into the process of human motivation.[88] But what the concept of suspension does stress rather forcefully is that some considerations of the moral kind can play a role in determining the will. The proponents of the hedonistic interpretation of Locke's ethics then go further and ask what kind of moral considerations fit best with the rest of what Locke says in the chapter "Of Power." Their answer is that, given the tie between the good and happiness on the one hand and pleasure and pain on the other, Locke's ethics resolves to a pursuit of pleasure and avoidance of pain.

There are two possible versions of the hedonistic interpretation and the choice between them depends on the way one understands the criterion upon which the comparison between two alternative courses of action, interposed by Locke between desire and the ultimate decision of the will, is based. Since Locke expressly stated that this criterion is man's happiness[89] and that happiness is "the utmost Pleasure we are capable of,"[90] everything centers around the understanding of these terms. The proponents of one version want to see "happiness" as a Hobbesian "felicity," that is, the continual progress of desire without end.[91] What one's considered judgment in practical matters is supposed to accomplish simply amounts, according to this reading, to avoiding the mistake of satisfying the most pressing desire of the moment, which would in the long run, as compared with some other course of action, decrease one's relative happiness. The other interpretation of the role of judgment in the matters of action treats it as a step away from the "pleasure principle" in the materialistic, Hobbesian

---

[86]II, 21, 47.

[87]II, 21, 50.

[88]See the preceding section. Cf. also Locke's statement that "whatever necessity determines the pursuit of real Bliss, the same necessity, with the same force, establishes *suspense, deliberation,* and scrutiny of each successive desire" (II, 21, 52); and his otherwise surprising explanation that "consideration" is not an "abridgment of Liberty" (II, 21, 50).

[89]II, 21, 51.

[90]II, 21, 42.

[91]Leo Strauss is the best example. See *Natural Right and History,* 249–51. Those passages in which Locke denies the existence of a *summum bonum* (II, 21, 52–54) give some credence to such a reading.

sense.[92] According to this reading, "real happiness" consists in the pleasures of salvation to come as a reward for following God's commandments. Man's capacity for not following the most immediate and pressing inclinations is supposed to direct him away from the so-called natural pleasures toward a higher or "moral" good.[93]

Despite their different interpretations of the meaning of happiness in Locke, what unites the two hedonistic readings—each of which abounds in textual confirmations, especially if passages are taken out of context—is the assumption that a fixed class of things considered "good," meaning capable of giving one pleasure, one-sidedly determines the direction of man's search for happiness. In fact, however, the key to a more sophisticated interpretation of Locke's theory of moral action, capable of reconciling both the hedonistic and the rationalistic view of his ethics, as well as the two versions of the hedonistic reading, lies in a better understanding of Locke's concept of happiness.

5.2. Happiness, Pleasure, and Hedonism

Ever since antiquity, philosophers have used the concept of happiness as a favorite *principium executionis* of their moral theories, for it was assumed that everyone, by definition, wanted to be happy. Thus, to prove that one will be happy if one's actions are directed toward the good specified by a given ethical system was always one of the main tasks of moral theorists. Plato wanted to show that only the harmony of one's mental faculties, which he called "virtue," was capable of making one truly happy, while Aristotle attempted to show the same about moderation, and although both believed that a man needed proper education to provide him with a sufficient motivation to act righteously, both also assumed as self-evident that the good cannot contradict the requirements of happiness. Even Kant—who was later to break the necessary connection between happiness and morality—in the early stages of his moral thinking and even as late as the *Critique of Pure Reason*, believed, exactly like Locke, that "reason finds itself constrained to assume" the existence of God who distributes punishments and rewards (i.e., happiness) "in exact proportions to morality," for "otherwise it would have to regard the moral laws as empty figments of the

[92]The proponents of the "rationalistic" view usually include this reading in their interpretation, without noticing that, as Lamprecht points out (*Moral and Political Philosophy*, 84), it constitutes a departure from the rationalistic position. For such a combination of the two readings, see the already mentioned works of Polin.

[93]For the distinction between "moral" and "natural" good, see King, *Life of John Locke*, 2:128. See also *Essay*, II, 28, 5.

brain, since without this postulate the necessary consequence which it itself connects with these laws [i.e., that we should act on them] could not follow."[94] In a very Lockean statement, Kant then adds that "without God and without a world invisible to us now but hoped for, the glorious ideas of morality are indeed objects of approval and admiration, but not springs of purpose and action."[95]

Thus, the inclusion of the concept of happiness in a moral theory does not by any means make the theory hedonistic, and we need not assume that Locke's ethics is different in this respect. To say that the good is what makes a man happy was, before Kant's *Critique of Practical Reason* with its concept of duty, a mere tautology, and the Stoic claim that a wise man is *happy* even under the most terrible tortures is a rather nice case in point. The problem of ethics, before the late Kant, was to define what makes man good *and* really happy, while the link between the two was considered to be *the* condition of the possibility of morality *in general*.

What makes an ethical theory hedonistic is, as Kant observed in his critique of the Epicureans, the confusion of happiness with pleasure or of their respective priority. "Happiness," says Kant, "is not something sensed, but something thought."[96] Translated into Locke's terms, this means that happiness, unlike pleasure, is a complex idea representing the order of one's practical priorities rather than a simple sensation. What a hedonist does is either to ignore this difference altogether, so that an indiscriminate pursuit of pleasure is seen to constitute happiness, or to take pleasure as a primitive term and define happiness in terms of a "calculus of pleasures," possibly opting for some more "refined" types of pleasure than the seven cardinal sins of old. In all this, however, "happiness" functions as an elusive concept, the meaning of which it is not easy to discern. The problem does not lie so much in the fact that the ideal of happiness varies from person to person and even within the same subject through time, since a hedonist is willing to admit this and explains it by assuming that people differ considerably insofar as their sense organs (and their responses to stimuli) are concerned. The problem lies rather with the hedonistic view that the relation between various objects considered good by the agent and his

---

[94]*Critique of Pure Reason*, A811; B839.

[95]Ibid., A813; B841. Compare this with the following statement by Locke: "To establish morality, therefore, upon its proper basis . . . we must first prove a law, which always supposes a law-maker: one that has superiority and right to ordain, and also a power to reward and punish according to the tenor of the law established by him" (King, *Life*, 2:133). It was only in the *Foundations* and the *Critique of Practical Reason*, that Kant, for reasons to be explained below, rejected his old view and substituted "duty" for "happiness" as his *principium executionis*.

[96]P. A. Schlipp, ed., *Kant's Precritical Ethics* (Evanston, Ill., 1960), 129.

feelings of pleasure and pain is simply "given" and that the concept of happiness is derived from it, since this view presupposes an extremely primitive account of human experience. Particularly, the stimulus-response model that must be used in this account ignores the involvement of man's cognitive apparatus (as opposed to reflexes, instincts, and so on) in the shaping of the very form in which the stimulus is received. According to a hedonist, a man can have an input into his happiness only by being able to predict future reactions to stimuli and by making a corresponding attempt to control the input of future stimuli. But clearly our view of what constitutes happiness regulates our ordering of objects on the pleasure-pain scale as much as the "natural" pleasure-pain scale influences our concept of happiness. Not even the most narrow residue of physical pain and pleasure can be safely ascribed to a "natural" constitution of our receptive organs, unless one wants to maintain that, say, a masochist has a different *physiological* reaction to torture than other human beings. If, on the other hand, pleasure and pain are not defined as purely physiological reactions, but are seen as responses involving habits, results of education, rational or moral considerations, and so forth, then the hedonistic view disintegrates, for a nonphysiological definition of pleasure and pain amounts to an admission that pleasure and pain are reactions guided by one's more or less rational ordering of practical priorities or, in other words, are informed by one's *ideal of happiness*, so that to try, in turn, to define happiness with reference to pain and pleasure as primitive terms is to move in a circle.

5.3. Locke on the Primacy of Happiness

Now, I wish to argue here that Locke's empiricism does not lead him either to a hedonistic moral theory or to the resultant moral skepticism or relativism. In his epistemology, to be sure, Locke postulates that all the elements out of which knowledge is constituted are essentially "given" and passively "received" by the mind, no innate concepts or even dispositions being necessary. In his theory of action, however, he seems to claim that action always presupposes an already accepted set of ends to be pursued and that these ends, far from being "given" or extracted by a simple generalization from the data of experience, are in fact adopted by the mind itself and, by informing the sense data the mind receives, render possible the practical experience of the actor. This is not supposed to imply any innate moral ideas or an unrestrained freedom for the agent in setting the ends for his actions. What is meant here is that the feeling of pain or pleasure involved in an action, unlike an epistemic sensation, is connected to a particular stimulus

only by virtue of the location of that stimulus in an overarch
of relations among stimuli; a network, that is, which is c(
the agent's rational life plan and his order of practical r
nonrepresentative character of the ideas of pleasure and p(
prevents their being tied unambiguously to any particular feature or u.
objective world (unlike the ideas of both primary and secondary qualities), allows, I believe, for Locke's giving an interesting account of moral
experience, combining without inconsistency the elements of both the
rationalistic and the empiricist theory of action. There is also, I am going
to argue, a kind of "dialectical" relation in Locke's philosophy between
the ends and the means of moral action and between the agent and his
environment.

The argument for all these claims begins with the crucial contention
that Locke, despite his statement that happiness is "the utmost Pleasure we are capable of," did not confuse the relative priority of pleasure
and happiness. I base this contention on: (1) Locke's saying that we
choose our happiness;[97] (2) his saying that it is "in a Man's power to
change the pleasantness, and unpleasantness, that accompanies any
sort of action";[98] (3) his saying that it is "happiness and that alone" that
"moves *desire*";[99] and (4) his "mixed-modes" theory of morality.

I shall bring all of these four pieces of evidence to bear on my
argument gradually. But to begin with, let us look again at the passage
from the *Essay* in which Locke explains his idea of "suspension" and
seems to go back on his previously unqualified rejection of the concept
of free will:

> ... there is a case wherein a Man is at Liberty in respect of *willing*, and that
> is the chusing of a remote Good as an end to be pursued. Here a Man may
> suspend the act of his choice from being determined for or against the
> thing proposed, till he has examined, whether it be really of a nature in it
> self and consequences to make him happy or no. ... And here we may see
> how it comes to pass, that a Man may justly incur punishment, though it
> be certain that in all the particular actions that he *wills*, he does, and
> necessarily does will that, which he then judges to be good. For though his
> *will* be always determined by that, which is judg'd good by his Understand-
> ing, yet it excuses him not: Because, by a too hasty choice of his own
> making, he has imposed on himself wrong measures of good and evil;
> which however false and fallacious, have the same influence on all his
> future conduct, as if they were true and right. He has vitiated his own
> Palate, and must be answerable to himself for the sickness and death that
> follows from it.[100]

[97]King, *Life*, 2:107.
[98]II, 21, 69.
[99]II, 21, 41.
[100]II, 21, 56.

We are still not in a position to explain fully the notion of moral *responsibility* that Locke advocates in this passage. But even on the assumption that the "liberty with respect to *willing*" merely refers to the fact that human understanding is capable of an input into the decision-making process leading to a given action, it is quite obvious that in the passage just quoted this input is greater than just an estimation of agreement between the action proposed and the overall happiness of the agent. The "remote Good" to be chosen here is not a "particular action," but rather a "measure of good and evil" that the agent is to "impose" upon himself, that is, not something designated by the agent's standard of happiness, but this very *standard itself*. The reason the act of volition is "suspended" in this case is not that the agent does not know whether a particular action is compatible with his happiness or that the "remoteness" of the end to be pursued simply lengthens the time allowed for the associative train of the understanding. The reason rather is that the decision in question is not a matter of mere calcula-tion, but concerns something that is not determined by what now gives the agent pain or pleasure, and requires the agent to ask what should or should not be included among the *criteria* that constitute his ideal of happiness itself, i.e., his life plan and his order of practical priorities. Indeed, whatever the more precise argument in favor of moral respon-sibility that Locke is making here, it would lead nowhere for him to say that a wrong or evil action is a result of a mistake in evaluating the amount of pain or pleasure attached to a given course of action and its consequences, that the actor could have used his judgment to a better effect. For as long as one holds to the view that the hierarchy of goods is beyond the control of the agent, there is hardly any reason, besides a truly unbounded confidence in the goodness of human nature, to suppose that if an agent does not make a mistake in his choice of the course of action capable of giving him the maximum of pleasure, then he will *not* do those things, such as murder, theft, or perjury, which most societies consider evil and for which they are going to punish him. In fact, the nearly infinite variety of human tastes should make us suspicious in the first place with regard to such a uniform abstention from criminal acts; an abstention allegedly forsaken through error and ignorance alone. To say, on the other hand, along Hobbesian lines, that the pain inflicted by the punishment itself should have entered into the agent's initial calculation is to say that the punishment *defines* the evil rather than punishes it. Neither of these views, I believe, can be safely imputed to the moral sense of John Locke.

Be this as it may, Locke's text makes it sufficiently clear that the foundation of responsibility lies not in a man's capacity to consider what will actually give him pleasure, but rather in his capacity for "choosing his own happiness" as a "measure of good and evil," that is, in his capacity for deciding what is and what is not supposed to give him pleasure. To commit a crime for which one is responsible is not to think that an act of killing or its consequences will give one pleasure while in fact it will not, but to "vitiate one's own Palate," that is, to establish one's order of priorities in such a way that one develops a disposition to find a criminal act pleasant and desirable. The power of suspension, of which so much has been made by Locke's commentators, turns out on reflection to consist in the fact that while the will is determined by desire, desire itself is in part a function of the idea of happiness which, in turn, is an ideal of the understanding. Thus, a deliberate formation of one's own standard of good and evil lies at the bottom of the will's determination.

Happiness, therefore, as that which "moves *desire*," is not a derivative of pleasure, but rather the logically prior criterion that determines what is and what is not capable of giving one pleasure. It is wrong to understand the pursuit of happiness as a consequence, rather than the cause, of man's search for pleasure or as an outcome of a "calculus of pleasures," be it *à la* Hobbes or *à la* Mill. Happiness, as I have said, is a *complex* idea of the understanding; like the constructs of mathematics, it is a *mixed mode*, and such that pain and pleasure are not even its components. Pain and pleasure, in turn, are *simple* ideas of the senses that habitually follow upon the realization that an element of one's happiness is either absent or present. Happiness, to quote the early Kant once again, is not "a thought which can be taken from experience [which means that it is not arrived at by a process of generalization], but a thought which makes its experience [i.e., pleasure] possible."[101] It is this understanding of happiness that Locke had in mind when he wrote that "that is morally good or evil which, by the intervention of the will of an intelligent free agent, draws pleasure or pain *after* it."[102]

This reading of the relation between happiness and pleasure reconciles, I believe, the mixed-modes theory of morality with the seemingly incompatible "executive" mechanism of human action Locke discusses in the chapter "Of Power." We have not yet analyzed how a man comes to forge those ideas which Locke calls "mixed modes." Insofar as the concept of happiness is concerned, however, several things should be immediately clear. First, if the concept of happiness is a logically prior condition of human action (since it is necessary for the very formation of desire that determines the will) then, as we have already observed, the ideal of happiness cannot be a simple product of an inductive

[101]Schlipp, ed., *Kant's Precritical Ethics*, 129.
[102]King, *Life*, 2:128.

generalization from past experiences of pleasure or, in fact, from any past experience of action. In order to act a man must always *already have* a set of ends he wants to pursue through his action. Second, since the components of the ideal of happiness have the character of *norms* that an agent accepts for himself, they are not *representative* of any outside reality and cannot be mere products of observation that yields such descriptive statements as "Swans are white."[103] Thus, as in the case of other mixed modes, such as mathematical constructs, there are in the case of the practical postulates of action no constraints of adequacy with respect to some outside reality (truth as correspondence) that account for the most important source of error in dealing with empirical knowledge. Third, while we do not yet know what kinds of considerations constrain our choices of practical priorities, we know that there must be some such constraints, if our actions are not to be ultimately a product of sheer arbitrariness. Although Locke sometimes speaks as if freedom were involved in some processes of ratiocination (and not only in carrying the results of such processes into action), his theory would be no advance over the old free-will conception if ethical responsibility (or, in fact, any human action) were to rely on a man's ability to engage in unconstrained, arbitrary behavior.[104] But if the constraints on our choice of practical priorities do not derive from the need of an adequacy with respect to an outside reality, then they must derive from the laws that govern our *thinking* about these priorities. Ethics, then, as an inquiry into the right choice of practical priorities, can be, like mathematics, a demonstrable science, since it deals with a subject of "maker's knowledge," in which no error can undermine our reasoning as long as proper rational procedures govern our choice of moral postulates and the drawing of their consequences.[105] At the same time, what was usually objected to the mixed-modes theory of morality, namely, that is was a game of definitions and consequences, rather than a theory of obligations, does not hold any longer, since the constructs of morality, being tantamount to the accepted ideal of happiness, are backed by the natural mechanism leading up to action. If I "define," say, generosity in such-and-such a way, and if I choose to call it "good," that is, for one reason or another include it in my concept of happiness, or rational life plan, then being generous is capable of giving me pleasure,

---

[103]In II, 22, 9, Locke does list "Observation" as one of the ways in which mixed modes are acquired. In our case, this simply means that some patterns of the behavior of other people can give rise to an idea in our minds. Still, the adoption of that pattern as a postulate to be included in *our* ideal of happiness is not a matter of generalization from such observations. As we shall see later, this does not mean that moral choices are made *in abstracto*, independently of all experience. All that is claimed here is that they are not *inductive* generalizations from experience.

[104]See above, section 3.

[105]IV, 4, 7.

so that not only should I, according to the principles of rationality, prefer generous behavior to all those actions that play a lesser role in my order of practical priorities; but also, in view of the fact that the pleasure or pain an action is capable of giving me is dependent on the action's position in my order of practical priorities, I am provided with what ought to constitute a sufficient *motivation* for following such and no other course of action. My not following what my rational life plan prescribes may be due solely to an impairment of rational faculties, suffered because of carelessness, bad habits, or a particularly strong deprivation. In this sense the mixed-modes theory of morality fore-shadows all the future theories of autonomy in that it makes *rational self-legislation* the principle of all morally commanded actions.

The mixed-modes theory, however, with its priority of happiness over pleasure, should not be understood to imply that one's reactions in terms of pain and pleasure do not develop their own momentum, so that changes in them would *immediately* follow any change in one's concept of happiness. An inclusion of something in one's concept of happiness initially determines its position in the hierarchy of pleasures only as an "ought" or a postulate of reason. An actual stimulus of a particular kind, however, is not in each individual instance referred to the agent's whole hierarchy of goods before a reaction in terms of pain or pleasure occurs. The ordinary life of the agent would be impossibly inefficient if each and every stimulus were to involve an extended consideration. Hence, a particular stimulus is most often taken care of with the help of a *disposition* to a reaction of a given kind—a disposition that results from a process of conditioning, long-standing habits, and so forth.[106] Such dispositions may sometimes be very hard to overcome, and a change in actual patterns of reaction may be very gradual and quite slow. Nevertheless, the basic framework of Locke's theory of moral action is not seriously affected by this fact, mainly because an agent's habits and dispositions are themselves a function of his choice of his ideal of happiness. Although a change in one's habitual responses may be at times very hard to effect,[107] the extent of the propensity to replace consideration with dispositionally determined behavior is itself one of the things that can, within certain limits, be subject to evaluation with respect to its inclusion in the concept of happiness.

5.4. The Process of Moral Development

How *does* a man come to have an ideal of happiness that is always presupposed insofar as he is an agent?

---

[106]II, 21, 69.

[107]While Locke tells us that such changes are possible in II, 21, 69, a contrary impression may be had from II, 21, 38.

The first thing to be stressed is that the acquisition of an ideal of happiness is a process of *reasoning* and thus, like all mental events for Locke, is *determined* by the laws that govern the processes of ratiocination. As we have noted before, Locke does not consider the laws of thought to be all that different from the laws of physics—the *reasons* that determine a certain outcome are simply *causes* in the associational mechanics of the mental. Therefore, while Locke's theory of moral action resembles future theories of autonomy in that it substitutes the concept of rational self-legislation for the "possibility of having done otherwise" associated with the old free-will theory, it must be clearly distinguished from Rousseau's and Kant's theories of autonomy in that it does not rely on the mind's "pure spontaneity" in producing the set of norms the agent will follow. Neither are the imperatives of happiness merely deduced from some immutable laws of reason, independently of an existing situation. Although these imperatives are not inductive generalizations, the process by which they are arrived at is nevertheless deeply rooted in the context of practical experience. Thus, a man is never, according to Locke, confronted with problems of moral and practical significance *in abstracto*; he never solves his problems either by mere fiat or by pure contemplation. On the contrary, the possibility of rational self-legislation, far from being predicated on a man's ability to begin his moral experience with a set of norms that spring like Athena from the head of Zeus, relies on the fact that moral life involves a *development*, that is, an open-ended process in which *all* norms of conduct (and not just strategies to achieve some preestablished ends) are open to revision.[108]

It is true, of course, that at any stage in his life, insofar as it makes

[108]Aaron (*John Locke*, 263) doubts that a reconciliation, such as I am now trying to establish, between the mental origin of mixed modes and their grounding in experience could ever provide a successful defense of the mixed-modes theory of morality. Nevertheless, there seems to me no doubt that Locke himself tried to do this and his problem has a significance beyond just the questions of morality. Mathematics, according to Locke, is also a science of mixed modes, in that nothing in reality directly corresponds to its constructs. At the same time, however, as the certainty of mathematical constructs derives from the fact of "maker's knowledge," the practical significance of mathematics depends on the use that can be made of it in the application to the problems we solve by using its constructs. Thus, without some experience of such problems we would never engage in a mathematical inquiry, but the constraints that this experience imposes on our inquiry do not change the nonrepresentative character (or the certainty) of mathematics. Whatever one wants to say about this insight in the context of mathematics, carried over to matters of morality it seems to me quite appealing: while we do not believe that moral questions have empirical answers, neither do we believe that one can really decide how to live in abstraction from the experience of life. The reason no contradiction is involved here is that moral experience (the experience of life) is not a mere collecting of data about ourselves: the data are "created" in the same process in which they are observed. The nature of this "dialectic" between our moral ideals and our moral experience will be analyzed to some extent in what follows.

sense to say that he is an agent, a man must *already have* an ideal of happiness and react with pain or pleasure to all kinds of stimuli, since otherwise all action would be impossible. But an agent does not start his moral life with an ideal of happiness arrived at through a proper application of the laws of reason; it cannot be arrived at *in abstracto* and his experience is too limited to allow for a considered choice. Thus, the agent's initial ordering of his priorities must come from some other source.

It is "the most usual way," says Locke, to acquire the ideas of mixed modes through language, and particularly "by *explaining the names* of Actions we never saw, or Notions we cannot see."[109] Hence, the initial acquisition of one's ideal of happiness, which is also a mixed mode, will "usually" take place through intercourse with other people who, in various ways, communicate to us during the formative stages of our development the meaning of moral categories. In other words, man is first of all *socialized* into a system of values prevalent in his environment, and even the ways of satisfying his basic natural needs are determined by prevailing customs and education.[110] Thus, human moral experience usually begins with a rather uncritical acceptance of an ideal of happiness prevalent in the social environment of the actor. In its most elementary stages, when a child is still incapable of understanding the more abstract moral categories, this process most often results in a chain of dispositions that make abundant satisfaction of bodily and emotional needs the chief element of happiness. In the later stages, education, combined with observation of other people's behavior (and "Observation" is, according to Locke, another way in which a man acquires the ideas of mixed modes[111]), adds some further elements to our ideal of happiness, thus completing the first molding of our "characters." At this stage,

> the ordinary necessities of our lives fill a great part of them with the *uneasiness* of *Hunger, Thrift, Heat, Cold, Weariness* with labour, and *Sleepiness,* in their Constant Returns, *etc.* To which, if besides accidental harms, we add the fantastical *uneasiness,* (as itch after *Honour, Power,* or *Riches,* etc.) which acquir'd habits by Fashion, Example, and Education, have settled in us, and a thousand other irregular desires, which custom has

---

[109]II, 22, 9.

[110]Given the importance of this process of socialization in moral experience, it is not entirely correct to say that Locke was a radical individualist who considered social intercourse irrelevant for the constitution of a human person. In fact, despite the prevalence of individualism in his theory of man, an interesting theory of civil (or prepolitical) society could be extracted from Locke's writings. Some other aspects of this theory will be pointed out in the next chapter, dealing with his conception of property.

[111]II, 22, 9.

made natural to us, we shall find that a very little part of our life is so vacant from these *uneasinesses*, as to leave us free to the attraction of remoter absent good. We are seldom at ease, and free enough from the solicitation of our natural or adopted desires, but a constant Succession of *uneasinesses* out that stock, which natural wants or acquired habits have heaped up, take the *will* in their turns; and no sooner is one action dispatch'd, which by such a determination of the *will* we are set upon, but another *uneasiness* is ready to set us on work.[112]

It can be seen, then, that the naive hedonistic identification of happiness with the satisfaction of the relatively "unreflected" inclinations does, indeed, constitute the first stage in the ontogenetic development of the human psyche. Moreover, the dispositional character of most human responses at this stage makes the pursuit of even those things which are *in abstracto* considered good, but for which no disposition exists, something very difficult and requiring a conscious effort on the part of the agent:

... absent good, though thought on, confessed, and appearing to be good, not making any part of this unhappiness in its absence, is jostled out, to make way for the removal of the *uneasiness* we feel, till due, and repeated Contemplation has brought it nearer to our Mind, given some relish of it, and raised in us some desire; which then beginning to make part of our present *uneasiness*, stands upon fair terms with the rest, to be satisfied; and so according to its greatness, and pressure, comes in its turn to determine the *will*.[113]

Still, even at this stage the unreflective character of human pursuits can be changed and some elements of rational order can be introduced, since

... by a due consideration, and examining any good proposed, it is in our power, to raise our desires, in a due proportion to the value of that good, whereby, in its turn, and place, it may come to work upon the *will*, and be pursued.[114]

But the crucial point here consists in the fact that "consideration" or "contemplation," when once begun, does not stop at a more rational pursuit of the already accepted values. On the contrary, "contemplation" begins a slow *learning process*, as a result of which the irrational and permanently unsatisfactory life of naive hedonism gives way to a

[112]II, 21, 45.
[113]II, 21, 45.
[114]II, 21, 46.

reordering of the agent's priorities. In the process of his moral development, not only the means of the agent's action, but also its ends, are constantly open to rational scrutiny and revision. Consequently, a man comes to "choose" his happiness in such a way that his dependence on self-perpetuating desires and absent or fleeting satisfactions is reduced and the Hobbesian "continuall progresse of desire" is replaced by a more rational order:

> Fashion and the common Opinion having settled wrong Notions, and education and custom ill habits, the just values of things are misplaced, and the palates of Men corrupted. Pains should be taken to rectify these; and contrary habits change our pleasure and give relish to that, which is necessary and conducive to our Happiness.[115]

Along this road, man is in fact capable of influencing, within certain limits, even his most physiologically conditioned responses, in order to reconcile pleasure with his rational life plan:

> ... 'tis a mistake to think, that Men cannot change the displeasingness, or Indifferency, that is in actions, into pleasure and desire, if they will do but what is in their power. A due consideration will do it in some cases; and practice, application, and custom in most. Bread and Tobacco may be neglected, where they are shewn to be useful to health, because of an indifferency or disrelish to them; reason and consideration at first recommends, and begins their trial, and use finds, or custom makes them pleasant.... Though this be very visible, and every one's Experience shews him he can do so; yet it is a part, in the conduct of men towards their Happiness, neglected to a degree, that it will be possibly entertain'd as a Paradox, if it be said, that Men can make things or actions more or less pleasing to themselves; and thereby remedy that, to which one may justly impute a great deal of their wandering.[116]

The reason a man can influence his sense responses to stimuli is, of course, that these responses, insofar as pain and pleasure are concerned, are informed to begin with by rational considerations and the latter are in part constitutive of the former. In this respect, Locke's theory of practical sense experience, underlying his theory of rational self-legislation, is in some ways more sophisticated than that of the later proponents of the concept of autonomy. For Kant, for example, rational self-legislation could constitute the foundation of morality only if intellectual activity was seen to represent an element of genuine spontaneity (à la Locke's "active power") and if actions determined by reason

[115] II, 21, 69.
[116] II, 21, 69.

were strictly opposed to those which followed the dictates of "inclinations." This was so because Kant, in his late critical period, came to accept the essentially Hobbesian argument that the mechanistic vision of modern science precluded a natural link between the requirements of happiness and a rationally founded moral order. "Inclinations" ("desires," Hobbes and Locke would say) are part of the natural world and must be viewed, according to Kant, as something merely *given*, rather than shaped by rational considerations. Consequently, Kant came to abandon the Lockean idea of happiness as a *principium executionis* of his moral theory, since the link between happiness and the "unreflected," "merely sensed" feelings of pain and pleasure convinced him that happiness could not be seen as an a priori condition of the experience of pleasure, and should be viewed as a concept of which "all components . . . are empirical, *i.e.*, must be taken from experience,"[117] rather than forged by the agent as a part of his autonomous life plan. Given his strict dichotomy between the rational and the sensible, Kant came to the conclusion that only an action which is *entirely* an effect of human spontaneity could be viewed as moral, and he located moral agency in the "noumenal" self that could not be guided by any considerations of pleasure or happiness.[118] Where such considerations do enter into the agent's motivational process, we can speak of his acting on a hypothetical, but not a categorical (moral), imperative. As a result, Kant reintroduced a radical break between moral action and actions connected with the fulfillment of natural needs and inclinations, reminiscent of the ancient distinction between *praxis* and *poesis*.

Locke's theory of mixed modes, however, allowed him to avoid most of the problems inherent in the Kantian account, since it provided a basis for viewing moral ideas as nonderivable from simple inclinations and at the time related to them in both origin and consequences. Because the intervention of reason in matters of action is not for Locke equivalent to an insertion of an entirely separate kind of "rational causation" into the self-enclosed order of nature, the relation between moral reasons and natural inclinations is one of mutual interaction and not one-sided dependence. Locke manages to avoid both a dualistic separation of reason from inclination and a simplistic reduction of one to the other. On the one hand, Locke—unlike Kant—does not separate the moral norm from the concrete needs and inclinations of man, so that the element of "universalization," which, according to Kant, made

---

[117]*Foundations of the Metaphysics of Morals* (Prussian Academy edition), 418.

[118]In the *Foundations* the idea of "worthiness of being happy" does not appear at all; in the *Critique of Practical Reason* (pp. 110, 134 of the Prussian Academy edition) it plays a minor role as a step toward a philosophy of religion.

the rational order so different from the sensual (and which tied the purely rational to the teleological and the moral, as opposed to the mechanical and the empirical), is *always*, according to Locke, tied to the material of the senses. Moral law, according to Locke, never becomes "pure," since its ultimate function is to guide the pursuit of happiness. But on the other hand, Locke's moral ideal is not simply parasitic on the biological requirements of life, since the relation between universal moral norms and sensual inclinations is more "dialectical" in Locke than in Kant. The input of the sense in matters of pain and pleasure, unlike in matters of knowledge (and here Locke's system is exactly the reverse of the Kantian), is never entirely uninformed by intellectual considerations (although we may not always be aware of that). Thus, while this input of the senses may always occasion a change in one's norms of conduct, these latter may always, in turn, change and influence the "immediate" reactions, seemingly based on inclinations alone. Therefore, the meaning of "necessity," or that which is imposed on human conduct by the requirements of "mere life," is always a flexible matter, insofar as human action is concerned. Not only is man capable of satisfying his physiological needs in ways not at all determined by these needs alone, but also most, if not all, of his needs are not in fact "physiological," that is, undetermined by rational or moral considerations.

For these reasons, the Lockean moral principles escape Kant's neat classification of all imperatives into "hypothetical" (pragmatic) and "categorical" (moral), since the whole classification is based on strict dichotomies between reason and senses, ends and means, mechanism and teleology—none of which Locke accepted without serious modifications. While the noninductive origin of moral ideals makes ethics into a demonstrable system of abstract obligations, the dispositional character of most human responses to stimuli (especially in the early stages of moral development) makes the process of the formation of, and the effective compliance with, the commands of morality a matter of training and development. Moral ideals are in this respect comparable to the constructs of mathematics: although both are not simply generalized from the data of the senses (and this ensures their certainty), neither are they arbitrary or unrelated to the world of sense experience, since their formation is traceable to practical concerns.[119] Hence, Locke's somewhat Aristotelian insistence on the role of education in matters of morality is directly related to his view that moral systems do not arise like a *deus ex machina*, but rather result from an "education of the senses," not unlike what the young Hegel was later to

[119]For the role of experience in reaching mathematical knowledge, see IV, 12, 15.

oppose as "love" to the ethics of Kant,[120] or what made the young Marx speak of the senses as "theoreticians."[121]

This integration of the sensual and the intellectual I consider to be an essential element of the Lockean foundations of the liberal theory of man. For although Locke makes every effort to reintroduce a moral dimension, the dimension threatened by Hobbesian reductionism, into human life, he preserves Hobbes's insistence on the central role of *interest* in the modern theory of human action. The fact that it is *happiness* that remains the focal point of morality and that its definition is rooted in the concept of *need* or *desire* provides an indispensable link between moral *praxis* and quotidian, earthly *poesis*. Insofar as moral theory then provides a foundation for the political order, the concerns of political action are not sidetracked into a nostalgic reconstruction of the leisurely *polis*, with its self-proclaimed indifference to the private, "household" concerns of economic life, but elevate the concerns of production to the status of a morally and politically relevant activity in which the creative aspect of modern man finds its most important expression.

5.5. Natural Moral Laws

I have talked about how moral considerations enter into the motivational circuit of human action and how an agent's acceptance of an ideal of happiness is subject to a development throughout the course of his life. But even if it is granted that men do form their own standards of good and evil and that these standards, by virtue of their being backed by an appropriate motivational mechanism described in the chapter "Of Power," constitute valid norms of individual behavior, it could still be argued that these facts by themselves do not guarantee any *uniformity* of moral values accepted by different subjects. The principal feature of mixed modes is that their origin is contingent on the conditions of life of a given individual. Consequently, mixed modes, unless they are artificially fixed by a convention (linguistic or otherwise), will vary from one person to another as well for the same person over time. The norms of behavior presented in the mixed-modes theory may then be said to be like figments of imagination or conventional theoretical constructs: they can be changed for all kinds of reasons and are in this respect unlike the principles of morality, which must preserve a con-

---

[120]See "The Spirit of Christianity and Its Fate," in Hegel, *The Early Theological Writings* (Philadelphia, 1971), 224–53.

[121]K. Marx, *Economic and Philosophic Manuscripts of 1844*, ed. D. Struik (New York, 1964), 139.

stant and intersubjective validity. In this way, something reminiscent of the Kantian problem of deducing substantive moral commands from the formal principle expressed in the categorical imperative could also be reconstructed in Locke's system as I have interpreted it.

The solution that Locke himself proposed to this problem (although he did little to connect it explicitly with the other components of his moral theory) is to be found in his conception of natural moral laws. The gist of this conception is that certain moral principles are "natural" for man in that they arise in accordance with the laws of nature (and specifically in accordance with the mechanism of association) in the course of "normal" human development.

This is to be understood as follows: The "choice" of moral ideals constituting one's rational life plan does not represent, as I have repeatedly stressed, any break in the chain of "natural causality." Although the moral experience of man differs from, say, perception in that it is holistic and not atomistic, the fact nevertheless remains that even if some combinations of ideas, relevant to human moral experience, are mixed modes to which nothing corresponds in the objective world, the *mental acts* in which such combinations are brought about are, in view of the mind's being essentially passive and originally a *tabula rasa*, ultimately traceable to external stimulation. Hence, the formation of one's ideal of happiness, and in general the whole of human moral development, must be *causally* accountable for. Consequently, given the uniformity of the laws of association (the "laws of reason" under the guise of the "mechanics of the mental") for different subjects, it is not unreasonable to suppose that in certain types of situations, which one may call "normal," people will, as a result of forces acting in accordance with the laws of nature, come to a far-reaching uniformity in their views of moral obligations. These may for this reason be called "natural laws," especially since Locke is prone to confuse (or to conflate) mental acts with their contents. A similar reasoning is, in fact, involved in Locke's account of the origin of all mixed modes, including the constructs of mathematics and other sciences, which are not for him either arbitrary or different for every subject. Clearly, the conditions of life are somewhat different for every knower, but they are sufficiently uniform to guarantee that the theoretical constructs produced in each mind in response to certain kinds of experiences manifest so far-reaching a similarity as to allow, for example, for the perfect intersubjectivity of mathematical knowledge. What makes some of the "natural laws" that have arisen in this way "moral" is not that the mental acts in which they are apprehended are not mechanically produced, but that these laws specify an ideal of life that a rational agent feels obliged to pursue. An additional feature that assimilates these natural laws to our usual conception of moral norms is that the commands of reason (as well as those of the inclinations, for that matter) are not mechanically executed; that is, being only *commands*, they cannot be "translated" back into action without the intervention of *freedom*. But the moral laws themselves, being a result of the "natural" mode of the mind's operation, are in such a sense a "necessity" for man, although this necessity is of such a kind that even God is under it.[122]

If moral laws are, in the sense just described, natural, then the principles of rationality will actually yield a set of substantive moral principles, namely, those that represent the life plan to be arrived at by a "normal" subject under "normal" conditions, in which no superstitious customs, wrong education, or bad social influences interfere with the process of moral development. The impossibility of deducing substantive moral norms from the purely formal canons of rationality, which has often been raised as an objection against the Kantian hopes connected with the principles of autonomy,[123] is usually seen to lie in the possibility of many incompatible, yet internally consistent, moral systems. In view of the Lockean "naturalization" of rationality, however—in view of his associationist account of the laws of reason—the scope of what is "possible" is sufficiently restricted to exclude those moral principles which, though not in themselves inconsistent, are not *in fact* going to be accepted by most rational agents. Hence, the uniformity of the laws of reason is all that is needed, according to Locke, to translate the principles of rationality into a system of substantive moral obligations, and such a uniformity (which distinguishes man's intellectual endowment from the haphazardly formed dispositions usually designated by the name of "tastes") is taken for granted. To search, therefore, for a model life plan, that is, to attempt to reconstruct the concept of happiness (the standards of the good embodying a system of substantive obligations) that is the most "natural," must constitute one of the main tasks of Locke's ethics.

Locke does not pretend that he, or anyone, is able to "deduce" a rule of action for every particular situation that may be morally relevant, and even less does he presume that there exists a *single* principle (like Kant's categorical imperative) which would take care of all such situations *in abstracto*. On the contrary, liberal that he was, Locke believed that the "natural morality" of the kind just referred to must necessarily underdetermine most morally relevant behaviors, thus leaving room for both some revealed commandments and a variety of legal systems and personal codes that "close" the natural indeterminacy of the moral laws

---

[122]II, 21, 50.
[123]See R. P. Wolff, *The Autonomy of Reason* (New York, 1973), 49–50, 162ff.

of reason. Nevertheless, he did undertake to specify a certain body of obligations representing the necessary moral foundation of every legal order or every system of personal preferences. Among these moral foundations, the acquisition of property represents for Locke the most "natural" component of every rational life plan, so that given the "normal" conditions of a "natural state," every man must, insofar as his actions follow the laws of reason and not the blind impulses of the moment, come to devote a substantial part of his energy to the process of appropriation.

6. Autonomy

We are finally reaching the stage at which the diverse strands of Locke's theory of action and his theory of moral motivation can be linked together with the crucial concept of appropriation in order to complete the reconstruction of Locke's theory of *responsibility*.

As I have so far presented it, Locke's theory of moral action is still obviously insufficient to meet the challenge posed by the Hobbesian claim that a scientific account of mental processes leaves no room for a full-fledged concept of freedom that could do the job the old conception of free will was supposed to do. It is true that Locke's theory of rational self-legislation, in its tying of the agent's moral worth to his obedience to reason, resembles the later theories of autonomy associated with Rousseau, Kant, and Hegel. But the theory of autonomy, as we know it from Locke's successors, involves more than the identification of moral worth with rational deliberation. The very ground of why obedience to reason could be seen as the source of moral responsibility is that rationally guided action was seen to follow a *self*-legislated principle and to constitute the foundation of freedom. But if rational deliberation is for Locke essentially of the same kind as all other casually determined systems and if the mind is for him a *tabula rasa*, such that *all* content of its cogitations, including all that goes into the formation of mixed modes in general and of the idea of happiness in particular, is ultimately due to the mind's receptivity, then tying human action to rational deliberation will still not allow for true responsibility and will make Locke's conception of autonomy a fiction. If reason is thoroughly passive (and despite Locke's confusion on this point, I think he is committed to this claim), then we shall never be able to locate a true *agency* in the human mind. The fact that external stimulation is ultimately responsible for everything that takes place in the human mind must make human behavior ultimately heteronomous (i.e., traceable to the effects of some events in the outside world that the agent does not control), despite the nonrepresentative character of moral concepts and despite the fact that Locke sees moral, unlike cognitive, experience as holistic and not atomistic.

In view of the fact that Locke's theory of autonomy, unlike its later "idealist" counterparts, is constructed against the thoroughgoing empiricist and naturalistic background of his philosophy and, consequently, does not involve an identification of rationality with spontaneity, we must look *elsewhere* for an explanation as to why a rationally guided action may be said to follow *self*-legislated principles and, thus, ground the notion of moral responsibility. Locke's solution to this dilemma—and here is the crucial move of my interpretation—comes from a conjunction of his theory of the rational determination of the will with his theory of freedom as a power of contingency. It is true that the decrees of the human will being "mechanically" determined and the mind's being originally a *tabula rasa* would indeed make all human action ultimately heteronomous, *were it not* for the fact that the dictates of human volition are not themselves mechanically executed, but require freedom, i.e., an active power of initiating the physical motion commanded by the agent's will. We have seen before that this freedom cannot be attributed *directly* to the will without bringing back the problems associated with the conception of free will that Locke so trenchantly criticized. But there is another, *indirect*, way in which freedom affects the will, namely, through the mediation of its effects on the outside world. The necessary intervention of freedom in the translation of mental commands into physical action constitutes, as we have seen, a break in the normal mechanical order of the natural world, and consequently, human action, insofar as it has an impact on the world outside, introduces an element of contingency into the natural environment; a contingency that has no mechanical explanation and constitutes a subjective reference in the objective world of nature. This means that a man's action on the world around him is capable of imposing on it a *human* order and transforming it in accordance with the dictates of the agent's will. A transformation of this kind takes place, according to Locke, when a man *appropriates* nature, i.e., "*humanizes*" it and makes it "*his own*" by subjecting it to the effects of his own freedom and making it into an extension of his own person. But the world of nature that a man transforms in this way and assimilates to his own person, is, of course, the same world that constituted the originally *alien* source of the determination of his own will. Consequently, the process of appropriation, insofar as it substitutes a human (or "humanized") environment for the alien, natural one, transforms the heteronomy of human action into *autonomy* or *self-determination*.

A more detailed analysis of the concept of appropriation will be taken up in the next chapter. But it is important to explain now how and why a man, in the natural course of his moral development, comes to include appropriation among the top priorities in his life plan or ideal of happiness.

Contrary to the opinions of most commentators, man's natural propensity toward appropriation does not resolve for Locke to a mere pursuit of survival; on the contrary, at least the mature form of ownership fulfills a moral function *par excellence*, since the essence of appropriation consists in the process of the "humanization" of nature that constitutes the foundation of man's autonomy. But, like all mature forms of moral ideals in Locke, the ethics of appropriation does not arise like a *deus ex machina*; it is shaped in the process of moral development. We have noted already that in the early stages of this development it is normal for a man to identify his happiness with the satisfaction of relatively "unreflected" inclinations. Even at this stage, some form of appropriation is necessary, for the satisfaction of the most basic needs of survival requires some application of *labor* that, according to Locke, removes objects from the state of nature and places them at man's disposal. But at this early stage, appropriation is essentially tied to the immediate purpose of *consumption* and, thus, merely serves the purpose of making nature "usable" for the fulfillment of basic needs. How is this function then transformed into the more general attitude underlying the concept of autonomy?

It is worth noting that at this crucial step in his argument Locke, once again, draws on an insight of Hobbes's. I have explained that human desires, according to Locke, are not uninformed by the operations of the understanding. In the preceding pages, I have for the most part stressed how Locke's development of this theme distinguishes his theory from that of Hobbes, but I also indicated that Hobbes was not entirely unaware of it, for he had connected with it his claim that human desire is transformed into a general desire for power as a result of the translation of the "Trayne of Thoughts" into a "Trayne of Words."[124] In this respect, Locke follows Hobbes in claiming that the insertion of rational considerations, insofar as it involves the capacity for *abstraction*, distinguishes human action from the merely instinctual or reflexive responses that an animal inherits or develops for the preservation of its life.[125] Locke agrees further with Hobbes that one of the main consequences of the human capacity for abstraction is the fact that a man is capable of reacting to dangers that are merely possible as if they were actual.[126] Because he has the ability to form a general conception of the

[124]See above, section 4. Also Chap. I, section 4.
[125]II, 11, 10.
[126]For a fuller development of this idea in Hobbes, see above, Chap. I, 4.2.

external world and its laws (thus allowing for science and prediction) and to distinguish it from the internal world of his own, a man is capable of realizing (is, indeed, bound to realize) that his dependence on the natural environment is fraught with dangers that are neither immediate nor concrete. Unlike Hobbes and Rousseau, Locke does not stress the threatening aspect of nature overmuch, for he believes that a remedy for it is always at hand, but it is clear that he holds the alien character of nature responsible for the initial precariousness of the human condition. The uncontrolled influence of the external world on man's behavior results, according to Locke, in an unceasing pressure of "uneasinesses" and the general feeling of insecurity that move a man to strive for ever new powers and satisfactions. A man is of course capable of realizing that he is in this situation, and it is one of the basic aspects of his moral development that he comes to see as one of the requirements of his happiness that he must attempt to eliminate the independent natural environment's control over his own volition and to replace the haphazard and *ad hoc* pattern of his responses to external stimulation with a more orderly system of rational behavior, designed to assure him of mastery over what appears to him the contingent external circumstances of his own life.[127]

This means that man, insofar as he is capable of rational action, must upgrade the role of appropriation in the order of his practical priorities, from an activity that serves the purposes of consumption to a more general attitude directed toward achieving mastery over the natural world.[128] Unlike an animal, man does not simply reach into nature for the requirements of his subsistence and survival. His awareness of the alien character of nature requires not only an interposition of appropriation between his need and its satisfaction, but also a generalization of the process of appropriation into an independent attitude characteristic of the specifically human relation to nature—an attitude without which a man is incapable of true happiness and civilized existence. When this attitude develops and man makes the alien environment *his*

[127]It is, of course, a very interesting question why Locke thinks that he can avoid the Hobbesian conclusion that man's insecurity in the face of the indifference of the natural environment of his action must spill over into a deadly conflict among men fighting over scarce resources. Part of the answer lies undoubtedly in the already discussed fact that human beings are, according to Locke, much more capable than Hobbes had supposed of restraining their immediate responses in favor of long-term planning. But another important part of the answer lies in Locke's argument concerning the nature of *scarcity*, which will be discussed in the next chapter. And, finally, Locke's state also functions to prevent conflicts among men, although its role is much more limited than that of the Hobbesian Leviathan.

[128]Once again, note Locke's adherence to the characteristically modern idea, introduced by Hobbes, of the self-realization of man in his conquest of the natural world.

174

own, the *indifference* of nature with respect to man's need is overcome. To the extent that the world is appropriated, it is also "spiritualized" and represents the embodiment of human freedom. As such, it is no longer an alien force, but the extension of human *power*. To put it briefly, appropriation ultimately "tames" the world, makes it "available," and puts it at man's disposal. This, in turn, makes man doubly free: first, an overly cautious attitude toward nature is no longer called for, so that one's order of priorities may allow for a diversity of the "higher" pursuits that characterize civilized societies; and, second, the remaining portion of man's dependence is transformed into a form of self-sufficiency or autonomy proper. Both these aspects of human freedom confer a preeminently moral significance on the activity of appropriation. For if the nature of appropriation reveals itself in the achievement of autonomy in the sense just indicated, then in its highest form appropriation aims not at consumption, but rather at the creation of a *permanent, subsisting* humanized environment, geared toward the achievement of self-sufficiency, and not the satisfaction of some *particular* need or interest. What we see here again is the Lockean "dialectic" of reason and desire. Although appropriation is an attitude that develops in the context of human needs, in the ultimate outcome it does not "follow" a need, but rather *anticipates* it, and most often eliminates it, by restricting the scope of possible deprivations. Although Locke starts from the Hobbesian concern with self-preservation and survival, his account of the evolution of appropriation frees it from its link to consumption and makes it into a higher principle that in fact integrates consumption into a broader context of the "ethics of production" that constitutes the basis of the Locke's own practical philosophy. In this process, "self-preservation" loses the morally indifferent status it had in Hobbes—that of a purely descriptive category referring to the mere struggle for survival—and acquires some of the Aristotelian overtones of an effort to achieve moral perfection. Self-sufficiency and autonomy come to define the content of self-preservation so understood.

Parallel to Locke's "dialectical" account of the interdependence between reason and inclination is, we find, yet another "dialectical" aspect of his moral theory: the relation between man and his environment which underlies Locke's account of moral responsibility. We have seen that in view of the mind's being originally a *tabula rasa*, the external world constitutes the first source of all man's ideas and provides the initial impetus for all his mental activities. This, in turn, determines the fact that the initial stages of man's moral development are characterized by his crucial dependence on the natural environment, and this heteronomy precludes a satisfactory reconstruction of

175

the full concept of moral responsibility. But in the process of his development, a process that is governed by the operation of *natural* laws, man's rationality imposes on him an ideal of self-sufficiency as an integral component of his life plan. By then acting in accordance with this life plan, man embodies his own freedom in the alien world of nature and transforms his dependence into autonomy. Although the potential for moral freedom is presumably inherent in every subject, the dignity that derives from it comes only as a *result* of a developmental process in which the relation of man to nature is turned inside out and reversed.[129]

The conception of responsibility that finally emerges from my account of Locke's theory does not, of course, rely on any simple ability of an agent "to have done otherwise." Rather, like the later theories of autonomy, Locke's belief that a man can justly be held responsible for his actions rests essentially on the possibility of identifying the person responsible as a true *agent*, i.e., someone who, according to his own light and the sense of right and wrong, causes his own actions, without undue external influence. The agent is, of course, determined to act the way he does, for otherwise his action would have to be arbitrary. But the source of the determination of his will is ultimately internal to him and subject to rational scrutiny. It is thus the conjunction of man's rationality with the at first rather bizarre conception of freedom as a power of initiating motions that have no mechanical explanation (the power of contingency) that allows for Locke's theory of an indirectly *self-referential* determination of the agent's will and provides the explanation of the meaning of moral responsibility. In all this, the link of autonomy to the function of appropriation results in a system of substantive moral norms that constitute Locke's new "ethics of production." What this ethic involves in a more properly social context will be the subject of the next chapter.

---

[129]This fact that the dignity of man comes only as a *result* of the conjunction of rationality and appropriation may be responsible for Locke's striking attitude toward the poor in his *Proposals for Reforming the Poor Laws*, in H. R. Fox Bourne, *The Life of John Locke* (London, 1876), 2:378.

IV. Locke on Property

1. Problems of Interpretation

So much has been written on the relatively short Chapter v of the *Second Treatise of Government* that one could expect the main issues concerning Locke's conception of property (to which the chapter is devoted) to have been at least clarified, if not settled. But although very few readers would disagree that the chapter on property contains some crucial claims of Locke's social theory and represents one of the most important pieces of political writing in general, until quite recently relatively little enlightenment could be gained from perusing the thousands of pages for which it had provided an occasion. Then, a considerable amount of fresh air was brought into the rather stale atmosphere of Locke scholarship by a lively discussion centering around C. B. Macpherson's book *The Political Theory of Possessive Individualism*.[1] Macpherson's quite unorthodox view was that Locke wrote the chapter on property not in order to justify private ownership as such, but rather in order to justify a transition from a traditionally limited idea of property to a new capitalist conception of unrestrained acquisitiveness.[2] Mac-

---

[1] C. B. Macpherson, *The Political Theory of Possessive Individualism* (Oxford, 1962). A slightly different version of Macpherson's views on Locke's theory of property had been published as "Locke on Capitalist Appropriation" in *Western Political Quarterly*, 4 (1951), 550–66. For a critique of Macpherson, see P. Laslett, "Market Society and Political Theory," *Historical Journal*, 6 (1964), 150–54; and A. Ryan, "Locke and the Dictatorship of the Bourgeoisie," in C. B. Martin and D. Armstrong, eds., *Locke and Berkeley* (London, 1968). Extensive polemics with Macpherson may also be found in J. Dunn, *The Political Thought of John Locke* (Cambridge, 1969), and J. Tully, *A Discourse on Property: John Locke and His Adversaries* (Cambridge, 1980).

[2] Macpherson, *Political Theory*, 194–262. A similar argument is made by L. Strauss in his *Natural Right and History* (Chicago, 1953), 238–49.

pherson's analyses (some of which will be discussed and criticized below) focus on the nature of the limitations imposed by Locke's theory on the extent of man's right to appropriate, and the thrust of his argument is that whatever these limitations are, Locke progressively abandons them as his account of appropriation develops. The Locke that emerges from the pages of Macpherson's book is no longer a moderate, if not a timid, critic of Filmer, Grotius, and other proponents of the religious or social legitimization of ownership, but an aggressive exponent of the developed form of capitalist appropriation. The theory he proposes is not just a defense of private property but an ideology of the capitalist system, together with its moral and political implications.

In part, perhaps, as a result of the Macphersonian attack, the more traditional reading of Locke's theory of property has received a new shot in the arm in the form of a thoroughly scholarly study by James Tully.[3] Tully's book derives its inspiration from the approach, advocated by John Dunn,[4] that views as anachronistic all attempts to see Locke as an ancestor of specifically modern political positions such as capitalism or socialism. Instead, Tully proposes to "recover" the original meaning of Locke's conception of property by placing it rigorously in its historical context. Against the background of the natural-law theories of Aquinas, Suarez, Grotius, and Pufendorf and in the context of Locke's own views on natural law, as Tully sees them, he argues that Locke did not intend to explain the origins of private property, but rather wanted to show that, contrary to the claims of Filmer, the "particularization of the natural common is possible,"[5] i.e., that the original gift of the earth to mankind in common[6] did not preclude creation of more special, private property rights. These derive, according to Tully, from a divinely ordained duty "to make use of the world to achieve God's purpose of preserving all his workmanship"[7] and, contrary to the claims of Macpherson, are always restrained by "the Christian duty of liberality or charity."[8]

Despite many very interesting historical analyses, Tully's Locke (as well as that of Dunn) emerges as a rather uninspiring figure who not only cannot tell us anything about our own political problems,[9] but also whose continuous influence on later liberal theory is a puzzling phenomenon. Deeply wedded to the theological perspective of his contem-

[3]See note 1, above.
[4]See note 1, above.
[5]Tully, *Discourse on Property*, 100. See also J. W. Yolton, *Locke and the Compass of Human Understanding* (Cambridge, 1970), 187.
[6]*Second Treatise*, §25. Paragraph numbers appear hereafter in the text.
[7]Tully, *Discourse on Property*, 175.
[8]Ibid., 176.
[9]See Dunn, *Political Thought of John Locke*, x.

poraries, pursuing his argument against the long-since-ignored Filmer, Tully's Locke is a figure thoroughly overrated by the posterity that has credited him with having inspired liberals from Madison to Nozick. In this respect, the Macphersonian claim that Locke was an ideologue of capitalist appropriation, despite certain overtones of anachronism, has more to recommend it.

The problem with Macpherson's interpretation is not its insistence on unlimited appropriation, for I believe that Macpherson is clearly right in insisting on it, but rather his misconstrual of the meaning of this concept and of the role it plays in Locke's political theory. The primary source of Macpherson's misinterpretation of Locke's conception of property is his deemphasis of the labor theory of acquisition, a deemphasis that Macpherson considered necessary to establish his claim that Locke was a defender of unlimited appropriation. As I shall try to show, Macpherson has failed to explore the possibilities entailed by Locke's grounding of ownership in human labor because he concentrated on the prima facie meaning of this term, as it appears in the *Second Treatise*, and failed to relate it to Locke's theory of human action, presented in the *Essay*, from which it derives its proper significance. In this respect, Macpherson has in fact followed those previous interpreters whose lack of acumen he so justly criticized, and has viewed Locke's general justification of property (both limited and unlimited) as based on the assumption that appropriation is simply a means by which men provide the requirements of their subsistence.[10] There is an element of irony in this oversight, for with his presumably Marxist sympathies, Macpherson should have been singularly well positioned to observe those features of Locke's theory of labor which made it simultaneously the main predecessor and the most important competitor of the Marxist philosophical theory of production.[11]

Because of the persisting controversy concerning the very meaning of Locke's theory of appropriation, I shall begin my own discussion by going over the main features of his theory of property and present my own reading of Chapter v of the *Second Treatise*. In particular, I shall analyze the role played by labor in property acquisition and the function of appropriation as a process of the transformation of nature and the achievement of human autonomy (section 2). I shall then concen-

---

[10]Tully adheres to a similar position (*Discourse on Property*, 132). But given his insistence on the religious underpinnings of man's duty to preserve himself and others, the concept of self-preservation acquires for him the status of a moral norm, whereas Macpherson makes it into a linchpin of his critique of Locke's alleged abdication of man's responsibility toward his fellow men.

[11]A similarity between Locke's and Marx's conceptions of labor is observed by W. Euchner in his *Naturrecht und Politik bei John Locke* (Frankfurt-am-Main, 1969), 82.

trate on the social aspects of appropriation, and especially on Locke's solution to the Hobbesian problem of conflicts generated by human aggressiveness in the face of limited natural resources (section 3). I shall, finally, conclude my discussion of Locke with some remarks concerning the general significance of his theory of appropriation and autonomy (section 4).

2. The Labor Theory of Property

Locke's statement in the *Second Treatise* (§124) that "the great and *chief end* . . . of Mens uniting into Commonwealths, and putting themselves under Government, *is the Preservation of their Property*" indicates not only a revolutionary theory of political government but also a new theory of property and its origins. It is quite clear that the word "Property," as Locke uses it, cannot always be understood to refer to the institution of ownership, since he often uses it in a more general sense, roughly corresponding to our term "right."[12] Nevertheless, property in its narrower sense plays a crucial role in Locke's view of the human condition, for as I have tried to show, appropriation is the fundamental activity which permits man to overcome his estrangement from the natural environment and to achieve his autonomy. In this way, all human rights—"property" in its broader sense—are tied to man's ability to transform nature into an objective correlate of his own freedom.

Locke's inversion of the normal relation between property and the state, i.e., his assertion that property, far from being an originally social institution, in fact precedes all political compact and serves as its foundation, means that property, according to him, originates in a natural, prepolitical relation between man and his environment. Moreover, if my account of the role played by appropriation in the life of the Lockean man is correct, then the theory of property Locke must provide has to stress the strong sense in which human action penetrates the natural environment and effects a significant change in the natural world. Property must appear not as a result of a conventional division of the resources available in advance for the satisfaction of human needs but as an effect of genuine human spontaneity which transforms preexisting natural reality. Only then will it be possible to see it as a foundation of human autonomy.

---

[12]In §123 Locke says that it is "Lives, Liberties and Estates, which I call by the general Name, *Property*." For contemporary usage, see Laslett's "Introduction" to the *Two Treatises* (New York, 1965), 115–16.

It is thus a species of an "ontology of property" that the Lockean system requires, an ontology in which the effects of human action cannot be reduced to a mere provision of the necessities of life but must be viewed in the light of the moral function fulfilled by the creation of a permanent humanized world. It will be argued here that Locke's labor theory of property provides precisely such an "ontological" theory of human activity. But Locke himself begins his discussion of property not with the labor theory, but with the idea that God had granted the earth to mankind in common, thus raising the possibility that the labor theory plays only a secondary role in his overall account of appropriation. This view has been recently reinforced by an interesting argument of James Tully, for whom the divine grant fixes the paramount function of property in Locke as the means by which men can provide for their own preservation and "fulfill their duty of protecting God's workmanship."[13] We may do well, therefore, to begin our own inquiry by looking into the Lockean meaning of the idea that God "has given the Earth to mankind in common."

2.1. Ownership in Common: Property and Dominion

Locke opens Chapter v of the *Second Treatise* with the statement:

Whether we consider natural *Reason*, which tells us, that Men, being once born, have a right to their Preservation . . . : Or *Revelation*, which gives us an account of those Grants God made of the World to Adam, 'tis very clear, that God . . . *has given Earth to the Children of Men*, given it to Mankind in common. . . . But I shall endeavour to shew, how Men might come to have a property in several parts of that which God gave to Mankind in common, and that without an express Compact of all the Commoners. [§25]

Before Tully wrote, the standard reading of this passage was that Locke, in opposing Filmer's view of the divine right of kings (who were supposed to have inherited the earth from Adam, to whom God had given it, via Noah and his son Japheth from whom in turn the Gentile rulers were supposed to descend),[14] based his own interpretation of the meaning of the original grant of the earth to mankind in common on Pufendorf's distinction between "positive" and "negative community."[15] Positively common ownership, which would involve a genuine,

---

[13]Tully, *Discourse on Property*, passim.

[14]R. Filmer, *Patriarcha*, chaps. iii–iv.

[15]Pufendorf, *De jure naturae et gentium* (Oxford, 1934), 363. For previous interpretations, see C. J. Czajkowski, *The Theory of Private Property in John Locke's Political Philosophy* (Notre Dame, 1941), 79–80, and R. Schlatter, *Private Property: The History of an Idea* (New Brunswick, N.J., 1951), 153.

full-fledged right of each man to the fruits of the earth, would make *private* property impossible without the consent of all mankind, according to Pufendorf, since if things are already owned, they cannot be appropriated by anyone else. When things are negatively common, on the other hand, they "are said to be *Nobody's*, . . . *i.e.*, they are not yet assigned to any particular Person . . . [t]hey are . . . free for any Taker." Locke was then thought to take over from Pufendorf the idea that prior to their appropriation things had been common to all men in the negative sense, i.e., available to all but not within anyone's property right. Unlike Pufendorf, however, for whom the transition from the original negative community to exclusive private property involved a series of necessary social agreements, Locke was believed to have provided his labor theory of property to explain how the transition could be effected "without any express Compact of all the Commoners."

Tully attacked this interpretation with an elaborate argument that Locke's theory was constructed in opposition to Pufendorf as much as to Filmer. Locke, according to Tully, opposes not only Pufendorf's requirement of a compact establishing private property but also his rejection of the idea that man's original right was that of positively common ownership.[16] Tully's Locke in fact accepts from the beginning the idea (derived from Aquinas and Suarez) that the divine grant had

[16]Apart from some deductions from the *First Treatise*, Tully bases his argument (*Discourse on Property*, 96) that Locke rejects the notion of negative community on Locke's statement (in §25) that "it seems to some a very great difficulty, how any one should ever come to have a *Property* in any thing" if God gave the earth to mankind in common and that he (Locke) would not rest content with the answer that if the original grant to mankind in common poses this difficulty then its alternative, namely, Filmer's Adamite theory, is even more unacceptable. Tully takes this to be a reference to Pufendorf, who simply assumes that Filmer's theory is unacceptable and, in view of the difficulty involved in the concept of positive community, proceeds to assume that the original divine grant had the meaning of negative community. This, according to Tully, means that Locke is prepared to start from the concept of positive community and, *pace* Pufendorf, derive from it the institution of private property "without any express Compact of all the Commoners." But this is a very improbable reading. First, it must be noted that it was *Filmer* who had first argued that the divine grant to mankind in common cannot be made into private property without universal consent (*Observations upon H. Grotius De jure belli et pacis* in Filmer, *Patriarcha and Other Political Writings* [Oxford, 1949], 273). Second, it was *Pufendorf's* derivation of private property from the original (negative) community that involved (as Tully himself points out on p. 88) a series of social agreements. Thus, the "some" who find a great difficulty in deriving property from the original grant probably refers to Filmer rather than Pufendorf. And Locke does indeed say that Pufendorf's answer to Filmer is insufficient—not, however, because Pufendorf rejects the concept of positive community, but because he does not respond to Filmer's objection concerning the impossibility of deriving property from the commons without the improbable series of agreements, and simply says that that difficulty is preferable to the consequences of the Adamite theory. Locke, in contrast, will provide his labor theory as an answer to Filmer's objection. As to whether Locke's own derivation of private property starts from the concept of positive or negative community the passage in question is simply silent.

created a form of common property for all men, on the basis of a right which each man has to his subsistence, and that the labor theory, far from being designed to explain "the origin of property"[17] or to give a "justification of private property," was supposed to work out the "problem of the natural distribution of common property,"[18] i.e., "to show that particularization of the natural common is possible."[19] The only problem for Chapter v of the *Second Treatise*, according to Tully, is to explain this transition from an inclusive right *to* deriving subsistence from the common to an exclusive right *in* particular things.[20] But even this demonstration is only provisional, for the natural right of exclusive property disintegrates as a result of the introduction of money and is replaced by conventional property established in society.[21]

There is not much point in battling over whether or not Locke actually took over from Pufendorf the idea of negative community. It might be noted instead that, so far as I was able to establish, nowhere in the *Second Treatise* (and nowhere unambiguously in the *First Treatise*) does Locke use the word "property" with respect to man's original title, derived from God's granting man the use of the earth and its products.[22] If he uses another locution, it is that of "dominion."[23] Now, though this term has many meanings and had often been used interchangeably with the word "property,"[24] Locke most often makes a distinction

[17]Tully, *Discourse on Property*, 96.

[18]Ibid., 4.

[19]Ibid., 100. See also Yolton, *Locke and the Compass of Human Understanding*, 187.

[20]Tully, *Discourse on Property*, 67.

[21]I shall deal with this last problem in my discussion of the role of money and of the sufficiency limitation. See below, section 3.

[22]The following passages may be checked: *First Treatise*, §§24, 29, 32, 36; *Second Treatise*, each paragraph of Chap. v (§§25–51). Neither is the word "property" used anywhere outside of Chap. iv of the *First Treatise* and Chap. v of the *Second Treatise* to refer to the original grant. The only potentially controversial places I was able to find are in §23 and §§38–39 of the *First Treatise*. In §23 (which Tully cites on p. 60) Locke seems to be saying that even if we *supposed* that God granted "property" to Adam, it would not follow that he gave Adam the monarchical right to rule over people, but he does not seem to *agree* to the premise. In §§38–39, Locke disputes Filmer's claim that the right of Noah and his sons jointly (deriving from Gen. 9:1–3) was less than that of Adam (deriving from Gen 1:26 and 28) and in the course of this says that their right was "Property." Again, however, the tenor of the statement seems more hypothetical than categorical: Locke says that "had it been his own *Case*, Sir *Robert* I believe, would have thought here was an *Alteration*, nay, an enlarging of *Property*" from Adam to Noah. But if Locke does not believe that Adam had had property in the earth by virtue of God's grant, then he does not have to adhere to the view of Noah's property either. (It is nevertheless an unusual place, in which Locke seems to identify property with a right to *use*. As we shall see, this is *not* his view in the *Second Treatise*.)

[23]See, for example, *First Treatise*, §§26–29. The term is used in the Bible, Gen. 1:26 and 28.

[24]Cf. Pufendorf's statement in *De jure naturae et gentium*, 363: "Sunt enim dominium et proprietas nobis unum et idem." Even Pufendorf, however, in various contexts uses the word "proprietas" only with respect to individual ownership.

between the two terms, as when he explains "the difference between *having Dominion*, which a Shepard may have, and having full Property as an Owner."[25] In its original Roman-law context, the term "dominion" denoted complete and exclusive control, and this meaning has reasserted itself in modern civil law. But for Locke the term is primarily associated with the feudal forms of property relationships: it is a vague term referring to all kinds of authority—political, ecclesiastical, familial, or property-related.[26] What it reflects, for Locke, is above all the medieval view that property ownership is of the same class as political and ecclesiastical authority and that property rights, far from being absolute and unconditional, are, like an "office," tied to all kinds of obligations with respect to the social order that confers them. Despite Tully's learned argument, it seems much more plausible that Locke's own naturalistic and anticonventionalist account of private property was consciously designed in opposition to, rather than in support of, the remains of the medieval theory of dominion. Its historical significance lies precisely in reversing the traditional order of dependence between a social system and the rights of ownership, and in thus founding the capitalist political doctrine that sets clear limits to the extent of communal interference with private economic initiative.

The meaning of the original "dominion" that men had in common over the earth as a result of God's grant Locke explains as a "Liberty of using" the fruits of the earth "to the best advantage of Life, and convenience."[27] This "Liberty" is certainly a "right" related to the general right of self-preservation.[28] What is the nature of this right?

It may be best to begin by pointing to what the right to self-preservation is not. First, then, it is clearly not the Hobbesian right to everything that a man may grab for his use, without any concern for what others may need. Tully is quite correct in pointing our attention to the fact that the divine grant assures everyone the ability to derive subsistence from the natural plenty and demands that everyone be *included* in the use of the common. This argument is present not only in the *First Treatise*; it reappears in the *Second* in the form of the "sufficiency limitation," which allows men to appropriate only so long as "there is enough, and as good left in common for others" (§27). But neither does the right to self-preservation amount to the establishment of a genuine *proprietary* relationship between man and nature. There are two reasons why this

[25]*First Treatise*, §39. He often identifies "property" with "*private* dominion."

[26]For various connotations of "dominion" see Czajkowski, *Theory of Private Property*, 53–72. Cf. also Schlatter, *Private Property*, 75–76, which provides a useful account of the history of "property" and "dominion."

[27]*First Treatise*, §39; *Second Treatise*, §26.

[28]*First Treatise*, §41.

cannot be. First, the idea of a truly common positive right is straightforwardly inconsistent with Locke's nominalism.[29] One does not have to believe in a very close link between Locke's philosophical views expressed in the *Essay* and his political theory in order to accept the contention that his nominalism is a pervasive feature of his whole system. And here, unlike most continental thinkers who considered the dominion theory, Locke faces the additional difficulty of reconciling his individualistic account of human nature with the existence of truly collective ownership. Second, if Locke wants to account for the strong sense traditionally conveyed by the word "property" (even if one were to conceive it as entailing less than an *absolute* mastery over the object), the right of *use* is clearly insufficient. The concept of common ownership expressed by God's grant of the earth to *all* men involves not only no exclusivity whatever but also no alienability. The transition from natural dominion to private property cannot, therefore, amount to a simple "distribution" of the right to use, but entails a more significant change from a mere right to use to a right to *control*. The distinction between the right to use and property is like the distinction between the right to continue staying alive and the right to decide how one wants to live.[30]

In positive terms, the right to self-preservation granted to man by God in the form of the original dominion over the earth and its products is best understood in terms of the basic *adequacy* of nature for the satisfaction of human needs. Despite the freedom which makes man capable of changing the natural course of events, the extent of human creativity is quite limited for Locke. The raw material man needs for his survival must come to him from outside, and this constitutes an ineliminable element of his dependence on the natural world. What God's grant ensures is, first of all, that the fruits of nature are essentially homogeneous with human nature and *nourish* man rather than leaving him entirely dependent on his own ability to sustain himself. Second, and equally important, the fruits of the earth are provided *richly* (§31), in

[29]Strictly speaking, Locke's position on universals is, to use medieval terminology, "conceptualist" rather than nominalist, since he thinks of concepts as existing in the mind. Nevertheless, only particulars exist for him in the objective world. I shall disregard this difference in my discussions.

[30]This argument is, of course, not conclusive against someone like Tully who claims that man's control over nature is always extremely superficial, since property is, for him, never more than a trust that God gives to man for his (God's) own benefit. My argument here is only that such a view of property does not account for some of the basic features of ownership clearly present in the world of legal relationships at the time of Locke's writing. (In the spirit of fairness, one must also point once again to §39 of the *First Treatise*, in which Locke does seem to identify property with the right to use.) A fuller refutation of Tully's position can come only with a more complete exposition of my alternative reading of Chapter v of the *Second Treatise*.

an abundance that makes possible ultimately unlimited individual appropriation, without exhausting the stock of goods and preventing others from appropriating as well.[31] Each man is thus assured of the possibility of survival which in another, less generously constituted world he would not have.

Whether this theory of the divine grant is or is not directly taken over from Pufendorf's notion of "negative community" is not particularly important. What is central, however, is that the content of the original "dominion" that man has over the world is very different from positive ownership and control, and refers instead to the mere availability, both qualitative and quantitative, of nature for the satisfaction of human needs. If there is more to it, I was unable, despite Tully's argument, to discover what it is.

2.2. Labor and Appropriation

The labor theory of property, with which Locke's name is indelibly associated,[32] is introduced in a straightforward fashion in the *Second Treatise*. "Whatsoever [a man] removes out of the State that Nature hath provided, and left it in, he hath mixed his Labour with, and joyned to it something that is his own." The natural object "hath by this *labour* something annexed to it, that excludes the common right of other Men" (§27). As a result, the object becomes "a part of him" (§26) and his "Property."

What is this "something of his own" that a man "annexes" to the object of nature to make it "a part of him"? Locke's conception of labor as the activity by which man transforms nature requires that labor fulfill two quite distinct functions. In one sense, labor is, according to Locke, an activity by which men (and other creatures) provide for the sustenance of their life. As such, labor must be understood as a physical effort and is given a physiological function. But if labor were to be conceived solely as a physical force, it could not account for the fact that uniquely man is capable of appropriation. The reason animals, and perhaps even machines, do not acquire property in those things upon which they exercise some physical influence is that human labor also has another function, namely, it is an activity by which men create the specifically *human* environment of their lives.[33] As such labor is understood as an

---

[31]This crucial argument will be discussed below, section 3.2.

[32]Despite Locke's clearly original contribution to this theory, P. Larkin, in his *Property in the Eighteenth Century with Special Reference to England and Locke* (Dublin, 1930), 80, points out that "Paulus, the Roman jurist, and John of Paris, had held that justification of private property was to be found in labour."

[33]In this sense, one could talk, in Locke, about something akin to H. Arendt's distinction between "labor" and "work." See Arendt, *The Human Condition* (Chicago, 1958), 79–81. J. P.

essentially "spiritual" operation by which men infuse things with value (§§40, 42) and impart to them something that material objects do not possess by themselves (§43). It is only in this second sense that labor gives man a title to ownership and constitutes the source of appropriation.

Realization of the distinctness of these two functions should help us avoid the mistake, common to most interpreters of Locke, of making the appropriative function of labor a derivative of the more general function of self-preservation. No one would deny, I presume, that Locke makes labor into the cornerstone of his conception of private property because labor is *productive*. The appropriative function of labor is thus its *economic* function. But it is a mistake to take an anachronistic view of economics and then interpret Locke's concept of production in its light. In modern economic theory, private property is often seen as a social arrangement that eliminates the externalities associated with the institution of the common and creates a situation in which an individual has undistorted incentives to use the resources within his control in the most efficient way. Given well-functioning markets, private property contributes in this fashion to the socially most efficient allocation of resources and their best productive use.[34] Throughout this account, production is always seen as ultimately geared to the satisfaction of the consumptive preferences of social actors, and if private property is the most efficient way of achieving this result, it is easy to conclude that its justification is that it, better than the commons, provides not only for the means of subsistence but also for human "comfort and support."

This, however, was not, and could not be, Locke's view. In a very emphatic sense, property is not a social arrangement for Locke. It is true, of course, that the modern economic theory of property rights does not have to base its explanation of the origins of property on any explicit social agreement, since it can resort to Adam Smith's ingenious "invisible hand" account. But still, even this account makes sense only as referring to a more or less spontaneous *social* division of roles, while Locke's account seems to imply a *natural* right to appropriation which exists regardless of any social arrangements. Even if only one man existed in the world, his "mixing his labour" with a natural object would make the object "a part of him." In other words, while Locke clearly

---

Day, "Locke on Property," *Philosophical Quarterly*, 16 (1956) distinguishes, in fact, *five* different meanings of "labor" in Locke.

[34]For the problem of the commons, see G. Hardin, "The Tragedy of the Commons," *Science*, no. 162 (1968), 1243–48. For an economic theory of property, see H. Demsetz, "Toward a Theory of Property Rights," *American Economic Review*. (Papers and Proceedings), no. 57 (79) (1967), 347–59; and R. Posner, *Economic Analysis of Law* (2d ed.; Boston, 1977), 27–64.

believes that labor gives title to property because it is productive, the concept of production he had in mind is quite different from the idea that by now seems natural to our economists.

The main difference between Locke's and our view of production comes to the fore when one considers his *mercantilist* economic outlook.[35] One of the most characteristic features of this outlook was a radical separation of the problems of production from those of distribution and consumption. The mercantilists' preoccupation with accumulation, which is often viewed as a form of gold-fetishism, was essentially a result of their paramount concern with production as basically the only self-sustaining process in which new *value* is created as a result of human activity. Consumption, on the other hand, they viewed as competing with the properly economic (value-creating) interests of production and as something which, because of its harmful effect on capital accumulation, had to be limited by a system of duties and tariffs.[36]

It is for this economic theory that Locke provides a philosophical foundation. One should not be surprised, therefore, that in justifying property as a result of productive labor he did not have in mind a concept of production primarily tied to the function of assuring man's subsistence and self-preservation.[37] Appropriation originates, of course, in man's desire to provide for his subsistence, but the "use value" of property is quickly transcended in the value of another kind. Consequently, property, according to Locke, is not founded in a physiological union between a man and a natural object, such as a model of consumption would suggest. The fact that property, as a product of

[35]A great merit of Macpherson was to connect Locke's theory of property with his economic writings and to show that Locke, as a mercantilist, had seen property—like money—not as something merely useful or (in the case of money) as a means of exchange. (*Political Theory*, 205, 207). It is particularly unfortunate, therefore, that Macpherson continues to claim that Locke's justification of unlimited appropriation abandons the labor theory in favor of the utilitarian defense based on the argument that unlimited appropriation better assures the subsistence of the greatest number of people.

[36]See E. Lipson, *The Economic History of England* (London, 1929–31), 3:62–116 (esp. 62–67 and 88–99). It is also to be noted that until quite recently, *value* was viewed by economists not as "use value" but rather as an *inherent* quality of the object. See in this connection C. Gide and C. Rist, *A History of Economic Doctrines* (2d ed., London, 1948), 91–93.

[37]In fact, I find no passage in either of the *Two Treatises* in which Locke unambiguously ties *any* form of appropriation to self-preservation (in doing so he would have to explain, for example, why animals are not capable of property ownership). On the contrary, both in §25 of the *Second Treatise* (which Macpherson, *Political Theory*, 200, cites as his reference) and in §86 of the *First Treatise*, Locke says that God gave to man the means of self-preservation in the form of nature itself, and he seems to oppose appropriation to this direct "grant" as something tied not to man's generic requirements but to factors connected with his *individuality*. For a link between self-preservation and appropriation, see also Strauss, *Natural Right and History*, 243–45.

labor, becomes a "part" of man does not mean, as Macpherson suggests, that appropriation has the "original sense of ingest,"[38] unless one confuses consumption with production and obliterates the distinction between labor as a physical force and as an economic operation, imposing value on natural objects. Similarly, Locke's idea of property is not to be explained in terms of a merely functionalist account, analogous to that which may be given of the relation obtaining between a tool and the man who uses it. A hammer is not "mine" in the sense of being a prolongation of my hand when I use it to drive some nails in; if I own it, then it remains mine (at least so long as it does not rust or otherwise "spoil") even if I leave it in my yard and, say, go to Australia. In other words, in accordance with the usual understanding of property as control, Locke's labor theory of property accounts for much more than a merely undisturbed use and looks to the permanent effect that the application of labor has on the objects of nature.

As was to be expected, Locke's justification of the independent significance of production is tied to his theory of autonomy. The "something of his own" that a man "annexes" to the object of nature by applying his labor to it is nothing less than his own *freedom*, his very *practical self* and *personhood*. In other words, labor appropriates nature and makes it a "part" of man because it "spiritualizes" the objects and makes them into an objective extension of the human person: it embodies man's own subjectivity, so that if my property is taken away from me without my consent, I am deprived of my very freedom (or of its objective embodiment, necessary for the purpose of my autonomy).

A proper understanding of this process is possible only when one connects Locke's conception of labor with his theory of human action in the *Essay*. Productive labor, unlike mechanically arising physical force, is an *action* in the literal sense of the word, because it involves the "active power" of the agent who *initiates* his bodily motion and through it introduces something genuinely *new* into the preexisting state of the environment. This "something new," being an embodiment and expression of human freedom, constitutes a break in the usual mechanical course of natural events and establishes man's title to ownership. Appropriation differs from mere use and consumption as knowledge

---

[38]Macpherson, *Political Theory*, 213. Macpherson refers here to §26 of the *Second Treatise*. There, however, Locke specifically says that the fruit an Indian picks must be "his, *i.e.*, a part of him ... *before* it can do him any good for the support of his Life" (emphasis added). He explains his meaning a few lines later (§28): "He that is nourished by the Acorns pickt up under an Oak ... has certainly appropriated them to himself. ... I ask then, When did they begin to be his? When he digested? Or when he eat? Or when he boiled? Or when he brought them home? Or when he pickt them up? And 'tis plain, if the first gathering made them not his, nothing else could."

differs from instincts: both are higher functions in terms of which humanity is defined. In becoming a man's property, natural objects, "almost worthless Materials, as in themselves" (§43), can be said to possess *value* because they are infused with man's freedom; "value" is an ontological category pertaining to the meaningful and the mental rather than to the mechanical and the material. In infusing things with value and making them his, man fulfills his God-given vocation;[39] his rights and liberties serve the realization of his autonomy, which he achieves by transforming the natural environment into a reflection of his own humanity.

2.3. The Abstractness of Ownership

But what is the connection—it could well be asked at this point— between the mere introduction of an element of contingency into man's natural environment and the general "availability" of nature for the purposes of man that appropriation was supposed to effect? Why should a simple infusion of contingency meaningfully affect the indifference of nature to the ends of human action? How can this contingency influence the suitability of nature for meeting human requirements?

On one level, these questions are rather easy to answer, as long as one remembers the *moral* significance of appropriation. Naturally, if one follows Hegel or Marx in viewing the effects of labor as bridging the gap between the essentially heterogeneous worlds of human need and inanimate nature, then Locke's analysis of appropriation does not adequately capture this aspect of man's relation to nature. But as I have stressed already, Locke views appropriation as not primarily *use-related*. The alien character of nature, which makes appropriation necessary, has the significance of making man dependent on the environment which obeys its own laws and is, *in this sense*, "indifferent" to human striving for self-sufficiency. But insofar as human needs are concerned, the indifference of nature means only that there is some *uncertainty* with respect to their satisfaction, and not that raw nature is in some way essentially *inadequate* for meeting human requirements. Thus, the connection between labor and the system of human needs is somewhat looser in Locke than it is in Hegel or Marx, since Locke envisages an essential homogeneity between the functioning of the human organism and the natural environment. The latter's basic adequacy for the former is, as we have seen, what he expresses by saying

---

[39]See, e.g., §26. Cf. also H. Schmidt, *Seinserkenntnis und Staatsdenken* (Tübingen, 1965), 213: "Produktion is . . . die Bestimmung des Menschen."

that nature as such had already been provided by God for the satisfaction of human needs, *before* any process of appropriation took place.[40] Consequently, the fact that man interposes appropriation between his needs and consumption is not supposed to make the world itself better or worse suited for satisfying his needs, but rather, by providing him with his private enclave of self-dependence, is meant to remedy the alienation of his self-consciousness as a *free* individual being from the external world ruled by *necessary* and universal laws. But this is accomplished precisely through his ability to embody his own freedom in the natural world, into which he thus introduces his own element of contingency.

On another level, however, the questions with which we are now dealing do point to a fundamental difference between Locke's conception of labor and that of later thinkers who followed Hegel and Marx. Moreover, the sources of this difference, which constitutes the focal point of the controversies as to whether the character of ownership is private or social, and alienable or inalienable, go deeper than the realm of political philosophy: they have their roots in broader epistemological and ontological commitments.

The questions at hand clearly point to the abstractness of the agency embodied in property in the Lockean account. In one sense, appropriation does away with the abstractness of human agency, since the practical self becomes "real" or "materialized" through its embodiment in property. This process is, in a way, the reverse of the one in which the theoretical counterpart of the practical self, the *tabula rasa* of Locke's *Essay*, acquires concreteness by being, in turn, influenced (through experience) by its natural environment. But in another sense, in which "abstract" is opposed to "rich in content" or "fully developed," the practical self remains the counterpart of the epistemological *tabula rasa*, despite its transformation into a property owner. For it is the legalistic, ahistorical, and abstract self, rather than a concrete human individuality, with all its wealth of particular characteristics, talents, skills, education, inventiveness, and so on, that constitutes the subject of ownership. In other words, it is the modern, capitalist form of ownership that Locke defends in his theory, a form of ownership in which the *nature* of one's holdings has nothing to do with one's particular personality. Were I a completely different type of person or a product of a completely different culture and society than I in fact am, absolutely nothing would be different in my property (*qua* property) and the *same* personhood would inhere in it.

This view of property draws its philosophical support from the em-

40See section 2.1, above.

piricist and nominalistic background of Locke's conception of labor. In fact, a "richer" conception of labor, such as Hegel's or Marx's, would be incompatible with the theoretical presuppositions of Locke's political thought. Both Hegel and Marx, relying on the Kantian revolution in philosophy, believed that the world of ideas, representing the specifically mental realm of existence, had a constitutive function with respect to the so-called objective world. After Kant, no epistemic experience, not even *observation*, was seen as a passive process of reception. On the contrary, Kant viewed the mind as always active in that it imposed a form on the manifold of sensations. Even though the manifold was seen as coming from the shapeless world of things in themselves, the form belonged to the ideal, intellectual world of concepts. The form of a particular object was only an instance of a *universal*, which ordered the manifold, thus giving it life and understandability. Hence, nature, with all its wealth of determinations, was for a post-Kantian partially a human product. The employment of labor upon it was then seen by Hegel and Marx as a prolongation of this process; the humanization of nature through labor was seen not as giving it an ideal form (for this it already had as an object of man's cognitive activities), but as making this ideal form subject to human freedom, i.e., as shaping it not merely in accordance with the necessary conditions of experience but also in accordance with the dictates of human will and human needs.[41] In this sense, the work of a laborer (in the broadest meaning of the word, including artists, technicians, and engineers) was considered a true *creation*, at least insofar as the form of the product was concerned. Consequently, the concept of property arising against the background of such a theory of labor reveals a much more intimate link between the product and the producer than that Locke believed in. As a result, in the case of Hegel, some problems may arise in connection with the alienability of property, while in the case of Marx, property (at least under communism) is clearly neither private nor alienable.[42]

Things are very different for Locke, however. Locke's nominalism undercuts much of the ontological significance of a distinction between "natural kinds" and "artificial collections," and in particular between the "products of nature" and the "artifacts of human industry." We can, of course, trace the origin of each object either to some "natural events" or to the intervention of human freedom, since the latter cannot be accounted for in purely mechanical terms. But although we can give

---

[41]For Hegel, see *The Phenomenology of Mind* (New York, 1967), 238f. For Marx, see, for example, *The Economic and Philosophic Manuscripts of 1844*, ed. D. J. Struik (New York, 1964), 114.

[42]See A. Rapaczynski, "Locke's Conception of Property and the Principle of Sufficient Reason," *Journal of the History of Ideas*, 42 (1981), 305–15.

generic names to (and form abstract ideas of) human products (such as "a house") and oppose them to those of the objects of nature (such as "a tree"), such generic names constitute no real essences of things. Hence, every classification of objects into "natural" and "artificial" is (like all classifications) merely subjective and nominal, while insofar as reality itself is concerned, we have to deal with every individual object case by case, and all we can say about it is that one "real essence" (an arrangement of invisible particles) was changed into another. There is nothing generically "human" (or even "natural") about natural objects themselves, before as well as after labor is applied to them. In other words, our concepts (ideas), which could possibly constitute a "human element" in the results of man's labor, never *penetrate* into the world of nature. This, in turn, poses a serious difficulty insofar as an "ontology of property" is concerned, since apart from the discoverable effects of freedom, there is absolutely nothing in the objects themselves that could carry an "imprint" of human personality. And it is such an "ontology of property" that Locke is, I believe, trying to provide, for only in this way can he claim that property is itself "natural," i.e., does not result from any conventional agreement (as nominal essences do), and that taking someone else's property constitutes a violation of a *natural law*.[43]

But as well as Locke's nominalism, his empiricism also restricts the scope of the possible "productivity" of the human mind. Unlike Kant, who believed that the process of ratiocination necessarily presupposes a system of innate dispositions which guide the process of synthesis with the help of rules that cannot be derived from experience, Locke was a radical antinativist and believed that the basic components of all ideas were empirical. Even when an idea is a product of the mind's activity, the combination does not require any guiding principle that could not be traced to sensations. Therefore, if the mind's ideas were then embodied in the natural world through the process of production (i.e., a process in which the world is shaped according to a human plan), the only thing that the mind could "add" to what could arise without any human intervention is not any new determination but only a new *modality*, that is, a *contingent* arrangement of objective qualities that

---

[43]This requirement of an "ontology of property" has an interesting consequence with respect to the concept of *tabula rasa*. As presented in the *Essay*, "*tabula rasa*" seems to be conceived as purely epistemological category, devoid of any ontological significance. Since, however, the practical self is, of course, simply another aspect of the theoretical self (and not a different subject altogether), the ontological significance of the subject of ownership transforms the *tabula rasa* into a *real* subject as well, so that it can no longer be viewed as a mere explanatory device. This could be used as an indication that the widespread view that Locke is concerned in the *Essay* with only epistemological problems may not be as accurate as it appears.

would eliminate the *necessary* status of all mechanically produced states of affairs.

The empiricist and nominalistic background of Locke's philosophy thus influences his analysis of the nature of human productivity and results in a theory of labor that fits with his defense of the individualistic, abstract theory of private property. Unlike Hegel and Marx, Locke does not view labor as through and through creative—the limitations of human productivity require that the adequacy of nature for the satisfaction of human needs be externally guaranteed. Far from raising man to a semi-divine status, as Hegel and Marx were to do, Locke's defense of human dignity presupposed a divine grant of the earth to mankind. And since human freedom is limited to the "power of contingency," the creative aspect of human labor resolves to the *initiative* that it expresses—something which corresponds to the economic function of *capital*, rather than to the concrete physical toil of the worker. Finally, since the "power of contingency" only numerically (and not qualitatively) differentiates among individuals, property created by human labor is essentially *fungible*: it is the abstract form of capitalist ownership.

2.4. Hired Services and the Labor Limitation

The relation between the appropriative character of labor and the initiative expressive of human freedom helps to explain how Locke views the use of hired workers by one who is engaged in the process of appropriation.

In making his claim that Locke wrote Chapter v of the *Second Treatise* not to justify property as such, but rather in order to justify the unlimited, capitalist form of appropriation, C. B. Macpherson has argued that one of Locke's assumptions in the chapter on property was that, contrary to what may be one's first impression, the labor theory of property does not imply the proviso that only the employment of his *own* hands and body allows a man to appropriate the objects of nature. For with such a proviso, Macpherson argues, the specifically capitalist form of ownership, arising out of the use of a hired work force, could never be established.[44]

As should be clear from what has been said already, I do not intend to dispute Macpherson's claim that Locke's theory of property was designed to justify the capitalist form of ownership in which the owner is not necessarily the one who engages in physical toil. I believe, however, that Macpherson is wrong in thinking that Locke must (and does)

[44]Macpherson, *Political Theory*, 214ff.

conceive of labor as a commodity in order to allow for unlimited appropriation.[45]

According to Macpherson, the requirement that one must use one's own labor in order to acquire title to the product is compatible with the employment of other people because Locke views labor as itself a property of the agent which the agent can freely sell and another may buy. To prove that Locke indeed allows for such buying and selling of labor, Macpherson quotes the passage usually cited as evidence that Locke violated the "labor limitation" supposedly implicit in his theory:

> Thus the Grass my Horse has bit; the Turfs my Servant has cut; and the Ore I have digg'd in any place where I have a right to them in common with others, become my *Property*, without the assignation or consent of any body. The *labour* that was mine, removing them out of that common state they were in, hath *fixed* my *Property* in them. [§28]

To Macpherson the implication that Locke allows for the "sale of labor" is so evident that he says: "I do not see how Locke could have been more specific: the labour performed by my servant is 'the labour that was mine.' "[46] And yet Locke never says that the servant has performed any *labor*, only that he "has cut" some turfs. In other places he talks about the "service" the servant "undertakes to do,"[47] but not about labor either. Macpherson's conclusion is, of course, perfectly understandable in view of both ordinary language usage and the conception of labor held by economists. We are dealing here, however, with one of those cases where an author has a highly innovative and specific concept in mind, so that our "natural" linguistic intuitions can easily lead us astray. Thus, if what I have said about the distinction between the two functions of labor—its being both a physical effort and a spiritual operation of infusing things with value—is correct, and if the imparting of value to the object is due to the *initiative* that expresses the essence of human freedom, then it becomes clear that the "service" performed by the "servant" does not qualify as "labor" in the sense that enables a man to appropriate. For the servant's action, being *initiated* by

[45]In other words, my disagreement with Macpherson is not over whether Locke allowed for the wage system (for I believe, as does Macpherson, that he did), but over the meaning of the concept of labor as the means of acquisition.

[46]Macpherson, *Political Theory*, 215n.

[47]§85. See also Laslett's "Introduction," 118n. But even if in other contexts, such as his economic writings, Locke uses the term "labor" in the ordinary sense, comprising a hired work force, it is significant that he does not use it *here*, for in the context of appropriation he has a very specific concept in mind. The parallel between the servant's "labor" and the work of a horse is quite significant as well. No one would argue, I presume, that "the Grass my Horse has bit" is a sign that the horse performed some labor that (had he not sold it) could possibly give him a property right in that grass.

the master, was not free: it was the *master's* will that the servant obeyed
and should he have for one reason or another decided not to perform
the service requested, the products of his work would have been
brought about anyway, as long as the master could find someone else to
employ. It is with the master's freedom, as embodied in the *capital*, that
the initiative rests, insofar as all the modern forms of production are
concerned, and this initiative is what gives the property title to the
master.[48] The servant, despite his share in the physical toil of production, is no more than an instrument (this is why Locke likens his action
to that of a horse), a conduit for a spiritual operation that is not his own.
Thus, although Locke clearly believes that one can use a hired work for
oneself, it is absurd, within the language of his theory, to say that one
can buy someone else's labor as a property-making activity. It would be
absolutely impossible to sell one's labor in this sense, since it would
automatically amount to losing one's own freedom in labor, and hence
one's capacity for appropriation.[49]

The mistake of saying that, according to Locke, one can sell one's own
labor also comes from a confusion of the two senses of "property" in
Locke's theory: one referring to the alienable possession of external
objects, and the other referring to the inalienable relation of a man to his
own person, natural endowments, rights, liberties, and the like.[50] Although Macpherson is trying to prove that Locke intended to identify
the two meanings and allowed for the alienability of the property
everyone has in his own person, he in fact simply presupposes this very
identification in his own argument. For it is only by interpreting the

[48]This is, in fact, the standard way of justifying profits in a system of free enterprise. Also,
it may be useful to point out here that on the basis of what I have said, it is seriously
misleading to attribute to Locke anything like a "labor theory of value" in the usual sense
of this expression. Although Locke clearly holds a "labor theory of property," and *in this
sense* also a "labor theory of value," the latter should not be confused with what economists mean by this expression. Far from believing that the *worker's effort* creates the value
of the product, Locke holds that value is attributable to the *capitalist's initiative*. In this
sense, he is, in economic terms, much closer to the cost of production, rather than labor,
theory of value. For instances of this confusion in Locke literature, see Day, "Locke on
Property," 211; and R. Polin, *La politique morale de John Locke* (Paris, 1960), 268–69.

[49]Tully's argument against Macpherson's view of labor as a commodity in Locke also
rests on the idea that labor is inalienable because "the labour of a person is defined as
actions determined by the will of that person" (Tully, *Discourse on Property*, 138). Tully
then proceeds, however, to argue that the servant (understood by Locke in terms of the
seventeenth-century theories of employment) has "a natural property in the turf he cuts,"
but the product becomes the conventional property of the master as a result of a contract
(139). Both because I believe that Tully overdraws the distinction between "natural" and
"conventional" property (see below, section 3), and because the sale of the product in
exchange for *wages* does not seem to me all that different from Macpherson's sale of labor,
I find Tully's account not fully persuasive. The concept of labor as a commodity is also
criticized in the works of Laslett and Ryan cited in footnote 1, above.

[50]See Laslett's "Introduction," 115, 116n.

phrase "properly his" in Locke's famous statement about man that "[t]he *Labour* of his Body and the *Work* of his Hands . . . are properly his" (§27) as an expression of Locke's belief that labor is an agent's property in the ordinary sense of alienable ownership that Macpherson can argue for the possibility of the worker's selling his labor. If such, however, were Locke's meaning, his derivation of property from labor would be a very uninteresting form of question-begging: he would in fact have assumed a concept of ownership and only extended it from one's person to external things. What is even worse, the idea of property *assumed* in this strange argument would be much more questionable than the one to be *derived*, for while the concept of alienable ownership is in general somewhat problematic in Locke,[51] at least the idea of an alienable property in things is intuitively understandable, while that of selling the attributes of one's personhood is not. In reality, however, Locke is very far from arguing that my labor is my property and hence what I mix it with is also mine, as a very cursory reading of §27 could, perhaps, suggest.[52] On the contrary, he intends to explain the *origin* and the *meaning* of both the inalienable and the alienable sense of property. This he begins by introducing the concept of inalienable property: not as ownership, however, but as an *identification*.[53] Thus, the last "his" in the sentence quoted above merely identifies a *person*, and Locke then proceeds with his justification of property in the usual (alienable) sense by showing that by uniting my labor with something I have mixed my *personhood* (and not another property of mine) with it. The reasons Locke uses the word "property" with respect to one's person are, apart from common contemporary usage,[54] twofold. The first is connected with the etymological affinity between the "properly his" and "property" (or "propriety," for which Locke substituted "property" in correcting his text)[55]—an affinity that lends linguistic persuasiveness to his argument. The linguistic ambiguity of "property" is still well preserved in the French "propre," which means not only that which I own as a property but also that which identifies what is a part of me or "properly mine," and something analogous obtains for the English words "own" and "to belong," as well as for all the possessive pronouns. No one, I hope, would claim, however, that by saying "This is

---

[51]For the difficulties posed by the problem of alienability in Locke, see my "Locke's Conception of Property."

[52]Should we accept such a superficial reading, we might be faced with pondering the following dilemma: if I sprinkle some still unappropriated piece of land with some salt I happen to own, should we then say that the land becomes mine because I mixed with it the labor that was mine or because I mixed with it some salt that was mine?

[53]A similar point is made by Ryan, "Locke and the Dictatorship," 244.

[54]See Laslett's "Introduction," 116n.

[55]Ibid.

my (own) head," I am also implying that I own my head in a sense that would allow for my free sale of it. The second reason Locke uses the word "property" with respect to one's own person is, indeed, connected with the central place that appropriation occupies in human life; not because, however, one's own person is for sale, but because a person's autonomy is, as I have tried to show, realized through the process of appropriation. Thus, the preservation of property, for the purpose of which men unite into commonwealths, is not just limited to the protection of men's narrowly understood economic interests but entails the protection of their freedom and dignity, which depend on their ownership of things.

3. Property and Society

Some readings of Locke deemphasize the importance of Chapter v in the *Second Treatise* by limiting its applicability only to the state of nature and insisting that in a civil society the natural law of appropriation is replaced by positive law. The first significant effort to interpret Locke in this fashion was presented some time ago by Willmoore Kendall in his provocative book *John Locke and the Doctrine of Majority Rule*.[56] Locke indeed says (in §50 of the *Second Treatise*) that "in Government the Laws regulate the right of property, and the possession of land is determined by positive constitutions." Kendall took this to mean that under civil society the majority rules supreme and takes it upon itself to legislate in all matters of social interaction, without any essential limitation by, or regard for, the laws of nature. Thus, in the case of property relations, the majority may wish to base the title on a positive law that no longer ties it to labor, and this is supposed to have in fact happened in most, if not all, societies.

Kendall's claim must appear rather strange in view of Locke's stated view that the *"Preservation of their Property"* is the "great and *chief end* . . . of Mens uniting into Commonwealths" (§124). Obviously civil society replaces the natural title to property with its "positive constitution" (i.e., a legal title), but there is very little evidence to support the claim that Locke believed that the laws of nature cease to be binding at this point.[57] Clearly, those who enter into a social compact in order to

---

[56]Urbana, 1941.

[57]The strongest statement in support of such a position comes from too early a period in Locke's development to count as valid evidence. In the *Essay* of 1667, when Locke was probably under the influence of Hobbes and had not yet developed his labor theory of property, he did indeed say that the magistrate "having a power to appoint ways of transferring propriety from one man to another, may establish any, so they be universal,

achieve better protection of their natural rights are not likely to relinquish them at that very moment.

Nevertheless, the argument that the labor theory of property is no longer operative in political society has been recently revived by Tully.[58] Tully's purpose in reviving it, however, is very different from Kendall's, for, far from viewing the abandonment of the labor theory as an expression of Locke's positivistic majoritarianism, he sees it as an effort to retain the spirit of natural law which is defeated by the introduction of money in the development of the labor-related form of ownership. It will be remembered that property, according to Tully, is originally common and guarantees each person an access to the resources necessary for his self-preservation. Private property is then introduced because it leads to a better use of these resources, but the institution of private ownership is always conditioned by a duty of charity toward others. A positive duty of this kind Tully believes is "integrated" into the labor theory;[59] a negative expression of it is to be found in the limitations that Locke imposes on the extent an individual may appropriate in the state of nature: what a man makes his is his property only so long as it does not spoil and there is enough left in common for others. However, the introduction of money, according to Tully, "brings with it the fall of man,"[60] since it allows for the kind of property which does not spoil, induces people to hoard more than they need, and undermines the foundation natural law provided for the introduction of private property in the first place: the preservation of oneself *and others*. Consequently, the introduction of money "furnishes the most powerful motive for entering into political society,"[61] since the reclamation of the original natural order requires that title derived from labor be replaced with a conventional one, which restores the principles of equity and justice.[62]

---

equal and without violence and suited to the welfare of that society" (from Huntington MS, quoted after Laslett's note to §120 of the *Second Treatise*). As Laslett observes in his "Introduction" to the *Two Treatises*, 118, the *Second Treatise* never explicitly contradicts that assertion. Nevertheless, the relevant passages (§§ 45, 51, 120, and 139), while admitting of the possibility of far-reaching regulation, are not sufficient to warrant the claim that the primacy of natural law (or at least of its spirit) is obliterated in a political society.

[58]Tully, *Discourse on Property*, 151ff.

[59]Ibid., 132.

[60]Ibid., 150.

[61]Ibid.

[62]On this last score, Tully's argument is particularly unpersuasive. Even on the assumption that the "Property," for the "Preservation" of which men unite in civil societies, is much broader than the simple ownership of things, Locke's account of the reasons that lead men to this step leaves no room for doubt that it is the illegitimate "Invasion" of an individual's right to control over his own "Person and Possessions" that makes him willing to abandon his natural freedom in favor of a secure protection of "Lives, Liberties and Estates" (§123). It is unlikely that any amount of interpretation could explain away the

I have argued extensively that, despite the fact that Locke's primary purpose in writing the *Two Treatises* may have been the refutation of Filmer's theory of the divine right of kings, Locke's deeper historical significance lies in his contribution to the intellectual origins of liberalism, and in this respect his relation to Hobbes is of greater importance. I have also argued that the concept of property bears a double burden in Locke's theory that ought to be compared to the function played by the concept of the state in the thought of Hobbes.[63] First—and demonstrating this has been my paramount concern so far—the concept of property is the keystone in Locke's reconstruction of the moral dimension in human life: the dimension threatened by Hobbesian positivism and only very partially remedied by Hobbes's account of political and civil obligation. Second—and this aspect will mainly occupy us in what follows—Locke's conception of property is supposed to explain how the insecurity that plagues natural man is remedied in the process of the transformation of nature through labor, thus avoiding the pitting of each man against his fellow human beings in the Hobbesian *bellum omnis contra omnem*.

In this respect, both Kendall's and Tully's view that the foundation of property in labor does not survive the establishment of the political community constitutes a special challenge to my interpretation. In particular, Tully's view that the introduction of money defeats the moral underpinnings of private property based on labor shifts back to the state the role of the Hobbesian guardian who stands to curb the aggressiveness of natural man. Although this does not seem to interest Tully (for whom Locke's philosophy has no enduring implications), such a shift threatens to undermine the basic liberal foundation of the Lockean system and to repoliticize those very aspects of human existence which Locke intended to remove from the scope of the government's legitimate concern.

Undoubtedly, Locke believed that peace is insecure in the state of nature and that governments are instituted to remedy that insecurity. It is one thing, however, to say that the natural order is disturbed either because some men refuse to observe the principles of human coexistence that every rational agent must recognize as binding even in the state of nature or because the absence of an impartial judge leaves room for numerous conflicts (which become ever sharper as the stakes grow with the increase of wealth produced by human industry) arising from diverse interpretations of natural law by fallible and often selfish indi-

---

clear statement that the preservation of the preexisting "Possessions" and "Estates" is among the "chief ends" of the state.

[63]See above, Introduction to Part Two.

viduals. It is quite another thing to say that natural moral order itself is inherently inconsistent and unstable, so that a state is needed to redefine the principles of natural justice and confer a *new* form of dignity on human beings. The admission of human imperfection and of the need for the state as an impartial arbiter is of essence of the liberal thought. The transformation of man into a *homo politicus* is its antithesis.[64] It is therefore of great importance for my interpretation to establish that no such breakdown of the natural order is envisaged in Locke's thought and that the transition to civil society does not entail a redefinition of the principles of natural justice. In particular, we must follow Locke's account of the evolution of natural property and show that the introduction of money, far from leading to "the fall of man," brings out the most fundamental moral features of appropriation. As we shall see, the unlimited appropriation that the introduction of money facilitates not only does not release the Hobbesian aggressiveness of man, but, on the contrary, creates the objective conditions that permit the widespread enjoyment of human autonomy.

3.1. The Self and Others—Language, Property, and Money

While Tully, following Lamprecht, believes that Locke "never considers a congeries of presocial and isolated individuals," and sees society as "an irreducible datum of human existence,"[65] a rather commonplace view of Locke is that he was an unabashed individualist who saw in social relations nothing but a form of joint-stock company, i.e., a form of cooperation among already fully developed, autonomous human beings. According to this view, which makes no distinction between political society and other forms of social interaction which later came to be called "civil society" (although this is not the way in which Locke uses the term), society does not introduce any qualitative change in human life; it is only a contractually established framework within which men agree to combine their power to police each other, so that each of them can now more safely pursue the very same ends he was pursuing individually before the creation of the state. The locus of human self-realization, according to this view, lies outside society al-

[64]This is not meant to imply, of course, that every liberal theory must be based on the idea of natural law. Though Locke's theory was indeed based on it, I believe that the absence of a historical dimension is one of the weakest points in his thought. Nevertheless, it is critical for any liberal theory to establish a system of political legitimation which locates the basic rights of individuals *outside* the narrowly political sphere.

[65]Tully, *Discourse on Property*, 49. S. P. Lamprecht, *The Moral and Political Philosophy of John Locke* (New York, 1918), 132. Among others who question the radically individualistic interpretation of Locke are Polin, *La politique morale de John Locke*, and Kendall, *John Locke and the Doctrine of Majority Rule*.

together: in the individual pursuit of wealth, happiness, salvation, and other aims.

Locke's conception of property has been seen in this context as a prime strand in his individualistic and atomistic theory of society.[66] Not only is property *private* in Locke, so that an individual has an exclusive right to something to which the whole society may have made an important contribution (because of the social nature of the production process),[67] but also the origin of property lies in a purely "natural" (nonsocial) relation between an individual and his environment, so that neither his right nor his title to ownership derives from a socially established order. Society does not even really sanction the original title, for its true sanction is a "law of nature"; society is designed to "regulate and protect" Lives, Liberties and Estates," but it does not have power to legislate against the natural law from which it derives its own legitimation.[68]

I do not intend to question the most basic premises of the individualistic reading of Locke. There is no doubt that Locke reverses the Aristotelian "natural priority" of the state over the individual[69] and attempts to provide a philosophical foundation for modern liberalism, with its insistence on the autonomy of economic and property relations, its "depoliticization" of human life, and its rooting of the state's legitimacy in the inviolability of the *natural* rights of individuals. There is no inherent "natural" necessity of political organization for Locke, in the sense of either a teleological or a mechanical order of the universe which would determine man to seek the establishment of a political community. But nevertheless, the usual individualistic interpretation of Locke's theory is too simplistic and the truth seems to me to lie somewhere between this view and that of Lamprecht and Tully, who see the Lockean man as naturally social.

The roots of Locke's individualism must be looked for, again, in his

---

[66]See, in this connection, D. G. Ritchie, "Locke's Theory of Property," *Economic Review*, 1 (1891), 39.

[67]That Locke was not unaware of this aspect of production may be seen from a Smith-like description of it he gives in §43 and its discussion below. Ritchie (ibid., 36–38) claims that private property is incompatible with the division of labor. Day ("Locke on Property," 210–11) expresses a similar view.

[68]The social contract establishes the state, including its legislative authority, for the purpose of executing the laws of nature. This essential limitation of even the legislative power of political institutions to the role of an "executive" with respect to the laws of nature and the protection of the inalienable rights of man contained in them makes the famous problem of "majority rule" much less important than it appears. Since the main locus of human self-realization lies outside the political sphere anyway, the question of majority rule becomes a matter of *administrative detail*—a far cry from the paramount problem it is in Kendall's account.

[69]See Aristotle, *Politics*, 1253a.

broader theoretical commitments. Locke's discussion of human nature, in the context of his epistemological views, reveals a significant absence of any constitutive role for an intersubjective dimension of human knowledge, and this aspect of his theory is undoubtedly related to, among other things, his empiricist and nominalist conception of language. In a marked contrast to the Aristotelian insistence on the intimate relationship between language and human rationality, which connected man's ability to think (the *differentia specifica* of his humanity) with his ability to use speech and the latter's social dimension, and even in contrast to Hobbes, who defined the understanding as "Imagination that is raysed . . . by words,"[70] Locke viewed language and communication as built upon a nonlinguistic, purely subjective process of thinking and thus as not at all constitutive of human rationality. For Aristotle, the human use of language was possible only within the context of a community of speakers, so that man's very rationality was predicated on his being a member of a political body (for it was only in the *polis* that Aristotle saw the truly human, i.e., noninstrumental, use of speech). On the other hand, Locke, as we have seen, shifted the locus of man's self-realization from an interaction with other people to a relationship with nature. He saw, of course, the intimate link between language and the social dimension of human existence, for in the *Essay* he called language "the great Instrument, and the common Tye of Society,"[71] and, conversely, saw the "Comfort and Advantage of Society" as the reason why "Man should find out some external sensible Signs, whereby those invisible *Ideas*, which his thoughts are made up of, might be made known to others."[72] But rather than making language, or at least its logical structure, constitutive of human thought, he saw the relation between them to be just the reverse: man uses "*Sounds, as Signs of internal Conceptions*; and to make them stand as marks for the *Ideas* within his own Mind, whereby they might be made known to others."[73] Consequently, the function of communication remains for him purely derivative from the more fundamental cognitive processes, which do not involve any essential relation to other people.

A not surprising parallel (and in fact more than a parallel) exists between Locke's essentially individualistic account of human knowledge and a similar absence of any constitutive reference to a social context in his account of labor and appropriation. As in the case of his account of knowledge, Locke reverses the usual priorities: the socioeconomic and political order is based on property relations, and not

[70]*Lev.*, 8.
[71]III, 1, 1.
[72]III, 2, 1.
[73]III, 1, 2.

vice versa. The primacy of property over society concerns not merely the political order that is founded to protect "Lives, Liberties, and Estates," but also all other forms of social organization. Locke was clearly not unaware of the fact that the social division of labor makes a great difference in man's productivity, but his essentially nominalistic and naturalistic account of appropriation convinced him that social cooperation is parasitic on individual ownership. He envisaged appropriation as primarily a private relation between man and his natural environment and believed that the network of intersubjective exchange and cooperation could be explained only with reference to man's interaction with nature. Like linguistic communication, which presupposes the private world of ideas, social cooperation, according to Locke, presupposes the private form of ownership. Social interaction is, for Locke, always founded in some kind of conventional agreement, and no form of society is perfectly "natural." But in order for us to speak of any society-founding agreement we must assume that the parties to the agreement are autonomous agents, capable of undertaking contractual obligations, and this we can assume only if we view them as property owners, capable of exchange and cooperation.

It is a mistake, however, to believe that Locke did not view society as introducing a qualitative change into cognitive or practical experience. On the contrary, he says that God created man as a "sociable Creature, [and] made him . . . with an inclination, and under a necessity to have fellowship with those of his own kind."[74] It is the meaning of this "necessity" that we must understand in order to grasp his very interesting conception of the effects of social interaction on the development of human individuality.

Locke, it is often assumed, made no distinction between political society and other forms of social organization that came to be subsumed under the term "civil society." But despite the fact that he often uses the two terms interchangeably, his system includes some important foreshadowings of a distinction. To begin with, a conventionally established linguistic community clearly precedes for him any political compact, of which it constitutes an important presupposition.[75] The impact of this convention does not have to be stressed: it allows for the sharing of experiences, without which the progress of human knowledge would be impossible. In the previous part of this study, I have also mentioned the role that socialization plays in the formation of an ideal

[74]III, 1, 1.

[75]In some places Locke speaks of language as a gift from God and a part of man's natural endowment (see III, 1, 1), but from the context it is evident that this refers only to those parts of man's nature that make him *capable* of speech, while the actual pairing of words with ideas is conventionally established (III, 1, 5).

of happiness that an agent is going to follow at various stages of his moral development. Certain forms of contractual agreements are also prior to political society, and the most obvious form of social organization arising out of such obligations is the institution of the family. Although family has some natural roots in man's physiological and emotional needs, as well as in the God-given desire to continue the species (§79), the particular union of particular individuals and their property arrangements are, according to Locke, established by a contractual agreement (§78). The form of prepolitical social organization which concerns us most here, however, is the economic order. This social bond is more interesting not only because of its direct link to property relations, but also because it is much more complex than the family union. As a matter of fact, the introduction of an economic community qualitatively changes man's life, being at the same time only loosely connected with any natural phenomena. Even though primitive forms of communal economics arise in connection with human needs that can be better satisfied through exchange, the significance of the developed forms of economic order very quickly transcends its immediate rooting in natural phenomena. This is so because any economic order worth speaking of takes its origin in a peculiar form of prepolitical convention, namely, the introduction of money (§37).

The role played by the introduction of money in the context of Locke's theory of appropriation is easily obscured by its ambiguous presentation. Locke ascribes to money two more or less obvious functions. On the one hand, it facilitates exchange and thus establishes the foundation of the developed form of market economy. On the other hand, money also provides a new form of ownership because it constitutes a type of property that does not "spoil," and thus allows for unlimited appropriation. Despite Locke's occasional condemnation of the *amor sceleratus habendi* (the wretched love of owning) for which the introduction of money provides a decisive impetus (§111), there can be no doubt that the second function is by far more important than the first.

The reason the exchange-facilitating function of money is relatively unimportant for Locke becomes clear if we view it, once again, in the context of his mercantilist theory of economic activity. We have seen that the mercantilist theory was characterized by its paramount preoccupation with production and its severing of the link between production and consumption. The mercantilists' view of exchange was part and parcel of the same outlook. While production was for them the paradigmatic economic activity, since it created new value and contributed to the increase of wealth, exchange they viewed as essentially sterile, since it presupposed that the exchanged objects were of equal intrinsic value and thus could bring about no important change in one's state of ownership. In fact, insofar as properly economic concerns are involved, there could be no rational motive for exchange as such; men engage in it for reasons connected exclusively with the personal *use* value that the exchanged objects may have for them, and not with their concern for increasing the state of their ownership as measured by intrinsic value.[76] This may sound paradoxical at first, in view of the mercantilist insistence on the importance of commerce, but the paradox is only apparent. The mercantilist concern with commerce was connected exclusively with *selling*, not buying, and hence not really with exchange.[77] Commerce resolved for the mercantilists to a need for markets where one liquidated one's assets and realized one's profits in order to be left with the purest form of value, *capital*. Exchange, on the other hand, by being tied to use and consumption, was of necessity seen as competing with the properly economic interests of production, and consequently the mercantilists did not (nor did they think one could) provide any economic theory of domestic trade. Their protectionist theory of international commerce reveals the same basic attitude: fair trade being absolutely sterile and economically irrational, duties must be imposed on foreign imports to defeat the economically "harmful" (because tied to use and consumption) effects of exchange as such.

We have seen that Locke's theory of appropriation was supposed to provide the philosophical foundation for mercantilist economic theory by showing that the mercantilist concern with production was not, after all, a mere *amor sceleratus habendi*, but rather an expression of the human quest for dignity and self-sufficiency. Locke's theory of money is only an extension of this theory. Although money is clearly introduced in order to facilitate exchange, its real importance lies elsewhere. Perhaps we may even speak in this context of something not unlike the Hegelian "cunning of reason." For once introduced, money and the market economy decisively mediate the relation between production and consumption, thus further separating appropriation from the use-related functions of production. Money introduces a quantitative measure of the value embodied in the products of human labor and, by

[76]The distinction between the intrinsic (or exchange) value and the use value, which was to be much celebrated in later classical political economy, may also be viewed as corresponding to the distinction between primary and secondary qualities in Locke's epistemology. Like a primary quality, exchange value is an objective feature of the product; by expressing the homogeneity of human labor it is a common quantitative denominator of products of all kinds. Use value, on the other hand, like a secondary quality, is merely subjective and unstable, varying from one subject to another as well as for each individual subject through time.

[77]Cf. Locke's statement that man has "hopes of Commerce with other Parts of the World, to draw *Money* to him by the Sale of the Product" (§48).

establishing a common denominator for the diverse forms of productive activity, makes possible the full development of the moral aspect of property ownership. The ownership of money that results from the capital-oriented form of appropriation (accumulation) constitutes the "purest" form of ownership, since money is a symbol of the "pure" productivity of human labor, free from all the factors obscuring the autonomy-related significance of ownership. The main function of appropriation consists in helping man to eliminate the tremendous pressure of desires connected with the insecurity engendered by his awareness of the alien character of nature and in enabling him to make his rational life plan solely responsible for the totality of his needs and desires. In order for this to be accomplished, the productivity of human labor has to be turned away from serving the purpose of immediately satisfying man's desires and channeled into the process of transforming nature into an environment that constitutes an extension of human personality. Thus, the meaning of accumulation is that by counteracting the forces of consumption, it allows for the *permanence* of the products of human labor and a creation of the lasting objectification of human freedom. Even though the "infinity" of desire is not overcome in this way (since accumulation does not have its limits either), the satisfaction of the appropriative drive becomes at least *cumulative* and *progressive*, since the products of labor directed toward accumulation are not subject to immediate consumption. The self-perpetuating and irrational cycle of production and consumption gives way to an orderly and rational progression of self-sufficiency. Thus, as the introduction of language as a means of communication transforms knowledge from a mere instrument into a vocation, the introduction of money as a means of exchange transforms property into capital and effects the transcendence of use through accumulation.

In this way, a highly intricate nexus of relationships develops between property ownership and society within the framework of Lockean individualism. What we see in the complicated structure of dependence between property on the one hand, and the economic order based on exchange (and thus necessarily involving each agent in a social context) on the other hand, is a rather fine nominalistic conception of civil society: society is contractually introduced and remains secondary with respect to individuals, and yet in transforming the natural functions of property ownership, it qualitatively changes human life.

3.2. The Problem of Scarcity and the Sufficiency Limitation

It will be remembered that God's original grant of the earth to mankind in common meant, for Locke, that each individual had a right to derive his subsistence from the natural plenty.[78] This implied not only that everyone had to be included in the use of the common, but also that the process of appropriation was limited by the obligation to leave "enough, and as good . . . in common for others" (§27). As long as still another limitation, preventing anyone from appropriating more than he could use before it spoiled (§31), was in effect, appropriation had a rather limited effect on the depletion of the common and everyone was assured the opportunity of providing for his needs. The introduction of money, however, introduced a form of property that does not spoil and, by thus making possible unlimited appropriation, led to the possibility—perhaps, indeed, the certainty—that sooner or later all of nature would be appropriated and nothing would be left for others. The increasing scarcity could thus produce a situation of growing conflict and, as Tully noted, undermine the moral foundations of the natural order. How does Locke deal with this problem?

An interesting attempt to answer this question was made by Macpherson. According to Macpherson, Locke suspended the sufficiency limitation, which derives from each man's right to self-preservation, on the basis of an essentially utilitarian argument that land under cultivation provides subsistence (the means of self-preservation) to more people than when it lies waste.[79] Once the common is entirely appropriated, those who no longer have an opportunity to become landowners can still hire themselves out as laborers and derive their livelihood in this way.[80]

Macpherson's argument would be persuasive perhaps if all that Locke meant was that appropriation should not deprive others of their right to self-preservation, understood as a right to subsistence. As Locke formulated it, however, the sufficiency limitation seems to imply something more. By saying that a man may appropriate only so long as "there is enough, and as good left in common for others," Locke seems to imply at least that a sufficient amount of resources must be left *unowned*, so that others may also *appropriate*. Some such implication appears especially necessary if appropriation is, as I have argued, primarily related to the achievement of human autonomy and not to the purpose of mere subsistence, for then the fact that one is capable of

[78]See section 2.1, above.

[79]Macpherson, *Political Theory*, 212–13.

[80]An argument similar to Macpherson's is made by R. Nozick in his *Anarchy, State, and Utopia* (New York, 1974), 174–82. Nozick claims that all that remains of the sufficiency limitation following the elimination of the common is that a propertyless individual may have a claim for compensation amounting to a difference between what he could have had under the commons system and what he has as a result of benefiting from social cooperation. In most cases, Nozick claims, this amount would not be positive, presumably because of the increase in productivity that appropriation effects.

preserving oneself in no way compensates for the inability to become a property owner. And, indeed, Locke does not seem to tie the sufficiency limitation to the purpose of self-preservation. It is true that he allows for the fact that the introduction of money leads to a situation in which unequal possessions arise and in which some people may be left without the possibility of becoming landowners (§50). He also does say that land under cultivation produces much more than when it lies waste (§43). But nowhere in the chapter on property was I able to find a place where he *justifies* the former by the latter. The passages in which the benefits of cultivation are discussed, so far as I can see, serve only to justify land appropriation in general by showing that *"Labour . . . puts the greatest part of Value upon Land"* (§43), and I do not see any meaningful connection between this and the argument concerning the elimination of other people's right to appropriation.[81] After all, even if Locke attempted to argue as Macpherson thinks he did, one could still always reply that under conditions of scarcity the land of which the propertyless are deprived would not cease to be cultivated if it were left to them rather than taken over by others.[82]

Where does all this leave us, then, insofar as the sufficiency limitation is concerned? The answer, in my view, is that the limitation by its own very nature operates only in the earliest stages of economic development. In the later stages, the limitation is replaced by what we may call, perhaps, the "sufficiency principle," based on a form of antiscarcity argument which allows Locke to show that in advanced or civilized societies no one is left without the means to achieve individual autonomy.

That the sufficiency limitation operates on appropriation only in a society in a backward state of economic development is clear from the fact that it applies only to *uncultivated land*. In a very primitive society, such as that of some American Indians Locke uses as an example (§§ 26, 30), the only object of appropriation consists of land and its products. Now, in such a society, lack of available land might deprive some men

[81]On the contrary, Locke seems to claim that by increasing the productivity of land by appropriation, the individual draws less from the pool available to all and thus *facilitates* other people's appropriation (§37).

[82]There are of course, theoretically speaking, several ways in which one could counter this argument. One is to say that the land would indeed lie waste because the propertyless are too irrational to cultivate it without being forced to by someone else. Another would be to say that big holdings are more productive than small ones and thus ownership by a few is more efficient. But Locke uses neither of these arguments in the *Second Treatise*. Macpherson (*Political Theory*, 222–23) does refer us to some places in which Locke takes a very harsh view of the poor. But it is one thing to view the poor as responsible for their own poverty and quite another to say that the poor's indolence allows others to do what they otherwise have no right to do, i.e., appropriate so much as to leave nothing for others.

not so much of their subsistence (for this, as Macpherson rightly observes, they could always earn by working for others) as of the possibility of becoming property owners, i.e., of the full realization of their dignity or moral agency. In a more advanced society, however, such as the England of Locke's time, a situation of this kind could never arise, for in such societies the primary form of property is *capital*, i.e., a realizable monetary value of *all kinds* of products resulting from the application of labor. The attribution of a basically physiocratic outlook (that is, of linking productivity to land ownership) to Locke is quite out of place here; even with respect to land cultivation Locke makes clear that it is labor and not land that is productive (§43). But still more important is his view, reflecting his basic mercantilism (with some foreshadowings of the most important insights of later classical political economy), that nonagricultural production plays a crucial role in a developed economy, even when a seemingly agricultural product is considered:

> For 'tis not barely the Plough-man's Pains, the Reaper's and Thresher's Toil, and the Baker's Sweat, is to be counted into the *Bread* we eat [note that even here not land but labor is mentioned]; the Labour of those who broke the Oxen, who digged and wrought the Iron and Stones, who felled and framed the Timber imployed about the Plough, Mill, Oven, or any other Utensils, which are a vast Number, requisite to this Corn, from its being seed to be sown to its being made Bread, must all be *charged on* the account of *Labour*, and received as an effect of that: Nature and the Earth furnished only the almost worthless Materials, as in themselves. 'Twould be a strange *Catalogue of things, that Industry provided and made use of, about every Loaf of Bread*, before it came to our use, if we could trace them; Iron, Wood, Leather, Bark, Timber, Stone, Bricks, Coals, Lime, Cloth, Dying-Drugs, Pitch, Tar, Masts, Ropes, and all the Materials made use of in the Ship, that brought any of the Commodities made use of by any of the Workmen, to any part of the Work, all which 'twould be almost impossible, at least too long, to reckon up. [§43]

What this description worthy of Adam Smith is designed to show is that in advanced societies value can be created and capital accumulated in an almost infinite number of ways, and since those are created by labor it is impossible to exhaust the basic natural material that God provided for man to appropriate. This impossiblity of a real shortage of things to which labor can be productively applied constitutes the core of the Lockean reading of 1 Timothy 6:17: "God giveth us richly all things to enjoy."[83] "Humane Industry," and not land, being the source of all

---

[83]In §31, where Locke specifically mentions this passage, he is mostly concerned with explaining the meaning of "to enjoy." But from his discussion of the source of all value, it is clear that the richness of God's gift lies primarily in its providing an inexhaustible supply

value (§42), even the smallest natural object will know no limit of the extent to which it can be productively transformed, and hence of the extent of property (value) that it can sustain.

We can thus see that the sufficiency principle does not, in the long run, impose any limitation on man's right to appropriate, and this not because unlimited, capitalist appropriation can provide the means of subsistence for a larger population, but because of an underlying change in the economic structure of advanced civilizations (of which the introduction of money is one of the most important elements) that radically alters the very problem of scarcity that was faced by primitive man. Contrary to the claims of Macpherson, the *principle* underlying the sufficiency limitation is never suspended or replaced—it always remains the case that a man cannot by his actions leave his fellow human beings in a position that precludes their becoming property owners as well. But the principle no longer limits appropriation because the scarcity of natural resources is not a normal human condition. This implicit antiscarcity argument, which reminds us of the one given later by Marx, is what allows Locke to complete his refutation of Hobbesian (but, of course, not only Hobbesian) absolutism. Aggressiveness was to Hobbes a fundamental feature of natural man because nature could never catch up with human ambition and thus universal conflict among men was an inevitable consequence of the scarcity that results from this gap. Only the absolute power of the state could be relied on to provide some foundation of peaceful coexistence. The main thrust of Locke's response, throughout his theory of appropriation, is that man is not just a consumer, but above all a producer and that the outcome of his encounter with nature is cumulative and progressive rather than fleeting and transitory. It is, of course, true that a man may (and usually does) aspire to more than he already has, but the source of *this* scarcity lies not in the limitation of natural resources so much as in the limitations of man himself—his need to labor for the realization of his goals. The extent to which a man can lead a life of dignity and comfort depends, then, not on how much he can snatch away from the grip of his fellows, but on the degree of his own diligence and perseverance. There will no doubt always be men who will try to ride on other people's efforts, and there will be conflicts of one kind or another in a world of dense social interactions and great wealth. A state is needed to make sure that these conflicts are contained. But the role of the state, in accordance with Locke's liberal view, is limited to enforcing

---

of raw materials for the production of wealth. The only way in which that gift could leave no opportunity for a man to appropriate would be for some men to be given a categorical dominion over *all* fruits of the earth, as Filmer thought was the case. See the *First Treatise*, §40.

the preexisting natural order that contains within it all the principles of justice necessary for peaceful cooperation.

3.3. The Spoilage Limitation

Locke's insistence on the importance of labor as the main source of value is a key not only to the recognition of the real significance of the sufficiency limitation, but also to a correct understanding of the other restriction that Locke imposes on the right to appropriate, the so-called "spoilage limitation."

Of this limitation—and it is undoubtedly one that persists throughout the development of property to its highest stages—he wrote: "As much as any one can make use of to any advantage of life before it spoils; so much he may by his labour fix a Property in. Whatever is beyond this, is more than his share, and belongs to others" (§31).

At first sight, one might be tempted to read the "advantage of life" as "self-preservation" and to interpret this passage as an injunction against appropriating more than one can *use*.[84] Such a reading would be wrong, however, since Locke makes it quite clear that the restriction limits appropriation to what will not *spoil* as a result of being taken away from the common and *not* to what the owner may actually, or even possibly, use. Similarly, we should not interpret the "belongs to others" as referring to other people's right to self-preservation or even their right to appropriate since in that case the second limitation would be reduced to no more than a specific case of the first one. Now, one could, of course, argue that the second limitation is, indeed, only a specific case of the first one,[85] by saying that if people were able to appropriate more than they could use before it spoils then nothing *would* in fact be left for others. But if my interpretation of the first limitation as really an

---

[84]This is Tully's view (*Discourse on Property*, 132), but for him the spoilage limitation is only "coincident" with a "due use" restriction, which Locke does not mention in the *Second Treatise* but Tully imputes to him on the basis of what Locke says about charity in §42 of the *First Treatise*. This seems to me an overinterpretation. There is no doubt that Locke subscribed to the Christian view that each man had a duty to help "his needy Brother." There is no evidence, however, that this duty constitutes any limitation on appropriation, short of a situation in which the other "has no means to subsist otherwise." That, according to Locke, would be the case if, as Filmer maintained, the rulers had a property in nature *as a whole*. In other situations, the duty of charity clearly forbids ostentatious consumption or simple miserliness, but has not been usually taken to interfere with other duties of man, such as the maintenance of one's dignity and autonomy.

[85]M. Seliger, *The Liberal Politics of John Locke* (London, 1968), 147, is in fact of this opinion. As support he quotes (151) a passage from the *Essay* which runs counter to the interpretation provided below.

implicit antiscarcity argument is correct, then the reading in question is obviously (except in the case of very primitive societies) incorrect.

Locke explains the real meaning of the spoilage limitation in the sentence immediately following the passage I have already quoted: "Nothing," he says, "was made by God for Man to spoil or destroy." It is very important to notice that it is *man* who is not to "spoil or destroy," so that the spoilage in question is not supposed to be *natural* (wild berries will rot anyway, if not picked) but man-related. What is really "protected" by the spoilage limitation, therefore, is neither other people's rights (at least not primarily) nor nature as such (since otherwise the spoilage limitation would imply an obligation to appropriate everything that could in this way be prevented from spoiling), but rather that which is the real gift of God to man, i.e., *human labor*. What is prohibited by the spoilage limitation is the squandering of labor by appropriation that does not contribute to the *permanent* transformation of nature by man. Thus, when as a result of advancing civilization, and of the introduction of money in particular, capital takes the place of land as the most important form of ownership, the spoilage limitation is *in principle* overcome (although it is, of course, still possible to waste one's own labor by its irrational application). It seems, then, that the introduction of money, by which both the spoilage limitation, and the sufficiency limitation, are rendered ineffective as restrictions on the extent of appropriation, far from being the road to damnation, is in fact a crucial step in the process of the *civilization* of man, i.e., the process that allows for a fuller development of man's creative potential and the progress of his autonomy.

4. The General Significance of Locke's Theory

The standard critique of liberalism, whether it comes from the political right, nostalgic for the ancient or medieval model of a closely integrated social order, or from the political left, hopeful of a future society based on universal brotherhood, is that liberal individualism is predicated on a philosophical theory that makes moral and political obligations into functions of man's (mostly material) interests and that its lofty ideas are but a thin cover for a brutal system of competition and exploitation. The basic argumentative strategy of this critique was discovered by Rousseau, whose theory of man will be the next subject of our discussion, and it was later developed by Hegel, the utopian socialists, Marx, the ideologues of nationalism, and many contemporary social critics. The positivistic or utilitarian approach to moral and political issues that these critics have seen as characteristic of capitalist society and its liberal doctrine leads, according to them, to ultimately nihilistic consequences. Its alleged elimination of "higher" moral standards of human action in favor of concentration on material comfort is seen as resulting in a senseless pursuit of ever new satisfactions of artificially created needs that are never subjected to a rational scrutiny. Hobbes, Locke, the thinkers of Enlightenment, the pragmatists, and the utilitarians are among the favorite *bêtes noires* of these critics. Because they attacked the concept of *summum bonum*, in the absence of which human life is supposed to become a purposeless and unhappy form of vegetation, the liberal thinkers are viewed as responsible for having laid the ground for a thoroughgoing moral relativism. The outcome of the atrophy of moral sense, characteristic of the liberal theory so interpreted, is that, as one prominent critic of Locke put it, "life is a joyless quest for joy."[86]

It is often claimed, especially among some contemporary Marxist critics of this kind, that the moral nihilism of liberal theory is linked to the very conception of rationality that stands behind it. This model of rationality, derived from modern mechanistic science, is seen to be predicated, on the one hand, on a strict separation between description and value judgments, and on the other hand, on locating the essence of knowledge in man's ability to manipulate nature and other men for the satisfaction of his unreflected needs. As a result, reason of this kind is viewed as purely "instrumental" and, like the Aristotelian *techne*, ultimately incapable of a disinterested inquiry into the purpose of human activities. In becoming more and more critical with respect to the foundation of all value judgments, such reason is responsible for the nihilistic exclusion of all moral questions from the reach of rational justification, and it makes adherence to any system of values a matter of an uncritical and *ad hoc* decision.

With respect to Locke, an argument of this kind has been most consistently pursued, perhaps unexpectedly but not surprisingly, by the conservative ally of the Marxist critics, Leo Strauss.[87] Strauss believes that Locke was essentially a Hobbesian and that he proposed an atomistic theory of society in which there is no room for any meaningful concept of obligation. Looking back to antiquity for a model of the "true" natural-right tradition which, on the basis of its teleological world view, implied an intimate link between right and obligation, Strauss sees Locke's modern view of man, oriented around the mechanistic science

---

[86]Strauss, *Natural Right and History*, 251.

[87]In *Natural Right and History*, 202–51. For a critique of Strauss's interpretation of Locke, see C. H. Monson, Jr., "Locke's Political Theory and Its Interpreters," in Martin and Armstrong, eds., *Locke and Berkeley*.

of the seventeenth century, as a hypocritically disguised form of extreme moral nihilism. This judgment of Locke is based on Strauss's general belief that no concept of obligation is genuinely compatible with the modern concept of natural right. "Natural" is, for Locke and his contemporaries, related to the "mechanical" and the "material," and thus explicable only in terms of "force." Therefore, in the modern conception of natural right, "right" becomes indistinguishable from "might" and (especially in Locke's version of the theory) provides a license for an unbridled development of egotistic passion, without any regard for the rights of other people. In an argument parallel to that of Macpherson, Strauss interprets Locke's theory of unlimited appropriation as a crucial social expression of the same general attitude.[88]

As should be clear from the preceding pages, I have not attempted to argue that Locke's was not a philosophy of liberal capitalism, based on a practically unlimited right of appropriation as a crucial factor in man's quest for dignity and freedom. As a matter of fact, with certain qualifications, I am closer here to Locke's opponents than to his defenders. What I wished to dispute, however, was the view that Locke's liberalism is *ipso facto* nihilistic, that under the pernicious influence of positivistically understood mechanistic science, he attempted the construction of a philosophical system in which the concepts of authentic value and obligation give way to a mere "calculus of desires." Although the standard objections to the modern natural-right tradition may have some applicability to Hobbes, for example, since Hobbes had indeed identified right with might, eliminated the concept of purpose not only from natural but also from human phenomena, and reduced moral concerns to a quest for mere security, Locke's "ethics of production" seems to me to avoid all of these extreme positions. His individualism does not result from a substitution of passion for reason as the determining factor in human behavior. On the contrary, its source seems to me to lie in a quite sophisticated synthesis of modern scientific rationality with a basically moralist attitude to human life. Locke's conception of natural moral law, in which his whole system is grounded, rests on his general belief in the compatibility of mechanistic science with a rational system of norms. In other words, I have tried to argue that in Locke's understanding of human rationality, reason is not what came to be called "instrumental," as opposed to the ancient *Logos* or the Marxist "dialectical" *Vernunft*. His ethos of capitalism may not be to everyone's taste, but it is an *ethos* nevertheless.

Where Locke does, indeed, break with the ancients is, above all, in their *separation of action and production*. His theory of property is not

[88]Strauss, *Natural Right and History*, 238ff.

meant as a theory of production in the Aristotelian sense. Rather, it is designed to show that production, insofar as it involves and, indeed, requires *appropriation*, contains *within* itself the element of praxis, that which is "done for its own sake," and which Aristotle saw as inhering only in a political organization of those whose basic needs are already satisfied. In comparison with the *polis*, "labor takes the place of the art," as Strauss put it so well, even while thoroughly mistaking the meaning of his own words.[89]

It is in this sense that Locke is a modern thinker, not in his alleged rejection of all moral quality in human life. Production, as the domain of necessity, is no longer separated from the "good life" and left outside the category of truly human activities. Locke is a man living in the post-Copernican era when the automatic subordination of nature to man is no longer to be taken for granted. The vast expanse of inanimate nature is without an immanent purpose, and if God gave the earth and its products to man it was only in the *virtual* sense of providing him with something which man can, by his own effort, appropriate and make his, and not in the *actual* sense of making nature dependent on man. Hence, Locke's theory of appropriation is designed to reverse the loss sustained as a result of the Copernican discovery; like the Kantian "(anti-) Copernical revolution" it clearly prefigures, his theory of property aims to explain how man is the coauthor of his environment and how he can transform his dependence on nature into an expression of his autonomy. Acquisition of property is not hoarding, not mere *auri sacra fames* and *amor sceleratus habendi*; the capitalist, for Locke, is not a Harpagon but a man in search of freedom and dignity.

In viewing production not as just a subordinate effort to provide the means necessary for the reproduction of "mere life," but as a liberating and morally significant activity, Locke clearly anticipated Hegel and Marx in their attempt to provide a truly philosophical account of man's concern with production. Unlike them, however, he at the same time rooted his philosophical world view in the modern tradition of empiricism and nominalism. Consequently, while his general understanding of the task of moral theory was, after all, not widely different from that of Hegel and Marx, the substantive system of norms he advocated was much less removed than theirs from the prevailing self-understanding of modernity. His theory of asocial labor, giving rise to his abstract and legalistic conception of private property, has been seen by many as a poor counterpart of the later Hegelian and Marxist analyses of human

[89]Ibid., 250. Even though Strauss brings in Hegel here, he still claims that the substitution of labor for art means a move away from the pursuit of "good life" and toward a purely hedonistic and utilitarian morality.

activity, based on the much more mature theories of the classical political economists. But despite its mercantilist background, the individualism of Locke's theory of property, together with its rooting in contemporary empiricist and nominalistic philosophy, is one of the strongest points of his system. By adopting this more realistic perspective and not attempting to reconstruct more fully the ancient *agora* within the confines of the modern marketplace. Locke, in his search for a modern counterpart to Aristotle's *Politics*, may have erred much less than·either Hegel or Marx.[90]

[90]See above, Introduction, note 11.

PART THREE: ROUSSEAU

Introduction

It has often been said that with Rousseau the modern conception of natural right and natural law comes to a crisis.[1] It has also been remarked many times that, in his search for an alternative to the natural-right tradition, Rousseau looked back to antiquity for a model of good social order.[2] But still it is obvious to most of Rousseau's interpreters, including those who have observed his nostalgia for the constitutions of Sparta and republican Rome, that he was a thoroughly modern thinker. He was a passionate lover of liberty and individual independence; he did not believe in the natural sociability of man; and he inspired nationalisms of left and right (a concept unknown even to Aristotle who, although a Greek patriot, never envisaged a nation-state of all Greeks).[3] He has been seen both as a spiritual father of the French Revolution and as a forerunner of totalitarianism[4]—again, despite Pop-

[1] See, for example, C. E. Vaughan's "Introduction" to his edition of *The Political Writings of Jean-Jacques Rousseau* (Oxford and New York, 1962), and L. Strauss, *Natural Right and History* (Chicago, 1953), 252–95 passim. For a different view of Rousseau's relation to the natural-law tradition, see R. Derathé, *Le rationalisme de J. J. Rousseau* (Paris, 1948), 74ff., and Derathé, *J. J. Rousseau et la science politique de son temps* (Paris, 1950).

[2] See, for example, L. Strauss, "On the Intention of Rousseau," *Social Research*, 14 (1947), 455–87.

[3] See A. M. Cohler, *Rousseau and Nationalism* (New York, 1970). For Rousseau's own ignorance of the concept of nationality, see below, Chap. VII, note 11.

[4] The literature on Rousseau and totalitarianism is quite extensive. The most influential presentation of the totalitarian implications of his doctrine is that of J. L. Talmon, *The Origins of Totalitarian Democracy* (New York, 1970). See also J. W. Chapman, *Rousseau—Totalitarian or Liberal* (New York, 1968). A short review of the subject is given by J. McManners, "The Social Contract and Rousseau's Revolt against Society," reprinted in M. Cranston and R. S. Peters, eds., *Hobbes and Rousseau* (Garden City, N.Y., 1972).

per's claims,[5] a thoroughly modern idea, conceivable only against the background of the modern liberal conception of individuality and the technological revolution of recent times. He also gave us a romantic description of the blessed life of *l'homme de la nature* which, despite the fact that the dream of a Golden Age may be as old as civilization, is a strikingly modern vision in its critique not of a corrupt society but of human civilizations as such. Although each significant previous conception of the Golden Age, be it in the Bible or in Ovid, had extolled the simplicity of mankind's infancy, none of them had gone so far in its praise of innocence as to equate it with such a lack of self-awareness that only an entirely nonrational, nonsocial, and subhuman machine would be capable of it. Yet this is precisely what Rousseau did: in his vision of the infancy of man, he opposed the "noble savage" not to man corrupted by society but to humanity *tout court*, that is, to all those features that differentiate human from animals.

It is because Rousseau was a *critic* of liberalism and of the natural-right tradition that this paradoxical mixture of antiquity and modernity comes to the fore in his thought. Indeed, much of Rousseau's famous penchant for paradoxes can be explained if we see his criticism of post-Hobbesian political thought as an integral part of his own philosophy. "Who resorts to paradox. . . ," says John Plamenatz in his essay on Rousseau, "is ordinarily not concerned to deny the received opinion which his paradox appears to challenge. His purpose is to jolt the reader or listener into recognizing something which he might otherwise overlook."[6] Similarly, a real critic does not simply dismiss the views that he criticizes. Views to be dismissed ought to be either passed over in silence or perhaps ridiculed, and only lesser minds derive satisfaction from total annihilation of their opponents. For a mind of Rousseau's quality, to enter into a polemic against someone is to take his views seriously and to appreciate the sources from which they spring.[7] We may immensely enjoy the wit of Voltaire's *reductio ad absurdum* of Leibnizian theodicy, but we learn more about the truth of Leibniz's views from Kant's critique of metaphysics. For even while rejecting the absolute truth of Leibniz's system, Kant, unlike Voltaire, is far from deeming it absurd: he shows that unless one sees something that

[5]K. Popper, *The Open Society and Its Enemies* (Princeton, 1966), vol. 1, makes the claim that Plato was the father of totalitarianism.

[6]J. Plamenatz, "C'est qui ne signifie autre chose sinon qu'on le forcera d'être libre," *Annales de Philosophie Politique*, 5 (1965), reprinted in Cranston and Peters, eds., *Hobbes and Rousseau*, 320.

[7]Cf. Rousseau's remarks on his critiques of J. Leszczynski and the Archbishop de Beaumont in *Confessions*, 1:607. (All page references to Rousseau's works are to the 4-volume Pléiade edition of *Oeuvres complètes*.)

Leibniz himself could not see, Leibniz's reasoning is irrefutable, and that even its ultimate refutation, which Kant believed to have himself provided, will only restrict the validity of Leibniz's claims and reformulate their meaning by showing they have a regulative and not a constitutive function with respect to experience. Similarly, Rousseau's critique of the natural-right tradition, like the later critique of liberalism by Hegel and Marx, is designed not to obliterate Hobbes and Locke in favor of a reactionary nostalgia or a future utopia, but to uncover the inherent limitations of their theories and assign the proper place to their undoubted discoveries. In fact, Rousseau himself, despite his many opponents and defenders, may still be awaiting as perspicacious a critique of his own theories as the one he himself provided of the natural-right tradition.

V. Man and His Nature

1. Natural Man

The first and the most important point of agreement between Rousseau and the philosophers of the natural-right tradition concerns the concept of nature itself. Rousseau differed very strongly from both Hobbes and Locke in his estimate of what the nature of *man* is. "The Philosophers, who have examined the foundations of society, have all perceived the necessity of tracing it back to a state of nature, but not one of them has ever got there," he wrote in the Introduction to his *Discourse on the Origin and Foundation of Inequality among Mankind.*[1] Hobbes and Locke, as well as other thinkers such as Grotius and Pufendorf, had smuggled into their descriptions of natural man all kinds of characteristics that did not belong there, and consequently they had found natural man in possession of the faculty of reason, a fully developed language, the urge and capacity to appropriate, a whole set of moral concepts, and all the prerequisites needed for either a deadly conflict or cooperation with other men.

But much more basic than these differences between Rousseau and his predecessors is the point of agreement between them, namely the fact that they all found it necessary to trace the origins of society "back to a state of nature." For by "going back to a state of nature," Rousseau had in mind a very specific concept of nature, namely the world view implied in the system of modern science. To go back to a state of nature meant for him primarily not to isolate those features of human life which accorded with the essence of man and were not brought about

[1]*Second Discourse*, 3:132.

by some contingent circumstances of life, but to isolate those features of man which could be captured by a conceptual apparatus similar to that used by Galileo and Newton. According to the spirit of his time, Rousseau viewed science as nominalistic and mechanistic;[2] and his main objection to Hobbes, Locke, and others was that they had not properly grasped the conception of man that this type of science implied.

With this view of science and of the concept of nature that it involved, Rousseau placed himself in a decidedly modern perspective and focused his attention on bringing back certain elements of ancient political ideals that were in need of an entirely new foundation. The model of social integration that he found in ancient theories and constitutions rested on a teleological world view that he could no longer accept, since he had unequivocally accepted the superiority of modern science over the old philosophical speculation. Yet he found that in both moral and political terms, the model advocated by the ancient theories and constitutions pointed to a nobler and more just way of life than the competitive struggle for survival among the isolated, atomized individuals of the liberal tradition. A lesser mind than Rousseau's might have effected an eclectic mixture of these traditions without seeing the elements of their incompatibility. But Rousseau saw clearly the difference between a compilation and a synthesis: he realized that if he was to bring back some of the ancient political ideals as a corrective for the ills of liberal society he had to show first how they would fit with the broad outlook of modernity. And this meant that he first had to show the insufficiency of the philosophical foundations of liberalism not by merely contrasting its consequences with the ancient ideal of politics, but by placing himself *within* the modern tradition and exploring its advantages and limitations from that perspective. Moreover, he had to work out a broad new philosophical conception of man that, while different from those of both ancient speculation and modern mechanistic reductionism,

---

[2]This statement has to be qualified somewhat to take into account what Rousseau says about mechanism in Book ii, Chap. 1 of his *Institutions chymiques* (written around 1747, and published by M. Gautier in *Annales Jean-Jacques Rousseau*, 12/13 [1918–21]). He states there that it is "chimerical" to try to explain "the construction of an organic body (*corps organisé*) solely in terms of the laws of motion" (p. 47). Nevertheless, even there, Rousseau speaks of nature as an "immense machine" (p. 44), and says that Newton "came close to explaining all natural phenomena by the principle of attraction alone" (p. 47) (which, on the other hand, does not stop him from equating attraction with "occult qualities" on p. 45). Without ruling out the possibility of a unitary theory of science, Rousseau opts in the *Institutions chymiques*, much as Kant was to do later in the *Critique of Judgment*, for a special treatment of organic matter in nonmechanistic terms. No trace of this view is visible, however, in the later *Discourse on the Origins of Inequality* (1755) which, together with *Emile*, constitutes the main basis of my reading of Rousseau's views on the nature of man. (I wish to thank Patrick Riley for turning my attention to the *Institutions chymiques*.)

would still permit him to accommodate the advantages of both modern liberalism and the ancient political ideal. Only then could he finally attempt to bring the two views together in a thoroughly original philosophical effort.

The task may seem too great for one man; and Rousseau, living in a climate more favorable to brilliant journalistic exercises than to genuine philosophical analyses, may be seen as particularly ill suited for an enterprise on such a scale. Indeed without the later work of Kant, Hegel, and Marx, who gave a more systematic form to Rousseau's intuitions and gradually rid his theory of some of its dualistic elements, we might not have been able to appreciate fully the fertility of his genius. But within all these limitations, Rousseau acquitted himself surprisingly well in his enormously difficult task, and the most important insights of his successors can already be found in his unsystematic and sometimes chaotic thought. Even if, after having carefully studied his own work and that of his most illustrious successors, we should finally come—as I think we must—to reject his vision as ultimately resting on an illusion and as extremely dangerous in its consequences, we cannot deny that his illusion was grand indeed and that it is impossible for us to understand the political and moral predicament of our age without coming to grips with most, if not all, of the issues that animated the thinking of Rousseau himself and of those whom he guided in their reflections.

Although it is for Hobbes that Rousseau reserved some of his most pointed criticisms, his own concept of nature and the method he uses to analyze "natural man" are closer to Hobbes's than to anyone else's. For it is Hobbes's strictly mechanistic view of natural phenomena that Rousseau considered to be the *differentia specifica* of the natural. "I can discover nothing in any animal but an ingenious machine, to which nature has given sense to wind itself up, and guard, to a certain degree, against everything that might destroy or disorder it. I perceive the very same thing in the human machine, with this difference, that nature alone operates in all the operations of the beast, whereas man, as a free agent, has a share in his. One chooses by instinct; the other by an act of liberty. . . ."[3] Thus, if we are to speak of a "natural man," it is only on the condition that the animalistic features of man's life can be realistically separated from the specifically human capacity for liberty which is "purely spiritual, and cannot be accounted for by the laws of mechanics."[4] Without going into a detailed exposition of how the mechanism of the human machine is constructed, Rousseau believes that we can indeed envisage certain aspects of man's constitution as indis-

[3]*Second Discourse*, 141.
[4]Ibid., 142.

tinguishable from that of a machine. This Gedankenexperiment is not to be taken as a "historical truth" (although we shall see later that it does in *some sense* represent the initial stage in man's "history") "but merely as hypothetical and conditional reasonings."[5] The procedure to be used here Rousseau significantly compares to scientific idealization; his own reflections are "like those systems, which our naturalists daily make of the formation of the world."[6] Such an abstraction or idealization is possible because we can envisage a man who, for reasons to be discussed later, makes little or no use of his liberty. We can think of liberty as merely virtual and not actual in the savage; as merely "the perfectibility,"[7] which has not yet developed to any significant degree. This means that we shall consider the savage as "abandoned by nature to pure instinct, or rather [if we cannot entirely abstract from his perfectibility, as] indemnified for the instinct which has perhaps been denied to him by faculties capable of immediately supplying its place." Even if these faculties are, in the long run, "capable of raising him ... a great deal higher," the idealized savage "would begin with purely animal functions; to see and feel would be his first condition, which he would enjoy in common with other animals."[8] All that will follow in the First Part of the *Second Discourse*, despite substantive differences between Rousseau's and Hobbes's accounts of human nature, will agree with the formal limitations imposed on the concept of nature by Hobbes's mechanistic theory. Man's actions in the state of nature will be viewed as passive responses to external stimulation, and "self-love," or the desire for self-preservation, will be the dominant feature of human motivation. Even when Rousseau takes issue with Hobbes's postulation of the absolute egoism of natural man, his own concept of pity has nothing to do with the moral category of altruism. Pity is "the pure impulse of nature, anterior to all manner of reflection." The commiseration of a savage "is no more than a sentiment, which puts us in the place of him who suffers" and thus, contributing to the suffering of the one moved by it, is disturbing to his own *amour de soi*.[9]

It is only on the basis of this agreement as to the "nature of nature" that the question of disagreement between Rousseau and Hobbes comes into play. The bone of contention between them is not so much the question of the natural goodness or evil of primitive man, but the question of the extent to which the important characteristics of a human being can be accounted for in terms of mechanistic science.

[5]Ibid., 132–33.
[6]Ibid., 133.
[7]Ibid., 142.
[8]Ibid., 142–43.
[9]Ibid., 155.

Their disagreements concerning the description of the actual character and behavior of presocial man are merely consequences of their prior disagreement concerning the limits of the mechanistic account.

In some sense, Rousseau must, of course, be impressed by the consistency of Hobbes's theory. Unlike Locke, who read back into the state of nature all the moral concepts dependent on the existence of freedom that he himself believed to admit of no mechanical explanation, Hobbes consistently carried through his thoroughgoing mechanistic reduction. If liberty involved mechanistically unexplainable phenomena, it had to be denied or transformed into a completely innocuous "absence of external impediments to motion." If natural man was to be capable of reasoning, speaking a language, and contracting obligations toward other men, then all these features had to be accounted for in a way compatible with mechanistic science. As a result, however, Rousseau believes Hobbes's concept of nature to be no longer a term of opposition. The reason the concept of nature is so useful in an investigation of human phenomena is that it can provide a contrast to the concept of *artifact* and especially to the concept of *corruption*. "We should consider what is natural," says Aristotle in a precept that Rousseau chose a motto for his *Second Discourse*, "not in things which are depraved, but in those which are rightly ordered according to nature."[10] In matters concerning inanimate objects or animals there may be no need for the nature-artifact distinction, since no questions of *value* are apt to arise in such contexts. We may safely say that nothing truly "unnatural" could take place among these things, unless it has something to do with the consequences of human action with respect to them. But when we speak of the nature of man, we always mean to oppose it to what men themselves can bring about as their *own* creation. Unlike Aristotle, who identified nature and norm, Rousseau no longer looks to nature as a guide to human behavior. Many, if not most, of his interpreters have missed his point on this score: Rousseau's nostalgia for the noble savage was never meant as a program for action, and he never regarded "going back to nature" (in the sense of "nature" discussed in the *Second Discourse*[11]) as an option for modern man. When one understands nature as a mechanical system, one must immediately realize that it offers no indication as to what one *should* do, and Rousseau was not simple enough to confuse these things. We may bemoan our civilized state and long for the dissolution of our individuality that "going back to

---

[10]Aristotle, *Politics*, 1254a.

[11]In *Emile*, for example, Rousseau uses the terms "nature" and "natural" in a less precise sense.

nature" would bring us, but we can no longer argue that this is a natural (in the normative sense of "natural") way out of our predicament.

Nevertheless, Rousseau still needs the concept of nature as a term of opposition, because with its help he can delineate the scope of that which is *morally indifferent*. In a paradoxical reversal of the Aristotelian attitude, for Rousseau to say that something (and society in particular) is a human artifact is to say that it is a subject of moral concern. Since an artifact is something that is our own free creation, it is something for which we are responsible; an act of spontaneity involves us in the reality of the question about *norms*. If we want to say that certain forms of society are morally wrong, we must first show that the words "right" and "wrong" apply here and then explain why they do. And the first step in showing this is to prove that the making and remaking of society are in our power.

Hobbes himself believed that society was a human artifact and not a natural creation. But since there is nothing about men, according to Hobbes, that could make us believe them to be capable of true creativity, human artifacts must be ultimately seen as more or less indirect natural consequences of the way in which the human machine functions. The appearance of political obligations that to some extent correspond to our moral intuitions made Hobbes distinguish the social state of man from his presocial behavior, but in a fundamental sense nothing could qualify as "unnatural" within the framework of his total philosophical commitment to mechanistic science. Consequently, in arguing against Hobbes, Rousseau wished to show that there are some features of man's behavior the account of which absolutely requires the acknowledgment of human freedom and spontaneity. Since Hobbes specifically denies the existence of free will, Rousseau could not convincingly begin his critique of Hobbes by claiming that the mechanistic account is incapable of accounting for human freedom. But he believed the Hobbesian theory of man to be vulnerable on another score, namely, in its reduction of rationality to a set of mechanical phenomena. It is this aspect of Hobbes's theory that Rousseau attacks first, and he follows his attack with a presentation of what is to him a more adequate method of describing the rational animal.

The cornerstone of Rousseau's claim that rationality is irreducible to mechanical phenomena is his distinction between sensation and ideas. It is in *Emile*, rather than the *Second Discourse*, that Rousseau gives the most cogent exposition of his views on this subject:

Before the age of reason the child receives images, not ideas; and there is this difference between them: images are merely the pictures of external objects, while ideas are notions about those objects determined by their relations. An image when it is recalled may exist by itself in the mind, but every idea implies other ideas. When we have images we merely perceive, when we reason we compare. Our sensations are merely passive, our notions or ideas spring from an active principle which judges.[12]

Without the sophisticated apparatus of Kant's epistemology, Rousseau makes an essentially Kantian point: to reason is to judge, to judge is to compare; to compare the individually disparate sensations and to bring them together ("to synthesize," Kant would say) is a spontaneous activity of which no passive mechanism is capable. Moreover, without this synthesis, sensation is meaningless (Kant would say "blind"), since meaning comes from judgment and comparison. Concepts or judgments express *relations* and not objects; they refer to "functions" and not "substances." Hence, it is absurd to represent them as forms of material existence. Rather than paraphrasing Rousseau's expressions, I shall let him speak; there could hardly be a more clear and succinct exposition of this aspect of his thought than the one he gave himself.

To perceive is to feel [sense]; to compare is to judge; to judge and to feel are not the same. Through sensations objects present themselves to me separately and singly as they are in nature; but comparing them I rearrange them, I shift them so to speak, I place one upon another to decide whether they are alike or different, or more generally to find out their relations. To my mind, the distinctive faculty of an active or intelligent being is the power of understanding this word 'is.' I seek in vain in the merely sensitive entity that intelligent force . . . I can find no trace of it in its nature. This passive entity will be aware of each object separately, it will even be aware of the whole formed by the two together, but having no power to place them side by side it can never compare them, it can never form a judgment with regard to them.[13]

The first time a child sees a stick half-immersed in water he thinks he sees a broken stick; the sensation is true and would not cease even if he knew the reason for this appearance. . . . But when deceived by his judgment he goes further and, after saying he sees a broken stick, he affirms that it is really broken he says what is not true. Why? Because he becomes active and judges no longer by observation but by induction, he affirms what he does not perceive, that is, that the judgment he receives through one of his senses would be confirmed by another.[14]

[The] comparative ideas, *greater*, *smaller*, together with number of ideas

<hr>

[12]*Emile*, 4:344.
[13]Ibid., 571–72.
[14]Ibid., 482–83.

of *one, two*, etc., are certainly not sensations, although my mind produces them only when my sensations occur.[15]

The more I consider thought and the nature of the human mind, the more likeness I find between the argument of the materialists and those of the deaf man. Indeed, they are deaf to the inner voice which cries to them, in a tone which can hardly be mistaken. A machine does not think, there is neither movement nor form which can produce reflection; something within you tries to break the bonds which confine it; space is not your measure, the whole universe does not suffice to contain you; your sentiments, your desires, your anxiety, your pride itself, have another origin than this small body in which you are imprisoned.[16]

In the *Second Discourse*, Rousseau relates his attack on Hobbes's mechanistic reductionism to a point concerning the relation between rationality and speech. A savage (a man of whose behavior a mechanistic account could be given) may be capable of a rudimentary language of proper names, but he is in no condition to distinguish a genus or a species.[17] General ideas, which constitute the core of every developed language, "cannot be conveyed to the mind without the assistance of words, nor can the understanding seize them except by means of propositions."[18] This is to be a powerful argument against Hobbes's identification of understanding and imagination, for Rousseau sees the connection between language and thought as transcending any empiricist account. "Every general idea is purely intellectual," he says; "let imagination tamper ever so little with it, it immediately becomes a particular idea."[19] One will never be able to form an "image of a tree in general," since beings that are "perfectly abstract" are not *perceivable*; they are only "*conceivable* by the assistance of speech." "We must therefore make use of propositions; we must therefore speak to have general ideas; for the moment imagination stops, the mind can continue to function only with the aid of discourse. If therefore the first inventors could give no names to any ideas except those which they already had, it follows that the first substantives could never have been anything more than proper names."[20]

Thus, Hobbes's mistake, according to Rousseau, was to overestimate the power of "natural man." It is difficult to evaluate in detail the merit of Rousseau's arguments on this score, and this is certainly not the place to make the attempt, since one of the most contentious issues in

[15]Ibid., 572.
[16]Ibid., 585.
[17]*Second Discourse*, 149.
[18]Ibid.
[19]Ibid., 150.
[20]Ibid.

philosophy in general is involved. Hobbes's reductionism was certainly crude and could not remain unmodified if it were to be made defensible. On the other hand, whether one finds Rousseau's critique persuasive depends on a broad range of philosophical commitments, not the least of which is our evaluation of the merits of Kant's arguments, which were clearly prefigured in Rousseau and which extended Rousseau's position into a full-fledged philosophical system. Also, Rousseau's critique may be more applicable to Hobbes than to Locke. Clearly, Locke also used the term "nature" in such a broad sense that hardly anything could be viewed as "unnatural" in his system. But the "naturalization" of human behavior in Locke is no longer tied to a simple mechanistic, and even less to a simple materialistic, reductionism, since Locke's understanding of the commitment implied by modern natural science was much less clear-cut than either Hobbes's or Rousseau's. Whereas Hobbes and Rousseau have given us a quite positivistic reading of modern science, with its insistence on physicalism, nominalism, and (causal) determinism, Locke was not a very strict adherent of the latter two doctrines and rejected the first altogether. Naturally, his own account of thought processes left no room for a genuine spontaneity of the human mind; but because his "mechanics of the mental" allowed for an association of ideas in which the semantic features of ideas were not necessarily irrelevant to the process of association, Locke may, perhaps, have provided a more complex causal account of rationality, which would not automatically collapse when confronted with Rousseau's objections. This, in fact, applies to Locke's naturalism in general; since Rousseau's belief in the necessity of transcending the limits of naturalism and bringing in a heterogeneous account of human phenomena depends on his rather narrow interpretation of modern science, Locke's broad understanding of "nature" may exempt him from many of Rousseau's objections. Where Rousseau believed that matters of politics and morality must be given complete independence from natural science, and where he consequently found the liberal tradition lacking in philosophical foundation, Locke could perhaps claim that Rousseau misunderstood what these foundations were supposed to be.

Be that as it may, it should be clear that the gist of Rousseau's disagreement with the natural-right theorists lies in his methodological belief that the natural is equivalent to the mechanical and that a mechanistic theory is incapable of accounting for the specifically human phenomena of freedom and rationality. We can—indeed we must— delineate the bounds of nature with respect to humans, but the only result attainable by this inquiry is that "man is by nature subhuman."[21]

[21]L. Strauss, *Natural Right and History* (Chicago, 1953), 271.

By reading back into the state of nature the specifically human charac-
terstics of man we can only miss their true meaning, obscure the issue
of moral responsibility, and mistake the character of social relationships.

2. Reflection and Alienated Man

The crucial characteristic of postnatural man, which truly takes man
out of the state of nature and explains all the features of his constitution
that elude the grasp of a mechanistic account, is his capacity for
reflection. "I dare almost affirm," says Rousseau with uncharacteristic
modesty, "that a state of reflection is a state against nature, and that the
man who meditates is a degenerate animal (*animal dépravé*)."[22] The
word "reflection" has an ambiguous meaning which Rousseau finds
very suitable for his purposes: it connects the detached character of
thinking (reflection in the sense of "meditation") with an act of intro-
spection and self-consciousness (*re-flectio* as bending backward or
turning inward). The precedent for this link between rationality and
self-consciousness is, of course, to be found in Descartes's *cogito*.
Indeed, in his "Confession of Faith of the Savoyard Vicar," Rousseau
clearly follows the broad lines of Cartesian *Meditations*. In the *Second
Discourse* he is less explicit, but the Cartesian parallels are nonetheless
there. "Man's first feeling was that of his own existence, his first care
that of preserving it," he says in connection with his account of appropriation.[23] It is the transformation of the prerational "feeling" into a full-
blown phenomenon of self-consciousness that will finally take man out
of the state of nature altogether. The self-love of the savage is merely an
impulse of self-preservation, and natural man has no finer sense of self-
identity. To begin with, he is apt to confuse himself with other members
of the species, and this is the foundation of his natural pity, a mere
sentiment or "impulse of nature, anterior to all reflection."[24] Pity consists in an immediate identification with the sufferer. "It is evident that
this identification," says Rousseau, "must have been infinitely more
perfect in the state of nature than in the state of reason. It is reason that
engenders selfishness (*amour propre*), and reflection that strengthens
it; it is reflection (*elle*) that bends man backward into himself (*replie
l'homme sur lui-même*)."[25] The facility with which a savage could satisfy

[22]*Second Discourse*, 138.
[23]Ibid., 164.
[24]Ibid., 155.
[25]Ibid., 155–56.

his needs made him ignore even the difference between himself and his environment: stones and branches were for him his "natural arms."[26] The world presents itself to the savage as "constantly the same order, constantly the same revolutions" and "his soul which nothing disturbs, gives itself up entirely to the sentiment of its present existence, without any thought of even the nearest futurity."[27]

The simple immersion in the world present to the savage gives way to the most acute estrangement and anxiety the moment a man acquires all the prerequisites for saying "*I* am" and for opposing his self-consciousness to the existence of things and people around him. Rousseau gives a rather appealing genetic account of the origins of self-consciousness, an account that corresponds to his version of the original sin or the termination of the Golden Age. What is distinctive in his view, as compared with biblical and mythological tales, is that he sees the "fall" from nature as the last significant event (or rather a long series of events) in a human evolution that was still fundamentally *prehistorical*, in that it was the last time that men were shaped by the natural course of events and had no responsibility for their own fate. There is a certain paradox about this transition: nature acts here to release the very capacity of man that it can no longer shape and that makes man enter a new, "unnatural" mode of existence. It is "many different accidents"[28] that make men reach the state of reflection, and at the present stage men are still *drifting* toward their destiny. These accidents fall, roughly, into two interrelated categories: natural disasters and overpopulation. "In proportion as the human species grew more numerous, and extended itself, its difficulties likewise multiplied and increased." Whereas the previous conditions of life had been characterized by plenty, scarcity began now to appear, so that "bad harvests, long and severe winters, and scorching summers . . . required a new resourcefulness and activity (*industrie*)."[29] Finally, "great inundations or earthquakes surrounded inhabited districts with water or precipices. Portions of the continent were by revolutions of the globe torn off and split into islands," and this in turn concentrated large populations in smaller territories and inexorably released the forces implicit in human "perfectibility."

The evolution of man toward a self-conscious being involves four essential characteristics: (1) the crucial distinction between oneself and the whole environment (including other people), which results in the

[26]Ibid., 165.
[27]Ibid., 144.
[28]Ibid.
[29]Ibid., 165.

formation of a radically *egocentric view of the world*; (2) the appearance of a *moral* dimension of man's life in that human action becomes largely independent of "natural impulses"; (3) the introduction of *anxiety*, which results from the perception, implicit in the egocentric view of the world, of the general estrangement and hostility of the environment; (4) the consequent aggressive attitude of man toward nature and other men, with the concomitant development of reason, pride, property, and inequality.

Rousseau tries to capture the process of the formation of man's radically egocentric view of the world by describing it as a transformation of the savage's *amour de soi*, or self-love, into a civilized man's *amour propre* or selfishness: "We must not confuse selfishness with self-love," he says in an important note in the *Second Discourse*; "they are two very distinct passions both in their nature and in their effects. Self-love is a natural sentiment, which inclines every animal to his preservation.... Selfishness is but a relative and factitious sentiment, engendered in society, which inclines every individual to set a greater value upon himself than upon any other man, which inspires men with all mischief they do to each other...."[30]

Amour de soi is tied to the self-preservative activity of the savage. The requirements of self-preservation—as long as self-preservation is viewed as a natural phenomenon, explicable with reference to the laws of mechanics—are, according to Rousseau, very different from what Hobbes had imagined them to be. In particular, Rousseau believes, self-preservation cannot involve, to any significant degree, the capacity for *reasoning*; consequently, it cannot become a generalized attitude toward the environment as such. Hobbes, according to Rousseau, did not see the full consequences of his linking self-preservation to the fear of violent death. The savage "fears no evils but pain and hunger; I say pain, and not death; for no animal, merely as such, will ever know what it is to die, and the knowledge of death, and of its terrors, is one of the first acquisitions made by man, in consequence of his deviating from the animal state."[31] To say that a man or an animal fears death is to endow him with a capacity for making a general distinction between "I" and "not-I," for comparing and opposing the self and the world, and for realizing the temporal dimension of his own existence, which can be ended by death. Death is one of the most abstract concepts, and man's realization that he is mortal requires a type of awareness that subordinates the particular events of the present to a general vision of the world

[30]Ibid., 219.
[31]Ibid., 143.

in which a very special place is assigned to a continuous unity of one's own disparate acts and states.

Similarly, the capacity for responding to possible dangers as if they were actual—which both Hobbes and Rousseau (and Locke, for that matter) take to be a distinctively human characteristic—is, according to Rousseau, incompatible with mechanical activity, no matter how complicated the machine in question. To speak about a hypothetical event requires that an abstraction be made from everything that is actually present to the senses and that the one who expects something to happen be able to compare and analyze past events, think in terms of an analogy between the past and the future, and correct the evidence of the senses with a judgment formed on the basis of such comparisons and analyses. The data of the senses, according to Rousseau, are always unambiguous and concrete; ambiguity (and possibility) appears only with interpretation, for which a genuine generalization (and hence understanding) is indispensable. Hobbes must be given credit for not ignoring the connection between language and generalization; but he must also be blamed, according to Rousseau, for not noticing the radical break that linguistic generalization involves with respect to all natural phenomena. When an animal responds to a sign of danger, it acts according to a natural impulse that unambiguously ties certain types of sensations to certain kinds of responses. But when a man hypothesizes about future events, he interprets and judges his sensations, and no naturalistic account could be given of these activities. Within the stimulus-response model of behavior, ambiguity is tantamount to *neurosis*; and neurosis, being a clear case of *dysfunction*, cannot be made into a principle defining the functioning of the human machine. To identify neurosis as such a principle is to say that man is not a creature of nature, since the natural mechanism defining his constitution grossly underdetermines his actual behavior.

So long, therefore, as one thinks of self-preservation in naturalistic terms, *amour de soi* does not involve either the concept of the self or that of the world as such. It merely rests on a set of instincts that unambiguously define each particular behavior of the animal as a response to a particular present stimulation. When changes in the environment suddenly make this set of instincts counterproductive with respect to an animal's self-preservation, the individual becomes neurotic and the species perishes. Only man is an exception here, since his dormant "perfectibility" is at this point awakened and takes over the function of his instincts. The new set of principles by which man is now guided in his actions is not comparable to a new organ arisen as a result of a genetic mutation but is due to a purely *spiritual* and nonnatural faculty of reflection. Thus, to give a further account of human action, including an account of interpersonal relations and of social and political phenomena, we must find another *method* of analysis, a *new science*, different from mechanistic natural science and capable of doing justice to the subject matter. The transition between the state of nature and the civilized state is not merely a break between the individual and society or between presocial and social man; it is, rather, a break between two heterogeneous kinds of entities and two correspondingly heterogeneous kinds of analyses. Rousseau is not afraid of the inherent dualism involved in this parting of ways between *Naturwissenschaften* and *Geisteswissenschaften*; it is a dualism that he finds characteristic of modern man's predicament. It will not do, according to him, merely to postulate two kinds of "nature," one for man and another for other living and inanimate objects. Such a way was still open to previous philosophers who separated "soul" and "matter," for they did not realize that, with respect to man, there arises a fundamental question concerning the *authorship* of his actions which makes it no longer possible to speak of his "nature" at all. When, after the publication of *Emile* (1762), the civil and religious authorities in Paris began their campaign of persecution against Rousseau, they were not moving against what would today appear merely minor infractions of the rules of orthodoxy. The scholars of the Sorbonne, the *Parlement* of Paris, and Archbishop de Beaumont were reacting against Rousseau's total emancipation of man from all constraints of an external order, be it natural or divine. The nineteenth-century theories of an omnipotent Man-God (as opposed to the Christian doctrine of God-Man) were to bring out what was already quite distinctly present in Rousseau.

Amour de soi gives way to *amour propre* when a man begins to reflect. Overpopulation and natural disasters make men scramble for available resources. The first change in a man's attitude connected with these situations is his turning his attention to the relation between himself and his environment. While the savage was incapable of making a clear distinction between himself and his environment and lived completely immersed in his immediate needs, of which the external world provided the natural means of satisfaction, a prolonged state of nonsatisfaction made him realize the difference between his volition and the effects it produced in combination with the external conditions of his life. A cataclysmic flood or an earthquake made him realize that nature, far from being in total harmony with his bodily needs, was in fact an alien force that could threaten his very existence. The development of his rational ability progressed along lines exactly parallel to the development of his self-consciousness: only by clearly delineating the bounds of what he could call his own could he define the scope of that which constituted the source of his dependence and which his knowledge was to examine and conquer. The first "kind of reflection" of which the savage was capable was only "mechanical prudence,"[32] but by gradually experimenting with his power, he acquired a full realization of his own distinctness. "The first look he gave into himself produced the first emotion of pride in him: thus it was that at a time he scarcely knew how to distinguish between the different orders of beings (*rangs*), in considering himself the highest by virtue of his species, he prepared his later claim to preeminence as an individual."[33]

The full development of *amour propre* results in a world indelibly stamped with a *value* placed on the subject. Self-preservation is gradually transformed from a merely instinctive reaching for what is self-evidently assumed to "be there" into a complex vision of the world in which the agent tries to secure the means of his survival from what appears to him a hostile, external world. Self-preservation is now a conscious *norm* for his actions, and he can no longer be sure of his success in implementing it. He orders the world in such a way as to prevent the occurrence of danger, reasoning from past observations to general laws and to future events.

Like Descartes, then, Rousseau makes the self a foundation of all that is human in man. Like Descartes too, he makes self-consciousness the pivotal point around which other human characteristics are to be explained and a pillar around which man constructs the edifice of his knowledge. But there are at least three important differences between Rousseau's and Descartes's treatments of self-consciousness. First, Rousseau's main concern is not epistemological. He is interested not in founding knowledge on self-certainty but in locating an ontological or existential principle of human freedom and rationality. "What is man?" is his question, not "What can be known with certainty?" Second, Rousseau's account of the self ties it inherently to man's *practical* attitudes and to his struggle for survival. Self-consciousness is not an attitude of a knower who may doubt the existence of the external world, but a form of self-assertion by a subject who is threatened with extinction. It is not the "I *think*" that provides the emphasis of the Rousseauean *cogito*, but the "I am."[34] Finally, self-consciousness is the origin of man's struggle and misfortunes, and not the first step toward security, even if only toward the security of a knower. Rousseau is, of course, aware of the optimism of the rationalist tradition, both in its Cartesian form and in the form of the exuberant confidence of the Enlightenment. He was himself of the opinion that rationality and self-

[32]Ibid., 165.
[33]Ibid., 166.
[34]See B. Baczko, *Rousseau: Solitude et communauté* (Paris, 1974), 213.

consciousness finally raise man to the most exalted position among creatures. But like Hobbes, who made absurdity the balance for the blessings of reason, Rousseau emphasized that by raising man to the level of morality, reflection is equally responsible for all the evil, as well as all the good, things in this world. And in many of his writings, such as the *Second Discourse*, he indeed appears as a Cartesian *à rebours* who traces all the misfortunes of human life to the *cogito* and the principle of rationality that it expresses.

When a dog looks at itself in the mirror, it barks at an unexpected companion. When a man sees his own image, his pride may be affected, but his loneliness is not. Rousseau was the first political thinker (Pascal being his forerunner in the area of religion) who saw this loneliness and alienation as a direct consequence of man's emancipation from the forces of nature. For Aristotle, man was by nature social, since only a beast or a god could live alone.[35] Living alone was for him a condition expressing a certain kind of perfection, for it implied self-sufficiency. Rousseau, on the other hand, believed that both man's happiness and his moral rectitude involved a relation to other people, and yet he asserted that the first consequence of self-consciousness and rationality was the radical estrangement of man both from his natural environment and from other men. As we shall see, man's happiness and moral rectitude require a generalization of his conduct and a subjection of passions to reason—both of which are possible only within the context of a human community.

Amour propre, however, is only a middle term of human development, the extremes of which are the prereflective unity with nature and the formation of a new supraindividual totality constituted by the general will. A man is free at the stage of *amour propre*; and by virtue of this freedom, he is responsible for his actions. But since his reason is entirely devoted to the task of perpetuating the existence of that particular individual which he happens to be, it does not guide, but follows, the *ad hoc* dictates of passion. Reason emancipates man from nature, but the meaning of this emancipation is one-sided at the stage of *amour propre*: it gives man those means of gratifying his desires which he could not possess before, but the only result of this acquisition is an enormous increase in the scope of his wants and desires. Something quite analogous to Hobbes's constant regeneration of desire is ascribed by Rousseau to the vicious circle into which a man is introduced by his rationality:

> It is by the activity of our passions, that our reason improves; we covet knowledge merely because we covet enjoyment, and it is impossible to

[35]*Politics*, 1253a.

conceive why a man exempt from fears and desires should take the trouble to reason. The passions, in their turn, owe their origin to our needs, and their increase to our progress in science, for we cannot desire or fear anything, except in consequence of the ideas we have of it, or of the simple impulses of nature; and the savage man, destitute of every species of knowledge, experiences no passions but those of this last kind.[36]

In other words, reason, which gives man the capacity to order his life in accordance with the principles of morality, is initially used by man merely as an *instrument* for the gratification of passions that it itself engenders. It is the truly fallen condition of man that is defined by *amour propre*.

The greatest factor in this increase of the number and strength of passions is the phenomenon of alienation that self-consciousness produces. The very fact of the radical division of the world into self and everything-outside-self makes man radically *alone* in the world. This feeling of loneliness is less a result of any particular dangers that threaten man's existence than of his general world view, in which there is room for only one independent subject. Where a savage had felt a vague communion with nature, a civilized man feels the uniqueness of his own existence and sees nature *as such* as a threatening or at best an indifferent element. Only a union with other people could provide him with a way of reestablishing some form of fellowship, but he is incapable of that at this stage, since he views other men as competitors for scarce resources. Although even complete mastery over nature would only make his isolation more acute, the anxiety connected with his inability to foresee all the contingencies of estranged nature makes for a constant increase in the scope of what is in his eyes indispensable to his security, and thus aggravates the competition with, and alienation from, other men. In pursuing his independence he increases his own isolation, which brings new insecurity and hence new wants and new dependence.

[36]*Second Discourse*, 143.

VI. Morality and Politics

1. Autonomy

There has been some controversy as to whether Rousseau's ideas of morality should be read in the light of Kant's doctrine. Serious differences between their moral philosophies certainly go beyond the fact that Kant had at his disposal a very sophisticated philosophical apparatus, still lacking in Rousseau.[1] Rousseau's thought has a strong tendency to what one opponent of the Kantian interpretation calls "sentimentalism," an insistence on the role of feeling in morality, which is lacking in Kant.[2] Rousseau also exhibits a clear element of "eudaimonism," an insistence on the intimate bond between morality and happiness, which Kant finally came to reject.[3] Finally, there are clear elements of "Hegelianism" in Rousseau, especially in his connecting morality with politics and education and in his view that moral action involves a supraindividual totality embodied in the general will.

Those interpreters of Rousseau who have read his moral theory exclusively through Kantian glasses were certainly wrong in eliminating these non-Kantian elements of his thought, even if they believed they were actually doing Rousseau a service in cleansing his discoveries of what they viewed as "romantic nonsense." Nevertheless, it is equally indubitable that Kant took up a certain *aspect* of Rousseau's moral

---

[1]A pronounced Kantian reading has been presented by E. Cassirer in *Rousseau, Kant, Goethe* (Princeton, 1945) and *The Question of J. J. Rousseau* (New York, 1954). For a review of scholarship on this matter, as well as a critique of the Kantian interpretation, see P. Pasqualucci, *Rousseau e Kant* (Milan, 1974), vol. 1.

[2]Pasqualucci, *Rousseau e Kant*, 1:142.

[3]Ibid., 143.

theory and gave it a very cogent and persuasive form, so by following a Kantian reading of Rousseau we may be able to clear up certain ambiguities in Rousseau's own formulations. That Rousseau influenced not only Kant but also Hegel and Marx is obvious, but it is equally obvious that the latter two were influenced by Kant as well and that they returned to those aspects of Rousseau's moral theory that Kant had not considered because they believed that they could thus remedy what they saw as errors and limitations of Kant's own moral philosophy. It is only a sign of the fertility of Rousseau's genius that the full reception of his theory required the work of a whole succession of great philosophers. In my own effort to capture in Rousseau's work the main features of a whole tradition of moral and political thought to which it gave impetus, I shall feel free to draw from all those thinkers who consciously followed the path he had indicated.

The most important element that Rousseau and Kant share is their understanding of freedom. Even if Rousseau had no other merit, his introduction of the concept of autonomy would have placed him among the very greatest moral philosophers. One should recall that among the most important reasons Hobbes and Locke undertook to provide a new theory of action was the fact that they both found the concept of free will absurd. Given their world view, shaped by the methodological and philosophical assumptions of modern science, the concept of free will appeared to them to equate freedom with arbitrariness and thus to make free action incompatible with morality understood as obedience to a system of norms. Responsibility seemed to call for a possibility of "doing otherwise," but the assumption of such a possibility seemed to conflict with an action determined by moral principles. Hobbes decided to make a clean sweep of the whole problem. He postulated a uniformly mechanistic account of human action and reconstructed the behavior of man usually associated with morality as an interplay of external compulsion and an internal force of motivation. He would preserve the *political* sense of obligation and responsibility, but only at the price of eliminating their properly *moral* sense. Locke's approach was much more ambiguous. He left some room for a nonmechanical freedom, for he thought that even in nature there must be some beginning of motion and, in particular, he could not see how human action, which clearly follows the dictates of volition, could be brought about mechanically by what is only an idea, and not a material form of existence. But since he was at first incapable of connecting this sense of freedom with any processes of volition, he could not see how it could stand in any meaningful relation to morality. Only a madman could disobey the commands of his will, and since Locke saw the will as strictly determined, he thought that basing responsibility on this kind of freedom would be to found morality on the possibility of insanity. After much hesitation he seems to have stumbled on the type of solution that Rousseau was to discover after him, namely, the possibility of self-legislation. Paradoxically, his theory may even have some significant advantages over Rousseau's and Kant's or Hegel's. Rousseau once said that "upright and simple men are difficult to deceive precisely because of their simplicity; . . . they are not indeed subtle enough to be dupes."[4] It would certainly be preposterous to call Locke a "simple man," but in this particular case, his ignorance of the vistas that Rousseau and Kant were to open up made him not "subtle enough" to become entangled in the new metaphysical speculations that placed man in two totally separate dimensions of being and made morality independent of the modern scientific outlook. Where Kant and Rousseau remained at the level of radical dualism, and where Hegel and Marx fought to synthesize the rational and the natural, Locke may have found his way to a theory of autonomy that did not involve a radical break between the mental and the material or the pure and the empirical. Consequently, the system of values that he arrived at, in opposition to a system based on the ancient political ideal that his part-opponents-part-successors wanted to reinstitute, may have been more realistically tailored to the conditions of life of the modern *homo oeconomicus*. But Locke was still groping in the dark, and it is not clear to what extent he realized the novelty of his move. "His" theory of autonomy must still be read into his work, while Rousseau is clearly conscious of breaking new ground and substituting a new conceptual framework for the old inconsistency-ridden theory of free will.

> The passing from the state of nature to the civil society produces a remarkable change in man; it puts justice as a rule of conduct in the place of instinct, and gives his actions the moral quality they previously lacked. It is only then, when the voice of duty has taken the place of physical impulse, and right that of desire, that man, who has hitherto thought only of himself, finds himself compelled to act on other principles, and to consult his reason rather than study his inclinations. . . . We might also add that man acquires with civil society, moral freedom, which alone makes man the master of himself; for to be governed by appetite alone is slavery, while obedience to a law one prescribes to oneself is freedom."[5]

Freedom is "obedience to a law one prescribes to oneself." How does this view of freedom resolve the antinomies of free will? Rousseau

---

[4]*Social Contract*, IV, 1 (3:437). All references to *The Social Contract* are to the appropriate Book (roman numerals) and chapter (arabic numerals). Where an additional specification is needed, the page number of vol. 3 of the Pléiade edition is referred to in parentheses.
[5]Ibid., I, 8 (364, 365).

provides his answer to this question in the most philosophical part of *Emile*, the "Confession of Faith of the Savoyard Vicar." The problem with the materialist critique of the free-will conception is that in this account "it is not the word 'freedom' that is meaningless, but the word 'necessity.' "[6] At first sight, Rousseau's argument does not seem to offer anything new: the word "necessity" is absurd because "to suppose some action which is not the effect of an active motive power is indeed to suppose effects without cause, to reason in a vicious circle." But Rousseau's point is not that every movement must have its origin in a first impulse that can have no antecedent cause in turn, and that *hence* there is nothing absurd in the concept of free will. If that were his point, his theory would be of no interest. But his point is that an action's being free does not imply its arbitrariness. Those who, like Hobbes and Locke, identify free will with arbitrariness do not understand the distinction between the way in which a man's will is "determined" by a *cause* and by a *reason*. In other words, they do not distinguish between sensations and ideas. "I have a body," says Rousseau, "which is acted upon by other bodies, and it acts upon them in turn; there is no doubt about this reciprocal action; but my will is independent of my senses; I consent or resist; . . . and I know very well in myself when I have done what I wanted [willed] and when I have merely given way to my passions."[7] Rousseau makes a very Kantian distinction here between passions, which are merely effects of external pressures and the will, which is the result of reasoning. Despite his rather clumsy terminology, he also makes another Kantian point, that the distinctive feature of a moral action has its locus in a corresponding intention,[8] and since the acts of volition are those of an "immaterial substance,"[9] they are not *empirically discoverable*. It is only I "in myself" who know whether a given action had a moral character (since "I know the will only through the consciousness of my own will"[10]), and no dissection of my body will ever be able to discover it. But the most crucial similarity between Rousseau and Kant lies in their identification of will and reason. So far as it is possible to distinguish between the *will* and *reason* (that is, between practical and theoretical reason), it is possible to speak about the will's being "determined": "What is the cause that determines [a man's] will?" we can ask. The answer is: "It is his intelligence [*faculté intelligente*], his power of judging." Nevertheless, the will is only a parallel power to reason

---

[6]*Emile*, 586.
[7]Ibid., 585–86.
[8]Ibid., 595; *Moral Letters*, 4:1106.
[9]*Emile*, 587.
[10]Ibid., 586.

and their operation is the same: a man "chooses between good and evil as he judges between truth and falsehood; if his judgment is at fault, he chooses amiss."[11] Thus, to will is to follow one's reason in deciding upon one's course of action. But since the most fundamental characteristic of reason is its operation in accordance with universal principles, and since only that is rational which is *justified* according to general norms, an act of volition can be wrong, but it *cannot* be arbitrary.

But if the will is the same as practical reason, Hobbes would ask why this is grounds for calling it "free." It is here that Rousseau brings in his distinction between nature and reflection. As long as reason is seen as something "natural," that is, part and parcel of the objective world, being determined by a law of reason is not different in kind from being determined by a law of mechanics. Even if rational processes are not reduced to events subject to a mechanistic explanation (as when, for example, our theory of man involves a teleology), the situation remains the same with respect to the problem of freedom as long as the origin of rationality is not to be found in human spontaneity. It is by no means a novel idea that reason is active; in fact it was a common view throughout the whole rationalist tradition, from Plato and Aristotle, through Christian philosophy, to Descartes and Leibniz. But in all these doctrines the process of thinking was conceived of as a rediscovery of the principles encoded in the human mind, whether as a result of a divine act or as a result of the homogeneous nature of the mind and the world. One way or another, the activity of the mind was seen as guided by principles the authorship of which was not man's but God's or nature's. For Rousseau, however, reason is not at all a part of the natural order, so that "if you understand clearly that man is active in his judgments, that his intelligence is only the power to compare and judge, you will see that his freedom is only a similar power derived from this; . . . the determining cause [of his judgment and volition] is in himself." Thus, a rational action follows the dictates of human spontaneity and "what [a man] does freely is no part of a system marked out by Providence and it cannot be imputed to Providence."[12]

There is a further important similarity between the moral systems of Rousseau and Kant: Rousseau's account, like Kant's, makes freedom itself the supreme moral value. Freedom is not simply a necessary condition of virtue in a man; it is also its sufficient condition. "What is meant by a virtuous man?" Rousseau asks his pupil in *Emile*. And he provides the answer himself: "He can conquer his affections; for then he

[11]Ibid.
[12]Ibid., 589.

follows his reason, his conscience; he does his duty; he is his own master and nothing can turn him from the right way."[13] This statement, the political corollary of which is Rousseau's claim that the general will never errs, has often been misunderstood. It says not that freedom always leads in the right direction, but that insofar as *moral* rightness is concerned, freedom itself *is* the right direction—the statement expresses what, for Rousseau, is a tautology. This has a significant bearing on Rousseau's view of moral responsibility. Since in some sense *taking* responsibility for one's own actions, that is, acting according to reason and hence freely, is itself the supreme moral value, responsibility cannot imply that an immoral action is done freely. Immorality is more in the nature of abdicating responsibility and abandoning oneself to the influence of passions than freely done evil. Hence, attachment of praise and blame is not inseparable from moral agency, but is rather tied to human imperfection. "There is no ... virtue without a struggle. The word virtue is derived from a word signifying strength, and strength is the foundation of all virtue. Virtue is a heritage of a creature weak by nature but strong by will; that is the whole merit of the righteous man; and though we call God good we do not call Him virtuous, because He does good without effort."[14] Nevertheless, while there can be moral agency without praise and blame, the reverse does not hold: the "natural weakness" of man is not in itself evil but becomes such only when a man is capable of freedom. As Rousseau puts it, it is only "in the world of morals" that "the door to vice is open."[15] For not only are predicates such as "good" and "evil," strictly speaking, inapplicable to natural phenomena, but also the source of most passions that lead men to harm one another goes back to the vistas opened by the progress of rationality. It is passion exaggerated and abandoned by reason, instead of guided by it, that is responsible for most evil actions.

But what is the guidance that reason offers to passion? The basic feature of rational action, according to Rousseau, is that it follows a general principle and not an *ad hoc* inclination. Reason develops together with self-awareness, that is, a realization of one's own uniqueness and a positioning of one's own self at the center of the subject's vision of the world. Nevertheless, the ultimate point of arrival of rational development is the concept of *objectivity*, in which the egocentric position is abandoned in favor of a world view organized by general principles. Rationality, in its true form, is a perspective that places the particular within the framework of a law. The practical counterpart of

[13]Ibid., 818.
[14]Ibid., 817.
[15]Ibid., 334.

rationality is justice and moral equality; it is an ordering of one's actions according to general principles that do not assign any privileged position to this or that particular subject or interest, but point to a type of action that is in itself worthy of approval, simply by virtue of its being in accordance with a rational law. It is this principle that, carried over into political matters, will identify social justice with the rule of law. The concept of public good or public interest, which becomes the foundation of the Rousseauean state, is defined by nothing other than the generality of the law: "The first and foremost public interest," Rousseau says in his *Lettres écrites de la montagne*,[16] "is always justice. Everyone wants the conditions to be equal for all, and justice is nothing but this equality. The citizen wants only laws and laws that are being observed." In individual morality, the basic principle of rational conduct, "that sublime maxim of rational justice," is "Do to others as you would have others do to you."[17] Hence, moral goodness is designed to remedy the radical alienation brought about by man's separation from nature. The unreflective identification with other men which characterized the savage's behavior based on pity is reconstructed at the level of reason through the imperative of overcoming the depraved selfishness of the reflecting man and of instituting a moral community of agents who treat each other as equals.

So far the parallels with Kant are nearly complete. As for Kant, morality consists for Rousseau in obedience to a self-prescribed rational law and in resistance to the forces of passion, which give a priority to the particular over the universal.[18] The command of Rousseau's highest moral norm is for many purposes identical with Kant's categorical imperative, and they also agree in their insistence on intention as the locus of moral worth. At this point, however, the roads of the citizen of Geneva and the Koenigsberg philosopher diverge. For while Kant believes that it is possible to derive a complete set of substantive norms of behavior from the formal description of moral worth contained in the categorical imperative, Rousseau is more skeptical with respect to the powers of human reason. One of Kant's formulations of his categorical imperative was: "Act as though the maxim of your action were by your will to become a universal law of nature.[19] What he implied

---

[16]*Lettres écrites de la montagne*, 3:891.

[17]*Second Discourse*, 156.

[18]This statement will be qualified somewhat in what follows. Strictly, speaking, Rousseau's mature ethic is not universalistic, since we shall see that the norms that give content to ethical life are the norms of a particular community, rather than principles binding on all rational agents. One could express this distinction by saying that for Kant moral norms are universal, while for Rousseau they are "general." For reasons of convenience, however, I shall sometimes disregard this distinction.

[19]Kant, *Foundations of the Metaphysics of Morals* (Prussian Academy edition), 441.

in this statement was that a system of purely rational laws, springing from practical reason, could theoretically provide a basis for a system of nature—that reason alone could unequivocally determine every event to take place. Clearly, the nature of which Kant speaks is not the nature we know from experience, but he wants us to suppose that if we accept the categorical imperative as the supreme law of rational behavior we should be able to derive from it another "nature," another dense order in which every concrete action of a rational being would be unambiguously indicated. A perfectly rational creature, such as a disembodied angel, would, according to Kant, be capable of agency, for its reason alone would in every morally relevant situation dictate to it a certain course of action. In other words, Kant believed that reason alone could sufficiently determine the will, and he viewed as properly moral only actions which are in fact so determined.

It is well known that this aspect of Kant's moral doctrine met with severe criticism from Hegel, who believed that because it did not ground moral action in ordinary, *natural* human life functions, Kant's categorical imperative remained an empty, formal principle. As several commentators on Kant have observed, the categorical imperative underdetermines the system of substantive moral principles that a man may follow, and many mutually incompatible, but internally consistent, ethical systems would be compatible with the categorical imperative. Kant believed, for example, that a prohibition of murder could be deduced from his supreme moral principle. It may be that men in fact fear death so much that they could not wish a system of life-and-death struggle to be introduced among them. But it does not follow that such a system would have to be necessarily unacceptable for *all* rational beings, and some daredevils may actually find it preferable to our sedate mode of life. If we choose a less drastic example (such as norms of economic competition or norms pertaining to sexual behavior), it will become clear that given different circumstances, men do in fact accept different, mutually incompatible systems of moral norms and still remain *moral*, since they base their behavior on adherence to general principles rather than only *ad hoc* inclinations.

It is this insufficiency of reason for an unequivocal determination of a system of substantive moral norms that Rousseau had already observed, and it is this observation that marks his parting of the ways with Kant as well as his anticipation of the moral and political philosophies of Hegel and Marx. Rousseau's writings abound in passages that speak of reason's limitations: "Justice and kindness," he says in *Emile*,[20] "are

---

[20]*Emile*, 522–23.

no mere abstract terms, no mere moral conceptions framed by the understanding, but true affections of the heart enlightened by reason; . . . by reason alone, unguided by conscience, we cannot establish any natural law, and . . . all natural right is a vain dream if it does not rest upon some instinctive need of the human heart." In a note he adds that "it is false to say that the precepts of natural law are based on reason only; they have a firmer and more solid foundation." In the "Confession of Faith . . ." Rousseau offers an even more pertinent formulation, without the confusing reference to natural law:

> Reason alone is not a sufficient foundation for virtue; what solid ground can be found for it? Virtue we are told is a love of order. But can this love prevail over my love for my own well-being, and ought it so prevail? . . . Their so-called principle is in truth a mere playing with words; for also I say that vice is love of order, differently understood. Wherever there is feeling and intelligence, there is some sort of moral order. The difference is this: the good man orders his life with regard to all men; the wicked orders it [*tout*] for himself alone.[21]

It would be wrong to take these statements as testifying to Rousseau's alleged antirationalist sentimentalism or naturalism and to read them as contradicting what I have said so far about the connection between morality and rationality. There is nothing in these passages that could really undermine Rousseau's commitment to the view that moral worth comes from a generalization of the maxims of one's own behavior as a result of the application of reason. What Rousseau does in these passages is to address himself in an anticipatory fashion to two problems endemic to the later Kantian system: the problem of the *motivational* insufficiency of purely rational grounds for action and the problem, already discussed, of the underdetermination of a system of substantive moral norms by the categorical imperative. The last quotation in particular (concerning the difference between a good and a wicked man) points to a problem that a Kantian must ponder: even the most selfish kind of attitude can be made into a matter of *principle*; the maxim of unabashed egoism is absolutely compatible with the categorical imperative, so long as one does not limit its application to oneself alone. If I am willing to grant other people the same right I presume for myself, the Hobbesian *bellum omnis contra omnem* is as much legitimized by pure rationality as is universal cooperation. This is what Rousseau considers a perversion of reason, for a maxim of this kind is equivalent to putting reason in the service of passions rather than providing a guidance for

[21]Ibid., 602.

them. Naturally, no one who acts in this way *in fact* does so *by virtue* of the principle he adopts, for his actual motivation is interest and not the principle with which he justifies his behavior. Consequently only a wicked man (one who really abdicates his responsibility) can appeal to such an argument. This is what Rousseau means by saying that the "love of order" has not really "prevailed" over this man's "love for [his] own well-being," and he is simply being polemical in representing the wicked man's action as a matter of principle. But the very fact that the wicked man is *capable* of providing such a flawless justification for his action testifies to an important limitation of reason itself. Another such limitation, only briefly mentioned so far, is the weakness of any motivation, even though unambiguous, if it is based on reason alone. Kant was not unaware of this problem, as his wrangling with the relation between morality and happiness indicates, but he finally postulated a certain inner force of rationality that filled the rational agent with "reverence" for the moral law. Rousseau, however, could not have been satisfied with this solution, even if he had considered it. The reasons for his position here have nothing to do with a mechanistic view of volition *à la* Hobbes or the Lockean claim that the strongest uneasiness of the moment always determines the will. Having once granted man his freedom, Rousseau does not intend to take it away by an argument of this kind. His doubts as to the motivational strength of reason come rather from his belief that reason itself strengthens and diversifies the passions, so that the natural *amour de soi*, by becoming perverted into *amour propre*, channels the "rational energy" into immoral rather than moral behavior. Consequently something more than reason alone is needed to extricate man from his fallen condition, namely, the identification of happiness with rational moral action.

2. The General Will

In his search for a solution to the problems connected with his identification of morality with rationality, above all, the problem of reason's underdetermination of the set of substantive moral commands and the problem of the motivational insufficiency of reason with respect to human action, Rousseau developed his theory in two different directions that may not be easily compatible. The first type of solution, which is presented in *Emile*, points to conscience and education as the means of supplementing the powers of reason in moral matters. The second solution, described in *The Social Contract*, points to an integration of man in the context of a community of rational agents as an indispensable element of moral life.

2.1. The Individualist Solution

The solution to the problem of limitations of pure rationality offered in *Emile* is both the less attractive and the less interesting for us in the present context. *Emile* deals with the education of an individual who, though living among men, is supposed to achieve a degree of self-sufficiency that will make it possible for him to fit into every society and belong to none. He will obey the laws of the country in which he is going to live, but he is intended to be a private person who infuses his life with meaning independently of any political context.[22] Rousseau leads his pupil until the time of his marriage and fatherhood, but family relations are to be the only significant bonds with other people that Emile will ever experience. The analogy with the person of Rousseau himself comes irresistibly to mind when we follow Emile's development. It is the cosmopolitan Rousseau that is being shaped in this book: a citizen of Geneva who, though he sees in his city an heir of Sparta and Rome, cannot live in his country without coming into conflict with its authorities; an *habitué* of Paris salons whose inner withdrawal and need for solitude make him a *"citoyen bien singulier"*;[23] an author of constitutions for countries that he has never seen; a fiercely independent individualist who is at one time a Protestant, at another a Catholic, and then again a Protestant—but always a rather suspect Christian. As long as there is no truly legitimate government on earth, an individual must be able to live anywhere but to shape his life alone. In these conditions, the only answer that Rousseau can provide to the problems involved in his moral system is education. Rousseau the tutor leads his pupil Emile through an ontogenetic concentration of the history of mankind, and in the process he draws on the *natural* inclinations of his charge. The "trick" played on Emile is that his *amour propre* is never given an adequate chance to develop. As he grows, his *amour de soi* is given ample time to guide his actions (it is only amazingly late that Rousseau augments the upbringing of his pupil with any genuine education), and he is being dosed with reason in amounts sufficient only to transform his natural benevolence into moral goodness. "If . . . we desire Emile to be a lover of truth, if we desire that he should indeed perceive it, let us keep him far from self-interest in all business."[24] Hence, what helps Emile to become a good man is really ignorance of evil, so that the

---

[22]For an analysis of some problems to which this may lead in connection with trying to relate Rousseau's political views to his views in *Emile*, see J. Charvet, "Individual Identity and Social Consciousness in Rousseau's Philosophy," in M. Cranston and R. S. Peters, eds., *Hobbes and Rousseau* (Garden City, N.Y., 1972).

[23]This is how Diderot addressed Rousseau in a letter to him of 16 March 1757.

[24]*Emile*, 547.

strength of his *natural* inclinations is immediately channeled to support his moral stand. When he encounters the first *conflict* between passion and reason (when he falls in love with Sophie), his moral sense is already sufficiently formed to keep him from yielding to passion.

It is in this context that Rousseau introduced his theory of conscience. In its paradoxicalness, the concept of conscience recalls the Kantian "reverence for the law." It is not a principle of reason, but a feeling. As such it is on a par with other natural impulses and not with the constructs of reason.[25] But at the same time "conscience is the voice of the soul, the passions are the voice of the body."[26] It is this hybrid that is brought in to aid reason: "Too often reason deceives us; . . . but conscience never deceives us; she is the true guide of man; it is to the soul what instinct is to the body; he who obeys his conscience is following nature and he need not fear that he will go astray."[27] We are as close here to "natural morality" as we ever get in Rousseau. But the theory of moral sentiment that he is trying to rehash is as little in agreement with the theoretical framework of autonomy as is the Hobbesian mechanistic reduction of morality. In fact, the same *Emile* abounds in statements that Rousseau's pupil should "own no sway but that of reason."[28] The painlessness of Emile's education into moral agency is possible only because his guardian angel Rousseau makes him forgo the bitter opposition between morality and nature perverted by reason. In fact, Rousseau himself may have been aware of the illusoriness of this solution. In an unfinished sequel to *Emile*,[29] he shows how the glasshouse of Emile's happiness is shattered the moment his mentor abandons him and he is confronted with the reality of social life. When the experience of evil reasserts itself against Emile's greenhouse education, he becomes no more than a moving misfit.

The real answer to the problems inherent in Rousseau's identification of morality with rationality is provided in *The Social Contract*. Even in *Emile*, Rousseau states that "those who desire to treat politics and morals apart from one another will never understand either."[30] In the *Confessions* he makes an even more general statement: "Everything is at bottom dependent on political arrangements."[31] The main thrust of Rousseau's identification of politics and morality lies, I believe, in his

[25]Ibid., 599.
[26]Ibid., 594.
[27]Ibid., 594–95. *The Moral Letters*, which Rousseau rewrote into the "Confession of Faith," contains a similar conception.
[28]*Emile*, 551. See also 586–87.
[29]*Emile et Sophie, ou les Solitaires*, first published in 1780.
[30]*Emile*, 524.
[31]*Confessions*, 404.

view that the insufficiencies of pure reason, insofar as either its emotional strength or its inability to determine unambiguously a set of substantive moral commands is concerned, are remedied by putting an individual's action in the context of a community of agents. It is in this light that Rousseau's theory of the general will should be understood, and before we can continue with our main problem, some general remarks must be made in connection with this most misunderstood aspect of Rousseau's political philosophy.

2.2. The Concept of the General Will

I have already emphasized that Rousseau's political theory and the broader philosophical justification that it entails should be read in light of the fact that Rousseau was a critic of the natural-right tradition. This point must be constantly kept in mind in interpreting Rousseau's theory of the general will, for he developed the very concept of a general will in response to what he saw as the most fundamental problem of liberalism: the problem of alienation and social atomization. Early liberal political theories (in the broadest sense, which includes Hobbes's philosophy, despite its authoritarian solution to the problem of social cooperation) rest on an investigation of the nature of man. The common element in all these theories is the claim that "life according to nature" does not involve sociability as a fundamental human characteristic. The nominalist background of modern science, which the natural-right theorists use as a foundation of their political theories, inclines them to think of society as an artificial product of men's will and not as an Aristotelian totality within which the very essence of human individuality is constituted. The whole problematic of the contractual origin of society is based on the conviction that men are fully constituted, autonomous, and self-enclosed entities before they come to make any political arrangements among themselves. Before the creation of a political society they are already as much *rational* agents (at least in kind, though not perhaps in degree) as they are ever going to be. They are also as capable of moral agency (although this may not mean much in practice for someone like Hobbes) as they are ever going to become. The *meaning of their lives* may lie in their self-preservation, as in Hobbes; or in their moral self-sufficiency achieved through property ownership, as in Locke; or in the independence from all interpersonal arrangements in their search for a direct relation to God and salvation, as in the Puritan tradition. Yet, no matter what its source, the meaning of men's lives is fully determined before they ever come to institute a political commonwealth. Consequently, social organization is above all a form of cooperation between autonomous agents, according to the natural-right theorists, and not a higher-order totality with its own goals and meaning independent of the realization of individual pursuits. Even if, as in Hobbes, stress is laid on political unity and not a loose form of association, the very essence of the natural-right conception is that political legitimization must ultimately refer to the benefits of society accruing to an individual. When such benefits are sacrificed for the sake of goals that transcend the values of an individual, the natural right of this individual is violated; and even if society can legitimize such a violation in the eyes of other people, the individual in question is no longer bound by any obligation to the community.[32] As a result, the natural-right theorists no longer see active participation in politics as indispensable to a meaningful life: an individual's goals may in some cases be furthered or thwarted by society, but they are not constituted by it. Because the locus of the meaning of human life is to be found elsewhere, politics is no longer a *sine qua non* of one's humanity.

Rousseau's criticism of liberal theory is based, as explained above, on his agreement with the natural-right theorists that man's nature, insofar as it must be understood within the conceptual framework of modern science, leaves no room for sociability. But Rousseau's further reasoning goes in the direction of showing that there is more to man than his nature, and that only on the basis of this "more" can a meaningful theory of society be founded. If this point is overlooked, and if all the features of humanity are reduced to natural phenomena, the ensuing theory of political cooperation will be unable to account for the fundamental aspirations of man and for the expectations he has of a political community. A man expects from his association with other men to overcome his "fallen condition"; he expects to reintegrate his individual activity into a broader context that will take the place of his original unity with nature. He expects that in a community with other men he is going to find the cure for the cosmic solitude to which his *amour propre* has exiled him from the womb of nature. He looks not for the mere security of his own individual existence, but for a moral fraternity that will remedy the insecurity and anxiety so fundamental to the very mode of individual existence that they will persist regardless of whether or not he enters into some forms of cooperation with others. An individual's insecurity is an expression not of his fear of any concrete danger that he could overcome by obtaining other people's cooperation, but of an "existential anxiety" attached to his very human condition. He looks to other people not for help in achieving the goals

---

[32]Cf., for example, Hobbes's insistence that no man can alienate his right to self-defense, even if he is to use it against the state (*Lev.*, 70).

he has set for himself, but precisely for the sake of life with them, that is, for the sake of society *as such*.

It is easy to dismiss Rousseau as a romantic dreamer and forerunner of totalitarianism if, like J. L. Talmon, one does not see that he strikes an extremely sensitive chord in a man brought up in a liberal society.[33] Rousseau's protest against liberalism is not merely an expression of his inability to think of progress in terms of piecemeal and gradual changes. Neither Talmon nor Burke (Talmon's clear forerunner in the critique of Rousseau) has noticed that Rousseau can sometimes think in very conservative and traditionalist terms.[34] But in his critique of liberalism he is not simply impatient; he demands a revolution in the liberal assumptions concerning the nature of society, because he believes that the very framework of liberal theory leaves no room for a society capable of remedying the isolated, atomistic character of modern life. One may agree or disagree with Rousseau's vision of what society is supposed to be (and I think that his vision cannot be sustained), but it will not suffice to reduce his objections to liberalism to his lack of social pragmatism. With reference to a mere temporal duration of change, Rousseau could be—and sometimes was—a pragmatist. But in his vision of the role of society as such, he consciously attacked the very premise of liberal pragmatism: society, according to him, is not a pragmatic but a moral creation; it is designed not to solve problems essentially preexisting and independent with respect to it, but to respond to an inner need to which it *itself* is the answer. Rousseau may be wrong in his claim that the inner need for a tightly integrated social system is compatible with freedom, but he is not wrong that such a need exists and that a liberal society can never fully satisfy it. The unceasing hold that Rousseau retains over the minds of modern thinkers, the fact that throughout the two centuries since the publication of his work he has been a constant source of inspiration for both leftist and rightist critics of liberalism, the periodic waves of dissatisfaction with what liberal society has to offer, despite its enormous success in emancipating one class and nation after another—these are the best witnesses that Rousseau, with his theory of alienation, touched on the most sensitive weak spot of the liberal system. Unless this problem is dealt with directly, rather than

[33] J. L. Talmon, *The Origins of Totalitarian Democracy* (New York, 1970), 38–49 passim.
[34] See particularly the conservative character of Rousseau's proposals in his *Constitution for Poland* and those parts of *The Social Contract* in which he excuses the institution of slavery in ancient Greece (III, 15). See also the studies devoted to the similarities between Rousseau and Burke: D. Cameron, *The Social Thought of Rousseau and Burke* (London, 1973); A. M. Osborn, *Rousseau and Burke* (London, 1940). See also W. Pickles, "The Notion of Time in Rousseau's Political Thought," in Cranston and Peters, eds., *Hobbes and Rousseau*.

being explained away as a temporary or unreal difficulty, no philosophical defense of liberalism is possible. This is what I meant by saying that Rousseau is still awaiting as perspicacious a critique of his own philosophy as the one he himself provided of the liberal tradition.

Rousseau's critique of the natural-right theory that underlies the contractarianism of Hobbes and Locke makes him only a qualified contractarian himself. As the *Second Discourse* clearly shows, Rousseau does not envisage the origins of society in a contractual agreement. The evolution of the "unnatural man" is from the very first connected with the introduction of social relations. In the state of nature man has only casual encounters with other members of the species,[35] and he establishes no meaningful relations with them. Even family life, according to Rousseau, is a product of civilization, since love, unlike sexual drive, is not a natural feeling.[36] Reason, which distinguishes man from animals, develops only with the introduction of language, and both are immediately connected with a meaningful intercourse with other people brought about as a result of overpopulation. Thus, Rousseau believes that it is impossible to speak about a man's contracting into society, for the development of human agency, which is indispensable for his entering into any kind of obligation, comes about only concurrently with the development of society. It is only a legitimate, political society that has its origin in a contract, whereas social cooperation (or competition) precedes any contractual arrangements. Thus, Rousseau is one of the first thinkers to make a strong distinction between civil society (which he most often calls "civilization" or simply "society") and political institutions. In a somewhat Aristotelian fashion, his objection to liberalism is that what it refers to as the "state" is in reality nothing but a form of civil society: a private association devoid of the truly general character of the state. But unlike Aristotle, Rousseau does not view this prepolitical association as subhuman, on a par with the "society" of ants or bees, but rather as a typically human phenomenon, involving intercourse between rational, self-oriented individuals.

Thus, the problem of an individual's isolation and alienation at the stage of *amour propre* is, despite the seemingly self-sufficient nature of the self, inherently connected with social interaction among many individuals. A political community of equals is already implicit in the self-enclosed world of the civilized man; it is a misperceived ideal norm of his relationships with other men, which an individual unconsciously longs for but consciously defeats. His rationality being *par excellence* a social phenomenon, his egocentric world view is obviously an illusion.

[35]*Second Discourse*, 140, 146–47, 159–60.
[36]Ibid., 157–58; *Emile*, 493–94.

The reason an individual is alienated and unhappy under the conditions of civilization is that the self-sufficiency he ascribes to his ego is in fact spurious. Reason involves a relationship to other people, without which it is ineffective. When an individual believes that he can rationally establish his own self-identity, that he can establish himself as a private moral cosmos, independently of both his subhuman, natural existence and his relationship to other people, reason is deprived of the context on which it thrives. As a result, an individual falls prey to antinomies. The purely formal character of individual rationality is responsible for the emptiness of an individual's moral life, the emptiness that must be filled by particular, *ad hoc* arising passions. These passions, on the other hand, involve man in the endless and meaningless pursuit of gratifications that only remove him further and further from self-sufficiency and from a communion with other agents. Rousseau differs from Aristotle in his insistence that human happiness and self-sufficiency are not fulfillments of a natural order; they are, according to him, results of a consistent realization of an ideal of life of which man himself is the author and which he brings about through his own freedom and spontaneity. Man does not have a nature and is himself the author of what he is. But in *political* terms, Rousseau's critique of liberalism is Aristotelian: the Hobbesian "continual progress of desire" appears to Rousseau a perversion of both nature and reason.

2.3. The Political Solution

The moral significance of Rousseau's concept of the general will consists in the fact that the overcoming of an individual's alienation by a process of reintegration in a broader, intersubjective community simultaneously remedies both the difficulties described earlier: that of the motivational insufficiency of reason, and that of the underdetermination of a substantive moral system by the formal rationality of the Rousseauean counterpart to Kant's categorical imperative. The replacement of the unjust social order based on inequality with an institution of legitimate political authority is supposed to preserve an individual's freedom while ensuring the content and motivational viability of his moral system. To replace a state in which man is a moral agent, but only in the sense of being capable of evil brought about by his *amour propre*, with a state in which he can realize his true moral worth is the main purpose of political association. Entering a political society, as I have said, is not primarily a prudent step designed to assure an individual of his security. Neither is it a matter of compromise in which the satisfaction of certain interests is traded for a renunciation of others. Rather, political association rests on the acceptance of a form of interaction with other men in which no one stands to lose and everyone stands to gain. It is in this light that we must read Rousseau's presentation of his own task and of the "fundamental problem to which the social contract holds the solution": "How to form a form of association . . . under which each individual, while uniting himself with others, obeys no one but himself, and remains as free as before."[37]

It is not very difficult to see how, within the context of the human community, reason acquires, according to Rousseau, the motivational power that it does not have for an isolated individual. To begin with, social relationships developing on the basis of individual pursuits of interest result in an arrangement that virtually all people must see as basically unjust and inhuman. Like Marx after him, though more intuitively than "scientifically," Rousseau viewed the liberal model of society as bringing forth an ever sharper inequality and ever sharper polarization between the haves and the have-nots. Ultimately, the interests of most people are thwarted by the very system that allows their unhampered development. Rousseau is a Hobbesian in this respect, with one significant difference: the Hobbesian state of nature very well describes for Rousseau the state of prepolitical civilization. Rousseau's complete lack of awareness of what Mandeville called the "public benefit of private vices," and of what Adam Smith described as the "invisible hand," may be one of the weakest points in his system.[38] But in any case, once Rousseau has postulated ever increasing social antagonisms within civil society, it is not surprising that he postulated the need for a revolutionary change that would restructure the ends, and not just the means, of social intercourse. The development of social antagonisms, he held, will have to bring an ever increasing realization of the self-defeating character of *amour propre* and provide a decisive impetus for subjecting passions to reason.[39] Furthermore, once the political order envisaged in *The Social Contract* is established, the power of the sovereign—and here again Rousseau reminds us of Hobbes—will provide a counteracting force to the centrifugal forces of interest. This includes both direct intervention of the state in cases where parties and other private associations are being formed[40]

[37]*Social Contract*, I, 6, (360). The purely moral significance of the concept of general will does not allow, therefore, for an interpretation of Rousseau's distinction between the general will and the will of all with reference to the prisoner's dilemma, since the prudentialist "collective interest" is still a *particular* interest for Rousseau.

[38]Surprisingly enough, Smith himself was not always particularly conscious of this difference between himself and Rousseau, and in one of his reviews he compared Rousseau to Mandeville.

[39]I do not mean to deny that Rousseau was often very pessimistic about the chances of establishing a legitimate state in any of the large European countries of his time. For more details, see Chap. VII, below.

[40]*Social Contract*, II, 3 (371–72).

and a long-term educational effort directed at the citizenry (of which the establishment of public religion is only one example).[41]

But the main problem of Rousseau's political philosophy, besides discovering what brings about the harmony between collective policies and individual freedom, is the problem of explaining exactly how the communal context of life will translate the formal principle embodied in Rousseau's counterpart of the categorical imperative into a system of substantive moral commands. In other words, how will the fact that a citizen votes in an assembly of his compatriots rather than in the solitude of his own mind enable him to fill reason with the content that it previously lacked?

It would be a vain effort to look in *The Social Contract* for a fully elaborated solution to this problem. Compared to Hegel and Marx, Rousseau is working under a serious disadvantage in that he has so sharply drawn his nature-reflection distinction that he has no way of mediating between passions and reason or between interest and morality. Whereas Hegel and Marx went one step further than Rousseau (and Kant for that matter) in their reception of liberalism and tried to provide a synthesis of what Aristotle called "action" and "production," Rousseau was bound to view the state as nearly exclusively an instrument of moral perfection and, in an Aristotelian manner, to eliminate the concerns of the market from the properly political domain. Consequently, the political program of *The Social Contract* is in a certain sense truly reactionary: having made political participation absolutely indispensable to the moral dignity of a citizen, and having limited it to the traditional forms of voting and deliberation, Rousseau was forced to offer the ancient *polis*, with its unrealistically small size and ignorance of economic concerns, as his alternative to the modern liberal state. What is even worse, perhaps, is that the remaining elements of the formalism entailed by his view of political morality made his proposal dangerously thin and one-sided. His call for fraternity was vacuous enough to make his system susceptible to immediate abuse at the hands of Robespierre and later proponents of terror in the name of a nation or humanity.

Nevertheless, certain features of Rousseau's politicization of the categorical imperative render it more robust than the later Kantian version. The content that the commands of reason receive upon becoming translated into the commands the general will is fraternity itself. Rousseau thinks of the general will as the moral substance of the community, much as Hegel thinks of his "objective spirit." The requirements to be satisfied in order for the outcome of an assembly vote to represent the

[41]Ibid., iv, 8.

general will are: (a) that each individual consider only the public good and not his private interests;[42] and (b) that all the decrees of the assembly have the form of general laws.[43] The problem that remains, of course, is what substantive criteria the citizen is to use when he asks himself what is in the public good. The dilemma becomes apparent when we see that Rousseau believes that "when a law is proposed in the people's assembly, what is asked of them is not precisely whether they approve of the proposition or reject it, but whether it is in conformity with the general will which is theirs."[44] On the face of it, it would seem that as a citizen I am obligated to ignore the content of the law being proposed, second-guess how the others are going to vote, and then cast my vote accordingly. As well as extreme opportunism, such a procedure also implies that the result of the voting will depend on chance alone. Having nothing else to go by, I might assume that the chances of acceptance or rejection of the proposed law are exactly equal. As a rational agent, I would then toss a coin and vote accordingly. But this, of course, is not what Rousseau has in mind. When he says that the question asked of the people is "not *precisely*" whether they accept or reject the proposed law, he does not mean that I cannot take the content of the law into consideration. A citizen has a right—indeed a duty—to be pragmatic and to consider whether the law contributes to the stability of the community and even to its members' interest; in the narrow, materialistic sense. He is prohibited from considering his private interest above the collective interest, so as to avoid the pernicious consequences of the prisoner's-dilemma type of situation. He is further prohibited from considering the collective interest of all the individuals involved if its increase were to contribute to the demise of the political bond that unites them (for example, a certain decision may greatly contribute to the wealth of the whole community, but at the same time undermine the civic spirit of the citizenry; in this case for *moral* and not merely pragmatic reasons, I should oppose such a decision). Still, pragmatic considerations do in fact determine the content of a citizen's decisions. But his pragmatic or utilitarian calculations are not "precisely" what is asked of him, because the good that he is primarily supposed to aim at is not what accrues to the community from its decisions but the *community* itself. When Rousseau says that the general will is always right,[45] he does not mean that it is pragmatically right, and he is not repeating Aristotle's doubtful claim that among a great

[42]Ibid., IV, 1 (438).
[43]Ibid., II, 6.
[44]Ibid., IV, 2 (440–41).
[45]Ibid., II, 3 (371).

number of people the extremes of opinion balance each other out and the remaining mean is most often closest to the truth.[46] On the contrary, Rousseau believes that people are very often wrong in the pragmatic sense[47] and this is why they need a wise legislator to guide them and why even the best states finally disintegrate.[48] But the "right" and "wrong" that apply to political decisions are moral and not pragmatic terms. And this moral rightness consists in the merging of individual wills into one universal will that eliminates the isolation and alienation of each person in the fraternal bond of the community.

To understand how the concept of the general will remedies the emptiness of the formal principle of individual morality, it is useful to set it against the Kantian kingdom of ends. A Kantian moral agent is a self-sufficient rational being whose reason dictates to him a specific type of behavior in each concrete situation. In particular, it dictates to him a respect for every other rational agent, whom he treats as an end in itself. Now, in a community of perfectly rational agents there will arise a necessary coincidence of individual wills, since the reason of each agent will provide him with a standard of behavior identical to everyone else's and will include a mutual respect for other members of the community. But the "kingdom of ends" that then arises is still no more a community than a Leibnizian collection of monads: it rests on an external coincidence of wills like preestablished harmony, but not on a real *communication* between the agents in question. The agents understand each other because each sees in himself what others reveal of themselves, but they can never speak with one will. In Rousseau, on the other hand, each agent in separation from others may come to an entirely different system of substantive moral values, for his individual reason underdetermines the content of his actions. In coming together agents will probably differ on most issues concerning the policies that they should follow. But what brings them together is the very moral insufficiency of their individual existence. The community itself is the main value of their moral system, so that as long as the expression of their will takes the form of a law that unites them by providing a common standard of behavior, the exact content of the law is of secondary importance. Clearly, insofar as pragmatic considerations must be taken into consideration, the laws of a given community represent a certain particular set of interests, although they are collective and not individual interests. But when a given standard of behavior is made actually binding on all the citizens without exception, and not (as in the

[46]*Politics*, 1282a.
[47]*Social Contract*, ii, 6 (380).
[48]Ibid., iii, 10–11 (esp. 424).

case of individual morality) only potentially applicable to other men, the equality implied in the categorical imperative becomes *more than a purely formal requirement*: it becomes a real political bond and an object of emotional attachment to be preserved for its own sake. The fraternity that Rousseau aims at is not a formal equality of all citizens, but the very *content* of justice and the supreme command of morality. Its sense does not lie in a mere conformity with a universal principle, but in an actual love of one's neighbor, so that its relation to the Kantian categorical imperative is not unlike that of the Christian *caritas* to the formal canon of Judaism that the former was supposed to "fulfill."[49]

Rousseau strongly insists that a political law must be universal in character. His point, however, does not concern the merely formal character of the general will. Laws must contain an element of particularity, since they are not empty; they order or prohibit something, and they will always affect some people differently from others. That they contain no existential quantifiers does not mean much, for one can phrase everything that matters without those and still single out the particular object that one wants to single out. The universality of law that Rousseau has in mind rests in the intention of the assembly, the intention to attend to the public interest in such a way that the bond uniting the people become stronger and not weaker. This is why a law cannot be inimical to any particular citizen, even if his particular interest is being thwarted; it is always designed to integrate him further into the community, which gives him his moral worth. He himself may believe that the result of the law will be the opposite of the one that its authors desire—and he may even be right. For this reason, he is given the opportunity to argue against it in the assembly and to bring it for reconsideration when there is a chance that others may have come to agree with him. But to disobey the law would be to bring about immediately what he claims he wants to avoid, since disobedience to a law amounts to breaking the unity of the general will here and now and not only in the future. It means either that one wants to secede from the state—a form of moral suicide for Rousseau—or that one wants to impose one's will on others and destroy the autonomy of the community. But since the moral quality of the community consists in its autonomy, "the worst of laws is still better than the best master."[50] People have a right to legislate bad laws as much as good ones, and "if they choose to do themselves an injury, who has the right to prevent them from doing so?"[51] They can be advised against, but not forcibly

---

[49]Matt. 5:17. Cf. also Hegel's *Early Theological Writings* (Philadelphia, 1971), 215.
[50]*Lettres écrites de la montagne*, 842–43.
[51]*Social Contract*, II, 12.

prevented from, harming themselves; for the practical harm that they might cause to themselves could never be greater than the moral damage they would suffer by being deprived of their freedom.

It is with this type of consideration in mind that Rousseau formulates his controversial theory of majority rule. To Locke, for example, majority rule is a pragmatic solution to the problems of legislation, and the limitations of political power in general leave the basic rights of the minority protected by delegitimizing any fundamental encroachments of positive law on the natural rights of individuals. To Rousseau, on the other hand, the problem of majority rule is crucial, since political participation is the main locus of moral life and the power of the sovereign is absolute (in the sense of not being limited by any nonpolitical constraints, such as natural law). Hence no minority is protected *qua* minority; its only consolation is that it is not singled out arbitrarily by the law. There are no doubt dangerous political consequences implied in this state of affairs, and no amount of explaining the famous phrase "on le forcera d'être libre" will eliminate its totalitarian implications.[52] But even if to understand is not to forgive, we should try to understand Rousseau's meaning. A man who enters the social contract—and the original pact requires unanimity—has renounced his individual freedom for the sake of social integration. The structure of the general will thus created is such that in participating in the political process and in obeying the laws of the community, the individual is finally able to live according to reason and not according to the dictates of passion. In one of the less brilliant passages of *The Social Contract*, Rousseau represents the relation of an individual to the general will as a proportion of one to the number of citizens, and he draws the conclusion that "the more the state is enlarged, the more freedom is diminished."[53] If that were indeed to be the case, Rousseau's whole scheme would fall to pieces. Not only would the citizen not be "as free as before,"[54] but in fact he could hardly be said to be free at all. To say that he has 1/10,000th part of the power to decide about his own life (and we are speaking of a small community indeed) is the same as saying that he is 9,999/10,000 unfree, and no tyranny could probably make him more of a slave. But Rousseau makes these naive calculations only in the context of his consideration of the size of the executive authority that a state needs. In the context of his discussion of the social pact itself, he clearly states that in obeying the law a citizen "obeys no one but himself."[55]

[52]Ibid., i, 7 (364). Cf. also the article by Plamenatz cited in note 6 to the Introduction to Part Three.
[53]*Social Contract*, iii, 1 (397).
[54]Ibid., i, 6 (360).
[55]Ibid.

True autonomy being possible only in a truly communal action, the general will expresses not a collection of wills but one will of the whole community of which I am as much a part as a totality, since my moral agency is realized only in the common decision. I may disagree with the *contingent* content of any particular law, but I cannot disagree with the *necessary* unity of the community. Such a disagreement would amount to a disagreement with myself, that is, a disagreement between my passions, which enslave me, and my reason, which emancipates me. In other words, by being forced to obey my reason I am forced (by the community that embodies *my own* moral agency) to be free.[56]

[56]The problem of majority rule may of course be pursued much further. Even assuming that every social contract must designate some kind of majority as sufficient to pass a law (and if the sufficient majority is defined minimally, it is not immediately clear what is supposed to be so magical about 51 percent that one should be persuaded to give it a crucial power over the remaining 49 percent, to say nothing of cases of plurality), the invalidity of all those votes that are cast with a private rather than public interest in mind may give a justification for a small minority's claim that it speaks for the people as a whole. This problem constitutes the central theme of Talmon's *Origins of Totalitarian Democracy*.

VII. The Historicity of
Human Development

One of the most important consequences of Rousseau's polemic against the natural-right tradition is his view that the understanding of the meaning of human existence requires an introduction of the concept of history. As Leo Strauss has keenly observed, the very fact that, according to Rousseau, "man is by nature subhuman" and "almost infinitely perfectible" means that "man's humanity is a product of the historical process."[1] Despite Rousseau's borrowing from the Aristotelian model of politics, the theory of autonomy that he used as a philosophical background for his political proposals was a thoroughly original and modern creation. The break between nature and society became in Rousseau's thought more radical than ever. That society is not natural had been claimed by Hobbes, Locke, and many others before Rousseau. But that the very set of problems to which a legitimate social order is supposed to provide a solution has itself nothing to do with nature is probably original with Rousseau.[2] Man is different from animals, according to Rousseau, not only because he does not have a "nature" that unequivocally determines his self-preservative responses to external stimulation (so that he can spontaneously respond to an entirely new situation in which an animal would be doomed to perish), but also because he is himself the author of his "second nature," that is,

[1] L. Strauss, *Natural Right and History* (Chicago, 1953), 271, 274.
[2] Rousseau's most important predecessor here was, of course, Vico, whose historicism was in many ways more refined than Rousseau's. That Vico (the first edition of whose *New Science* was published in 1725) may have had some actual influence on Rousseau is conjectured by M. H. Fisch and T. G. Bergin in their introduction to Vico's *Autobiography* (Ithaca, N.Y., 1975), 72–73.

of the nearly whole context within which his life is situated.[3] It is true that, unlike Marx, Hegel, or even Locke, Rousseau did not provide a modern theory of production that would make man responsible for the transformation of the natural world around him, so that even the external environment of his life would have to be viewed as an artificial, human creation. Consequently, he did not take the last step in the direction of the "denaturalization" of man, which would make it entirely impossible to analyze even a single aspect of human life in terms of a theory of nature. It was still possible, for Rousseau, to distinguish between a man's "natural" and "unnatural" needs and to designate the basic nucleus of human requirements that are independent of human freedom and of the social arrangements designed to satisfy them— something that was not to be true for either Hegel or Marx. Nevertheless, this remnant of human nature and the nucleus of basic needs that it entails is relatively unimportant, according to Rousseau, with respect to those problems that give real meaning to human existence. One of the main reasons Rousseau altogether ignored the relation of rational man to nature and gave us no modern theory of production was that he did not recognize any real problem of scarcity. In this respect his views were quite anachronistic and Aristotelian: he saw production as concerned merely with the satisfaction of natural necessities which, unless human nature is "perverted" by reason, are so modest and easy to satisfy that they present no serious obstacles to the realization of man's more important, moral concerns.[4] All nonphysiological requirements of human life, however (all those requirements that constitute the overwhelming majority of man's concerns after his departure from the

[3]If one were to trace the origin of this idea, one would be inevitably led to a beautiful vision of Pico della Mirandola, at about the beginning of the modern epoch. In his *Oration on the Dignity of Man* (1487), Pico says that God, having created the world and filled it with all possible kinds of creatures, bethought himself to create a being who "might comprehend the meaning of so vast an achievement" and "might be moved with love at its beauty and smitten with awe at its grandeur." "Truth was, however, that there remained no archetype according to which He might fashion a new offspring," since "[a]ll space was already filled; all things had been distributed." At last, when God created man, this is what He said to him: "We have given you, oh Adam, no visage proper to yourself, nor any endowment properly your own, in order that whatever place, whatever form, whatever gifts you may, with premeditation, select, these same you may have and possess through your own judgment and decision. The nature of all other creatures is defined and restricted within laws which We have laid down; you, by contrast, impeded by no such restrictions, may, by your own free will, to whose custody We have assigned you, trace for yourself the lineaments of your own nature. . . . We have made you a creature neither of heaven nor of earth, neither mortal nor immortal, in order that you may, as the free and proud shaper of your own being, fashion yourself in the form you may prefer" (trans. A. R. Caponigri, South Bend, Ind., 1956).

[4]In this sense the last stage of historical development does indeed constitute a certain form of "return to nature."

state of nature) are not in any way determined by man's natural constitution. Beyond the relatively unimportant nucleus of physiological
requirements, the scope of those things that a man may need, fear, or
desire—above all, the whole situation that leads to the most painful
dilemmas of human existence, to which the political order is supposed
to provide a solution—is to be explained with reference not to man's
essence or species, but only to his freedom. Consequently, Rousseau
believes, a theory of man, insofar as it is to deal with the specifically
human aspect of man's existence, must entail a theory of history rather
than a natural science.

Historicism, despite its obvious attractions, has been one of the most
misunderstood and criticized aspects of modern theories of man. It has
been, among other things, identified with relativism and blamed for the
origins of totalitarianism.[5] Yet it is interesting to note that, at least
insofar as Rousseau is concerned, historicism was designed to provide
a background against which human rights could be defended in the
absence of a theory that would ground them in a natural order. The
objections to historicism are very often based on the assumption that
the "laws of history" are either nonexistent or incompatible with human freedom. In the latter case, history is viewed as a brand of natural
science, seeking to discover the laws determining human behavior in
the same way as physics seeks to discover the laws determining the
behavior of natural objects. In the former case, history is viewed as a
mere collection of events and a historian as a mere accountant. If
history is a branch of natural science, human behavior is necessarily
determined and freedom is only an illusion; if it is a mere collection of
events, human behavior is arbitrary and human values are relativized to
a particular time and place.

Historicism was introduced, however, to escape precisely this naive
alternative; Rousseau designed it as a social counterpart to his theory of
freedom as autonomy. The simple nature-chaos alternative Rousseau
has already rejected in connection with his discussion of the problem
of free will. Nature represents, for him, only one kind of order and by no
means the only possible one. The science of history, according to
Rousseau, does not consist in discovering a set of laws rigidly determining the shape of every event, but its subject matter is not at all arbitrary: a
historian discovers certain principles of human development in events
that chroniclers only relate, in the same way that an economist explains

[5]For the identification of historicism with relativism and totalitarianism, see Strauss,
Natural Right and History, passim. For an identification of nonrelativistically understood
historicism with totalitarianism, see K. Popper, *The Open Society and Its Enemies* (Princeton, 1966), and the same author's *Poverty of Historicism* (London, 1957).

events that an accountant only notes in his ledgers. To be sure, these principles do not express the *mechanism* of human development; they express its *logic*. Men are free and they are the authors of their "second nature." But they do have a "second nature" (although the term is apt to be misleading), since their authorship of their own destiny, while not subject to any external constraints, has inner dynamics deriving from the order of human rationality. In the same way that a free agent does not act arbitrarily because his freedom expresses his obedience to reason, the human species does not develop haphazardly, because its history expresses the unfolding of human rationality. The successive stages of human development are neither arbitrary nor causally related to one another. They are not externally (mechanically or providentially) determined; if they were, by knowing the state of humanity at one point in time one could predict its future and reconstruct its past. The relation among them is, rather, comparable to that between premises and conclusions in an argument: they follow logically from one another; but whether or not the conclusions are actually drawn or whether they can be reached only on the basis of these particular premises is a matter of historical contingency.[6] Still, this view of history implies a clear order of human development and the failure to distinguish between this order of freedom (reason) and the order of nature leads to a misunderstanding of the meaning of the concept of humanity.

The order of freedom implies an inherent historicity in human existence, according to Rousseau, because the unfolding of human rationality has the character of a development and involves a succession of stages. This is to some extent true of individual as well as social phenomena, although Rousseau's treatment of the subject in *Emile* obscures many of the relevant parallels. Similarly, certain important anachronisms in Rousseau's model of the ideal state make his treatment of the subjects' moral education in *The Social Contract* run counter to a much more interesting account of individual development that he gave outside the political context. Despite his nearly obsessive preoccupation with the problem of education, Rousseau is so intent on proselyting and convincing the reader of the unique correctness of the system of values he proposes as his ultimate solution to man's dilemmas that he seems to forget that such an *ultimate* system of values can be arrived at only as a result of a long process of moral evolution. In nearly all his expositions of the problem of education the process of

---

[6]To qualify this parallel, however, we must add that reason itself is not "eternal" for Rousseau, so that not only the material content of the premises and conclusions constitutes the matter of historical development. Instead, human rationality itself is a historical product, and we cannot ultimately separate the purely formal rules of inference from all the concrete instances of actual reasoning.

moral growth is presented as strictly controlled by some guardian who leads his pupils by the hand. As a result, despite Rousseau's insistence on spontaneity as a necessary element of learning, his program of education is more often than not a blueprint for indoctrination.[7] In *The Social Contract*, the moral beliefs of the citizens are manipulated by the government with the help of lies, censorship, and so on. In *Emile* and the *Moral Letters*, Rousseau himself leads his pupils into the temple of moral truth by way of quite incredible shortcuts. Only from auto-biographical (or pseudobiographical) contexts do we get a glimpse of the real nature of individual moral development. It is not the education of Emile or Madame d'Houdetot, but of their mentor Rousseau himself or his projection of himself into his own teacher, the Savoyard Vicar, that provides us with an account of an immanent and not externally imposed moral development. The most important feature of this process is determined by the crucial difference between innocence and moral goodness. True moral worth can come about only as a result of a struggle in which the forces of evil (passion perverted by reason and reason used as an instrument of passions) are overcome in favor not of a return to the simplicity of childhood but of a rational order of life. Morality is something of which only a rational agent is capable. But reason develops initially in the service of unsatisfied needs or passions, and its first result is the opposite of morality: the proliferation of uncontrollable passions and desires. Thus, moral worth is neither natural nor innate; nor is it something that can be acquired without an experience of evil. Consequently, the way to morality is an indispensable element of morality itself, and moral worth can come about only as the culmination of a long process of evolution. Its superiority over innocence lies precisely in the stability of a man's purpose due to his consciousness of his development.

The process of history, according to Rousseau, is the same process of moral evolution as experienced by the human species. Rousseau was a rather poor historian, but his interest in the problem of human development was more historiographic than historical; he was interested not in detailed expositions of historical problems, but in revealing the sense of history itself. This, he thought, could be explained by pointing to significant stages of the historical process, which capture the most important aspects of human evolution. The view that history involves a succession of stages is, of course, not new with Rousseau. Classical antiquity had its conception of golden, silver, and bronze ages, and the Christian Middle Ages were at times deeply shaken by the expectation

[7]See L. G. Crocker, *Nature and Culture: Ethical Thought in the French Enlightenment* (Baltimore, 1963), 476.

of the coming millennium which, as the Age of the Holy Spirit, was to follow the Ages of the Father and Son. But Rousseau's postulation of the inner historicity of human existence is intended to refer not to a symbolic or mythological history, but to man's actual, worldly development. What he attempts is a secularization of the concept of sacred history, and he seeks to give an analysis of human development that no longer refers to any transcendent conditions of man's existence. In this respect Rousseau's theory of historicity is related to most previous conceptions of the ages of mankind in a way similar to that in which Darwin's natural evolution is related to the biblical story of creation. The ages of mankind, in Rousseau's account, no longer reflect the journey determined for it by Providence, but represent stages in the progress of man's emancipation from nature due to the inner development of his rationality.

There can be many ways of distinguishing among the various stages Rousseau saw as indispensable for an account of man's present condition, and different inquiries will find a differing number of stages involved.[8] For our purposes, it is not necessary to distinguish more than three major stages, which have been discussed in previous parts of this book: the stage of nature, civil society (or civilization), and the political stage envisaged in *The Social Contract*. Rather than going back over the detailed characteristics of each and the nature of the transitions between them, I shall now limit myself to some general considerations concerning Rousseau's theory of historicity and above all to an outline of his views on the nature of progress.

The reason history, according to Rousseau, can replace natural order as the foundation of human rights is directly related to those features of historical development that give rise to the idea of progress. The most important among them is the fact that crucial historical developments are irreversible and that each significant step along this road constitutes a stage in the development of reason and human moral worth.

"It is not easy for a man to begin to think," says Rousseau in *Emile*, "but when once he has begun he will never leave off.... The natural progress of the mind is quickened but never reversed."[9] The crucial transition that Rousseau has in mind here is, of course, the radical break in the continuity of human life that takes place when man leaves the stage of nature and enters the stage of reflection. As indicated previously, the state of nature is, properly speaking, still prehistorical, since

---

[8]Cf. W. Pickles, "The Notion of Time in Rousseau's Political Thought," in M. Cranston and R. S. Peters, eds., *Hobbes and Rousseau* (Garden City, N.Y., 1972), and J. Starobinski's "Introduction" to the Pléiade edition of the *Second Discourse*.

[9]*Emile*, 550–51.

we cannot speak in it of man's being the author of his own actions. But we can speak of the transition from this stage to the next as the hypothetical beginning of human history, because the impetus that natural events provide for the unfolding of human perfectibility is not really a cause, but only an occasion, of the development of reason. Although it is too early at this stage to speak of human freedom in the true sense of the word, the mechanical action of nature can only create the conditions that make the development of reason necessary for man's survival; it cannot influence this development more directly because of the heterogeneous character of nature and rationality. It was certainly not necessary for reason to have developed, if by "necessity" we mean any design or pattern that human development was externally bound to follow, or if it implies that each step in this development had to take place exactly when it actually did. The fact that certain external conditions accelerated or even began the evolution of humanity was purely contingent with respect to the course that it was to follow, even though, within the order of nature, the events that actually did precipitate man's alienation from nature were mechanically determined to take place. Nevertheless, once the coincidence of overpopulation and natural disasters had its effect on human development, the change they occasioned in man's *modus operandi* was irreversible by any act of human volition. The achievements of reason and civilization are, of course, not absolutely indestructible, since societies can regress into the "dark ages" from which they had emerged. Historians dealing with departed civilizations are quite familiar with such phenomena, and they have come up with many ideas as to why they take place: even very advanced civilizations may disappear as a result of certain social or demographic factors, natural disasters, or unintentional damage to vital organs resulting from faulty nutrition or poisoned environment. Theoretically one cannot even exclude a case of intentional collective suicide, although so far we know of no such instance on the scale of a whole civilization. But the irreversibility entailed by Rousseau's idea of historical progress is not the one intended by the proponents of the deterministic view of history. Instead, Rousseau claims that no effects of human volition, short of some form of self-maiming that would make men organically incapable of thinking, can make them forgo the opportunities opened by their rationality, even if they are aware of the dangers involved. As a result of his use of reason, man can provide for his needs in new and more efficient ways, and his needs themselves are transformed beyond recognition. It is a dominant feature of this new *modus operandi* to open up new possibilities and not to close them. To act in one way when one is aware of another, more efficient solution to the same problem can only be a matter of play or make-believe, not a matter of historical reality. Once men discovered agriculture, domesticated animals, and so forth, they could not go back to the carefree life of their ancestors, who had provided for themselves by picking berries or hunting, since such primitive "economy" was no longer adequate to their needs and expectations. Once emotional attachments were formed and men began to live in families, it was no longer possible for them to go back to roaming in the woods in solitude, even if the independence of the savage sometimes seemed preferable to their own condition. The same is true of most later developments. Men may devise some means to avoid wars once they have invented machine guns or atomic weapons, but they cannot return to sword fighting, no matter how much they might be convinced of the superiority of the medieval code of honor over our prosaic system of values. They may invent some way of dealing with pollution, for example, but they cannot go back to a preindustrial way of life. And the reason for this inability to regress is not connected with the operation of any natural laws, but constitutes a consequence of man's ability to think.

The irreversibility of progress does not mean, however, that progress is inevitable. This may be best seen by examining Rousseau's view of the transition from civil society to the state. The pessimistic strain in Rousseau as to the chances of establishing a truly legitimate state[10] could, at first sight, be considered incompatible with his own view of the nature of historical progress. Upon closer inspection, however, it turns out that Rousseau is not committed to the claim that no cul de sac can be reached in the process of human development. Within the age of civil society, it is indeed the case that new rational means of satisfying men's needs necessarily breed new needs and new methods of satisfying them, and so on, possibly *ad infinitum*. This potentially endless repetition of human effort, however, is not what Rousseau refers to as "progress," since beyond a certain point it neither adds anything essentially new to human experience nor contributes to a further sharpening of the perception of inequality that may lead to the overcoming of the deplorable consequences of *amour propre* by making men move toward establishing a community based on a higher (moral) principle. Insofar as *this* step is concerned, on the other hand, there is no inherent

---

[10]This pessimism may indicate that Rousseau, in *The Social Contract*, does not take upon himself the role of a universal legislator who puts forth practical proposals that may transform any society into a legitimate state. Instead, he appears as a theorist who investigates what a good state may look like, without pretending to offer much practical advice. This view of the task of *The Social Contract* may invalidate at least some objections to Rousseau's political philosophy, especially those concerned with the fact that it does not provide sufficient safeguards against tyranny: Rousseau's answer may be that no *theory* could provide them.

necessity for it ever to take place. On the contrary, civil society can be transformed into a legitimate state only when many independent conditions are simultaneously present, and whether or not such a situation obtains is, as in the case of the transition from nature to civil society, a matter of historical contingency. For a legitimate state to be founded, there must exist a realistic possibility of organizing a viable political unit of relatively small size,[11] the great majority of people must become aware of the injustices of civil society, and an exceptional individual must be found to provide the necessary leadership and guide the people in the choice of their future constitution. If any one of these conditions is absent—and they may only very rarely occur simultaneously—no real progress is possible. What might in fact have been the case, according to Rousseau, in the Europe of his time was that civil society had grown to such dimensions (the nation-state) that the chance to establish a legitimate political community had disappeared for the foreseeable future.[12]

The inevitability of progress makes it into a normative and not a descriptive concept, and it is precisely its normative character that allows for Rousseau's historicist foundation of human rights. The overall sense of human history is the general rationalization of life. But the progress of reason does not resolve to a mere quantitative increase in the scope of human knowledge or to devising ever new means of satisfying human needs, since in the absence of other considerations, this only gives rise to an unlimited increase of man's further needs and desires. The progress of reason refers to the *moral* development of mankind, which involves a series of qualitatively distinct stages. Each stage in this series is ruled by a different principle arising as a result of the inadequacies and internal inconsistencies in the dominant principle of the previous stage. In the state of nature, the dominant principle of human behavior is the law of nature (self-preservation), which defines man as an amoral being and constitutes the basis of his innocence. The behavior of the social or civilized man is ruled by the principle of egoism (*amour propre*). Finally, the political stage is characterized by the fact that man's actions are governed by the principle of moral

[11]The small size of the legitimate state is evidence that Rousseau, even though he may have inspired many nationalists, was not one himself; in fact, his *polis*-like form of political organization is incompatible with a nation-state.

[12]This view of Rousseau does not contradict his claim that *should* the institution of a legitimate state take place, the move would be irreversible in the same sense as is the move from nature to civil society. Legitimate states do, of course, disintegrate, and much faster than civilizations. But such a dissolution is never an *option* for self-conscious agents constituting the community. This is the meaning of Rousseau's claim that the general will is indestructible (*Social Contract*, IV, 1).

equality. Like every sweeping generalization, Rousseau's distinction of the three basic ages of mankind is somewhat thin and not very helpful in analyzing actual historical problems. But we must remember that we are witnessing only the *birth* of modern historicism and that Rousseau meant his distinctions as only the roughest of approximations. As such, they are very telling as to what a historicist aims at. Each of the stages of history presupposes those which precede it and arises out of certain developments that take place within them. These developments do not have the character of causal determinants, but rather represent the inadequacies of the status quo with respect to the very principle that is supposed to characterize the given stage, that is, with respect to the dominant form of self-consciousness of the people of the time. It is true that neither a government nor an individual, in trying to legitimize its moral and political claims, has the possibility of appealing to some natural, unchanging norms regulating human relations. However, if the "laws" of social organization are not like the laws of physics, but specify a system of rational norms organizing the modes of human coexistence, then an individual can point to an internal inconsistency between the professed system of legitimization and the results of its practical application, and derive from this a legitimizing force for his criticism of the status quo and his demand for change. As soon as a viable alternative can be found to the existing order, he can claim that the irrationality of the status quo makes it illegitimate and in violation of his rights. The most fundamental right of a citizen is that he be allowed (and helped) to organize his life in accordance with the principles of reason. Even if reason itself is a historical product, its *normative* character always creates a tension between what is perceived as a fact and what is accepted as a norm. The essence of progress, according to Rousseau, lies precisely in man's ability to perceive such discrepancies and contradictions and to strive toward their resolution.

Naturally, there is another side to the same coin. Although Rousseau is sometimes reluctant to acknowledge this, when there is not viable alternative to the status quo in sight, a government can also legitimize its power by appeals to this fact, even though it may be admittedly far from perfect. Rousseau lived at a time when this aspect of historicism could not have been foremost in his mind. He believed that the governments around him were all patently illegitimate and that his own system provided the only standard of justice capable of rescuing man from his misery and degradation. But he was not entirely blind to the dangers of destructive revolutions. Although in *The Social Contract* he flatly declared that all existing governments persisted only by keeping their subjects in chains, in his project for the constitution of Poland he tried to build as much as possible on already existing, traditional institutions, even though the result of his proposals was a far cry from the universal equality that he advocated as a norm in *The Social Contract*.[13]

It does not seem, therefore, that Rousseau's historicism is particularly responsible for whatever totalitarian tendencies there may be in his thought. In fact, from a consistently historicist point of view, one could provide a very pertinent critique of Rousseau's antiliberalism, so that by blaming his historicism for his antiliberalism we may deprive ourselves of one of the most potent weapons in the defense against totalitarianism. One of the advantages of the historicist position is that it allows us to share Rousseau's admiration for ancient political institutions and at the same time claim that the irreversible development of the modern conception of individualism makes the attempt to restore the ancient model of social integration inherently reactionary and totalitarian in its implications. An effort at reimposing a tightly ordered political system on the developed form of civil society cannot result in the restoration of the unity of the *polis*, since it ignores the prevailing system of values and the technological development of modern society. An attempt to realize the nostalgic longing for an old order could be successful only if one were to enforce the preindustrial mode of political legitimization with the most modern methods of social control, deriving from the very technological reason one wants to destroy. But the resulting hybrid is what constitutes the most appalling and also the most typical characteristic of totalitarianism.

The main problem with Rousseau's elaborate attack on the early foundations of liberalism and the natural-right tradition lies not in his historicism *per se*, but in his lack of sufficient historical acumen and the consequent deficiency in his analysis of civil society. Rousseau, the born *contestateur avant la lettre*, though he very well understood the intellectual background of early liberal theory, did not understand the fundamental nature of the social changes that were taking place during his lifetime. Most important, he missed the historical meaning of the industrial revolution that was beginning in England, and, moving between the political climate of obsolete absolutism in France and the theocratic republic of Geneva, he did not realize the fundamental role that economic production would play only a few years after his death. His analysis of civil society was essentially that of Hobbes, who had written a hundred years before, and, unlike Locke, Rousseau did not attune his political proposals to the coming age of capitalism. Consequently, even though he tried to give civil society its due and recognized it as an indispensable stage of transition to political life, he left us only a

[13]Even there Rousseau makes a few exceptions. See note 34 to Chap. vi, above.

very anachronistic and essentially Aristotelian account of the concept of human needs. On the one hand, civil society represents an important step in man's moral development, but on the other hand it constitutes only an unfortunate detour insofar as the satisfaction of the ordinary necessities of life is concerned. The development of human productive capacity that takes place in civil society contributes absolutely nothing to the establishment of the legitimate social order described in *The Social Contract*. In this respect the ultimate point of human development is merely a *return* to nature: one of the dominant features of Rousseau's political society consists in its suppression of private interests and a reduction of human needs to the basic nucleus of physiologically determined necessities. In his account of human freedom Rousseau provided a decisively modern analysis of the nature of man's activity. But in his radical separation of moral freedom and the productive effort required to assure man of comfort in his life, Rousseau missed the most basic trend of modern political thought, that toward a synthesis of the Aristotelian *praxis* and *poesis*. As a result, his model of the state based on fraternity and devoted exclusively to moral concerns was itself politically anachronistic. His vision of historical stages was too abstract to provide an even apparently realistic account of historical complexity. It was only with Hegel and, especially, with Marx that Rousseau's historical triad was to achieve apparent (though only apparent) realism.

Nevertheless, where Rousseau, the still anachronistic utopian, anticipated Marx, the most realistic of all visionaries, was precisely in his insistence that the age of civil society be given its due. Anticipating both the Hegelian and the Marxist concept of dialectic, Rousseau, despite his repeated insistence on the political illegitimacy of all but a few states before his time, made it abundantly clear that civil society (to become capitalism in Marx) was not merely a perversion of reason. The unbridled development of egoistic passion, according to Rousseau, is a necessary prerequisite of virtue. "If man's soul had remained in a state of freedom and innocence," says the Savoyard Vicar in *Emile*, "what merit would there have been in loving and obeying the order he found established . . . ? He would be happy, no doubt, but his happiness would not attain to the highest point . . . ; he would be but as angels are, and no doubt the good man will be more than they."[14] Morality differs from innocence by the experience of evil and cannot come about without it. In political and historical terms, this means that the political stage of moral freedom is impossible without the preceding stage of civil society. The experience of extreme alienation and loneliness is a neces-

[14]*Emile*, 603.

sary prerequisite of the consciousness that finds its happiness in a free and uncoerced recognition of other people as not only worthy of respect but also indispensable to one's own self-fulfillment. Like the later Hegelian slave and the brutalized worker of Marx, the Rousseauean man, whose selfishness brings him to the depths of suffering and deprivation, is the future citizen of a free republic.

Conclusion

The three-way dispute among Hobbes, Locke, and Rousseau is like a battle among the pioneers who chart and divide a new territory of political philosophy, to be followed by generations that settle within their own borders. If the successors are forced to pay attention to their neighbors, it is only because they perceive them as external threats that have to be dealt with. In cultivating their own fields, they often bring home a very impressive harvest, but they lose sight of the tensions that gave rise to their respective dominions. The phenomenon of cross-fertilization becomes ever more rare.

To see how strange this outcome can be, it is enough to look at what happened to Rousseau's most important insights. The most fundamental challenge that Rousseau directed against his liberal opponents was his thoroughgoing attack on their naturalism. This attack was two-pronged. First, in the spirit of Pico della Mirandola,[1] Rousseau denied that man's freedom and rationality were compatible with his being a "natural" creature governed by laws of which he is not himself the author. Second, he rejected the notion that man's interaction with his natural environment could possibly infuse human existence with meaning sufficient to establish a moral dimension in our lives. Either of these arguments, according to Rousseau, leads to a rejection of liberal individualism. Man's "unnatural" condition makes him desperately alone in the universe, and his relation to nature is one of egotistic instrumentalism. The conclusion Rousseau drew from this is that the sense of estrangement and moral degradation plaguing modern man could be overcome only by a fusion of the individual and the commu-

[1]See note 3 to Chap. VII, above.

276

nity that would allow for a development of the moral dimension of human rationality.

As I have tried to show, Rousseau's critique of naturalism is more applicable to Hobbes than to Locke, and in fact Locke's theory of action seems to grope toward a conception of the person that shares many features with Rousseau's vision of autonomous man. Moreover, although Locke's reconciliation of natural science with the view of man as a free producer may be far from definitive, his effort points in the promising direction of an analysis of human phenomena in terms compatible with the general empiricist character of modern science. To be sure, the possibility of free action may never coexist easily with the deterministic implications of an explanation of every event in terms of antecedent efficient causes. The value of modern science, however, lies not in the metaphysical assumptions that some philosophers have taken it to presuppose, but in its ability to reformulate the questions raised in the course of our lives in such a way that we may begin to answer them to our satisfaction. Viewed in this perspective, science is neither positivistic nor deterministic, but, above all, pragmatic. What gives science its character is not an a priori conception of nature, but rather its approach to the problems that nature poses for human beings. Only when this pragmatic approach is misconceived as a metaphysical world view do the perennial metaphysical paradoxes reappear: how to reconcile freedom with determinism, how to derive norms from factual descriptions, and so on. The switch from the methodological to the metaphysical understanding of what science is about is a .change of *discourse*, a change from a search for a way of living to a search for absolutes. When we adopt this latter mode of inquiry, not only are we asking questions to which there are probably no satisfactory answers, but also the other approach, based on a rejection of questions that go beyond the problems that we actually encounter in the course of living our lives, must appear "relativistic."

Clearly, neither Hobbes's nor Locke's philosophy avoids treating the presuppositions of modern science as a metaphysical system. What primarily occupies their attention is the task of fitting a theory of man into the essentially metaphysical theory of nature they see as implicit in the mechanistic theory of modern science. Insofar as this is the case, Rousseau is probably right that whatever value such a metaphysical theory may have for analyzing natural phenomena, its value for explaining human freedom and rationality is highly questionable. But insofar as the modern scientific world view made Hobbes and Locke look for a theory of man rooted in human *interests* and insofar as they try to provide an elaborate theory of the nature of those interests and of their relation to the concerns of justice and politics, Rousseau's objection that a man has no "nature" misses the point, at least to some extent. For it is not just man as an *object* of modern science that fascinates Locke but also, and primarily, man as the *author* of science and its *user*. It is the characteristic attitude of modern man toward his environment, the attitude expressed in the enterprise of modern science, that Locke takes as paradigmatic and attempts to defend and justify. In the process, he also uses the tools of that same science to analyze the nature of human interests and the forms of their expression in human action, but in doing so he makes sure that the specific characteristics of human action, which distinguish it from the behavior of inanimate objects, are given their due. In this respect, then, Rousseau's objection that the application of modern science to human phenomena necessarily implies the view that man is a machine is not nearly as devastating to Locke as Rousseau imagines. On the contrary, it is a serious flaw in Rousseau's own philosophy that he misunderstood and summarily rejected the basic pragmatic attitude expressed in the enterprise of modern science.

But on another level, Rousseau's critique of the early liberals' naturalistic philosophy does point to a significant deficiency in their position. For Rousseau clearly saw that if man is himself the author of the laws that determine the shape of his actions, then the analysis of human action requires a historical dimension. Locke's theory is least satisfying in its attempt to defend the rights that an individual may have vis-à-vis the state by appealing to a rigid notion of natural law, where "natural" does indeed assimilate the human propensity to appropriate to the immutability of the laws of the physical universe. It may perhaps be the basic condition of man that he is dependent on the resources of nature for preserving himself and that the insecurity of their availability imposes on him the necessity of "taming" natural forces by a process that shares some features with Lockean appropriation. But that the specific form of this process which results in the regimen of *private property* is itself "natural" is a proposition hardly acceptable to anyone familiar with anthropological or historical evidence. Even Locke sees that the moral development of an individual has its social dimension, and the peculiar design of property relations must have some relation not only to the need for shaping the man-nature interaction, but also to the need to shape the interaction among human beings. It is more than likely, therefore, that individual life plans will take quite different forms depending on the various social contexts of individual moral development and that the "natural" problem of achieving some sort of human control over the environment will in fact underdetermine the particular distribution of individual control over the socially available resources that will become prevalent in a given community. By making *private* property into the universal condition of human freedom from subjection to the forces of nature, Locke has misperceived the extent of the creativity of which man may be capable in shaping his relationships with other men and has ignored the peculiar dynamics of social interaction.

In part this may result from Locke's nominalism, which precluded his giving proper attention to the fact that collective action may require a special kind of account, not reducible to a simple sum of individual decisions, and that the placing of an individual within the context of other individuals may qualitatively change the nature of his behavior. If this was, indeed, the reason for Locke's neglect of the constitutive role of social interaction in the life of an individual, it is rather unfortunate, for as we have seen from Hobbes's account of collective action or even from Locke's own account of the role of money (a social convention) in bringing out the moral aspects of appropriation, nominalism is not incompatible with an acknowledgment of the peculiar nature of social phenomena, an acknowledgment that does not require the conferring of a separate *ontological* status on the human collectivity. On the other hand, however, Locke's underestimation of the importance of the so-cial, and hence historical, dimension of the process by which men shape the contours of their lives may also result from his liberal pre-dispositions. By failing to distinguish sharply between civil society and the state, Locke may have been led to believe that acknowledging the constitutive nature of the social dimension of individual existence would force him to recognize the constitutive nature of the *state* and thus to go back to the Aristotelian politicization of those very aspects of life which his liberalism was designed to immunize from collective decisions backed by the instruments of state power.

This, in fact, is precisely the thrust of Rousseau's argument: if the life of an individual is inevitably intertwined with the lives of other individ-uals, then the only way in which a man may be made truly free is by the integration of his actions into the process of omnipresent collective, *political* decision making. But this move is by no means unavoidable; in fact, Rousseau himself makes it only because his analysis of *civil society* is such that it makes him believe that the behavior of individuals, in the absence of collectively imposed decisions concerning all the minutiae of human lives, leads to a universal conflict among men and to the moral degradation of each individual. It is true, of course, that once the radical interdependence of individuals is acknowledged, no a priori argument that some aspects of individual life are necessarily immune from political intervention can be given. But to want such an a priori argument may be to want too much: the price to be paid in misrepre-senting the forces that shape the individual may simply be too high. Nevertheless, it might be possible to argue that at a certain level of historical development some aspects of human interaction become sufficiently self-regulating to exclude them from the purview of state action and to narrow the dominion of politics to those issues that still require a collective decision to be imposed. And here Locke's theory of production, supplemented by a more mature conception of the market, may, unlike Rousseau's anachronistic account of civil society, provide a solid foundation for the defense of the liberal idea of individual rights and individual autonomy.

We can thus see that the impact of Rousseau's critique on the liberal position, as it crystallized in Locke's thought is far from unambiguous. Rousseau pointed out that the residuum of the metaphysical presuppositions seen as implied by the conceptual tools of modern science threatens to undermine Locke's attempt to give a theory of man that would allow for man's authorship of his own actions. But on the other hand, Rousseau is wrong in believing that the remedy for this problem requires abandoning either the conceptual tools of modern science in accounting for human behavior or the basic attitude toward the environment implicit in the scientific enterprise. Further, Rousseau is right in pointing to the absence of a social and historical dimension of human action in Locke, and he is right in claiming that this lack made Locke unjustifiably universalize (or "naturalize") the institution of private property and the liberal state. But Rousseau is wrong in believing that the recognition of this dimension requires us to abandon the nominalistic account of collective action and to start thinking of the collective interest in terms of a distinct entity called "the people" or "the general will." Moreover, he is wrong in believing that the recognition of the social dimension of individual life leads to the recognition of the omnipotence of the state and undercuts all defense of liberal institutions. Finally, Rousseau's critique of the order of civil society points to the endemic problems of "alienation" that plague a liberal society, and he is right in thinking that these problems were only aggravated by the radical individualism of the early liberals and their neglect of the fundamental link between the individual and the collectivity. But his own analysis of civil society is extremely impoverished by his inability to perceive the importance of production in human life and of the self-regulating aspects of the productive process that allow for the moral enrichment, rather than degradation, of individual life. Consequently, he failed to perceive that a certain amount of "alienation" may simply be the unavoidable price to be paid for the dignity and autonomy achieved by a modern individual.

In light of all this, one could expect that the further development of political philosophy would have involved a far-reaching refinement of the liberal theory *in answer* to Rousseau's challenge. What happened, however, was on balance the exact opposite: proponents and opponents of liberalism alike have generally entrenched their positions and attempted to fortify some of their most questionable territory. There are some partial exceptions, of course. Thus, on the liberal side, for example, both Burke and Tocqueville—two of Rousseau's harshest critics—generally assimilated Rousseau's historicist perspective, although neither of them had sufficient philosophical ambitions to give a systematic form to their borrowings from their principal adversary. On the opposing side, Hegel and Marx to some extent refined Rousseau's account of the nature of civil society by recognizing the importance of the process of production and acknowledging at least some achievements of the liberal model, but neither of them ever really opened his eyes to the intellectual caliber and potential of liberal individualism.[2]

The general absence of cross-fertilization between the two traditions manifests itself in the persistent rejection by liberals (for reasons alternating between ignorance and outright hostility) of the social and historical perspective on human action and the equally persistent belief (resulting intermittently in either outrage or simple scorn) among their opponents that the introduction of that perspective would spell the inevitable doom of liberal philosophy. In other words, critics of liberalism seem to believe that naturalism is the only possible moral underpinning of liberalism, while liberals seem to believe that historicism is the moral underpinning of totalitarianism.

The earliest response to Rousseau's critique of liberalism comes from Kant—philosophically the most sophisticated thinker in the liberal tradition, but not particularly attuned to the properly social and political consequences of his theory. Despite his paramount preoccupation with natural science, Kant is essentially persuaded by Rousseau's argument that a scientific account of human action necessarily reduces it to mechanically determined behavior. In order to preserve at least the possibility of morality, Kant follows Rousseau in giving a dualistic account of human action and in fact goes much further in this direction than his predecessor. Where Rousseau claimed that a mechanistic

[2]The most interesting exception, perhaps, may be found in the thought of the American "founding fathers," especially Madison's. Although the founding fathers failed to provide any overt acknowledgment of Rousseau's historicism and repeatedly invoked the idea of natural law, their common-law training made them quite attuned to the historical peculiarities of the community for which they devised the Constitution. Moreover, while clearly favoring the liberal, individualistic model of politics for everyday life, they at the same time attempted to preserve some room for the Rousseauean model of "republican virtue," which seemed to them necessary at a time when the foundations of established political practice need serious rethinking. Given, however, the predominantly practical nature of the founding fathers' enterprise, it is not clear to what extent one may infer from it a coherent theoretical justification of their attempted synthesis. (I owe most of my appreciation of the founding fathers' thought to my colleague Bruce A. Ackerman.)

account was simply inadequate to explain human behavior, Kant believes that all phenomenal manifestations of action must conform to the mechanistic, scientific description. But while no empirical observation, including the data of inner experience, can break out of the causal pattern of natural events, Kant believes that it is still meaningful to suppose the reality of an entirely alternative, unobservable world in which the laws of morality replace the principles of natural causation. To explain how freedom could reign in this alternative world, Kant takes up Rousseau's theory of autonomy but modifies it in a radically individualistic and universalistic direction. Morality, according to him, derives its content not from the merely general interest of a (particular) community, but from reason alone, and it extends universally over all rational beings. Moreover, each rational agent is individually capable of discerning the moral imperatives implicit in his rationality and ordering his life in accordance with their demands. The philosophical presuppositions of liberalism are thus seemingly vindicated: not only is the moral dignity of the individual independent of the community (as Locke had wanted it to be), but also the autonomy of the individual makes him into a self-enclosed cosmos—even the natural world constitutes no limitation on his freedom.

With all due respect and admiration for Kant's philosophical achievements, however, a closer inspection of his theory must show that it abandoned the most promising aspects of both Locke's liberalism and its Rousseauean critique while picking up the most questionable elements of both. The radical bifurcation of the moral-rational order of the noumenal world and the causal order of nature not only abandoned the Lockean effort at reconciling morality and freedom with human interests, but also removed the liberal theory of the person to a level of such metaphysical abstraction as to make it largely irrelevant for any ordinary social theory. The Marxist jeer that the Kantian concept of freedom, tied as it is to the idea of the noumenal self, allows the capitalist to claim that a worker remains "noumenally free" while all the particular, "empirical" aspects of his personality (his talents, capacity to labor, and the rest) are as much for sale as if he were a slave, contains—despite its crudeness—a kernel of truth. For the Kantian concept of the moral dignity to be respected in each individual is as thin in content as the categorical imperative in general: it is in fact quite hard to conceive of any substantive set of rules governing human interaction that could in principle be incompatible with its requirements. Kant, of course, did not conceive of the categorical imperative as so thin. But because he did not consider a theory of human interests relevant to his moral theory, he was left with at most a thin concept of consent ("at most" because it is not even clear that the principle of respect for other agents is genuinely entailed by the categorical imperative[3]) as the only barrier against unlimited exploitation. What the Marxist jeer shows is how manipulable such a thin concept of consent may become.

While the Kantian theory abandoned the Lockean attempt to tie the conception of freedom to a theory of human interests—thus exacerbating Rousseau's neglect of the concept of production[4]—Kant's individualistic theory of autonomy did not pick up Rousseau's insistence on the social and historical dimension of morality—thus exacerbating the Lockean confusion of political individualism with social atomism. To be sure, the social atomism of Kant is no longer based on a *naturalistic* account of human action; in fact it shows that the link between ahistoricism and naturalism is not automatic. It remains nevertheless true that the Kantian theory of the self, in both its theoretical and its practical aspects, is more or less oblivious to the difference it makes for an individual to live among other individuals. Even those aspects of human development which Locke still perceived as implicated in human interaction, whether involving the acquisition of moral categories or connected to the development of the autonomy-related significance of appropriation, disappear entirely from the Kantian picture. In fact, the very concept of *development*, even aside from its social dimension, is pushed out by Kant's transcendentalism. On the surface of the observable world is the "empirical man," who does not interest Kant. Whatever can be said of him, of his interests, talents, predilections, and evolution, is left entirely to natural scientists, whose research can never yield anything of interest to a moral philosopher. Behind the scenes, there is another, "noumenal man," who may be a moral agent, immutable in his freedom and rationality. Though we should focus around him our whole moral and political attention, it is a mark of his irrelevance that, as Kant himself tells us, we shall never *know* whether his freedom is real or only a fiction of our speculative imagination.

It was Kant's antinaturalism, for which he had provided an extremely powerful philosophical justification, that was picked up by his immediate successors and put to further use in the development of political philosophy. And given the nearly automatic association of liberalism

[3]It may not be incompatible with the principle of universalization to follow the maxim that other people may be trampled upon, if one does not intend to except oneself from the receiving end of the maxim's operation. To be sure, even in this maxim there is an implicit recognition of another person's formal moral *equality*, but it strains the use of the term to call this recognition "respect."

[4]Rousseau's neglect of the role of production was simply a result of his deficient analysis of civil society, which pointed only to the conflicts generated by competition and remained blind to its self-regulating character. Kant's concept of production, on the other hand, tied as it is to a pursuit of ends dictated by mere inclination, becomes *in principle* irrelevant to the concerns of a moral theory.

Conclusion

with naturalism, it is not surprising that the main impetus of the Kantian theory was felt on the antiliberal side of the argument, especially since the liberals were by then losing interest in philosophical speculation. Kant's successors—Hegel and Marx, above all—abandoned from the start the anti-Rousseauean elements of his philosophy—his individualism and ahistoricism—and generally modified Kant's transcendentalism by injecting into it a developmental dimention. This last step, in particular, allowed them to go beyond both Rousseau and Kant in presenting an apparently realistic and fully developed political alternative to liberal philosophy.

We have seen that Kant had radicalized the Rousseauean bifurcation between the order of nature and the order of freedom. Where Rousseau had believed that a naturalistic account was simply inapplicable to human action, Kant maintained that such an account of observable human behavior must be possible, but that another account could be given (in terms of freedom) from the noumenal perspective. Although the relation between these two accounts is never quite clear, they were supposed to be compatible with each other because the natural order of the phenomenal world was itself the product of human spontaneity. Still, and in this sense the Kantian reconciliation of freedom with determinism remains a puzzle, the subject's authorship of the formal elements of the natural world is not a product of his will, but rather a necessary condition of the possibility of any experience the subject may have. The laws that the subject imposes on the natural world are thus fixed and immutable, amounting to transcendental conditions defining any rational being's ability to make the world intelligible to himself. It is at this point that Hegel introduces his most significant modification of Kantian theory. The process by which a subject imposes an order on his experience of the world is not for Hegel, as it was for Kant, merely an activity designed to make the world intelligible, but an intensely *practical* experience in which the subject attempts to *subordinate* external reality to the requirements of his own freedom. Man's encounter with the world is thus not a theoretical experience for the knower, but a process of his gradual self-assertion over the environment of his action. Moreover, the agent does not approach this task with any ready-made tools, such as the Kantian system of a priori categories of the understanding, but rather must learn how to achieve his aims, indeed, what concrete shape to give to his aims themselves, by a process in which his expectations are frustrated and earlier, failed strategies are modified. Thus, the process by which man shapes the world according to his plan is also the developmental process in which his own plan, indeed, the concrete forms of his own subjectivity are constituted. Still further, one of the fundamental lessons that a man learns in this process is that the enterprise is impossible for an individual agent, that the experience of remaking the world in the image of freedom involves an encounter with others which shapes each of us as much as the encounter with nature, and that only the human *species* is the ultimate agent in the development of freedom and rationality.

The far-reaching transformation of the Kantian doctrine at the hands of Hegel remedied so many problems in Rousseau's philosophy that it made the theoretical alternative to liberalism seem impregnable, even as the practical successes of liberalism were making it indifferent to philosophical speculation. By reinterpreting the theoretical experience of the Kantian subject into the practical experience of man, Hegel was seemingly able to bridge the gap between moral freedom and the world of natural needs and inclinations. Unlike the Kantian noumenal self legislating in the invisible realm of the world of things in themselves or the Rousseauean citizen who must submerge his concern with material well-being in order to participate in the liberating process of communal self-legislation, the Hegelian subject pursues his autonomy through a process in which his material needs and his encounter with nature are fully objects of legitimate concern. The activity of production, neglected by Rousseau, has thus been made into a fully constitutive element of human autonomy, and its theory, which Kant deemed irrelevant to moral concerns, became an important component of a general theory of freedom. Hegel vindicated the social nature of human agency, as conceived by Rousseau and rejected by Kant, and integrated its concept into a developmental and historicist perspective of a much more solid kind than the one Rousseau had provided. In making all these moves, Hegel could claim to have "superseded" liberal theory by incorporating the truth of its insight concerning the importance of man's productive activity for the achievement of moral freedom, while rejecting its naturalism and its theory of individualism, and vindicating a theory of the public sphere (including the state) as the embodiment and a necessary condition of genuine autonomy.

The properly political implications of Hegel's philosophy and the degree of his antiliberalism have been much discussed. Clearly some distinctly modern elements in his philosophy are not inimical to the liberal outlook, particularly his distinction between civil society, in which many human aspirations are realized outside the political realm, and the state. Nevertheless, the prevailing tenor of his thought is that of the advocacy of a much greater degree of social and political integration than is compatible with the liberal theory of individual dignity. Despite his attempt to do justice to the liberal concern with production, he viewed the productive process primarily in social, rather than individual, terms. Still more significant, an individual's most important moral aspirations are for Hegel, as for Aristotle, bound up with that person's recognition by the other members of the community, whose acknowledgment of the validity of his self-image is constitutive of the individual's own dignity. Finally, while some elements of this recognition can be achieved outside the political realm, in the economic or family sphere, only the status of citizenship gives one access to the public sphere in which the process of mutual recognition is complete and man's moral aspirations are fully realized. The structure of mutual recognition with crowns the development of human autonomy thus recreates the Rousseauean concept of the general will and places politics and the state at the apex of morally significant institutions. Although the Hegelian individual is never as immediately dissolved in the community as his Rousseauean counterpart, Hegel's political philosophy ultimately preserves the Aristotelian insistence on the primacy of the state, the opposition to which defines the liberal enterprise.

Another feature of Hegelian philosophy which separates it from the liberal outlook is somewhat more amorphous but no less important. This is the generally metaphysical tenor of Hegelianism and its total contempt for modern science. Throughout this book, I have tried to show how fundamental for the development of liberal thought was the spirit of empirical pragmatism permeating the cultural formation that shaped Hobbes and Locke. Hegel's whole effort, on the other hand, despite his recognition of the importance of human interests, is to replace the analytical model of modern science with an a priori argument and to restore the primacy of philosophical speculation. The open-endedness of liberal theory and its underdetermination of the concept of the good life, which leave room for each individual to fill the gaps left by the common framework of moral action, are swept away in a doctrine for which there is only *one truth*, to be established by a priori means. The meaning of each action is determined by the omniscient philosophical observer for whom the action's social and historical significance exhausts what can be intelligible in it and relegates the idiosyncratic motivation of the individual to the domain of error and confusion or, at best, irrelevance. No amount of empirical evidence could move the sage of Jena and Berlin to modify his Olympian position.

It was only with Marx that an heir of Rousseau's critique of liberalism descended for a while from the heights of a priori arguments to revive Rousseau's own spirit of meeting the liberals on their own terms. Liberal theory had by then gone through its marriage with political economy, and a few words should be said about this.

By the end of the eighteenth century the promise held out by Hobbes and Locke that a truly scientific theory could be extended to human phenomena seemed to have entered a new phase, with the economic theory of Adam Smith purporting to show that the apparently uncoordinated actions of individuals, undertaken with purely self-interested motives, far from leading to a universal conflict among men, are invisibly coordinated by the market to the benefit of all (or nearly all) the participants. What Locke had only somewhat indistinctly envisaged—namely, that the productivity of human labor enables the state to stay out of the economic sphere and limit itself to the role of impartial umpire— seemed to have been confirmed by Smith's systematic analyses. Had a liberal philosopher of Locke's caliber then appeared on the scene, we might have seen a very significant refinement of liberal theory, for Smith's theory of the invisible hand was a ready-made answer to Rousseau's analysis of civil society. Rousseau's critique of the system of human relations entailed by the order of civil society was, of course, not limited to his condemnation of conflict over the resources that become ever more scarce as human covetousness grows beyond any limits. What he objected to above all was the very process of the unreflected-upon growth of human needs, to the neglect of what he saw as the moral demands of man's rationality. Nevertheless, his idea that civil society necessarily involves relentless conflict among men was extremely important in his theory, for he saw the moral degradation of man as largely its result. Rousseau had really no other explanation of why men constantly desire more than they already have, except for his hypothesis that their self-consciousness generates the overwhelming sense of aloneness and insecurity. He did not deny, of course, that nature provides a potential threat and that it needs to be controlled to *some* extent to enable man to exist. But the main source of human insecurity in the advanced stages of civil society comes not from the threat that nature as such represents, but from the fact that an individual is pitted against *other men* in his struggle for survival. Now, Smith's theory (before some of its darker consequences were brought out by Malthus and Ricardo) undermined much of the strength of Rousseau's argument, for it presented an optimistic vision of the market in which the self-interested effort of one individual not only does not detract from the efforts of another, but ultimately supports them. Clearly, an individual may still be concerned that he may be left behind his fellows in achieving the comforts of life, but this picture is quite different from the one Rousseau had envisioned. Behind the façade of competition, there appears a structure of cooperation: in competing with our fellow men we are really searching for the way in which we may best contribute to the good of society.

Given this theory, Rousseau would have found it much harder to argue that civil society necessarily leads to human moral degradation. The only way left open for him would be to argue that the good of the

Conclusion

society that a self-interested individual contributes to is not that of the general will but of the will of all, a mere aggregate of still atomized individuals. But even that distinction becomes more problematic, for it can no longer be claimed that self-interested behavior is automatically destructive of the spirit of the community. In fact, the problem is even deeper: why do we still need a concept of the general will, if the attitude of self-interest generates social cooperation? What Rousseau would need at this point is a new argument that the *values* pursued by self-interested individuals are wrong and need to be replaced by the fraternal values pursued by selfless citizens. Rousseau's previous argument was twofold: he claimed (1) that a communal, intersubjective context for human action was necessary for giving a moral quality to individual behavior and (2) that the pursuit of self-interest had only a divisive, alienating effect on the individual. The standard liberal response was (and still often appears to be) to deny both these components and to claim instead that: (1) an individual contains within himself a self-sufficient moral cosmos and (2) self-interested behavior leads, except for some special cases warranting political intervention, to a viable form of social cooperation. It is the second of these issues that Smith argued had been decided in favor of the liberals. But if we assume that he was right (which is, of course, open to question), then something of great importance follows with respect to the first issue. On the antiliberal side, there arises the possibility that even if Rousseau's first claim is correct, i.e., that moral action requires a social context, it may still not be the case that *politics* (communal decision making backed by coercive powers) is the most important social context in question. In other words, the so-called private sphere, together with what appears to be a merely self-interested pursuit of economic advantage, may in reality be a social sphere of another kind in which the individuals express their mutual interdependence in a noncoercive atmosphere. "Production" may thus be not an inherently alienating activity, but—as liberals of the Lockean persuasion would claim—an important component of moral action. On the liberal side, on the other hand, the argument that man is a self-enclosed moral cosmos may, in the light of Smith's argument, amount to overkill. For even if it is granted that moral action is meaningful only in a social context, it can still be true that political coercion is inappropriate in most situations and that the replacement of voluntary cooperation by political decision making requires a special justification.

No such implications are automatic, of course, and drawing them out would require a new version of the liberal theory. Rethinking of this kind would involve not only abandoning the social atomism of the early liberals but also an elaboration of a more plausible theory of man

288

entailing a historical perspective on the rise of the conditions that call for a liberal (individualistic) *political* system. Integrated into such a perspective would be an account of the process of production which would defend the role of individual autonomy without denying that this autonomy makes sense only in the context of social cooperation. A refined response to Rousseau would thus be elaborated which would grant his point that moral action necessarily involves a *community* of agents, but would present the productive process as a form of modern human interaction in which a rather complex network of relationships replaces the immediate fraternal unity of the citizens. Within this framework, it would also be possible to deal with the Rousseauean problem of alienation as a characteristically modern tension between the common enterprise and the diversity of individual pursuits.[5]

Despite some partial efforts, no systematic theory of this kind was brought forth by the defenders of liberalism. Instead, the achievements of economic theory and, to an even greater extent, the practical success of liberal politics (particularly in England and the United States), made liberals by and large uninterested in refining the philosophical foundations of their world view. Economics itself was largely seen as a new ahistorical science, revealing a more or less "natural" order of things. Its analysis of social cooperation was viewed as confirming the theory of social atomism, and pragmatic concerns have tended to push the moral meaning of production into the background. Nothing reveals this more clearly than the philosophical paucity of the utilitarian perspective associated with the dominance of political liberalism: the purpose of human action is the maximization of "happiness" understood in terms of the feeling of "pleasure" and ultimately incapable of providing a coherent theory of human personality.

Critics of liberalism did not follow the path of conversion either. Their position was more problematic, however, and they could not long ignore the impact of Adam Smith on their theory of politics. I have argued that the optimism of Smith's political economy provided a powerful argument against Rousseau's analysis of civil society. But I have also mentioned that Smith's optimism was, of course, open to question, and the immediate followers of the great Scotsman brought out some of the blacker implications of his analysis. It is from these that Marx was to derive his new version of the antiliberal critique. The basic philosophical foundations of his position had already been worked out by Hegel, who had integrated the concept of production into his political philosophy but attempted to show that liberal theory ignores the

---

[5]Some of these themes are elaborated in the sociological studies of Emile Durkheim, especially in his conception of organic versus mechanical solidarity.

intersubjective dimension of human life, constituting the necessary basis of autonomy. But whereas Hegel's theory had remained tied to the old philosophical vocabulary, inimical to the discourse of modern science, Marx undertook to translate its main insight into language that was familiar to the liberals and to bring his arguments to the heart of liberal territory. Relying on the deeply pessimistic arguments of Malthus and Ricardo, which he himself further elaborated, Marx argued that Rousseau had been right, after all, in claiming that the values inherent in the self-interested actions of individuals are in fact inimical to the orderly development of human autonomy. According to his analysis, the competitive pressures of the market do indeed pit man against man in a life-and-death struggle in which the collective outcome ultimately redounds to everyone's disadvantage. This is so because after the initial contribution of the free market to the development of human productive capacities, the capitalist system must in the long run grind to a halt and hamper further achievement of the prosperity it promises. Progress on both the economic and the human front will then be possible only if the communal nature of human agency is recognized and a transition to a new society based on this recognition. Though the Marxist critique of liberalism modifies the views of both Hegel and Rousseau (particularly in refusing ever to separate politics from the productive process), its basic point of arrival is to modernize their approaches without giving any ground to their common opponents.

It would be pointless to pursue this story further, especially because the two sides have only drifted much further. Given the failure of Marx's economic predictions, his followers, having defended them for a while, started to retranslate their communitarian insights into the familiar language of a priori philosophical speculation and, in exchange for their intellectual alienation from mainstream political thought, regained their immunity to empirical refutation. Liberals, on the other hand, have oscillated between utilitarianism and the recently popular revivals of Kantianism without having to come to terms with the heritage of the Rousseauean critique. It may be, of course, that we are past the time when a philosophical synthesis capable of providing a global picture of our social and political predicament, whether that picture were to provide a defense of something like liberalism or its comprehensive critique, could be within the ability of any one person. Economics alone, which would have to figure prominently in any such synthesis, is a complex discipline that few philosophers know much about. The complexities of modern historical research make most generalizations shaky and suspect. Political theory has become a vast and often arcane field of inquiry with its own specialists. Human life itself may indeed have become so fractured and diverse that a "theory of man" may be an anachronism. And yet the need for a more comprehensive notion of self-understanding is not something easily given up. Philosophers still exist and they seem to plow the same field over and over again. And amazingly enough, they learn from each other as little as in the past. Or less?

Index

Index

Benn, S. I., 52, 55n, 57n
Bergin, T. G., 263n
Blame, 70, 94, 100, 132, 244
Bowle, J., 17n
Burke, Edmund, 6, 11, 13, 72, 253, 281

Calvinism (see also Puritanism), 63
Capital, 188, 194, 196, 206, 207, 210, 213
Capitalism, 25, 63, 117, 178, 125, 177–79, 184, 191, 194, 196, 211, 213, 215, 216, 273, 274, 290
Cassirer, Ernst, 239n
Charles I, 27n
Charles II, 66
Charvet, J., 249n
Choice (see also Autonomy; Freedom; Free will; Liberty), 44, 71, 80, 81, 89, 94, 101, 126–30, 134, 147–49, 152, 157, 160, 161, 163, 169
Christianity (see also Puritanism; Religion), 12, 19, 47, 73, 104, 105, 127, 178, 212, 235, 243, 249, 260, 267
Civilization, process of, 213, 235, 254–56, 269, 271
Cogito (see also Descartes, René; Res cogitans), 48, 231, 236, 237
Communal institutions (see also Community; Society), 62
Communal values or norms, 13, 117, 245
Communication (see also Language; Speech), 43, 203, 204, 207, 259
Community (see also Society), 61, 93, 203, 204, 237, 248, 256, 257, 270, 271, 278, 281; economic, 205; and the individual, 12, 50, 62, 63, 65, 74, 75, 114, 120, 121, 184, 251, 252, 255, 259–62, 282, 286, 288, 290; interest or stability of (see also Interests, collective), 62, 258, 259, 282; political, 72, 75, 83, 107, 118, 200, 202, 252, 254, 271; positive and negative, 181–83, 186
Competition, 9, 35, 50, 51, 56, 89, 116, 213, 223, 238, 246, 254, 283, 287, 290
Conceptualism, 185
Conquest (see also Sovereignty), 96, 102, 106, 108, 109
Consciousness (see also Person; Self-consciousness; Soul), 49, 136, 143, 242, 267, 275
Consent, 61, 68, 73, 83, 89, 96, 97, 99, 102, 106, 108, 109, 182, 195, 282, 283
Consequentialism, 73
Consumption, 173–75, 188, 189, 191, 205–7
Contract (see also Agreement; Consent; Covenant; Obligation, contractual; Promise), 21, 66, 83, 93, 196; social c., pact or compact, 23, 36, 70, 72, 73, 83, 95, 98, 100–102, 106, 108–11, 119, 198, 201, 202, 207, 251, 254, 256, 261, 262; social c. as historical event, 73, 100, 101, 107
Contractarianism (contractualism), 8, 9, 12, 61, 62, 70, 73, 101, 108, 109, 120, 254
Convention (see also Agreement), 38, 41, 168, 180, 183, 184, 196, 199, 204, 205, 279
Covenant (see also Agreement; Contract; Promise), 90, 91–95, 107–9
Crocker, Lester G., 267n
Cromwell, Oliver, 66

Darwin, Charles, 39, 268
Day, J. P., 187n, 196n, 202n
Deliberation, 22, 39, 42, 79, 153, 171
Democracy, 4, 25–27, 102
Deontology, 61, 73
Derathé, R., 219n
Descartes, René, 28n, 48–49, 127n, 136, 137, 231, 236–37, 243
Desire (see also Interests; Passion; Will), 9, 20, 23, 27, 29–36, 39–43, 64, 79, 82, 91, 94, 122, 124, 131, 135–37, 140–43, 145–50, 153, 157, 159, 163–66, 168, 173, 175, 188, 205, 207, 215, 225, 237–38, 241, 255, 267, 271, 287; for power, 35, 36, 44–51, 55, 103, 116, 142, 173
Determinism (deterministic), 47, 54, 55, 65, 70, 71, 81, 89, 122, 126, 134, 135, 139, 140, 149, 230, 269, 277, 284
Development: economic, 7, 209, 212; historical, 16, 263–75, 280, 283, 286, 290; human, 37, 225, 233, 235–37, 244, 254, 263, 265–75; of liberalism, political theory or philosophy, 6, 15, 24, 27, 61, 62, 64, 65, 82, 280, 283; moral, 16, 161–76, 205, 266, 267, 271, 274, 278
Dialectic, 101, 162, 175, 274
Diderot, Denis, 249
Disposition(s), 21, 32, 121, 159, 161, 163, 164, 167, 170, 193
Dominion (see also Property): paternal, 92, 97, 106–8, 181; and property, 183–86, 210
Dunn, John, 2n, 3n, 115n, 120n, 177n, 178n
Durkheim, Emile, 289n
Duty, 60, 66–68, 85, 91, 155, 178, 179, 181, 199, 212, 241, 244, 258

Economics (see also Mercantilism), 9, 125, 187, 188, 205, 206, 210, 286, 289, 290
Education, 22, 32, 43, 99, 154, 156, 163, 165, 167, 170, 239, 248–50, 257, 266, 267
Egoism, egotism, egocentrism (see also Amour propre; Selfishness), 215, 225, 233, 244, 247, 254, 271, 276

Index

Index

Moral motivation, 150, 153, 155, 171
Moral norm: *see* Norm(s), moral
Moral obligation: *see* Obligation, moral
Moral reasons (*see also* Reason, and morality), 147, 166
Moral responsibility, 80, 123, 130–32, 134, 135, 140, 158, 160, 171, 172, 175, 176, 227, 231, 244, 248
Moral theory or philosophy, 12, 13, 15, 18, 29, 30, 87, 91, 116, 118, 122, 131, 150, 154–57, 159–62, 166, 168, 169, 175, 216, 239, 240, 246, 282, 283
Moral values, 168, 243, 244, 259
Moral worth, 116, 171, 245, 247, 255, 260, 267, 268
Moses, 101
Motivation: *see* Mechanism, of human action or motivation; Moral motivation
Mozart, Wolfgang Amadeus, 81

Napoleon I, 26
Nationalism, 213, 219, 271
Nation-state, 219, 279
Natural equality or inequality of men, 50, 52, 66, 69, 84, 89, 103–7, 110, 119
Natural law: *see* Law(s), natural
Natural morality, 170, 171, 250
Natural obligation: *see* Obligation, natural
Natural right: *see* Right, natural
Natural science: *see* Science, natural
Nature, 7, 8, 11, 25, 30, 31, 34, 36, 47, 54, 55, 80, 174, 222–27, 230, 232, 243, 246, 265, 269; forces of, and man, 36, 50, 237; human, 19, 23, 25, 29, 33–35, 41, 42, 48–50, 58, 60, 62–65, 90, 101, 110, 122, 140, 150, 158, 185, 203, 222, 225, 226, 230, 235, 251, 252, 255, 263, 264, 266; man's relation to, transformation of, or mastery over, 14, 47, 48, 116–24, 172–76, 179, 180, 181, 184, 185, 186, 188–94, 200, 203, 204, 207, 211, 213, 214, 216, 233, 237, 238, 245, 252, 264, 276, 278; state or stage of, 7, 8, 11, 16, 19, 23, 44, 50, 58, 60, 70, 72, 76–78, 80, 82, 83, 85, 86, 89, 92, 93, 95, 98, 100, 107, 110, 173, 186, 198–200, 222, 225, 226, 231, 235, 241, 254, 256, 265, 268, 271
Needs, human (*see also* Interests), 47, 64, 116, 117, 119, 124, 163, 166–68, 173–75, 180, 185, 186, 190–92, 194, 205–8, 214, 216, 232, 235, 238, 247, 253, 264, 267, 269–71, 274, 285, 287
Newton, Isaac (and Newtonian thought), 6, 136, 137, 223
Nihilism, 13, 14, 65, 117, 214, 215
Noble savage (*see also* Primitive man; Savage man), 220, 225, 226

Nominalism, 8, 37, 38, 50, 51, 55, 63, 99, 127, 185, 192–94, 203, 204, 207, 216, 217, 223, 230, 251, 279, 280
Norm(s), 13, 26, 30, 33, 37, 79, 88, 89, 119, 144, 160, 162, 226, 227, 236, 243, 254, 272, 273; of conduct or behavior, 167, 168, 245, 246, 272; and fact, 3, 9, 40, 67, 79, 272, 277; legal, 50, 100; moral, 8, 21, 30, 50, 72, 77, 166, 167, 170, 176, 179, 245–47; normative theory or account, 13, 14, 19, 30, 37, 41, 123, 271; normative vs. descriptive inquiry, approach, etc., 61, 65, 66; of prudence, 12, 20, 22; social or political, 94, 109–11, 117; system of, 21, 77, 215, 216, 240
Noumena: *see* Self, noumenal
Nozick, Robert, 1, 3, 179, 208n

Obligation, 8, 19, 21, 50, 52, 57, 60, 66–70, 74–76, 79, 80, 82–100, 110, 119, 160, 167, 171, 184, 208, 213–15, 226, 252, 254; adherence to, 84, 88–90, 94, 95; civil, 84, 87, 94, 97–100, 200; contractual, 19, 41, 100, 204, 205; filial, 92, 106–8; moral, 11, 21, 41, 86, 109, 121, 151, 152, 169, 170, 213; natural, 70, 71, 83–92, 94, 96, 97, 100; physical, 84–86, 88; political, 17, 70, 71, 83–85, 87, 92, 94–100, 109, 200, 213, 227, 240; prepolitical, 70, 84, 93, 96, 102; and right, 74–76, 86–88, 100, 214
Ontology (ontological), 10, 11, 36–38, 48, 49, 81, 181, 190–93, 236, 279
Ovid, 220
Ownership (*see also* Appropriation; Property), 89, 125, 173, 177–91, 193, 194, 197–99, 202, 204–7, 209, 210, 213, 251

Pain, 124, 137, 142–47, 149, 151, 153, 156–59, 161, 163, 165–67, 233
Parfit, Derek, 21n
Participation, political, 8, 118, 252, 257, 261
Pasqualucci, P., 239nn
Passion(s) (*see also* Reason, and passions), 19, 35, 90, 215, 233, 237, 238, 242, 244, 245, 247, 250, 261, 267, 274
Paternal dominion: *see* Dominion, paternal
Paulus, 186n
Peace (*see also* Security), 34, 41, 51, 69, 73, 90, 91, 98, 200
Pepys, Samuel, 115n
Perception (*see also* Sense(s)), 7, 46, 136, 137, 142, 169
Perfectibility, human, 225, 232, 234, 263, 269

Index

Index

Teleology (teleological), 11–13, 17, 28, 30, 33, 34, 36–38, 56, 137, 147, 167, 202, 214, 223, 243
Theodicy, 220
Theology, 7, 18, 28, 47, 63, 104, 168, 178
Tocqueville, Alexis de, 11, 281
Totalitarianism, 16, 219, 220, 253, 261, 265, 273, 281
Transcendental apperception, 64
Tully, James, 2n, 120n, 177n, 178–79, 181–86, 196n, 199–202, 208, 212n

Understanding, faculty of (see also Reason), 39, 42, 124, 129, 133, 135, 139, 142, 144, 145, 148, 149, 150, 153, 157–59, 173, 203, 229, 234, 247, 284
Uneasiness, Locke's concept of, 123, 124, 137, 141, 143, 145–49, 163, 164, 174, 248
Unger, Roberto Mangabeira, 1
Use value, 188, 206
Utilitarianism, 7, 61, 117, 124, 144, 147, 188, 208, 213, 216, 258, 259, 289, 290

Value(s) (see also Moral values), 2, 13, 17, 18, 50, 51, 70, 76, 77, 118, 146, 163, 164, 168, 214, 215, 226, 236, 241, 243, 244, 252, 259, 265, 266, 270, 273, 288, 290; economic, 187–90, 195, 205, 206, 209–12; exchange, 206; and fact (see also

Norm(s), and fact), 14, 36; labor theory of, 196; use, 188, 206
Vernunft (see also Reason), 215
Vico, Giambattista, 263
Volition (see also Will), 22, 32–35, 49, 82, 102, 122, 127–32, 134–42, 148, 152, 158, 172, 174, 235, 240, 242, 243, 248, 269
Voltaire, 220

War: of all against all, 44, 49, 50, 70, 82, 98; English Civil, 27, 60, 104
Warrender, J., 18, 28n, 83, 84, 93
Watkins, J. W. N., 38n
Weber, Max, 63
Will (see also Choice; Reason, and will): act of (see also Volition), 88, 128, 129, 137, 141; and desire, 137, 140–42, 147–50, 153, 159; determination of, 22, 33, 79, 123, 124, 126, 127, 130, 131, 135, 140, 141, 143, 153, 159, 172, 176, 242; faculty of, 32, 33, 39, 42, 46, 58, 59, 123, 127–30, 139–43, 147, 148, 149, 150, 240, 242, 284; freedom or liberty of (see also Free will), 44, 122, 127–32, 134, 137, 138, 158, 172; not an active power, 134, 139; of the people (see also General will), 25, 26; suspension of, 123, 152, 159; and understanding, 142, 148–50; and uneasiness, 123, 141, 143, 149, 164
Wolff, Robert Paul, 170n

Library of Congress Cataloging-in-Publication Data

Rapaczynski, Andrzej, 1947-
  Nature and politics.

  Includes index.
  1. Liberalism. 2. Hobbes, Thomas, 1588–1679—Contributions in political science. 3.
Locke, John, 1632–1704—Contributions in political science. 4. Rousseau, Jean-Jacques,
1712–1778.   I. Title.
JC571.R36   1987   320.5′12′01   87–5451
ISBN 0-8014-1992-1 (alk. paper)